INNER EARTH PEOPLE
OUTER SPACE PEOPLE

Is There A Golden Paradise
Inside Our Earth?

Are The Residents Of The
Subterranean World
Angels Or Devils?

Who Pilots The Craft
We Call UFOs?

Are They Here To
Hurt Or Help Us?

By William L. Blessing
A Minister Reveals The Truth About
These Explosive Topics!

Additional Updated Material by Timothy Green Beckley,
Tim R. Swartz and Dennis Crenshaw

POST OFFICE BOX 753
NEW BRUNSWICK, NJ 08903

Inner Earth People—Outer Space People

By

William Lester Blessing

Preface by Timothy Green Beckley

Edited and Updated from the 2008 Edition
Copyright 2013 by Timothy G. Beckley
dba Global Communications
and Inner Light Publications

EAN: 978-1-60611-036-2

ISBN: 1-60611-036-5

Nonfiction

No part of this book may be reproduced, stored in retrieval system or transmitted in any form or by any means, electronic, mechanical, photocopying, recording, or otherwise without the express permission of the publisher.

Timothy Green Beckley: Editorial Director

Carol Rodriguez: Publishers Assistant

Sean Casteel: Associate Editor

William Kern: Editorial Assistant

Front Cover Art: ©Dreamstime.com

If you are the legitimate copyright holder of any material inadvertently used in this book, please send a notice to this effect and the "offending" material will be immediately removed from all future printings. The material utilized herein is reproduced for educational purposes and every effort has been made to verify that the material has been properly credited and is available in the public domain.

Printed in the United States of America

For free catalog write:
Global Communications
P.O. Box 753
New Brunswick, NI 08903
Free Subscription to Conspiracy Journal E-Mail Newsletter
www.conspiracyjournal.com

CONTENTS

Foreword—Inner and Outer Space Beings and The Good Book

Chapter I—The Outer Space People And The Inner Earth People

Chapter II—Invasions Of This Earth By Outer Space People

Chapter III—Cities In The Sky

    The City In The Sky

Chapter IV—Invisible People In The Sea And Air

Chapter V—Treasure Mountain

Chapter VI—Our Three Bodies

Chapter VII—The Double Senses

    Introduction

    1. The Sense Of Hearing

    2. The Sense Of Sight

    3. The Sense Of Feeling

    4. The Sense Of Tasting

    5. The Sense Of Smell

    - Conclusion

Chapter VIII—Our Past, Present And Future Life

Chapter IX—Parapsychology

    There Is One God

Chapter X—Articles Republished From "Drift Of The Times"

    Extra Sensory Perception

    The Second Experience

    The Third Experience

    The Fourth Experience

    The Fifth Experience

    The Birds And Deer Attended My Lectures

    Christian Evidence

    Superstition And Magic

    The Scripture That Is Alleged To Stop Bleeding

The Scripture That Answers Your Questions

Issue Of Showers Of Blessing?

Extra Sensory Perception Works

Have A Pencil Ready For Word From Space

The Angels Of Mons

The White Cavalry

But It Was God Who "Won The War"

Further Visions Of The White Cavalry

Angels

Giants

The Devil's Wife

The Moon In Prophecy

Bible Predicts Sputniks With Mechanical Brain

The Sky Will Soon Be Full Of Sputniks

The Seven Last Plagues Are Upon Us

Disappearance From The Earth

Don't Be Surprised!

The Earth Turned Upside Down

Sputnik Information

"Turneth It Upside Down"

Pysicist Would Revamp Solar System

Look Out For Falling Ice

Earth's Surface Weather Originates At The South Pole

Origin Of Northern Lights

The Planet Mars

The Inside Of The Earth Is To Be Explored

A Round Earth Has Not Been Proven

Are We Hearing Creation?

Our Solar System

Sky Has More Stars Than Earth Has Grains Of Sand

  New Galaxy May Hold Earth's Creation Key

  Science Affirms Immortality

  Astronomer Describes Huge Star Explosion

  We Live Beneath A Fantastic Sea

Chapter XI—Thoughts That Influence Us

Chapter XII—Time And Balance

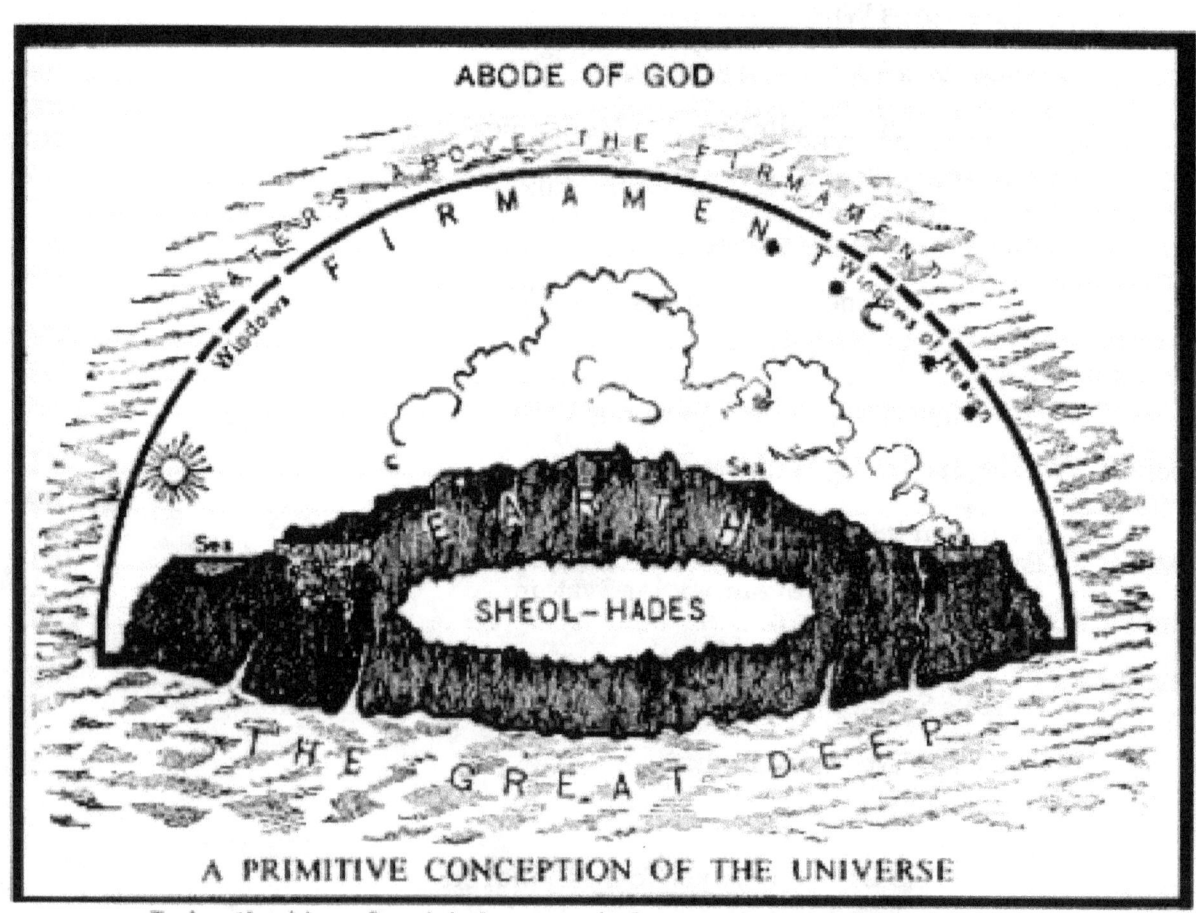

Today the idea of a global canopy is frequently met with ridicule, but it is still accepted among some Biblical students.

FOREWORD

TAKE A TRIP LIKE YOU'VE NEVER TAKEN BEFORE

By Timothy Green Beckley

This is going to turn out to be a hell of a road trip.

Mankind in the last couple of hundred years — give or take a century or two — has supposedly settled and explored pretty much every place on the surface of the earth, and we have even gone to the Moon and back.

BUT WE HAVEN'T EXPLORED THE LAST FRONTIER!

According to those who have studied such matters, there is a vast unexplored land right here on earth, right below our very feet.

Yes indeed, some maintain that the globe we live on is hollow and that a "secret civilization," exists here along side us and most of us know nothing about it at all.

Hail the Inner Earth. And so join our merry band of adventurers as they head for parts unknown. Come with the late Rev. William Blessing, Dennis Crenshaw and Tim R. Swartz as they take us down a path seldom walked. We have much to thank them for. Why? Well, despite what scientists and a hoard of government "authorities" tell us, we are about to crack open a whole new field of endeavor - we are about to enter the "twilight zone" of humanity — literally the new frontier.

Tim Beckley, Publisher

December, 2012

MRUFO8@hotmail.com

For a free subscription sign up at www.ConspiracyJournal.com

Inner and Outer Space Beings and The Good book

A Brief Introduction To A Very Fine Work

Offered Up By Timothy Green Beckley

The idea that the earth is hollow has fascinated me since I was a kid. While growing up, I must have owned five different editions of Jules Verne's, ***Journey To The Center of the Earth***. I even had model dinosaurs that I had glued together based upon the beasts that were said to still roam inside the earth (if not on the surface).

And like everyone else I was so intrigued I could not wait to get my hands on a copy of the book **The Hollow Earth** by Raymond Bernard that was advertised in every tabloid and pulp magazine (yes! even in Fate).

But I went one step further, I actually corresponded with Bernard from his conclave in the jungles of Brazil. He believed strongly that an entrance to the inner earth could be found and entered somewhere in the hot and steamy Amazon region of our planet.

Somewhere along the line I was sent a small book by William L. Blessing on what the Bible says about such a place. Now I am not much into Scriptures, but I was intrigued and Rev. Blessing wrote in such a matter-of-fact way that I felt this was at least evidence that the concept had been around for a hell of a long time.

William Blessing is now with the Lord, but we recently uncovered a copy of a very lengthy discourse he originally published on this very topic in the 1960s. I jumped at the opportunity to latch onto this work so that it could be preserved and offered to the legions of hollow and inner earth fans. William Kern has done us a fantastic new cover (the original edition had a very ordinary looking globe with a hole at the North Pole that has been used a hundred times or more) and has helped us organize it into a book we can be proud of.

Inner Light/Global Communications is the only publisher today who continues to present news of this fantastic land beyond the poles that Admiral Richard Byrd even seemingly spoke of. My own Subterranean Worlds Inside Earth has gone into many editions and has been translated into several languages (there is even a Korean and a Japanese edition out there as the subject is immensely popular in Asia). And you can find a complete list of available titles in the back of this book for those who would like to research the topic more thoroughly. We have a few other "lost" works on the subject we will release over the next few months so be on the look out for more material of this nature. But now on to what William Blessing has to say.

Tim Beckley, Publisher

MRUFO8@hotmail.com

Creationists believe that the earth was created in seven days and that the planet was surrounded by a protective canopy.

WHAT WAITS BELOW?

by Dennis Crenshaw

Anytime I tell someone about the Hollow Earth Theory the inevitable question is 'how can I get there? Hopefully this issue of THEI will help to answer this question. Of course, the first thought when seeking to enter the interior of our planet is to plan a trip through one of the two pole-holes which are alleged to be located at the north and south poles. I disagree with this idea. First, for those who would try to go over the lip into the interior by land the hardships would be unbearable. I lived in Alaska for six years and I found, operating in the cold without proper clothing etc. to be impossible. The amount of equipment and cold weather gear needed to make such a trip would be staggering. For this reason, most people who would try to gain entrance to the inner lands feel that an airplane would be the answer.

Those who feel this is the best avenue of exploration should get in touch with "The Society for a Complete Earth.". This group is currently planing a trip to re-create Admiral Byrd's alleged 1947 flight to the lands beyond the pole. For more information you can contact the director of the society, Danny Weiss, P.O.Box 890, Felton, CA 95018, 1(408)335-9329. However, I believe that these much-talked-about pole-holes, if they exist, have been hidden from view through the use of advanced technology which would prevent us from detecting their hole. It could be through the use of holograms, mind blocks, a space-time curve, or methods not even imagined by our limited knowledge. Of course, I could be wrong. At any rate, the north and south pole are probably the best protected areas of the world.

Another "plane down" is a realistic scenario for any "unauthorized" travel in these controlled areas. The best route to the interior of our earth is to be invited. Of course there's being invited and there's BEING INVITED! There are many documented cases of people being taken into areas of the interior of our planet, unfortunately, most are taken against their will. One such person was Kaye Kizziar who was abducted from her home and taken to "magnificent caverns beneath Fish Creek" in Arizona's Superstition Mountains. Another person who was kidnapped and taken by a "UFO" into the inner world was Katharina Wilson. Her experiences are accepted as one of the best documented abduction cases and can be read about in her excellent book The Alien Jigsaw (1993).

In his "must read" book Alien Update (1995), British UFO Researcher Extrodinare Timothy Good reports on UFO phenomena from around the world. On page 27, "They Took Me To Their Base" he tells of an interview with Carlos Manuel Mencado in Puerto Rico. Mr. Mencado was abducted by the Aliens commonly called the little grays who escorted him aboard a "flying saucer". Then; "The craft shot up, and I believed we would go far away, but instead, it seemed to veer to the left and descended toward the Sierra Benmeja. I was afraid we would crash, but a hole appeared in a depression to the side of El Cayul mountain and the craft went all the way down it through a tunnel and came out in a big place that seemed to be like a long, large cavern".

Those of us who are patient can wait till we're invited (hopefully not abducted). However, I know there are those people out there who can't wait. They are action people! For them, probably the best way to get to the inner earth is through one of the thousands of natural cavern entrances. With a lot of research and cave searching, plus a little luck, you just might find a "backdoor" into the subterranean lands.

Probably the best written account of a trip through the subterranean lands into the inner kingdom was reported in the 1895 book "Etidorhpa". Secret Societies, conspiracy, a strange alien guide, suppressed earth sciences - it's hard to believe that this book is a hundred years old! Yet, is it fact or fiction?

A few years ago long time inner earth researcher Bruce Walton made some startling discoveries. With his kind permission I am happy to reprint his complete and important research report, "Is William Morgan The Man" in this issue of THEI. After making the decision to seek out an entrance to the inner realms through one of the many cavern entrances it might be a good idea to go to one of the commercial caves around the country to get an idea what it will be like underground. These "open to the public" caves can be found in almost any state including, believe it or not, Florida. With a little research, and a weekend get-a-way, I'm sure you can locate one near you. The newspaper clipping, "Caves Not Far From Interstates", included with this issue should help you start your search. While many of these well known caves contain connecting passages to the inner lands, unless you "know someone", it's doubtful that you could use them. However, by studying and understanding the known caves, you just might find the clue you need to find your own entrance.

One man who may well have found a entrance to the lands inside the earth was Jack Mitchell, discoverer of Mitchell's Caverns, now a California State Park. Mitchell's Caverns is located 18 miles north of the small town of Essex which is 28 miles west of Needles California and 111 miles East of Barstow California on Route 66. The report, "The Cave Of The Winding Stairs", was filed by Hollow Earth researcher Ollie Mork. One of the best know areas where entrances to one of the inner realms is unarguably located somewhere in the vicinity of Mt. Shasta in northern California. Long known as the location of the subterranean city of Telos, Mt. Shasta is the best bet for serious searchers. Recently Michael Theroux director of Borderland Sciences and writer Michael P. Elsey conducted an expedition to the famous mountain in search of some answers. Their findings were published in Volume L1, Number 4 of BORDERLANDS which was issued during the fourth quarter of 1995. With Mr. Theroux's permission I am proud to reprint their report on the 1995 Mt. Shasta Expedition in Volume 3 #5 of The Hollow Earth Insider.

THE DOWN SIDE

Of course if you do decide to venture along a long, lonely, dark path leading to uncharted subterranean kingdoms it will not be a stroll in the park. There are many dangers underground. If one of your party should fall and, say, break a leg, - there are no doctors handy. Many times just moving forward will seem to be impossible. I highly recommend to anyone planning such an adventure to make it a point to read Subterranean Climbers (1951) by Pierre Chevalier. (Subterranean Climbers is available from: Cave Books, 756 Harvard Av., St. Louis MO 63130).

Written from the famous mountain climber and speleologist, Pierre Chevalier's on site journal, it tells of his groups' twelve years spent exploring the Trou du Glaz cave system in France. Not only does this book walk you through many of the problems these brave men met, but it also tells you what equipment you'll need for all kinds of situations. These gentlemen invented many of the caving solutions and special equipment used by professional cavers worldwide. There is one major problem that you will have right from the start. Unknown by most people as of November 18, 1988 both the Senate and House of Representatives passed Public Law 100-691 commonly referred to as the "Federal Cave Resources Protection Act of 1988". According to a copy of this law supplied by Hollow Earth researcher Tal LeVesque , the government has decided that caves located on "Federal Lands" are a natural resource and must be protected from you and I, America's citizens. The laws defines a cave as "any naturally occurring void, cavity, recess, or system of interconnecting passages which occurs beneath the surface of the earth or within a cliff or ledge (including any vug, mine, tunnel, aqueduct, or other manmade excavation) and which is large enough to permit an individual to enter, whether or not the entrance is naturally formed or manmade. Such term shall include any natural pit, sinkhole, or other feature which is an extension of the entrance". This translates into - any hole in the ground, natural or manmade.

Another interesting provision, under Section 5, "Confidentiality Of Information Concerning Nature and Location of Significant Caves" states; "Information concerning the specific location of any significant cave may not be made available to the public under section 552 of title, United States Code" The law states further; "Any person who, without prior authorization from the Secretary knowingly destroys, disturbs, defaces, mars, alters, removes or harms any significant cave or alters the free movement of any animal or plant life into or out of cave(s) located on Federal Land shall be punished". The use of the word "disturbs" disturbs me. Is leaving foot prints a disturbance? What about yanking one of those slimy reptilians out of their lair? Does that constitute "altering the free movement of any animal" or do reptiles count? Which brings us to the most important danger of all. Be aware that all creatures which inhabit the inner lands are not neighborly towards humans. Enter the subterranean realms at your own risk. And please do it cautiously. I also strongly suggest that before making any serious attempts at locating and entering a passageway into the subterranean depths you read the conclusion of John

Rhodes report "The Human-Reptilian Connection" in this issue of THEI.

* * * * *

Dennis Crenshaw has been the editor/Publisher of The Hollow Earth Insider Research Report since 1992. Now available on the internet at thehollowearthinsider.com. The site was upgraded last year and is now your online source of underground Alternative News.

Dennis is Also the Author of "Secrets of Dellschau: The Sonora Aero Club and the Airships of the 1800's" (A True Story available from Amazon.com, Barnes & Nobles etc.).

Brooks Agnew – Scientist in Search of Hollow Earth Reality

By Tim R. Swartz

Brooks A. Agnew, PhD is a commercial scientist and engineer with more than 17 years of field research in Earth Tomography. He also has 15 years of experience creating more than $500 million in process improvements for numerous industries.

His patents have revolutionized photopolymer applications, digital imaging, and high-speed manufacturing processes creating more than five thousand jobs. His technology is used on at least two planets to explore for water and other compounds.

Raised in Pasadena, California Dr. Agnew spent most of his youth hanging around Cal Tech and the folks who worked at the Jet Propulsion Labs. He entered the Air Force in 1973 where he became an electronics engineer. After earning an honorable discharge he attended Brigham Young, Western Kentucky, and Tennessee Technological Universities.

Dr. Agnew has a BS Degree in Chemistry, an MS Degree in Statistics, and a PhD in Physics. He also graduated as class valedictorian in Entrepreneurial Studies and produced a training video on raising money for non-profit ventures.

As a commercial scientist, he has produced thousands of technical papers and numerous patents. He was a featured scientist in the video documentary on *HAARP: Holes in Heaven* directed by Emmy Award Winning Wendy Robbins. He recently co-authored the two national best selling volumes of *The Ark of Millions of Years*.

Dr. Agnew has recently received substantial attention from the press because of his planned expedition to the Arctic, North Pole Inner Earth Expedition (NPIEE), to hopefully discover the Northern Polar opening to the hollow Earth. The Kentucky based physicist and futurist hopes to board the commercially owned Russian icebreaker Yamal in the port of Murmansk, and to sail into the polar sea just beyond Canada's Arctic islands.

Dr. Agnew is the latest in a long line of people to examine the theory that humans live on the surface of a hollow planet, in which two undiscovered openings, near the North and South poles, connect the outer Earth with an interior realm. However, the original idea to mount a modern-day quest for the Polar opening belongs to the late Steve Currey, a Utah adventure guide who organized rafting trips to the world's wildest white-water rivers. Currey knew how to hype exotic destinations and recruit would-be explorers on trips of a lifetime.

Dr. Brooks Agnew

Currey pinpointed the Arctic opening at 84.4 degrees north and 41 degrees east, roughly 250 miles northwest of Ellesmere Island. The inner Earth expedition was scheduled for the summer of 2006, with spaces offered for $20,000.

When Currey died unexpectedly of brain cancer, Dr. Agnew stepped in to take his place. The trip was postponed and while he insists the journey has a genuine scientific purpose; Dr. Agnew also says the expedition will include several experts in meditation, mythology and UFOs, as well as a team of documentary filmmakers.

However, if nothing is found, Dr. Agnew still promises a grand polar adventure, no matter what the outcome.

"If the polar opening isn't there, the voyage will still make an outstanding documentary," he says. "But if we do find something, this will be the greatest geological discovery in the history of the world."

Dr. Agnew says that much of the Arctic area of planet Earth has never been seen or properly analyzed by humans. Utilizing leading-edge science such as side-scan sonar, dynamo sensing, and gyroscopic global circumference tracking, the team expects to precisely measure the crust and the oceans physical properties to reveal unprecedented features about our planet. Sea-water chemistry, marine life cataloging, and even magnetic measurements will be collected during the 13-day expedition to see if there is any hard evidence that might support the hollow Earth hypothesis.

Now, no experiment on this subject would be complete without the other components so vehemently demanded by millions of paranormal prognosticators. There is a multidimensional aspect to this subject matter.

Many believe that there is a void in the interior of the Earth, but that it is fourth, and perhaps even fifth dimensional. These dimensions may require the observer to access higher vibrational levels than the vast sea of seeing-is-believing folks that clog our freeways. There will also be observation effects from the very measurement of these never before seen regions of planet Earth. Something or someone might be disturbed by this process. In other words, if the side-scan sonar sends a pulse across the bow of a 200-foot ship peacefully parked on the floor of the 4200-meter deep ocean, it might relocate itself. Besides being graphed by the sonar software, when that craft moves someone is going to get that movement on film.

QUESTIONS AND ANSWERS WITH BROOK AGNEW

Q: What is your background (education, profession, interests)?

Agnew: I was sort of a permanent student from 1970 until 2000 when I completed my PhD. I started out working as a lab assistant at UCLA Brain Research Institute while my brother was working on his PhD. I have been involved with science or engineering every since. I got my bachelor's degree from Tennessee Technological University in Chemistry. I went to work full time to support my family and worked through the Masters and Doctoral programs using extension and online courses.

My main interest has been manufacturing systems. I have worked for nearly every major auto maker in the U.S., as well as numerous suppliers for the industry. I am a certified quality engineer with a Black Belt in Six-Sigma quality systems.

I co-authored a book on the creation of the Earth in 2005, called *The Ark of Millions of Years*, which rapidly became a national best seller. I began doing radio interviews by demand, and soon was asked to host my own radio program. I founded X-Squared Radio in 2005 and have been growing every since with that wonderful hobby on the BBSRadio Network. We are modeled after Coast-to-Coast AM, but have a distinctly scientific theme with the best guests on Earth.

Q: How did you get interested in the hollow Earth theory?

Agnew: I joined the Inner Earth Expedition in 2005 as a team member to build a gyroscope and help with water sampling and analysis. I was happy to be part of the team. Steven Currey tragically and unexpectedly passed away in the summer of 2006, and I was elected to be the project leader.

Our team looked at the most likely way to fund a $2 million expedition and figured that a documentary film would be the best bet. We did not want to make the film the goal, but then again the world would probably best experience the expedition through film. We calculated that someone with financial backing would see the same incredible value that we did. So far, it has worked out that way.

Q: There is a long history on the idea that the Earth could be hollow, is there any modern science that could suggest the reality of the hollow Earth?

Agnew: The history of the hollow Earth is certainly fascinating and entertaining, but until recently lacked any credible scientific data to back it up. Satellite photos of the Earth have allowed the formation of serious questions and thus hypothesis to be formed about the structure of the planet.

Two things in particular showed up. The first was a photo of the Aurora Borealis over both planetary poles at the same time. This virtually ruled out the idea that this particular phenomenon was caused by the solar wind, a previously assumed source. Second, the USGS seismic data repeatedly, for more than 600,000 reports, produced data inconsistent with the current plate tectonic theory.

Q: Seismic research has shown anomalies that some scientists say could indicate a crust of 800 to 900 miles thick with an open area and then possibly a core of hot iron/nickel – how is this type of research done and who has made these suggestions?

Agnew: When the seismic data is recalculated, using the accelerometer as the starting point and the point of Earthquake as the endpoint, the results are stunning. A clear picture of a planet with a 900 mile thick crust appears in the math models. This, coupled with Washington University study by Dr. Wysessions, produced evidence that another entire ocean may exist underneath the Atlantic Ocean.

There is more. The magnetosphere around Earth is generated by a counter-rotation between two metal bodies. The first is the crust, which is now three times its original post-accretion disc diameter.

The second is the iron core, which was left behind during the overspin condition once the Earth began cooling. The crust is still in a slow expansion, filling with molten magma where the openings to the magma below are formed. By now, as the reader might notice, the crust is stable and cool enough to support liquid water and thus life.

Q: There have been astronomical observations that suggest the Earth is not alone in being hollow. Is there any theory that could explain how the Earth, and other planets, could form with a hollow center?

Agnew: The prevailing theory is that planets form from large accretion discs. These are huge slowly spinning discs of dust and rock. As this mini-galaxy of material becomes attracted to the center, planets begin to form. The Newtonian idea that mass attracts mass, through his concept of gravitation, denotes that in the center, the largest mass collects where the centrifugal forces are weakest. The gravity is believed to be enough to generate enough crushing power to light off the sun.

Now, as we zoom into a single planet, we see a really interesting dynamic process. The dust and rock coagulates into a single body. Obeying the law of conservation of momentum, this little rock spins faster and faster as it gets smaller. We have evidence that one of three things happens.

First, the planet can spin so fast that it explodes. The evidence of this is the plethora of asteroids and free-floating planets we have observed. Second, the planet can spin fast enough to throw off a chunk of itself. This usually exists as a moon. Sometimes that moon can be small enough to stay in orbit, and sometimes it is large enough that it breaks off and forms its own orbit around the central sun. We have evidence of both in our own solar system. Of course, we observe dozens of moons in our own solar system. And, Venus' moon broke off and became Mercury.

The third condition is the gray area in between these two extremes. The crust expands through upheavals, thinning, and cracking. The force releases in the form of heat which melts the inner layers to magma under extreme stress. As the crust cracks open, the magma flows to the outside, cools, and cements the crust back together.

We have clear evidence of this as rock assumes the planet's magnetic alignment at the instant it cools. As the crust expands, the alignment shifts. We have observed igneous rock with a gradient of magnetic fields. This could very well support this theory of crustal expansion.

Why is this important? Because if the crust is expanding, there is another interesting dynamic happening below; let's throw in an Einstein idea here. Suppose you were standing on a bathroom scale in an elevator. That elevator is a shaft that goes to the center of the Earth. When you press the button to go down, you observe your weight on the scale. Sure enough as you approach the center of the Earth, your weight begins to drop. Why? Because all of the mass of the Earth is above you in every direction; like standing on the North Pole, every direction is south.

Now, couple these ideas, and you will see why planets form as spheres and not as solid balls. The crust expands, leaving behind a molten ball of metal, probably iron. The crust is clearly three times its original size, as can be easily seen by fitting all the continental shelves together. The gap left behind is an open void. It filled with air and water. We have historical evidence of cataclysmic periods when the interior of the Earth vented to the exterior of the Earth.

The idea that planets form as hollow spheres is scientifically plausible, but not generally canonized by the high priests of science. Hence, we are mounting an expedition to gather enough observational evidence to either refute or prove the theory.

Q: Why do you think that most geologists ignore such findings preferring to "hang with the pack" refusing even to look at the evidence or speculate beyond the excepted theories of modern geology?

Agnew: It is not so much that they refuse to look at evidence. We have some of the best minds in the world joining our expedition. The problem exists because the approving authorities for PhD's are very conservative, but it goes beyond that. The previous degrees granted are based on things being a certain way. Upsetting that basis for "truth" negates all the previous degrees. In other words, if you got your PhD on the idea that Earth is flat and the sun revolved around the Earth, then sanctioning Galileo's ideas would put your tenure in question. No one wants to be the first to announce that heavier-than-air flight is now possible. Of course, that is irrelevant to those who are looking out the window of their aircraft at the degreed non-fliers below.

Q: What about the theorized holes at the poles? In this age of satellite photography and jetliners supposedly flying over the poles, how could something as obvious as polar openings be kept hidden?

Agnew: Actually, the evidence from both activities is lacking for two reasons. The first is the fact that polar satellites are looking at the Earth from about 260 miles away. They have visible, infrared, magnetic, and x-ray receivers. They are primarily used for weather reporting and thermal reviews of the Earth. The images of the poles don't really exist anymore. The Data Denial Act of 2006 prevents the release of data below 60 degrees latitude to the public. Google Maps animates their data above these areas.

The second reason is that the poles are almost always covered with clouds. This has been the main reason that there is still some credibility to Admiral Byrd's record-breaking polar flight. He flew at an altitude between 1,500 and 2,500 feet. At that altitude, your first mistake is your last.

However, Byrd very likely flew beneath the clouds giving him a clear view of the terrain below. He also would not have had the perspective to know that he was flying into an opening.

The apparent report that Admiral Byrd observed green grass, flowing water, and woolly mammoths where certainly none should have been was what really revived the age-old assertion that the Earth might be hollow. The modern plan to fly across the poles at low altitude is not practical. The cheapest aircraft that could make the 6,000 mile range is a Boeing 727. It would cost about $30,000 for such a trip. The major drawback is that no pilot is going to fly that aircraft for any period of time below 10 thousand feet in altitude. At that altitude, nothing would be visible except clouds.

Q: In your own opinion, do you think that past polar explorers encountered the openings or other anomalies associated with the polar openings?

Agnew: In my opinion, direct observation is excellent evidence. Scientifically speaking, lack of repeatability means the data is not legitimate. Edmund Haley was a strong advocate for the hollow Earth. He had very elaborate theories and great drawings of his ideas. In the 1830's another surge for the theory came out. We think it is about a time that someone went to the North Pole and gathered some real hard data and some really good film.

Q: Tell us about the upcoming Arctic trip that you are planning to try and find the Northern opening and other interesting mysteries.

Agnew: The expedition was originally planned by a group lead by Steven Currey. He had a good reputation for exotic and unusual expeditions. Tragically, he died during the preparation of this expedition. I was elected to be the new leader last October. The original funds collected were refunded by the Currey Estate, and we started over on funding.

The team consists of 100 experts in various fields. We are currently collecting scientists from major universities with expertise in polar research. We have signed experts in diving and arctic filmmaking. Then there is the Indiana Jones aspect of the expedition. In preparing for this trip, some rather powerful and esoteric events happened that convinced us there might be a higher-dimensional aspect to this entire venture. We were convinced, through various means, that we had to address these aspects or the expedition would fail.

Our leadership began training in meditation, light frequency and sound frequency chakra correlations, and even advanced physics for portal cognition. At long last, the project began moving forward extremely rapidly. The supporters for this project have come forth from every side. It seemed as though everyone got the message that we were somehow invited to visit this legendary opening. Perhaps there is an intelligence that knows we are coming and is paving the way and opening doors for us to get there.

There are two entities we have created to accomplish this voyage. The first is a non-profit company called Phoenix Science Foundation:

www.phoenixsciencefoundation.org/APEX.htm

This company is dedicated to bringing forth awareness of new sources of energy technologies and to do planetary explorations. That is where we formed the second company for profit called Advanced Planetary Explorations, LLC. This company owns the film rights, the copyrights and trademarks for the Inner Earth Expedition.

There is a new DVD documentary we produced called *The Inner Earth Expedition Part One*. It is filmed on location at Mount Shasta and in Tibet. There is remarkable footage never before seen in the West that proves beyond any doubt that the idea that the Earth is hollow has roots in ancient history. Couple that with the idea that ancient man has inextricably recorded his involvement with off-world beings, and you have a factor of this story that is simply stunning.

There are three books we have written, and one with which we are participating in a reissue. *The Ark of Millions of Years* has three volumes. They cover the creation and destiny of the Earth, the year 2012 mysteries, and a final book called *Unlocking the Secret*. These are all for sale at all bookstores and Amazon and Barnes & Noble as well as through our website at: **www.arkofmillionsofyears.com**

POST OFFICE BOX 753
NEW BRUNSWICK, NJ 08903

OUTER SPACE PEOPLE AND INNER EARTH PEOPLE

Chapter I

The Outer Space People

and

The Inner Earth People

(Study the charts, pictures and diagrams following this message.)

You are now beginning the reading and study of what I think is the most amazing, fascinating teaching that has ever been released in the last two thousand years. The very latest that YAHVEH has revealed to me is the truth about the three heavens that belong to this earth. The Apostle Paul tells us that he was "caught up to the third heaven" (ll Cor. 12:2) and, while in that heaven he "heard unspeakable words which it is not lawful for a man to utter." (II Cor. 12:4)

The Bible definition of "Heaven" is the word "FIRMAMENT" (Gen. 1:6) and means the air, atmosphere and sky. Therefore this earth has three heavens; that is, three skies.

The first heaven begins on the surface of the earth and extends upward 250,000 miles to the moon, and on past the moon for 250,000 miles. Therefore the first heaven extends from the surface of the earth upward and outward for 500,000 miles. In this we have the layers of atmosphere, stratosphere, ionosphere, etc. A ring of darkness begins about twenty miles above the surface of the earth. The darkness is inhabited by a very evil people. Beyond the darkness is the moon and then the asteroid or planetoid ring of inhabited places-inhabited by the outer-space people. Beyond this first heaven is a vaporous ring in which there are great quantities of ice. Light rays penetrating this ice account for the colors violet indigo, blue, green, yellow, orange and purple.

Beyond this first heaven (sky) is the second heaven (sky) which is much like the first except that it is much larger and grander than the first. Beyond the second heaven (sky) is the third heaven (sky) which is magnificent and beautiful beyond description. These three heavens belong to the earth and are inhabited. In each (sky) heaven there is an asteroid circle of land or planetoids. Actually the third heaven is the ultimate outer-

OUTER SPACE PEOPLE AND INNER EARTH PEOPLE

earth. We live away down under the third, second and first heavens. We are deep inside the earth proper, but there is an inner-earth people who are in the depths of the earth. They are separated from us by the mineral, metal and land shell of the earth which is about 600 to 800 miles thick.

All of the three heavens, as well as the surface of the earth on which we live and the inner earth, all belong to this globe. It is highly possible that not only the moon and asteroids in the first heaven (sky) revolve in a circuit around the earth, but that all of the planetoids or stars in the second and third heavens revolve around the earth. Instead of the earth turning on its axis from west to east at the rate of a thousand miles per hour and thus causing day and night it could be that the earth does not turn on its axis at all but that day and night are the result of the land areas in the first, second and third heavens (skies) which revolve around the earth.

But for the present, in this lecture, I shall not discard the theory which is generally accepted which is that the earth turns on its axis every twenty-four hours. But that theory may not be true. However, it is well established that the earth orbits the sun at the rate of 67,000 miles per hour. The sun is traveling toward the north in its orbit around the galaxy or central sun at the rate of 175 miles per second and, of course, taking the earth and all of its planetoids northward with it at the same rate of 175 miles per second.

The central sun that our sun orbits is taking all of its family of suns in its orbit around the hub of the universes at the rate of about 300 miles per second.

But in this lecture I shall confine what I say to this earth and the three heavens that belong to this earth and the inner earth.

The Bible teaches us that there are people dwelling in the inside of the earth. For want of a better name I shall call them Inner Earth people. I would estimate the population of the inner earth to be ten billion, or about five times more than those of us who live on the surface of the earth.

There are 200,000,000 pilots in the flying saucer corps in the inner earth. The name of their commander-in-chief is "Apollyon, whose name in the Hebrew tongue is Abaddon, but in the Greek tongue hath his name Apollyon." (Rev.9:11).

They will soon, very soon, invade the surface of the earth. In fact I believe that the invasion has already been begun by an advance reconnaissance force that is flying out over the surface of the earth, mapping the land areas and strategic places where they will strike in their all-out invasion.

"And the four angels were loosed, which were prepared for an hour, and a day, and a month, and a year, to slay the third part of men. And the number of the army and horsemen were two hundred thousand thousand: and I heard the number of them." (Rev. 9:15-16). That is two hundred million pilots or aviators of flying saucers. These pilots are "men" who look exactly like those of us on the surface of the earth. Their flying saucers are made of a type of iron that is plated with "gold" and "the sound of their wings was as the sound of chariots." (Rev.9 :9).

OUTER SPACE PEOPLE AND INNER EARTH PEOPLE

"And the fifth angel sounded, and I saw a star fall from heaven unto the earth: and to him was given the key of the bottomless pit. And he opened the bottomless pit; and there arose a smoke out of the pit as the smoke of the great furnace; and the sun and the air were darkened by reason of the smoke of the pit. And there came out of the smoke locusts upon the earth: "and unto them was given power, as the scorpions of the earth have power." (Rev.9:1-3).

They are bringing a cloud of darkness, a mist, a smog, a cloud over the cities that they are mapping out-such as Los Angeles, London and elsewhere. But when the all out invasion comes; they will blanket the whole surface of the earth with darkness. "It shall be one day which shall be known to the Lord, not day, nor night." (Zech. 14:7).

The type of vehicle that they use was well known to the ancient prophets. The best description that we have is that given to us by Ezekiel:

"And I looked, and behold, a whirlwind came out of the north, a great cloud, and a fire infolding itself, and a brightness was about it, and out of the midst thereof as the color of amber, out of the midst of the fire. Also out of the midst thereof came the likeness of four living creatures. And this was their appearance; they had the likeness of a man. And every one had four faces, and every one had four wings. And their feet were straight feet; and the sole of their feet was like the sole of a calf's foot; and they sparkled like the color of burnished brass. And they had the hands of man under their wings on their four sides; and they four had their faces and their wings. Their wings were joined one to another; they turned not when they went; they went every one straight forward. As for the likeness of their faces, they four had the face of a man, and the face of a lion, on the right side: and they four had the face of an ox on the left side: they four also had the face of an eagle. Thus were their faces: and their wings were stretched upward; two wings of every one were joined one to another, and two covered their bodies. And they went every one straight forward: whither the spirit was to go, they went; and they turned not when they went. As for the likeness of the living creatures, their appearance was like burning coals of fire, and like the appearance of lamps: it went up and down among the living creatures; and the fire was bright, and out of the fire went forth lightning. And the living creatures ran and returned as the appearance of a flash of lightning.

Now as I beheld the living creatures, behold one wheel upon the earth by the living creatures, with his four faces. The appearance of the wheels and their work was like unto the color of a beryl: and they four had one likeness: and their appearance and their work was as it were a wheel in the middle of a wheel. When they went, they went upon their four sides: and they turned not when they went. As for their rings, they were so high that they were dreadful; and their rings were full of eyes round about them four. And when the living creatures went the wheels went by them: and when the living creatures were lifted up from the earth, the wheels were lifted up. Whithersoever the spirit was to go, they went thither was their spirit to go; and the wheels were lifted up over against them: for the spirit of the living creature was in the wheels. When those went these went; and when those stood, these stood; and when those were lifted up from the earth, the wheels were lifted up over against them: for the spirit of the living creature was in the wheels. And the likeness of the firmament upon the heads of the living crea-

OUTER SPACE PEOPLE AND INNER EARTH PEOPLE

ture was as the color of the terrible crystal, stretched forth over their heads above. And under the firmament were their wings straight, the one toward the other: every one had two, which covered on this side, and every one had two, which covered on that side, their bodies. And when they went, I heard the noise of their wings, like the noise of great waters, as the voice of the Almighty, the voice of speech, as the noise of a host: when they stood, they let down their wings. And there was a voice from the firmament that was over their heads, when they stood, and had let down their wings." (Ezek. 1:4-25)

From these machines they will constantly radio messages to us. They fly on magnetic lines. Their flight is almost instant, They can instantly reverse their course or position. They understand the power of levitation; that is, how to use gravitation in reverse— the power of negative gravitation.

These inner earth people are of several different races and orders. Some of them originally lived on the surface of the earth just as you and I do. But some of them once lived above the earth in outer-space. In the ages long ago they invaded the earth from outer-space. The book of Genesis describes them first as the "serpent" people (Gen. 3:1-5) and secondly as follows: "And it came to pass, when men began to multiply on the face of the earth, and daughters were born unto them, that the sons of God saw the daughters of men that they were fair; and they took them wives of all which they chose.

And the Lord said, My Spirit shall not always strive with man, for that he also is flesh: yet his days shall be a hundred and twenty years. There were giants in the earth in those days; and also after that when the sons of God came in unto the daughters of men, and they bare children to them, the same became mighty men which were of old, men of renown. The earth also was corrupt before God; and the earth was filled with violence. And God looked upon the earth, and, behold, it was corrupt; for all flesh had corrupted his way upon the earth." (Gen. 6: 1-4, 11-12).

These outer-space invaders of the earth came originally from twenty-two different dwelling places in outer-space and the names of the leaders of each of the outer-space places that led a host of their people to the earth were as follows:

1. Samyaza, 2. Urakabarameel, 3. Akibeel, 4. Tamiel, 5. Ramuel, 6. Danel, 7. Azkeel, 8. Sarakuyal, 9. Asael, 10. Armers, 11. Batrael, 12. Anane, 13. Zavebe, 14. Samsaveel, 15. Etrael, 16. Turel, 17. Yomyael, 18. Arazyal, 19. Atnzarak, 20. Barkayal, 21 Barkayal Tamiel, 22. Asaradel. (Book of ENOCH, chapters 7 and 8).

Just exactly how many followers each leader brought with him to the earth is not known, but at any rate they materialized their bodies just like earth people and remained in the flesh and married women on the earth. The children of these invaders were great "giants", many of them malformed, having six fingers and six toes. (I Chron. 20:6). We do not say that all of the offspring were malformed, but many of them were. There was undoubtedly a race of giants ten to twelve feet tall and also a race of pygmies produced by the crossing of these outer-space people with the women on the earth. The first generation of these people were not sterile, but there is evidence that the second generation was sterile-hybrids which could not reproduce.

OUTER SPACE PEOPLE AND INNER EARTH PEOPLE

This crossing over and mixing of the outer Space invaders with the women on the earth continued for 1656 years-that is, from the time that Adam left the Garden of Eden until the final days of Noah. (Gen. 5 : 1-32). All the inhabitants of the earth had become sterile one hundred years before the flood.

The last children born on the earth before the flood were the triplet sons of Noah-Shem, Ham and Japheth. They were born on the 500th birthday of Noah, (Gen. 5:32). From that time on until the flood no children were born on the earth. Consequently no person on earth was drowned in the flood until one hundred years of age, for no children had been born in one hundred years.

Noah was 498 years old when he married Naamah, the daughter of Enoch, and she was 580 years old. (Book of Jasher 5: 15-16). She was 582 years old and Noah was 500 years old when Shem, Ham and Japheth were born. Noah was 600 years old when he went into the ark. (Gen. 7: 11). The sons of Noah-Shem, Ham and Japheth-married sisters who were of Eliakim-the great-granddaughters of Enoch.

Eliakim was a son of Methuselah, who was a son of Enoch. (Jasher 5: 35) Noah was 600 years old when he went into the ark. His sons, who were the youngest people on the earth at that time, were 100 years old when they went into the ark with their wives and with Noah and his wife.

Incidentally, in passing it needs to be stated that the degeneracy of the earth before the flood was indescribable. Not only had the outer-space people crossed with women, but men had corrupted themselves with animals also, "for all flesh had corrupted his way upon the earth." (Gen. 6: 12). Many of the unclean animals whose flesh we are forbidden to eat are part human. I could go into detail about this, describing the human marks in the bodies of each of the unclean animals, but suffice it to say that the serpent has a pelvic bone, also the remnants of arms and legs and gives birth to its young.

It is too long a story to point out the human marks in each of the unclean animals, but they all have them. The hog does not chew the cud and has a stomach like a human, etc.

The outer-space people who invaded the earth, fallen angels , if you wish to call them that, together with their hybrid offspring which were giants and pygmies, were all sent into the inner earth just before the flood came upon the earth. Later on and at intervals since the flood some of the earth people have been banished to the inner earth. "And the earth opened her mouth, and swallowed them up, and their houses, and all the men that appertained unto Korah, and all their goods. They, and all that appertained to them, went down alive into the pit and the earth closed upon them: and they perished from among the congregation." (Num.16:32 33).

The Bible gives us abundant evidence in regard to these inner earth people-from which I shall quote but a few more of the scriptures. "God spared not the angels that sinned, but cast them down into hell, and delivered them into chains of darkness, to be reserved unto judgment." (II Peter 2:4).

"And the angels which kept not their first estate, but left their own habitation, he

OUTER SPACE PEOPLE AND INNER EARTH PEOPLE

hath reserved in everlasting chains under darkness unto the judgment of the great day." (Jude 6).

The Bible plainly states that we are to judge these inner earth people: "Do ye not know that the saints shall judge the world? and if the world shall be judged by you; are ye unworthy to judge the smallest matters? Know ye not that we shall judge angels?" (1 Cor. 6: 2-3).

The Bible again and again speaks of men "under the earth" (Rev. 5:3) as well as men above the earth, and declares that they will all eventually be converted to Christ: "That at the name of Jesus every knee should bow, of things in heaven, and things in earth, and things under the earth, and that every tongue should confess that Jesus Christ is Lord, to the glory of God the Father." (Philippians.: 2:10-11).

We will actually hear those people: "Saying with a loud voice, Worthy is the Lamb that was slain to receive power, and riches, and wisdom, and strength; and honor, and glory, and blessing. And every creature which is in heaven, and on the earth and under the earth and such as are in the sea and all that are in them, heard I saying; Blessing, and honor; and glory, and power; be unto him that sitteth upon the throne, and unto The Lamb for ever and ever." (Rev. 5: 12-13.)

It is so emphatically evident in the Bible that Yahshua the Messiah (Jesus Christ) went into the inner earth and preached to those people, that no Bible believing person can deny it. "He also descended first into the lower parts of the earth." (Eph.4:9). "For Christ also hath once suffered for sins, the just for the unjust, that he might bring us to God, being put to death in the flesh, but quickened by the Spirit: by which also he went and preached unto the spirits in prison; which sometime were disobedient, when once the long-suffering of God waited in the days of Noah, while the ark was a preparing, wherein few, that is, eight souls were saved by water." (I Peter 3:18-20). "For, for this cause was the gospel preached also to them that are dead, that they might be judged according to men in the flesh, but live according to God in the spirit." (I Peter 4:6-7).

It was during the forty days between the resurrection of Christ and His ascension into heaven that he spent most of that time - most of those forty days were spent in the inner earth preaching to the inner earth people.

So far in this message I have not discussed the outer-space people, but I want to make it clear that there are many inhabited dwelling places in outer-space, and I do not mean on Mars, Venus, Jupiter nor some other planet. The outer planets are inhabited, but the outer-space people that I speak of in this message are those that belong primarily to this earth. There are people above the earth and on the earth and inside the earth, and all of these people belong to the earth realm. They will all be united in the near future: "Having made known unto us the mystery of his will, according to his good pleasure which he hath purposed in himself: that in the dispensation of the fullness of times he might gather together in one all things in Christ, both which are in heaven, and which are on earth; even in him." (Eph. 1:9-10).

The names of the prince leaders over these friendly people in six different outer-

OUTER SPACE PEOPLE AND INNER EARTH PEOPLE

space places are:

1. Uriel, 2. Raphael, 3. Raguel, 4. Michael, 5. Sarakiel and 6. Gabriel. (Book of ENOCH 20: 1 -7). These six leaders and their people are friendly and are holy followers of our Savior Yahshua the Messiah, but there are many other inhabited places in the immediate outer-space in which the people are not converted and are not friendly to us.

One of the surprises of my life was the discovery that "the heavens are not clean in his sight." (Job 15:15). And that we must invade the heavens and preach "the unsearchable riches of Christ" to them:

"To the intent that now unto the principalities and powers in heavenly places might be known by the church the manifold wisdom of God, according to the eternal purpose which he purposed in Christ Jesus our Lord:

In whom we have boldness and access with confidence by the faith of him. Wherefore I desire that ye faint not at my tribulations for you, which is your glory. For this cause I bow my knees unto the Father of our Lord Jesus Christ of whom the whole family in heaven and earth is named. That he would grant you, according to the riches of his glory, to be strengthened with might by his Spirit in the inner man." (Eph. 3:10-16).

At this time we are actually in a battle with these outer-space people, as it is written: "We wrestle not against flesh and blood, but against principalities, against powers, against the rulers of the darkness of this world, against spiritual wickedness in high places." (Eph. 6:12).

This battle is a dangerous one: "Wherefore take unto you the whole armor of God, that ye may be able to withstand in the evil day, and having done all, to stand. Stand therefore, having your loins girt about with truth, and having on the breastplate of righteousness; And your feet shod with the preparation of the gospel of peace; above all, taking the shield of faith, wherewith ye shall be able to quench all the fiery darts of the wicked. And take the helmet of salvation, and the sword of the Spirit which is the word of God: Praying always with all prayer and supplication in the Spirit, and watching thereunto with all perseverance and supplication for all saints; And for me, that utterance may be given unto me, that I may open my mouth boldly, to make known the mystery of the gospel, For which I am an ambassador in bonds; that therein I may speak boldly, as I ought to speak." (Eph. 6: 18-20).

This is a time of trouble as the battle rages between those in the different types of flying saucers from the inner earth and from outer-space; it is the time of the binding of Satan (Rev. 20:1-8) and also of the deliverance of the saints. "And at that time shall Michael stand up, the great prince which standeth for the children of thy people: and there shall be a time of trouble, such as never was since there was a nation even to that same time: and at that time thy people shall be delivered, every one that shall be found written in the book." (Dan. 12: 1).

The battle in the air is going on and many of the evil people from the inner earth and from outer-space are being cast down to the surface of the earth. The heavens will be purified and the battle will be won in the heavens before we get the complete victory

OUTER SPACE PEOPLE AND INNER EARTH PEOPLE

on the earth: "And there was war in heaven: Michael and his angels fought against the dragon; and the dragon fought and his angels, and prevailed not; neither was their place found any more in heaven. And the great dragon was cast out, that old serpent, called the Devil, and Satan, which deceiveth the whole world: he was cast out into the earth, and his angels were cast out with him. And I heard a loud voice saying in heaven, Now is come salvation, and strength, and the kingdom of our God, and the power of his Christ: for the accuser of our brethren is cast down, which accused them before our God day and night. And they overcame him by the blood of the Lamb, and by the word of their testimony; and they loved not their lives unto the death. Therefore rejoice, ye heavens, and ye that dwell in them. Woe to the inhabiters of the earth and of the sea! for the devils is come down unto you, having great wrath, because he knoweth that he hath but a short time." (Rev. 12:7-12).

These people now on earth who have come recently from outer-space and the inner earth are not all invisible persons. Some of them are literal, visible and are more dense and material than the average earth person. They are armed with fiery-tipped darts (Eph. 6:16) and with certain rays by which they can inflict us with terrible "stings" like "scorpions" (Rev. 9;10) unless we have on the whole armour of God. Actually, my opinion is that in many cases, those who are suddenly struck down with heart trouble and other sudden serious ailments are victims of the "stings" inflicted by these outer space and inner earth people. "And there shall be signs in the sun, and in the moon, and in the stars; and upon the earth distress of nations, with perplexity; the sea and the waves roaring; men's hearts failing them for fear, and for looking after those things which are coming on the earth: for the powers of heaven shall be shaken." (Luke 21: 25-26).

I believe also that much insanity is also caused by a brainwashing ray used by these invaders of the earth and mental diseases are increasing at an alarming rate. All that I can do is sound the alarm and give you fair warning about these things. I cannot at this time release to you all that I know about the outer-space and inner earth people, but I can tell you this much, that the one and only protection that you can have is the Divine Seal. If you are sealed in your forehead (that is, in your mind and heart) with the Sacred name (YHVH) YAHVEH, you will be absolutely safe. If you have that name they cannot hurt you.

"And the LORD said unto him, Go through the midst of the city, through the midst of Jerusalem, and set a mark upon the foreheads of the men that sigh and that cry for all the abominations that be, done in the midst thereof. And to the others he said in mine hearing, Go ye after him through the city, and smite: let not your eye spare, neither have ye pity. Slay utterly old and young, both maids, and little children, and women: but come not near any man upon whom is the mark; and begin at my sanctuary.

Then they began at the ancient men which were before the house. And he said unto them, Defile the house, and fill the courts with the slain: go ye forth. And they went forth, and slew in the city. (Ezekiel 9:4-7).

"And I heard a great voice out of the temple saying to the seven angels, go your ways, and pour out the vials of the wrath of God upon earth. And the first went, and poured

OUTER SPACE PEOPLE AND INNER EARTH PEOPLE

out his vial upon the earth and their fell a noisome and grievous sore upon the men which had the mark of the beast, and upon them which worshipped his image." (Rev. 16:1-2).

Those having his Father's name written in their foreheads (Rev. 14:1) are safe. They are protected.

"The name YAHVEH is a strong tower: the righteous runneth into it and is safe." (Prov. 18:10). The title "Lord" is, as you know, "YAHVEH."

"I will call upon the LORD, who is worthy to be praised: so shall I be saved from mine enemies. The sorrows of death compassed me, and the floods of ungodly men made me afraid. The sorrows of hell compassed me about: the snares of death prevented me. In my distress I called upon the LORD, and cried unto my God: he heard my voice out his temple, and my cry came before him, even into his ears. Then the earth shook and trembled; the foundations also of the hills moved and were shaken, because he was wroth. There went up a smoke out of his nostrils, and fire out of his mouth devoured: coals were kindled by it. He bowed the heavens also, and came down: and darkness was under his feet. And he rode upon a cherub, and did fly: yea, he did fly upon the wings of the wind. He made darkness his secret place; his pavilion round about him were dark waters and thick clouds of the skies. At the brightness that was before him thick clouds passed, hail stones and coals of fire. The LORD also thundered in the heavens, and the Highest gave his voice; hail stones and coals of fire.

Yea, he sent out his arrows, and scattered them; and he shot out lightnings, and discomfited them. Then the channels of waters were seen, and the foundations of the world were discovered at they rebuke, O LORD, at the blast of the breath of thy nostrils. He sent from above, he took me, he drew out of many waters. He delivered me from my strong enemy, and from them which hate me: for they were too strong for me. They prevented me in the day of my calamity: but the LORD was my stay. He brought me forth also into a large place; he delivered me, because he delighted in me." (Psalm 18: 3-19).

THE NAME YAHVEH IS ABSOLUTELY ESSENTIAL TO OUR SURVIVAL IN THE END TIME OF THIS AGE. The old evil world systems are being destroyed and the righteous new world order is coming in. With "YAHVEH" we can survive the disruption of the world and be safely and securely established in the new world order.

I believe the Bible! The Bible teaches that there are INNER EARTH people and OUTER SPACE people. I have already quoted the scriptures that show you clearly what the Bible teaches on this subject. I believe that the Bible is a book of pure, perfect exact science. The Bible in general and prophecy in particular is the one and only EXACT science. Mathematics and music come close to being exact science but are not as exact as the Bible.

Let me try to explain what I mean: There is ONE ETERNITY. Everything past, present and future is ETERNITY. The thing that we call time is the present. We have set up a wall between us and the past and a wall between us and the future and this present thing which we call TIME is like a prison in which we have shut ourselves off from the past and the future. But the wall between us and the past is breaking up, and the wall between us

OUTER SPACE PEOPLE AND INNER EARTH PEOPLE

and the future is breaking up. All of the past exists NOW and likewise all of the future exists NOW. ETERNITY IS NOW- without any past or future dimensions as such.

Prophecy is an exact science simply because the mind of the prophet was projected into the future. The mind of David was projected one thousand years into the future and he saw and experienced and wrote in detail the complete story of the crucifixion a thousand years before it took place. (See Psalm 22:1-31). This is just one example of all prophecy. If you could project your mind, let us say, for one year in advance and see and experience and write down the things in detail that will take place one year from today, that would be prophecy-which is a future projection. The future exists now. All of the future exists in eternity. Prophecy is exact history written in advance.

But let us remember that all of the Bible was written by DIVINE INSPIRATION. Men did not write their own ideas nor opinions. They wrote what the Spirit of Yahveh dictated to them. "Knowing this first that no prophecy of the Scripture is of any private interpretation. For the prophecy came not in old time, by the will of man: but holy men of God spake as they were moved by the Holy Ghost" (II Peter 1: 20-21). The words that they spoke and wrote were INSPIRED. It is true that we do not have any copies of their original writings. The Bible has come down to us, being copied through many languages and translations. The choice of words in some cases is not so clear; in fact, there are no words in our present language that are adequate to express the Divine revelation clearly. But allowing for human errors in translations, yet there is definitely a general INSPIRATION running through the whole Bible and by comparing scripture with scripture, with the help of the Holy Spirit the meaning of most of the Bible is clear to us.

As far as I am concerned, I believe the Bible. I believe that all that it teaches is true. I believe that all that it teaches on science is true, too. What it says about outer-space people and inner earth people and everything else that it teaches is true. The Bible came out of eternity into time by direct Divine inspiration to us, and I believe it!

All of the churches, every denomination, believes, in some kind of an underworld. Some call it "HELL". Others say that it is divided into "hell", purgatory" and "limbo." Most of them say that Jesus Christ "descended into hell" for a short time at least. LET THOSE WHO TEACH THAT THERE IS A HELL DEFINE IT. Is it a place? If it is a place, where is it? If it is not a place, What is it? If asked to point toward "Heaven" they usually point straight up. If asked to point toward "Hell", they point straight down. Are they right in their directions? I'm asking them. I have been severely criticized, persecuted and called "crazy" because of what I teach. I am not teaching anything except what the priests and preachers say they believe, but they refuse to locate or define it. Is it better to leave the people in total ignorance about "Hell"? That is a question for the ministers to answer!

In the study of the ten great religions, the Egyptian Book of the Dead, the philosophy of the Greeks and all the teaching of the ancient people I find that they all believed in the inner earth and inner earth people. I for one cannot disregard this teaching for modern atheistic material evolution which has been taught for only about one hundred years and which is nothing more than a theory, which the Bible calls "oppositions of science falsely so called: which some professing have erred concerning the faith." (I Tim.

OUTER SPACE PEOPLE AND INNER EARTH PEOPLE

6:20-21).

There are four words which, in the Bible, are translated "hell". They are: 1. Sheol, 2. Hades, 3. Gehenna, 4. Tartaros. It is true that in most instances the words "SHEOL" and "HADES" (translated "hell") simply mean the grave. But this is not true of "GEHENNA" (hell) in Luke 10:15 and 16:23 and "TARTAROS" (hell) in Second Peter 2:4 cannot possibly mean the grave. TARTAROS (hell) means the inner earth, the place of abode of the fallen angels who were the outer-space people that corrupted the earth before the flood. I have already explained by the scriptures that these people were banished to the inner earth before the flood in the days of Noah. Also that some earth people were also sent into the inner earth (Numbers 16: 32-33).

What I shall say now will not be accepted as a theory-not even as a hypothesis by the material scientists of this modern world but it is what the Bible teaches-therefore I believe it.

"IN THE BEGINNING GOD CREATED THE HEAVEN AND THE EARTH." (Gen. 1:1). How long ago that was we do not know. Science today says that the matter out of which this earth is made is three billion years old. That may be about right but not so many years ago Professor Walter Gregory of Scotland estimated the age of matter at eight billion years, while another scientist said it was twenty million years old. They disagreed 1,980,000,000 years. But I am inclined to believe that the present general opinion of three billion years is about right for the age of matter.

The earth has gone through six creative cycles and probably has been inhabited six different times. I do not know the length of a creative cycle. We are told that the earth at the present time turns on its axis from west to east at the equator at the rate of a thousand miles an hour. At the same time the earth is traveling in its orbit around the sun at 7,000 miles an hour. The sun and all of the planets in the solar system, including the earth of course, is traveling directly north at the terrific rate of speed of 175 miles per second.

When the sun and its planets, traveling north at 175 miles per second, completes its orbit around the central hub of the universes, then the earth and all the planets in this solar system will be disrupted. It has happened six times before. It will happen again. The day of the Lord will come as a thief in the night; in which the heavens shall pass away with a great noise; and the elements shall melt with fervent heat the earth also and the works that are therein shall be burned up. Seeing then that all these things shall be dissolved, what manner of persons ought ye to be in all holy conversation and godliness, looking for and hasting unto the coming of the day of God, wherein the heavens being on fire shall be dissolved, and the elements shall melt with fervent heat? Nevertheless we, according to his promise, look for new heavens and a new earth, wherein dwelleth righteousness." (II Peter 3:10-18).

On the earth (in the cycle) just prior to this present habitation, dwelt the man Lucifer and his wife Lilith and billions of people of the Luciferian race. The earth was much larger than it is now. The continents of Atlantis and Lemuria existed on the earth at that time. Actually there were mountains of gold and silver and of diamonds and rubies and precious stones which were magnificent beyond description. We have a description of

OUTER SPACE PEOPLE AND INNER EARTH PEOPLE

Lucifer in the following scriptures Under the symbol of Tyrus:

"The word of the LORD came again unto me, saying, Son of man, say unto the prince of Tyrus, Thus saith the Lord GOD; Because thine heart is lifted up, and thou hast said, I am god, I sit in the seat of God, in the midst of the seas; yet thou art a man, and not God, though thou set thine heart as the heart of God: Behold, thou art wiser than Daniel; there is no secret that they can hide from thee: With thy wisdom and with thine understanding thou has gotten thee riches, and hast gotten gold and silver into thy treasures:

By thy great wisdom and by thy traffic hast thou increased thy riches, and thine heart is lifted up because of thy riches: Therefore thus saith the Lord GOD; Because thou has set thine heart as the heart of God; Behold, therefore I will bring strangers upon thee, the terrible of the nations: and they shall draw their swords against the beauty of thy wisdom, and they shall defile thy brightness. They shall bring thee down to the pit, and thou shalt die the deaths of them that are slain in the midst of the seas. Wilt thou yet say before him that slayeth thee, I am God? but thou shalt be a man, and no God, in the hand of him that slayeth thee. Thou shalt die the deaths of the uncircumcised by the hand of strangers: for I have spoken it, saith the Lord GOD.

Moreover the word of the LORD came unto me, saying, Son of man, take up a lamentation upon the king of Tyrus, and say unto him, Thus saith the Lord GOD; Thou sealest up the sum, full of wisdom, and perfect in beauty. Thou hast been in Eden the garden of God; every precious stone was thy covering, the sardius, topaz, and the diamond, the beryl, the onyx, and the jasper, the sapphire, the emerald, and the carbuncle, and gold: the workmanship of thy tabrets and of thy pipes was prepared in thee in the day that thou wast created. Thou art the anointed cherub that covereth; and I have set thee so: thou wast upon the holy mountain of God; thou hast walked up and down in the midst of the stones of fire. Thou wast perfect in thy ways from the day that thou wast created, till iniquity was found in thee. By the multitude of thy merchandise they have filled the midst of thee with violence, and thou hast sinned: therefore I will cast thee as profane out of the mountain of God: and I will destroy thee, O covering cherub, from the midst of the stones of fire. Thine heart, was lifted up because of thy beauty, thou has corrupted thy wisdom by reason of thy brightness: I will cast thee to the ground, I will lay thee before kings, that they may behold thee. Thou hast defiled thy sanctuaries by the multitude of thine iniquities, by the iniquity of thy traffic; therefore will I bring forth a fire from the midst of thee, it shall devour thee, and I will bring thee to ashes upon the earth in sight of all them that behold thee." (Ezek. 28: 1-18).

"Hell from beneath is moved for thee to meet thee at thy coming: it stirreth up the dead for thee, even all the chief ones of the earth; it hath raised up from their thrones all the kings of the nations. All they shall speak and say unto thee, Art thou also become weak as we? art thou become like unto us? Thy pomp is brought down to the grave, and the noise of thy viols: the worm is spread under thee, and the worms cover thee. How art thou fallen from heaven, Lucifer, son of the morning! how art thou cut down to the ground, which didst weaken the nations! For thou hast said in thine heart I will ascend into heaven, I will exalt my throne above the stars of God:

OUTER SPACE PEOPLE AND INNER EARTH PEOPLE

I will sit also upon the mount of the congregation, in the sides of the north: I will ascend above the heights of the clouds; I will be like the Most High. Yet thou shalt be brought down to hell, to the sides of the pit. They that see thee shall narrowly look upon thee, and consider thee, saying, Is this the man that made the earth to tremble, that did shake kingdoms; That made the world as a wilderness, and destroyed the cities thereof; that opened not the house of his prisoners? All the kings of the nations, even all of, them, lie in glory, every one in his own house. But thou art cast out of thy grave like an abominable branch, and as the raiment of those that are slain, thrust through with a sword, that go down to the stones of the pit; as a carcass trodden under feet. Thou shalt not be joined with them in burial, because thou hast destroyed thy land, and slain thy people: the seed of evildoers shall never be renowned." (Isa. 14 :9-20).

"I beheld the earth, and, lo, it was without form, and void; and the heavens, and they had no light. I beheld the mountains, and lo, they trembled, and all the hills moved lightly. I beheld and, lo, there was no man, and all the birds of the heavens were fled. I beheld, and, lo, the fruitful place was a wilderness, and all the cities thereof were broken down at the presence of the Lord, and by his fierce anger. For thus hath the Lord said, The whole land shall be desolate; yet will I not make a full end." (Jer. 4: 26-27).

The above quoted scriptures from Ezekiel, Isaiah and Jeremiah describe the man Lucifer and his Luciferian race which inhabited the previous earth. When that earth cycle ended the earth was broken up by fire and later moved into chaos and darkness, being flooded many miles deep with water and darkness. Lucifer and all of his race of people were destroyed and I mean by that, their bodies died, but they survived as earth-bound disembodied spirits. Lucifer is now known as Satan, the devil. He is the disembodied spirit of the man who ruled over the previous earth. The "devils" are the disembodied spirits of the Luciferian men and women who lived on the previous earth. "Devils" are earth-bound. They are disembodied; they inhabit the air close to the surface land of the earth. They constantly seek to embody: -that is, to obsess and possess men and women of our race.

"AND THE EARTH WAS WITHOUT FORM AND VOID: AND DARKNESS WAS UPON THE FACE OF THE DEEP." (Gen. 1:2, first clause of verse 2.) The Devil and devils who are the disembodied spirits of the man Lucifer and his race of men and women who inhabited the previous earth, are permitted to exist in the air near this earth until the end of this age, at which time Yahveh will cause "the unclean spirits to pass out of the land" (Zech. 13:2) and will "take away the names of Baalim out of her mouth (that is, out of the mouth of his people), and they shall no more be remembered by their name." (Hosea 2:17). And the only name by which the Heavenly Father will be known will be "YAHVEH." For then will I turn to the people a pure language, that they may all call upon the name of the LORD, to serve him with one consent." (Zeph. 8:9). "And the LORD shall be King over all the earth: in that day shall there be one LORD, and his name one." (Zech. 14:9).

All of the fallen angels, that is, the outer space people, that are now in the inner earth, together with the hybrids and people of this earth who are in the inner earth, have to get out of there. They have to come out on the surface of the earth and are coming out (See Revelation 9:1-2 1) in order to prepare the way for the Devil and devils -to be put in

OUTER SPACE PEOPLE AND INNER EARTH PEOPLE

prison in the inner earth. The inner earth is being cleaned out and prepared for the Devil. "And I saw an angel come down from heaven, having the key of the bottomless pit and a great chain in his hand. And he laid hold on the dragon, that old serpent, which is the Devil, and Satan, and bound him a thousand years, and cast him into the bottomless pit, and shut him up, and set a seal upon him, that he should deceive the nations no more, till the thousand years should be fulfilled: and after that he must be loosed a little season." (Rev. 20:1-3

I suppose that after the Devil and devils are in prison for a thousand years, that sometime after they are released they will pass through the greater and more severe judgment of the lake of fire and will after that judgment be restored as Lucifer and Luciferians, just as they were on the original earth before they fell and became disembodied spirits.

Please do not confuse the Devil and devils with the fallen angels. The fallen angels were outer-space people that invaded the earth from outer-space. They were banished to the pit; that is, to the inner earth, in the days of Noah just prior to the flood. These fallen angels are not disembodied spirits. They are not devils.

Lucifer, the Devil, and all devils are the disembodied spirits of that race of men and women that lived on the earth prior to this present habitation on the earth. Devils are earth-bound spirits of a previous race of earth dwelling people. Beginning with the second clause of Genesis :2 "and the Spirit of God moved upon the face of the waters"-on to Genesis 2:4 is the story of the creation of the present inhabited cycle of this earth. Genesis 1:2-21 and Genesis 2:14 is the story of our earth as it emerged in this creation period.

The length of time of these seven days of creation is unknown. Each creative day may have been thousands of years long. They were not twenty-four hour days. This is evident from the fact that this earth (globe) was not set into the solar system until the fourth day of creation. (Gen. 1:14-19). There could not have been a solar day before there was a sun; nor a lunar week and month before there was a moon. Our seconds, minutes, hours, days, weeks, months and years are determined by the sun and moon and could not have existed before there was a sun and moon. There was no sun or moon until the fourth day of creation. That is, the earth was not set into and fixed in the family of the sun and moon until the fourth creative day.

Furthermore the word "GOD" in the first chapter of Genesis is ELOHIM and is plural. "GOD" is a plural body and is the heavenly sons and daughters of Yahveh. It was the Heavenly sons and daughters of Yahveh that created this earth and this heavenly family is called "GOD."

You can see this clearly and understand it perfectly by watching the context of the scripture. Notice "US" and "OUR" in this: "And God said, Let us make man in our own image, after our likeness: and let them have dominion over the fish of the sea, and over the fowl of the air, and over the cattle, and over all the earth, and over every creeping thing that creepeth upon the earth. So God created man in his own image, in the image of God created he him... male and female "created he them." (Gen. 1:26-27).

OUTER SPACE PEOPLE AND INNER EARTH PEOPLE

The natural man was created in the image of a son of Yahveh and the natural woman was created in the image of a daughter of Yahveh. That male and female man, and woman, in Genesis 1:26-27 were only earthly, mortal images of the ELOHIM, that is, they were images of the sons and daughters of Yahveh who created them.

All of the natural animal races of men who are of the earth, earthy-may have been on this earth for a million years before Adam and Eve were formed. When the Gods (ELOHIM) finished the creation, they rested on the seventh day. (Gen. 2:1-7). That simply meant that their work of creation was finished. The length of that period of rest is unknown.

The time came when Yahveh called all of his children before him in heaven and told these ELOHIM (Gods) who had created the world and the natural races of men, that they, the sons of God, would have to leave their spiritual bodies in heaven, give up their heavenly glory and be infolded in a seed and be born into the flesh on earth. They did not like that at all.

"The Spirit itself beareth witness with our spirit that we are the children of God: And, if children, then heirs; heirs of God, and joint heirs with Christ; if so be that we suffer with him, that we may be also glorified together. For I reckon that the sufferings of this present time are not worthy to be compared with the glory which shall be revealed in us. For the earnest expectation of the creature waiteth for the manifestation of the sons of God. For the creature was made subject to vanity, not willingly, but by reason of him who hath subjected the same in hope; because the creature itself also shall be delivered from the bondage of corruption into the glorious liberty of the children of God.

For we know that the whole creation groaneth and travaileth in pain together until now. And not only they, but ourselves also, which have the firstfruits of the Spirit, even we ourselves groan within ourselves waiting for the adoption, to wit: The redemption of our body. (Rom. 8:16-28).

"But we have this treasure in earthen vessels, That the excellency of the power may be of God, and not of us. . . Always bearing about in the body of the Dying of the Lord Jesus, that the life also of Jesus might be made manifest in our body. For we which live are always delivered unto death for Jesus' sake, that the life also of Jesus might be made manifest in our mortal flesh." (III Cor. 4:7, 10-11).

The first son of Yahveh that was made flesh was Adam. "And the Lord God formed man of the dust of the ground, and breathed into his nostrils the breath of life; and man became a living soul." (Gen. 2:7). ADAM was the first INSPIRED, heavenly son in the flesh on this earth. All in all there were actually 144,000 heavenly sons of Yahveh INCARNATED (born into flesh) from Adam to Christ. They were resurrected from the dead and ascended into heaven with Christ. (Matt. 27:50-58, Eph. 4:8, Heb. 2:9-18, Heb. 12:2-24, Rev.7:1-9, Rev. 14: 1-5). These are called THE FIRSTFRUITS. (I Cor. 15:23, Rev. 14:4).

Just how many heavenly sons have been INCARNATED, born into the flesh, in the last 1900 years since Christ and the 144,000 ascended, we do not know. But this we do know, that "Of his own will begat he us with the word of truth, that we should be a kind of

OUTER SPACE PEOPLE AND INNER EARTH PEOPLE

firstfruits of his creatures." (James 1:18). "And not only they, but ourselves also, which have the firstfruits of the Spirit, even we ourselves groan within ourselves, waiting for the adoption, to wit, the redemption of our body." (John. 8:28).

We who have the FIRSTFRUITS of the Spirit are the ELOHIM, sons and daughters of Yahveh. We are the Executive Body of Christ and are kings, priests and judges (Rev. 1:6, Rev.5:10, I Cor.6:1-8) who share equally with Christ in "THE HIGH CALLING." (Phil. 8:14). "The Spirit itself beareth witness with our spirit that we are the children of God: and if children, then heirs; heirs of God and joint heirs with Christ; if so be that we suffer with him, that we may be also glorified together." (Rom. 8:16-17). "For we are members of his body, of his flesh, and of his bones. . . . This is a great mystery: but I speak concerning Christ and the church." (Eph. 5:80, 82).

Those of us who are in the FIRSTFRUITS body do now share in and are now in the "BETTER RESURRECTION" (Heb. 11:85) which is to spiritual heavenly glory by which we will regain our heavenly bodies and return to the glory that we had with the Father before the world was. (John 17:5). Jesus said: "And all mine are thine, and thine are mine; and I am glorified in them. And now I am no more in the world, but these are in the world, and I come to thee. Holy Father, keep through thine own name those whom thou has given me, that they may be one, as we are. Neither pray I for these alone, but for them also which shall believe on me through their word; that they all may be one; as thou, Father, art in me, and I in thee, that they also may be one in us: that the world may believe that thou hast sent me. And the glory which thou gavest me I have given them; that they may be one, even as we are one." (John 17: 10-11, 20-22).

I do not say that every person in Adam's race is a son of Yahveh and preexisted, but I do say that every son of Yahveh who has been incarnated in the flesh has been born into Adam's race and never into any other. Also that every patriarch, prophet, priest, king and apostle and every person that Yahveh has ever called, chosen and used for his work in the earth has been of Adam's race. The race of Adam is the white race out of which the twelve tribes of Israel were chosen and also the twelve apostles and all of the Writers of the Bible. Likewise, all of the preexisting, foreordained, predestinated, chosen and elected sons of Yahveh that have come to earth have come here in and through the Adamic race and never through any of the natural earthy races of the first chapter of Genesis.

When Yahveh in person formed, inbreathed and inspired Adam (Gen. 2:7), he put Adam in The Garden which was Eastward in Eden. That area was 1200 miles long and 1200 miles wide. In other words the border was 1200 miles on the east side, 1200 miles on the west side, 1200 miles on the north side and 1200 miles on the south side. The distance around the boundary line of the Garden Of Eden Was 4800 miles. This area was at the top of the world. It was the capital ruling area of the world.

This area was shaped like a pyramid and from the base of it to the hotep or flat part was 1200 miles-that is it was 1200 miles high from the center of the base to the hotep. You will remember that in the center of this garden there was "THE TREE OF LIFE." (Gen. 2:9). Adam and Eve and many of the children of Yahveh may have been in that garden for

OUTER SPACE PEOPLE AND INNER EARTH PEOPLE

a thousand years or for as long as seven thousand years. We do not know. They had conditional immortality and were ageless and deathless while they were in the Garden. We do not begin to count the life of Adam by years until after he transgressed and was driven out of the Garden. When sin and disease and death set in, from that time on, we count the age of Adam by years. That was not too long ago—only 5,965 years ago that Adam left Eden.

We get this exact time element from taking the age of each father, when his son was born and adding up the years-beginning in Genesis 5: 1-82) and following through Genesis 11: 10-26 and Matthew I: 1-25), and in Luke 8: 28-88 we have two lineages or genealogies, from king to king and from father to son from Adam to Christ which was exactly four thousand years. It is now 1965 years since Christ or a total of 5965 years from the fall of Adam to the present time.

The earth, in the time of Genesis the first and second chapters, was upright at the poles. And there was an even tropical climate all over the earth. The energy from the sun was seven times greater than it is now and the energy of the moon was then equal to the present energy of the sun. (Isa. 80:26). The earth then was blessed with eight times more life-giving energy than it now has.

Six sevenths of the earth then was dry fertile soil. (II Esdras 6:42, Apocrypha). Four rivers flowed out from a fountainhead in the Garden of Eden, forming belts that crossed and thus divided the earth into "four quarters". These four rivers covered, all told, an area amounting to one-seventh of the earth's surface.

"And a river, went out of Eden to water the garden and from thence it was parted, and became into four heads. The name of the first is Pison: that is it which compasseth the whole land of Havilah, where there is gold.

And the gold of that land is good: there is Bdellium and the onyx stone: And the name of the second river is Gihon: the same is it that compasseth the whole land of Ethiopia. And the name of the third river is Hiddekel: that is it which goeth toward the east of Assyria. And the fourth rivet is Euphrates. (Gen. 2: 10-14.)

Immediately after Adam was driven out of the Garden of Eden the earth tilted and that pyramid-shaped area known as the Garden of Eden, which was 4800 miles around and 1200 miles high, was thrown off from the earth, hurled out into outer-space, and became a satellite, asteroid or planetoid of this earth. Yahshua the Messiah, during the last 1900 years, has built up that Garden of Eden which is now in outer-space into the New Jerusalem, the Holy City. The key to this truth is that in it is "THE TREE OF LIFE" (Rev. 22: 2) which proves that it was originally the Garden of Eden. (Gen. 2:9).

"And he that talked with me had a golden reed to measure the city, and the gates thereof, and the wall thereof. And the city lieth foursquare, and the length is as large as the breadth: and he measured the city with the reed, twelve thousand furlongs. The length and the breadth and the height of it are equal. And he measured the wall thereof, a hundred and forty and four cubits, according to the measure of a man. That is, of the angel. And the building of the wall of it was of jasper: and the city was pure gold, like unto clear

OUTER SPACE PEOPLE AND INNER EARTH PEOPLE

glass. And the foundations of the wall of the city were garnished with all manner of precious stones. The first foundation was jasper, the second sapphire; the third, a chalcedony; the fourth, an emerald; The fifth, sardonyx; the sixth, sardium; the seventh, chrysolite; the eighth, beryl; the ninth, a topaz; the tenth, a chrysoprasus; the eleventh, a jacinth; the twelfth, an amethyst. And the twelve gates were twelve pearls; every several gate was of one pearl: and the street of the city was pure gold, as it were transparent glass. And I saw no temple therein: for the Lord God Almighty and the Lamb are the temple of it. And the city had no need of the sun, neither of the moon, to shine in it: for the glory of God did lighten it, and the Lamb is the light thereof. And the nations of them which are saved shall walk in the light of it: and the kings of the earth do bring their glory and honor into it. And the gates of it shall not be shut at all by day: for there shall be no night there. And they shall bring the glory and honor of the nations into it. And there shall in no wise enter into it any thing that defileth, neither whatsoever worketh abomination, or maketh a lid: but they which are written in the Lamb's book of life". (Rev. 21: 15-26)

After the thousand years (millennium) when the earth is restored, the dead raised to life, death abolished and all men reconciled unto Yahveh, then the City of Heaven which is now in outer-space and which was originally the Garden of Eden will descend to the earth and will be the capstone or apex of the pyramid that will complete the perfect restoration and reconciliation of the earth and all things.

It was after the fall of Adam and all during those 1656 years from Adam to Noah that the angels who were outer-space people invaded the earth married women and corrupted the whole world. Those fallen angels and their hybrid offspring are now in the inner earth. Many of them are highly intelligent and farther advanced in science than those of us on the surface of the earth.

The energy from both the sun and the moon was greatly lessened when the Garden of Eden and other areas were thrown off from the earth. But 1656 years later when the outer-space water belt fell to the earth causing the flood (Gen. 1: 6-7 and Gen. 6th, 7th and 8th chapters), the earth turned upside-down. (Isa. 24: 1).

Dr. Warren Hamilton, a geologist living in Denver, Colorado, who just recently returned from the Antarctic, said on Feb. 10, 1959-Quote: "The Antarctic's geological features can best be explained by the continental drift theory." This theory, he explained, is that the earth's land area at one time was in a single mass, but for some reason the continents broke off and drifted to their present locations, "It appears logical that the Antarctic once was alongside of an upside down Australia in the Indian Ocean."

"Years ago the continent had a moist temperate climate, a study of rocks and plant fossils revealed," they said. "Temperature there has warmed up the past 50 years but glaciers essentially are in the same place as then. This is in contrast to the Arctic glaciers which have receded and are gradually dissolving. It's probably a good thing the Antarctic glaciers are not melting," Hayes added, "it would raise sea level about 800 feet."

When the earth turned upside-down (Isa. 24:1) and went out of its orbit in the solar system after that the Bible says: "all the foundations of the earth are out of course." (Psalm

OUTER SPACE PEOPLE AND INNER EARTH PEOPLE

82:5). The moon became a dead planet with its energy reduced 400,000 times. Six-sevenths of the energy from the sun was cut off from the earth. (Isa. 80:26). Consequently man, since the flood, has been living a very narrow span of life in a sick, sinful and dying world order.

However, since the flood there have been frequent visits by outer-space people to this earth. Most of them have been friendly. Most of those who have visited the earth since the flood have been holy people. The Bible mentions heaven, heavenly, heavens, angel and angels a total of 1025 times. The Bible literally records in detail the many visits by outer-space people to this earth; I shall cite but a few cases and only by brief outline.

WHO ARE THE ANGELS? The Hebrew word for "angel" is "MALAK". The Greek word for "angel" is "ANGELOS" and means a messenger, to bring tidings, ambassador, deputy, priest, teacher, king. The word "angels" as used in the Bible simply applies to outer-space and inner-earth people who have visited or contacted the people on this earth.

We know of four orders of angels: 1. Cherubim, 2. Seraphim (These have bodies composed of the element of light and fire and they dwell in the highest heavens). 3. Archangels, which are the kings and high-priests who are rulers over the outer-space dwelling places and they are always clothed in white. 4. Angels. These are outer-space men, exactly like the men on the earth. Some of them are of a little higher nature than we are, but there is very little, if any, noticeable difference.

Let us check up on a few of the visits that they have made to this earth. OUTER-SPACE PEOPLE HAVE VISITED THIS EARTH AND HAVE TAKEN PART IN EVERY MAJOR EVENT THAT HAS EVER HAPPENED ON THIS EARTH.

1. Three Outer-Space men visited Abraham and told him that they were going to destroy Sodom and Gomorrah. One of them told him that when he was one hundred years old and when Sarah was ninety, she would give birth to a son. (Gen. 18:1-8.)

2. Two Outer Space men rescued Lot and his wife and two daughters from Sodom. (Gen. 19: 1-23.)

3. An Outer-Space person visited Jacob and gave him the name "ISRAEL". (Gen. 32-28.)

4. The Law was "ordained by angels in the hand of a Mediator." (Gal. 8: 19.) Israel received the Law by the disposition of angels. (Acts 7:58). The law was spoken, that is, dictated by angels. (Heb. 2:2).

5. The children of Israel while in the wilderness were fed on angel food: "And had rained down manna upon them to eat and had given them of the corn of heaven. Man did eat angels' food: he sent them meat to the full." (Psalm 78:24-25)

"Thou feedest thine own people with angels' food, and didst send them from heaven bread prepared without their labour, able to content every man's delight, and agreeing to every taste." (Wisdom of Solomon 16:20. Apocrypha.)

OUTER SPACE PEOPLE AND INNER EARTH PEOPLE

THIS IS IMPORTANT. Hear it! If mortal man on this earth goes without food and water, he will die in a few days. Fasting is very dangerous. But if Outer Space people come here and give a man a meal of heavenly food, it completely satisfies his hunger and tastes better than any human food. Man can go as long as forty days on angel food without food or water. THIS IS THE KEY TO FASTING. If you are tired and weary, you need food from heaven.

"But he himself went a day's journey into the wilderness, and came and sat down under a juniper tree: and he requested for himself that he might die; and said, It is enough; now, O Lord, take away my life; for I am not better than my fathers. And as he lay and slept under the juniper tree, behold, then an angel touched him, and said unto him, Arise and eat. And he looked, and, be hold, there was a cake baked on the coals, and a cruse of water at his head. And he did eat and drink, and laid him down again. And The angel of the Lord came again the second time, and touched him, and said, Arise and eat; because the journey is too great for thee. And he arose, and did eat and drink, and went in the strength of that meat forty days and forty nights unto Horeb the mount of God." (1 Kings 19: 4-8.)

6. A general from Outer-Space led Israel to victory in the Promised Land.

"And it came to pass, when Joshua was by Jericho, that he lifted up his eyes and looked, and, behold, there stood a man over against him with his sword drawn in his hand: and Joshua went unto him, and said unto him, Art thou for us, or for our adversaries? And he said, Nay: but as captain of the host of the Lord am I now come. And Joshua fell on his face to the earth, and did worship, and said unto him, What saith my Lord unto his servant? And the captain of the Lord's host said unto Joshua, Loose thy shoe from off thy foot; for the place whereon thou standest is holy. And Joshua did so. (Joshua 5: 18-15.)

7. I would like to tell you in detail, but do not have the space to do so, how that Outer-Space man appeared to Gideon (Judges 6: 11-21) and to Manoah (Judges 18:15-28) and how that Outer Space captains destroyed 185,000 Assyrians (II Kings 19:35.) But I simply must give you now seventeen references in the New Testament showing the important part that Outer-Space people had in bringing the Christian Faith to this earth.

1. An angel announced the conception of John the Baptist and gave him the name "John" before he was born. (Luke 1 :1-19.)

2. An angel announced the Virgin conception to Mary. (Luke l: 145.)

3. An angel told Joseph that Mary had conceived by the Holy Ghost. (Matt. 1:18-24.)

4. An angel, together with a multitude of Outer-Space people, came to earth and announced the birth of Jesus Christ. (Luke 2: 8-16.)

7. An angel strengthened Jesus in the Garden of Gethsemane. (Luke 22: 41-42.)

8. Angels rolled the stone away from the tomb and announced the resurrection. (Matt. 28: 2-7.)

OUTER SPACE PEOPLE AND INNER EARTH PEOPLE

9. Immediately after his ascension angels came down and spoke to the disciples. (Acts I: 9-11)

10. An Angel told the Gentiles to send for the Apostle Peter to preach to them. (Acts 10: 30-42.)

11. An angel delivered the Apostle Peter from prison. (Acts 12: 8-11)

12. An angel struck Herod and killed him. (Acts 12: 20-28.)

13. An angel called the Apostle Paul to Europe. (Acts 16: 8-10.)

14. An angel announced to Paul that his life and those on board that ship, in that terrible storm at sea, would be saved. (Acts 27: 21-26.)

15. Angels rejoice when a soul is saved. (Luke 15: 7-10.)

16. Angels will gather the elect children of Yahveh together from all over this world. (Matt. 24:81.)

17. Angels will gather out the scoffers, sinners and ungodly and completely separate them from those who are saved.- (Matt. 13:40-48.)

There are so many other references to angels in both the Old and New Testaments that I say to you, if you do not believe that these Outer-Space people have frequently visited this earth over a period of 6000 years, then you had just as well throw your Bible away.

These Outer-Space people do minister to us. "Are they not all ministering spirits, sent forth to minister for them who shall be heirs of salvation?" (Heb. I : 14.) We also are compassed about with an innumerable company of angels." (Heb. 12:1-22.)

The Outer-Space people live in the area that begins twenty miles above the land of this earth. From twenty miles above the earth and extending to 250,000 miles beyond the moon, or a total of 500,000 miles beginning twenty miles above us, there is a ring 500,000 miles through in which the outer-space people dwell. That area completely surrounds us. (Remember the three skies, heavens, mentioned in the introduction to this message then multiply these figures by three.)

I am not talking about dwellers on Mars or Venus or other planets. (They are inhabited, too.) But I am talking about men above the earth.

THREE REALMS OF MEN BELONG TO THIS EARTH, namely: The men above the earth, the men on the surface of the earth and the men inside the earth. (Rev. 5:5, Rev. 5:18; Eph. 8: 940, Phil. 2:10-11, Eph. 1-10). Look up these scriptures and read them in your own Bible. We must get acquainted with and become friendly and cooperative with the men above the earth and with the inner-earth people before we can ever expect to reach the dwellers on other planets. As long as we know of only the people on the surface of the earth, that means that most of our earth people are unknown. Most of the earth people now dwell above the earth or inside the earth.

My contention is this! That in addition to the moon there are more than two thou-

OUTER SPACE PEOPLE AND INNER EARTH PEOPLE

sand planetoids or heavenly dwelling places which belong to this earth. They are fragments that were broken off from the earth in its many disruptions in the past. Everything in space extending to 250,000 miles beyond the moon belongs to the earth and is the earth. Maybe I can illustrate it this way: Let a hard-boiled egg represent the earth. The yolk of the egg represents the land on which we live. The white represents the air and immediate sky which the Bible calls "firmament." God called the firmament heaven". (Gen. 1: 8;. This is the "heaven" that belongs to this earth. The shell of the egg represents the outer rim or asteroid circle. The asteroid circle is broken up and forms an island archipelago or dwelling places which completely encase and surround the land and sky of our earth (and the earth has three skies), There are twelve gates, twelve magnetic fields or lanes through the asteroid circle by which we will someday travel from the earth to the outer planets. Jacob saw one of these gates or lanes:

"And he dreamed, and behold a ladder set up on the earth, and the top of it reached to heaven: and behold the angels of God ascending and descending on it. And Jacob awakened out of his sleep, and said, Surely the Lord is in this place: and I knew it not. And he was afraid, and said, How dreadful is this place! This is none other but the house of God, and this is the gate to heaven." (Gen. 28:12-16

That was one of the gates of heaven. There are twelve. A magnetic rocket launched from any one of the twelve magnetic fields of the earth, possibly could get through the three asteroid circles and perhaps reach Mars or Venus. But the men above the earth guard those gates with strong forces.

The Garden of Eden, which is now the New Jerusalem, is one of the more than 2000 Outer-Space dwelling places that are part of this earth. It is banked by fire and guarded by "Cherubims". (Gen. 3:24). It is 4800 miles around the boundary of that Eden. (Gen. 2:8, Rev. 21:16, Rev. 22:2.) The other inhabited places are guarded also but not as securely as Eden.

Those living closest to earth-that is, in "outer darkness" (Matt. 8: 12, Matt. 22:13, Matt. 25:30) are not friendly. They are wicked and very cruel. "Outer-Darkness" begins twenty miles above the earth. How far it extends I do not know, but perhaps from three to ten thousand miles. The righteous and friendly people above the earth live beyond the circle of darkness, but it is very hard for them to get through to us. It took a holy angel twenty-one days to come down through that darkness. He had to have the help of Michael to get through. (Daniel 10:. 12-14). Some of the fallen angels dwell in that realm of darkness just above the earth. They are able, it seems, to travel forth and back from outer darkness to the inner-earth. (2 Peter 2:4, Jude 6, Rev. 9:1-21).

We have been assigned the job of converting and judging them, and believe me it isn't any easy task. (Eph. 8:9-11, Eph. 6:12, I Cor. 6: 1-8).

The power of the Outer-Space people has been demonstrated twice in a mighty way. (Gen. 11: 1-9, Acts 2: 1-47). After the flood the land of the earth was still joined solidly together. There were no continents and islands as there now are. The family of Noah increased very rapidly. They were all of one race and spoke one language. They attempted to build a tower into heaven. More than 500,000 men were employed in the

OUTER SPACE PEOPLE AND INNER EARTH PEOPLE

construction of it. It was sixty miles around the base. Workers took materials up at the rate of ten miles a day. It took 365 days to transport the material from the base of the tower to the top. That tower rose 8650 miles high. The men on earth began an attack on the Outer-Space men. Blood rained down upon the earth. The Lords (leaders) of Outer-Space united their forces and invaded the earth. They brain-washed the men of the earth, took away their language, and planted or recorded in their minds more than a thousand of the outer-space languages. Then they scattered the earth men to every nook and corner of the land, threw down the tower and divided the land into continents and islands as it is today.

In the days of "Peleg" and "Joktan" the earth was divided, (Gen. 10:25). "Peleg" means "to divide", "Joktan" means "to lessen." Since the flood, and especially since the destruction of the tower of Babel and the dividing of the land, the land of the earth has been greatly lessened. In fact only one-tenth of the surface of the earth is inhabitable. The remainder being water, ice, deserts and rough mountains. The earth before the flood was six-sevenths fertile inhabitable land. Now it is only one-tenth inhabitable.

When the Outer-Space people invaded the earth, confused the tongues, scattered the people, destroyed the tower of Babel, and divided the land, they also transported a lot of the lowest and worst of their own races to this earth. The savage tribes and the Satanic serpent peoples of this earth did not originate here. They were dumped here by the Outer-Space people. They will be banished from the earth to "outer darkness", driven off the face of the earth. (Gen. 4:14, Matt. 8:12, Matt. 22:13, Matt. 25:30, Matt. 13:40-43). That is, they will be sent back to the place from which they came. Jesus Christ in person, together with an innumerable host of angels and spirits of just men made perfect (Acts 2:1-47, Heb. 12:22-24), came to earth on the day of Pentecost and gave to us the first signs that our pure and original language is to be restored. We have regained the name "YAHVEH" and "YAHSHUA" and will eventually get back all of our pure language. "In that day shall there be one YAHVEH and his name one." (Zech. 14:9). "For then will I turn to the people a pure language that they may all call upon the name of YAHVEH, to serve him with one consent." (Zeph. 8:9).

I have freely consulted the Apocrypha, the Book of Enoch, the book of Jasher, the book of Adam and Eve, the Egyptian book of the Dead, and hundreds of other ancient books, both secular and religious. I accept the Bible as absolute authority on science and all things. As long as I live I'm going to stick to the Bible.

The material scientists, university professors, colleges, universities and modernistic preachers will not accept anything that I write as truth. This message, like all of my messages, will be studied by classes in sociology and by students of psychology and even by psychiatrists-just to try to point out that I am a crazy fanatic. I have said before, and I say again that those in authority today will not even consider what I say as an hypothesis-much less as a theory, but I say that it is the Bible and that the Holy Spirit is my teacher. The wisdom of this world knows nothing about Yahveh and the Holy Spirit.

My own opinion is that the earth is shaped like a cube, with the top side and bottom being inhabited and the sides being an ice barrier. This is my idea of the shape of

OUTER SPACE PEOPLE AND INNER EARTH PEOPLE

this earth. The Inner earth undoubtedly has an even tropical climate and probably six or seven times more inhabitable land than our surface of the earth.

The ninetieth parallel where the needle of the compass points straight up and where the gyroscope stands still is not, in my opinion, the north or the south pole but only the magnetic rim or border where the earth becomes flat. We have no ascertained truth-so far only theories. Latitude and longitude and the poles are imaginary-theories which work to a given point. I predict that all the present ideas taught in the schools today about our globe and all of the ideas of the scientists today about this earth and the stars will be wholly discarded within less than forty years.

"Hast thou entered into the treasure of the snow?" (Job 88:22). From time immemorial in all sacred and profane literature of all the ancient nations they referred to the northernmost point on the earth as "the navel of the earth." The Bible says that Yahveh "stretches out the North over the empty place, and hangeth the earth upon nothing," (Job 26:7.) The circuit of the wind and water was well known: "Out of the south cometh the whirlwind." (Job 87:9) - In 1947 Admiral Byrd discovered an open warm water sea at, and stretching beyond, the region of the South Pole. The earth is flat at the South Pole over an area larger than North America of which a section of land larger than the United States of America is covered with ice two miles deep. There is no mould, rust, tarnish or decay in all that ice-covered area. Meat, fruit or food of any kind stored there would be kept fresh indefinitely. Machinery would not rust and would be kept bright and shining and as good as new for hundreds or even for thousands of years. This Antarctic "deep freeze" will eventually be utilized.

The Antarctic is a vast continent and the frozen trees, fruits, animals and buried cities under that ice will, when uncovered, astonish the world. The open water and dry land, near and beyond the pole is no mystery to anyone who believes the Bible. A great canyon slopes gradually into the interior of the earth. The outer edge of the rim of the canyon at the point where the slope begins possibly may be 6000 miles in circumference and 2000 miles across. It is definitely known and an established scientific fact that the weather, that is, the circuit of the winds originates at the South Pole. A constant strong current of wind comes out from the opening from the interior of the earth. "Out of the south cometh the whirlwind." (Job 87:9). "The wind goeth toward the south, and turneth about unto the north: it whirleth about continually and the wind returneth again according to his circuits." (Eccl. 1:6).

But the circuit of the waters undoubtedly originates at the North Pole. "All the rivers run into the sea; yet the sea is not full; unto the place from whence the rivers come; thither they return again." (Eccl. 1:7).

"For promotion cometh neither from the east nor from the west nor from the south. But God is the judge; he putteth down one, and setteth up another. For in the land of the Lord there is a cup, and the wine is red; it is full of mixture." (Ps.75:6-8).

God rules the universes from "the mount of the congregation, in the sides of the north." (Isa. 14:13.) Our sun and all planets in our solar system and all suns and solar systems move toward the north. The origin of matter and the central hub of all universes

OUTER SPACE PEOPLE AND INNER EARTH PEOPLE

is in the north. How long it takes all solar systems to complete their orbit around the central hub is unknown, but at any rate all stars and planets move northward at a terrific speed. For all we know there may be millions or even billions of suns, each with a family of planets. The Bible says that to man "the stars of the sky in multitude" are "innumerable." (Heb. I 1:12.) But Yahveh "telleth the number of the stars; he calleth them all by their names. (Ps. 147:4). And it was in and by and through Yahshua The Messiah (Jesus Christ) "by whom also he made the worlds." (Heb. 1:2.) What a great truth our Savior spoke when he said, "In my Father's house are many mansions. I go to prepare a place for you." (John 14:2.) And the prophet Amos said, "It is he that buildeth his stories in the heavens." (Amos 9:6.) All of the billions of worlds are inhabited by "an innumerable company of angels." (Heb. 12:22.) They are also inhabited by men and are being prepared for habitations for the men of the earth."

Let us look for a moment at our own universe as it is known today. There are probably at least three planets as well as thousands of asteroids and planetoids in our solar system that have not yet been discovered. But the facts as we now have them are as follows:

EDITOR'S NOTE:

The following statistics are found in Blessing's original text. Following these claims will be found updated information concerning the solar system and the star formations in Centauri.

1. The Sun. Diameter 886,000 miles. Circumference 2,658,000 miles. Turns on its axis in 25 days, 7 hours. 48 minutes.

2. Mercury. Diameter 3000 miles. Circumference 9000 miles. Turns on axis every nine hours. Goes around the sun, a distance of 36,000,000 miles, every 88 days. If you were on this planet you would be four times as old in a year as you are now. A year is 88 days.

3. Venus; Diameter 7600 miles. Circumference 22;500 miles. Goes around the sun, a distance of 67,000,000 miles every 225 days.

4. Mars. Diameter 4180 miles. Circumference 12,500 miles. Turns on its axis 24 hours, 37 minutes; 32.6 seconds. Orbit 686 days. Distance from the, sun 141,650,000 miles. Varies in distance from the earth from 25 million to 63 million miles. Most observable of all planets. If you were on this planet you would be only half as old as you are now.

5. Jupiter. Has three red belts. Has seven moons, is 483,000,000 miles from the sun. Orbit is 12 years. On Jupiter you would be only one-twelfth as old as you are on earth.

6. Uranus. Diameter 32,000- miles. Circumference 96,000 miles. Orbit 84 years. A man on earth 84 years old would only be one year old on Uranus. Is it any wonder that God says that a man on earth, age 100, is a child. (Isa.65:20.) We are ail infants now. Our real life begins in the world to come. Uranus has three red belts, several red spots and has four moons.

OUTER SPACE PEOPLE AND INNER EARTH PEOPLE

7. Saturn. Most interesting of all. Diameter 75,000 miles. Circumference 225,000 miles. Orbit 29-1/2, years. Distance from the Sun 885,900,0.00 miles. Has nine moons chartered, measured and weighed, by the astronomers. Has three outer water rings? The first ring, 175,000 miles from the surface of Saturn is 10,000 miles thick. The second ring 145,000 miles from The surface is 16,000 miles thick. The third ring, 113,000 miles from the surface is 11,000 miles thick, (The earth once had a water ring or belt above the sky. This fell to the earth, 1656 years after the present creation and caused the Flood. Genesis 5th to 9th chapters tells the story.

8. Neptune. Diameter 30,000 miles. Circumference 90,000 miles. Orbit 16 years. In that time it travels. 18-billion, 859-million, 800-thousand miles-rate of 2000 miles per second, fastest of all the planets. Distance from the sun -2,700,800,000 miles. Has one moon that circles it every five days and twelve hours.

9. Pluto. Was discovered Jan. 28, 1930 by astronomer C. W. Tombaugh. Circles the sun every 248 years. Solid substances are only one-tenth as heavy as earthly solids. If you weigh 100 pounds on the earth you would weigh 1000 pounds on Pluto. But since one year there is as long as 248 of our years the oldest man now on earth, if taken to Pluto would have to wait at least 148 years to be born.

10. Alpha-Centauri. The nearest (sun) fixed star to our sun is 25,000,000,000,000 (trillion) miles away. If you got in an airplane on earth and flew toward Alpha-Centauri at the rate of a mile a minute, it would take you 48,000,000 years to reach her. But, thought is instant and when in a celestial body like Jesus had after his resurrection we will be able to travel instantly at will to the various stars, the many dwelling places in our Father's house.

UPDATED FACTS ABOUT THE SOLAR SYSTEM

SUN:
- Diameter (miles)= 865,000
  - Volume= 1,300,000 times that of earth
  - Temperature= =10,000 degrees Fahrenheit 27,000,000 degrees Fahrenheit
  - Age=4,600,000,000
  - Rotation period=1 month
  - Revolution around Milky Way= 200 to 250 million years

Observation data

Mean distance from Earth	$1.496 10^8$ km
8 min 19 s at light speed	
Visual brightness (V)	26.74[1]
Absolute magnitude	4.83[1]
Spectral classification	G2V
Metallicity	$Z = 0.0122$[2]
Angular size	31.6 – 32.7[3]

OUTER SPACE PEOPLE AND INNER EARTH PEOPLE

Adjectives   Solar
Orbital characteristics
Mean distance
from Milky Way core   ~$2.50 10^{17}$ km
26,000 light-years
Galactic period $(2.25–2.50) 10^8$ a
Velocity   ~220 km/s (orbit around the center of the
Galaxy)
~20 km/s (relative to average velocity of other stars in stellar neighborhood)
~370 km/s[4] (relative to the cosmic microwave background)
Physical characteristics
Mean diameter $1.392684 10^6$ km[5]
Equatorial radius $6.96342 10^5$ km[5]
109 Earth[6]
Equatorial circumference $4.379 10^6$ km[6]
109 Earth[6]
Flattening $9 10^6$
Surface area $6.0877 10^{12}$ km²[6]
11,990 Earth[6]
Volume $1.412 10^{18}$ km³[6]
1,300,000 Earth
Mass $1.9891 10^{30}$ kg[1]
333,000 Earth[1]
Average density $1.408 10^3$ kg/m³[1][6][7]
Density   Center (model): $1.622 10^5$ kg/m³[1]
Lower photosphere: $2 10^4$ kg/m³
Lower chromosphere: $5 10^6$ kg/m³
Corona (avg): $1 10^{12}$ kg/m³[8]
Equatorial surface gravity   274.0 m/s²[1]
27.94 g
27,542.29 cgs
28 Earth[6]
Escape velocity
(from the surface)   617.7 km/s[6]
55 Earth[6]
Temperature   Center (modeled): ~$1.57 10^7$ K[1]
Photosphere (effective): 5,778 K[1]
Corona: ~$5 10^6$ K
Luminosity (L_{sol}) $3.846 10^{26}$ W[1]
~$3.75 10^{28}$ lm
~98 lm/W efficacy
Mean intensity (I_{sol}) $2.009 10^7$ W·m²·sr¹
Age   4.57 billion years[9]
Rotation characteristics
Obliquity   7.25°[1]
(to the ecliptic)
67.23°
(to the galactic plane)
Right ascension

OUTER SPACE PEOPLE AND INNER EARTH PEOPLE

of North pole[10]	286.13°
19 h 4 min 30 s	
Declination	
of North pole	+63.87°
63° 52' North	
Sidereal rotation period	
(at equator)	25.05 days[1]
(at 16° latitude)	25.38 days[1]
25 d 9 h 7 min 12 s[10]	
(at poles)	34.4 days[1]
Rotation velocity	
(at equator)	7.18910^3 km/h[6]
Photospheric composition (by mass)	
Hydrogen	73.46%[11]
Helium	24.85%
Oxygen	0.77%
Carbon	0.29%
Iron	0.16%
Neon	0.12%
Nitrogen	0.09%
Silicon	0.07%
Magnesium	0.05%
Sulfur	0.04%

The **Sun** is the star at the center of the Solar System. It is almost perfectly spherical and consists of hot plasma interwoven with magnetic fields.[12][13] It has a diameter of about 1,392,684 km,[5] about 109 times that of Earth, and its mass (about 210^{30} kilograms, 330,000 times that of Earth) accounts for about 99.86% of the total mass of the Solar System.[14] Chemically, about three quarters of the Sun's mass consists of hydrogen, while the rest is mostly helium. The remainder (1.69%, which nonetheless equals 5,628 times the mass of Earth) consists of heavier elements, including oxygen, carbon, neon and iron, among others.[15]

The Sun formed about 4.6 billion years ago from the gravitational collapse of a region within a large molecular cloud. Most of the matter gathered in the center, while the rest flattened into an orbiting disk that would become the Solar System. The central mass became increasingly hot and dense, eventually initiating thermonuclear fusion in its core. It is thought that almost all other stars form by this process. The Sun's stellar classification, based on spectral class, is G2V, and is informally designated as a *yellow dwarf*, because its visible radiation is most intense in the yellow-green portion of the spectrum and although its color is white, from the surface of the Earth it may appear yellow because of atmospheric scattering of blue light.[16] In the spectral class label, *G2* indicates its surface temperature of approximately 5778 K (5505 °C), and *V* indicates that the Sun, like most stars, is a main-sequence star, and thus generates its energy by nuclear fusion of hydrogen nuclei into helium. In its core, the Sun fuses 620 million metric tons of hydrogen each second.

OUTER SPACE PEOPLE AND INNER EARTH PEOPLE

Once regarded by astronomers as a small and relatively insignificant star, the Sun is now thought to be brighter than about 85% of the stars in the Milky Way galaxy, most of which are red dwarfs.[17][18] The absolute magnitude of the Sun is +4.83; however, as the star closest to Earth, the Sun is the brightest object in the sky with an apparent magnitude of 26.74.[19][20] The Sun's hot corona continuously expands in space creating the solar wind, a stream of charged particles that extends to the heliopause at roughly 100 astronomical units. The bubble in the interstellar medium formed by the solar wind, the heliosphere, is the largest continuous structure in the Solar System.[21][22]

The Sun is currently traveling through the Local Interstellar Cloud (near to the G-cloud) in the Local Bubble zone, within the inner rim of the Orion Arm of the Milky Way galaxy.[23][24] Of the 50 nearest stellar systems within 17 light-years from Earth (the closest being a red dwarf named Proxima Centauri at approximately 4.2 light-years away), the Sun ranks fourth in mass.[25] The Sun orbits the center of the Milky Way at a distance of approximately 24,000–26,000 light-years from the galactic center, completing one clockwise orbit, as viewed from the galactic north pole, in about 225–250 million years. Since our galaxy is moving with respect to the cosmic microwave background radiation (CMB) in the direction of the constellation Hydra with a speed of 550 km/s, the Sun's resultant velocity with respect to the CMB is about 370 km/s in the direction of Crater or Leo.[26]

The mean distance of the Sun from the Earth is approximately 149.6 million kilometers (1 AU), though the distance varies as the Earth moves from perihelion in January to aphelion in July.[27] At this average distance, light travels from the Sun to Earth in about 8 minutes and 19 seconds. The energy of this sunlight supports almost all life on Earth by photosynthesis,[28] and drives Earth's climate and weather. The enormous effect of the Sun on the Earth has been recognized since prehistoric times, and the Sun has been regarded by some cultures as a deity. An accurate scientific understanding of the Sun developed slowly, and as recently as the 19th century prominent scientists had little knowledge of the Sun's physical composition and source of energy. This understanding is still developing; there are a number of present day anomalies in the Sun's behavior that remain unexplained.

MERCURY

Type of Object : Solid Planet
Location : First planet away from Sun
Diameter : 4,878 kilometers (3031.04 miles)
Mass : 3.303^{23} kilograms (2.051^{26} pounds), or 0.0558 Earths
Temperature : Surface-179°C (354.2°F)
Rotation Period : 58.6462 days
Density : 5.42 gm/cm^3
Distance from Sun : 57.9 million kilometers

OUTER SPACE PEOPLE AND INNER EARTH PEOPLE

Mean orbital velocity: 47.89 kilometers per second
Length of mercurian year: 0.2408 Earth-year, 87.9 Earth-days
Length of mercurian day: 58.6 Earth-days
Rotational period : 58.6462 days
Orbital period : 87.969 days
Mean orbital velocity : 47.88 km/sec
Orbital eccentricity : 0.2056
Tilt of axis : 0.00°
Orbital inclination : 7.004°
Equatorial surface gravity : 2.78 m/sec^2
Equatorial escape velocity : 4.25 km/sec
Magnitude : -1.9 Vo

V E N U S

Orbital Distance: 0.72 Earths orbit
Orbital Period: 0.62 Earth years
Rotation: 243 Earth days (retrograde)
Mean Radius: 0.95 Earths radius
Mass : 0.815 Earth's mass
Surface Pressure : 90 atmospheres
Gravity : 0.91 Earths gravity
Orbit : 108,200,000 km (0.72 AU) from Sun
Diameter : 12,103.6 km
Mass : 4.869 x 10^24 kg

E A R T H

Mass (kg) : 5.98 x 10^24
Diameter (km) : 12756
Mean density (kg/m^3) : 5520
Escape velocity (m/sec) : 11200
Equatorial surface gravity (m/sec^2) : 9.78
Average distance from Sun (AU) : 1 (149,600,000 km)
Rotation period (length of day in Earth hours) : 23.93
Revolution period (length of year in Earth days) : 365.26
Mean orbital velocity (km/sec) : 29.79
Obliquity (tilt of axis in degrees) : 23.4
Orbit eccentricity (deviation from circular) : 0.017
Mean surface temperature (K) : 281 (15 degree Celsius)
Maximum surface temperature (K) : 310
Minimum surface temperature (K) : 260
Visual geometric albedo (reflectivity) : 0.39
Highest point on surface : Mount Everest (8+ km above sea-level)
Atmospheric components : 78% nitrogen, 21% oxygen, 1% argon

OUTER SPACE PEOPLE AND INNER EARTH PEOPLE

Surface materials : basaltic and granitic rock and altered materials

MARS

Mass : 6.42×10^{23} kg
Diameter : 6787 km
Mean density : 3940 kg/m^3
Escape velocity : 5000 m/sec
Average distance from the Sun : 227,940,000 km
Average distance from Sun : 1.524 AU
Rotation period/Length of day : 1.026 Earth days
Revolution period/Length of year : 686.98 Earth years
Obliquity/Tilt of axis : 25 degrees
Orbit inclination : 1.85 degrees
Orbit eccentricity/deviation from circular : 0.093
Maximum surface temperature : 310 K
Minimum surface temperature : 150 K
Visual geometric albedo (reflectivity) : 0.15
Magnitude : -2.01 Vo
Highest point on surface: Olympus Mons, 24 km high
Atmospheric components: 95% carbon dioxide, 3% nitrogen, 1.6% argon

ASTEROID BELT

The Asteroid Belt is made up of large and small rocks and chunks of ice called Asteroids that were left over from the creation of the solar system about 4.6 billion years ago. They are rocky objects with round or irregular shapes. Some are up to several hundred km across, but most are very small.

JUPITER

Mass : 1.90×10^{27} kg
Diameter : 142,800 km (88,731.8 miles)
Mean density : 1,314 kg/m^3
Escape velocity : 59,500 m/sec
Average distance from Sun : 5.203 Astronomical Units
Rotation period/Length of Day : 9.8 Earth hours
Revolution period/Length of Year: 11.86 Earth years
Obliquity/Tilt of Axis : 3.08 degrees
Orbit inclination : 1.3 degrees
Orbit eccentricity (deviation from circular): 0.048
Mean surface temperature : 120 K (cloud tops)
Visual geometric albedo (reflectivity): 0.44
Rings: Faint ring : Infrared spectra imply dark rock fragments.
<u>Halo</u>

OUTER SPACE PEOPLE AND INNER EARTH PEOPLE

Distance (From center of Jupiter) : 92,000 km (57,166.15 miles)
Width: 30,500 km (18,951.82 miles)
Thickness: 20,000 km (12,427.42 miles)

Main
Distance (From center of Jupiter) : 122,500 km (76,117.97 miles)
Width: 6,440 km (4,001.63 miles)
Thickness: Greater than 30 km (18.64 miles)

Inner Gossamer
Distance (From center of Jupiter) : 128,940 km (80,119.60 miles)
Width: 52,060 km (32,348.58 miles)
Thickness: Unknown

Outer Gossamer
Distance (From center of Jupiter) : 181,000 km (112,468.18 miles)
Width : 40,000 km (24,854.84 miles)
Thickness : Unknown

S A T U R N

Mass : 5.69×10^{26} kg (95.2 Earth masses)
Volume : 8.52×10^{23} m^3 (764 Earth volumes)
Diameter : 120660 km
Mean density : 690 kg/m^3
Escape velocity : 35600 m/sec
Average distance from Sun : 1,430 million km (9.539AU)
Gravity : 1.08 x Earth's
Rotation period/Length of Day : 10.2 Earth hours
Revolution period/Length of Year : 29.46 Earth years
Orbit Eccentricity : 0.056
Orbit Inclination : 2.5 degrees
Obliquity/Tilt of axis : 26.73 degrees
Orbit eccentricity (deviation from circular) : 0.056
Mean temperature : 134 K (1 bar level)
Visual geometric albedo (reflectivity) : 0.46

Rings
Rings are 270,000 km in diameter, but only a few hundred meters thick.
Particles are centimeters to decameters in size and are ice (some may be covered with ice); there are traces of silicate and carbon minerals. There are four main ring groups and three more faint, narrow ring groups separated by gaps called division.

U R A N U S

Minimum Distance from Earth : 2.57 billion km (1.6 billion miles)
Minimum Distance from Sun : 2.7 billion km (1.7 billion miles)
Maximum Distance from Sun : 3 billion km (1.87 billion miles)
Period of Revolution/Length of Year : 84.01 Earth years

OUTER SPACE PEOPLE AND INNER EARTH PEOPLE

Period of Rotation/Length of Day : 17.3 Earth hours
Orbital Eccentricity : 0.047 degrees
Orbit Inclination : 0.8 degrees
Diameter : 51,488 km (32,000 miles)
Mass : 14.5 Earths
Density : 1.3 (water=1)
Tilt of Axis : 98 degrees
Surface Gravity : 0.91 x Earth
Temperature : -200 degrees C (-328 degrees F)

NEPTUNE

Distance to Sun : 2.793 billion miles
Period of Revolution/Length of Year : 164.79 Earth years
Period of Rotation/Length of Day : 16.03 Earth hours
Orbit Eccentricity : 0.009
Orbit Inclination : 1.8 degrees
Mass : 1.024×10^{26} kg
Mass : 17.204 Earths
Diameter 48,598.97 km (30,198 miles)
Gravity : 1.19 Earths
Density : 1.76
Tilt of Axis : 29.6 degrees
Rings of Neptune
<u>1989N3R</u>
Distance From center of Neptune : 41,900 km (26,035.45 miles)
Width : 15 km (9.32 miles)
Thickness : Unknown
Mass : Unknown
Albedo : low
<u>1989N2R</u>
Distance From center of Neptune : 53,200 km (33,056.94 miles)
Width : 15 km (9.32 miles)
Thickness : Unknown
Mass : Unknown
Albedo : low
<u>1989N4R</u>
Distance From center of Neptune : 53,200 km (33,056.94 miles)
Width : 5,800 km (3,603.95 miles)
Thickness : Unknown
Mass : Unknown
Albedo : low
<u>1989N1R</u>
Distance From center of Neptune : 62,930 km (39,102.889 miles)
Width : 50 km (31.06 miles)

OUTER SPACE PEOPLE AND INNER EARTH PEOPLE

Thickness : Unknown
Mass : Unknown
Albedo : low

P L U T O

Distance to Sun: 5.899 billion km (3.666 billion miles)
Distance to Sun in Astronomical Units : 39.5
Average Surface Temperature : -230 degrees C (-446 degrees F)
Length of year : 247.69 Earth years
Length of Day : 6.3867 Earth days
Orbit Eccentricity : 0.25
Orbit Inclination : 17.2 degrees
Mass : 0.0026 Earths
Diameter : 2299.75 km (1,429 miles)
Gravity : .05 Earth or 1.27 x 10^22 kg
Tilt of Axis : 94 degrees
Year Discovered : 1930

O R T C L O U D

The Oort Cloud is a giant field of Asteroids and Comets that encircles the solar system. Discovered in 1950 when Jan Oort believed that since no Comets were coming from interstellar space, there must be some vast cloud where all our solar system's comets come from. The cloud could contain more than a trillion comets, and might account for a very large portion of the mass of our system. Not much is known about this or even if it exists, because seeing objects that small that far away is very difficult.

RETURN TO TEXT:

Light travels at the rate of 186,000 miles per second and until recently that was the measuring line used by astronomers, They often spoke of light years or "so many light years." Today the astronomers say "parsec" or "parsec universes." A "parsec" is 200,000 times the distance from the earth to the sun; that is 200,000 times 93,000,000 or 18,600,000,000,000 (18-trillion, 600-billion). There have been discovered 15,000 island parsec universes. 15,000 times 18,600,000,000,000 is 279,000,000,000,000,000 (279 quadrillion miles.) This is the diameter of all of our universes so far as it is known today.

This is; of course, incomprehensible, but now I wart to narrow it down to our Father's world, our earth. The earth occupies a diameter in space of 500,000 miles and a circumference of 1,500,000 miles. This is based on the earth's most distant satellite, the moon. The moon is 250,000 miles out from the center of the earth. In approximately twenty-eight days the moon travels in its orbit around the earth, a distance of 1,500,000 miles. The moon and everything within the moon's orbit belongs to this earth. (Since there are three Firmaments, Skies, or heavens that belong to the earth multiply this by three). The earth proper, as every school boy knows, is 8,000 miles in diameter and 24,000 miles in

OUTER SPACE PEOPLE AND INNER EARTH PEOPLE

circumference. It turns on its axis (at the equator) at the rate of 1000 miles per hour. The sun is 92 million miles from the earth. Therefore in 365¼ days the earth must travel 552-million miles in its orbit around the sun. The diameter of the earth's orbit is 184-million miles, the circumference 552 million miles, which means that the earth is traveling around the sun at a rate of 18 miles per second. (This is based upon the generally accepted theories.)

The long accepted Newton theory of gravitation is that gravity is something that pulls everything downward toward the center of the earth. That theory is now seriously questioned- Gravity is thought by many to be a pressure rather than a pull at the center of the earth a push in the entire solar systems which makes matter compact and holds all material things together-not a pull from within but a push from without. If this is true then there must be some power within the earth that is pressing outward, pushing things away from itself. This would explain the breathing of the earth-the expanding and contracting and this expanding and contracting may be the cause of the ebb and flow of the tides as well as the upheaval of the mountains, the volcanoes and the rising of new islands and land areas. The outward push from the center of the earth and the downward push of gravity may be a new theory that will completely revolutionize our thinking about both astronomy and geology.

Now as I have said before, the earth occupies all space within the orbit of the moon. Therefore, everything around the earth and upward for 500,000 miles belongs to the earth. The electrical current of the outward push extends upward for twenty miles and mingled with the positive rays of the sun it produces light. The light is due entirely to dust particles in the air. The air has weight. It is matter, the finest particles of dust-that is air.

The air, which is fine particles of dust, is charged with the negative electrical current which is the outward push from the earth. The air is twenty miles deep around the earth. The positive, electrical rays of the sun and the negative electrical rays of the earth combined and acting upon the dust particles which we call air produce light.

Twenty miles above the earth there is no light but a realm of darkness which the Bible calls "outer darkness." (Matt. 8:12, Matt. 22:18, Matt. 25:30.) This realm of darkness may be 3000 miles thick, a band of darkness that surrounds the earth beginning at the edge of the outermost air. There are inhabited places in this "outer darkness." Cain was afraid of being banished to that realm of darkness when he said, "Thou hast driven me out this day from the face of the earth." (Gen. 4:14.) Now the face of the earth is the surface on which we live, together with the air and light that extends upward for twenty miles. Radar detects solid objects in this "outer darkness." They cannot be seen but they are detected and for want of a better name the scientists call them "ghosts". They are the inhabited islands in "outer darkness." Some of the fallen angels are confined in this chain, of darkness (Jude 6, II Peter 2:4) for God has "delivered them into chains of darkness."

Many people now living on the earth are to be banished "into outer darkness." (Matt. 8:12). This realm of outer darkness is the present home of the dark and evil forces of both angels and men who are under condemnation from this and other worlds. So

OUTER SPACE PEOPLE AND INNER EARTH PEOPLE

strong is this evil force that it took Michael, one of the best and greatest of the angels, twenty-one days to get a good angel messenger from heaven through that "outer darkness to the earth to give a message to Daniel. (Dan. 10:12-14.)

Beyond the "outer darkness" above the face of the earth is what we now call the Halpuch-Bagby circle discovered in 1955, which evidently is a chain of small planetoids which move in an orbit around the earth at the rate of 17,000 miles per hour. This same Halpuch-Bagby ring was sighted in Mexico in 1880 but was discarded at the time by astronomers as a thing impossible. (Halpuch-Bagby circle does not exist. ED)

Within the earth's realm of space, there may be 10,000 or more inhabited planetoids-a regular island archipelago of little planets about 400 miles in diameter and 12,000 miles in circumference.

They are inhabited. They belong to the earth. The Bible speaks of the people who inhabit them as "men in heaven." (Rev.5:3, Rev. 5:18, Eph. 1:10). Phil. 2:10.)

There are three heavens that belong to this earth. Therefore, the earth has three skies. The moon is the largest and the most distinct satellite in the heaven of the earth. This naturally brings up the question, Is the moon inhabited? My answer to the question is an unqualified "Yes?"

Why not? It is almost a perfect sphere 2160: miles in diameter and 6480 miles in circumference. The New Standard Encyclopedia, says: "The Moon travels in its orbit with a velocity, of 3384 feet per second, and its equatorial velocity of rotation is ten miles per hour. Recent sightings on the moon show strange new lights in several of its craters. Gruithuisen in 1821 reported the discovery of a city on the moon. Recently thousands of objects, each appearing like a dome-shaped house and grouped together like a city, and which may move from place to place, have been reported. Some think that men from Mars have set up a base on the moon, but I think that the moon is inhabited in its own right by its own people.

The moon may be a captive planet of the earth. That is, a planet that came into the earth's realm and has been held by the earth's attraction. But more than likely the moon and all of the earth's planetoids were originally thrown off from a disruption of the earth. This seems to be corroborated by the Bible.

The Garden of Eden was the apex of the original earth. It was a perfect cube, 1200 miles square and extended upward from the face of the earth 1200 miles into the sky. (Rev. 21:16.) Out of each side-north, east, south and west flowed a river; four rivers in all. Like two belts that crossed in the North and South these rivers ran around the earth. They were equal to one-seventh of the earth's surface and they divided the land of the earth into "the four quarters of the earth." (Rev. 20:8, Jer. 49:36). Not only the Garden of Eden but all the earth at that time had an even semi-tropical climate.

The surface of the earth was six-sevenths dry, fertile, inhabitable land (II Esdras 6:42) and if the planetoids and asteroids now in the earth's orbit were later thrown off from the earth; then the earth at the time that the Garden of Eden was a part of it was much, very much, larger than it is now.

OUTER SPACE PEOPLE AND INNER EARTH PEOPLE

When Adam and his family were driven out of the Garden to thenceforth dwell with the natural earthly races of men, immediately the Garden of Eden, an area 1200 miles square, was thrown off from the earth and taken up into outer-space. The Garden of Eden may have been in the north or in the south. Eventually large areas at what we call the north pole and the south pole were taken up from the earth at the same time. The Bible indicates that at the time the earth turned "upside down." (Isa. 24:1). A complete reversal of poles. The south pole was originally the north pole and vice versa. For 20 years I have been teaching that the earth turned upside down, now here it is verified by scientists.

On Sept. 6, 1957, an (AP) report from Toronto said: "Ancient rocks are whispering fantastic stories, scientists reported to the International Union of Geodesy and Geophysics Friday.

The rocks tell of sudden flip flops in the north and south magnetic poles. They tell of continents drifting apart, or the whole crust of the earth skidding about to turn maps topsy-turvy. They say the United States and Europe once were 1,000 miles closer together; that India once was north of the equator, not south.

All this happened in the long ago past. But, it could happen again.

The stories come from the natural magnetism in rocks. Theories as to what the rocks and stones mean were described by the scientists.

Some rocks are natural compasses: They contain grains of magnetic minerals. When the rocks were formed, the grains lined up to point in the direction of the magnetic north pole, where it existed then.

Checking rocks formed at different times during the last 500 million years, scientists find some not only don't point to the present north pole; they even point in the opposite direction. The record seems clear that the magnetic poles mysteriously and completely reversed themselves at times in the past, said Sir Edward Builard of Cambridge University. The flip-flops came perhaps every 100,000 to one million years, he said, and the last was apparently a million years ago.

Rock records in England indicate the north magnetic pole 150 million years ago was where Japan is now, but it's doubtful Japan was right there then, said Dr. K. M. Creer of Kings College.

Rock records from different continents indicate the continents drifted apart even turned part way around, perhaps. And the earth's crust apparently slithered about, changing the position of land masses in respect to the poles. End quote.

In the disruption of the earth at that time, other large land areas may have been thrown off and thereafter formed the earth's planetoids and asteroids in the earth's outer ether. The tilt of the earth greatly diminished the life-giving rays of the sun, reducing the life span of man to less than 100 years. There was a period of exactly 1656 years from the time that Adam left the Garden until the time of Noah and the flood. (Gen. 5: 1-82, Gen. 7:11.) During that period of time the average age of man was from 700 to 900 years.

OUTER SPACE PEOPLE AND INNER EARTH PEOPLE

The flood was caused by the last of the great water rings (Gen. 1:7) or belts of water from the upper sky falling upon the earth. The flood reduced the face of the earth from six-sevenths land to more than two-thirds water, increased the frozen areas at the poles, and taking into consideration the uninhabitable deserts and mountains, the result since the flood has been that only about one-tenth of the earth's surface is inhabitable.

The earth was so terribly thrown out of balance and off its course by the flood that the psalmist wrote that "all the foundations of the earth are out of course." (Ps. 82:5). Before the flood the energy of the sun was seven times greater than it now is (Isa. 30:26) and the energy of the moon was then equal to the present energy of the sun. With a total reduction of more than seven-eights of the cosmic energy, it is easily understood how the life span of man was reduced to seventy years.

As before stated the Bible completed 2000 years ago, gives us incidences of visitors (angels) from outer-space who had visited the earth at intervals over a period of 4000 years then past. Often it describes in detail the type of vehicle that the outer-space visitors used. It also tells how both Enoch and Elijah were taken up into heaven. As late as the Apostle Paul we read that he was "caught up to the third heaven" (2 Cor. 12:2), and heard unspeakable words, which is not lawful for a man to utter." (2 Cor. 12:4). Yes, Paul visited the outer-space people and returned to earth. - He did, however, tell us that we must preach the gospel of salvation to those people in outer space, saying: "To the intent that now unto the principalities and powers in heavenly places might be known by the church the manifold wisdom of God." (Eph. 3:10.) "Principalities are different kingdoms. "Powers" are the political nations in the various places in outer-space. And furthermore we are told that the outer-space people and the people on earth are to be united. "That in the dispensation of the fullness of times he might gather together in one all things in Christ, both which are in heaven, and which are on earth, even in him." (Eph. 1:10).

The land areas of the outer-space people and the land of the earth will be join together. That is evident because that in the garden of Eden was "the tree of life." (Gen. 2:9.) The Garden of Eden ascended into heaven, but it is to come down out of heaven as the new Jerusalem, Camp of Saints and capital of the new world and in it is "the tree of life" (Rev. 22:2) and, that's the way it will be when all things are restored.

If you were in some areas of the far north you would see black snow and would be so terribly annoyed by a rain of black dust that you could hardly endure it. It has been analyzed and is known to contain sulphur, iron and carbon. Where does it come from? "He opened the bottomless pit and there arose a smoke out of the pit, as the smoke of a great furnace and the sun and the sky were darkened by reason of the smoke of the pit." (Rev. 9:2). That's exactly the way it is in some regions of the north. This black dust comes from the interior of the earth.

You would also, in other areas of the far north, see green and yellow and red snow. This is caused by an iron dust and by pollen in the air. There is more pollen and a thicker fine dust in the air around and above the north pole than in any other region on earth.

Yet it is an error to refer to this as snow, for no snow falls in Greenland or anywhere in the far north, but all the time there is a fine ice blowing all over Greenland and

OUTER SPACE PEOPLE AND INNER EARTH PEOPLE

the far north. Where does it come from? There are four rivers flowing out from the interior of the earth (north—east—south—west). The spray from these rivers gushing out like fountains freezes and blows all over the north. Greenland is as large as France and is covered with ice two miles deep. If that ice melted it would flood out every port city on earth, but for some unknown reason it never melts.

It is there that the great icebergs form. These are formed by warm fresh water that flows out from the interior of the earth. All icebergs are fresh water. All kinds of vegetation and animal life have been found frozen in these icebergs. Elephants with fresh blood in their bodies have been found in icebergs. This vegetation and these animals are washed out in the warm fresh water from the earth's interior. The icebergs pile up into enormous mountains in the north. When they break loose into the salt water of the ocean it is with such terrific force that the result is often tidal waves.

Under the snow and ice of Siberia are the richest ivory deposits on earth. Many species of tropic animals have been found frozen and in a perfect state of preservation, some with green grass in their mouths and stomachs, showing that the freeze was instant when the earth turned out of its course. Tropical trees, loaded with fruits, have also been found, and I am told that there are cities and people frozen under that ice.

The Aurora Borealis or Polaris which is the Northern lights is the most beautiful spectacle on this earth. Great curtains and draperies of light beautiful beyond description seem to rain down upon the earth. The northern heavens are a mirror which reflect in the sky all of that northern country. Fishermen use the sky as a way to guide their course. What are these lights? There is only one answer: There is a sun at the exact center of the interior of the earth. Its light, like that of a great flash of light shines out from the northern opening of the earth's interior and the northern sky reflects this light.

Now let us consider the shell of the earth. We know little about what is ten miles deep in the earth. We know that there is a surface layer of soil and sedimentary rock about three or perhaps five miles thick. Under this is granite perhaps from ten to fifty miles thick, and under the granite is a layer of basalt, such as dolerite, gabbro, eclogite and tochylyte. And under this is something we know not what! It may be a ring of solid iron. The shell leaves a vast area, a hollow or bottomless pit with more inhabitable land area than the surface or face of the earth.

There is an opening into the interior of the earth in the north. It is approximately 4800 miles in circumference, that is, around the rim of a canyon that slopes very gradually into the earth's interior. It was my privilege to meet Captain Roland Amunsen in 1926. He had just flown from King's Bay, Spitzbergen to Nome, Alaska. (He was the reputed discoverer of the South Pole and was beaten by Richard Byrd by an hour in a flight over the alleged North Pole.) You will remember that Captain Amunsen flew into the direct north in search of the lost Italian aviators and that neither he nor they have ever been heard of since. Likewise many ships have sailed out into the northern open waters and ships and crews have never been heard of again. They are probably now in the interior of the earth, unable to return.

The interior of the earth is definitely inhabited by INNER EARTH people. There

OUTER SPACE PEOPLE AND INNER EARTH PEOPLE

are several classes or races of these people. First there are the angels who kept not their first estate or order and materialized and married women on the earth. Before the flood these angels and also a race of prehistoric giants and also a race of pygmies were banished from the face or exterior of the earth to the interior of the earth. From time to time there were people on the earth who were sent into the earth's interior. Such as when "The earth opened her mouth and swallowed up" (Num. 16:30-32) certain people who went down into the pit alive. Jesus Christ himself descended into the interior of the earth and preached the gospel to those people. "He also descended first into the lower parts of the earth." (Eph. 4:9). He preached the same gospel to them that he preached to us:

"For Christ also once suffered for sins, the just for the unjust, that he might bring us to God, being put to death in the flesh, but quickened by the Spirit: by which also he went and preached unto the spirits in prison; which sometime were disobedient when once the long-suffering of God waited in the days of Noah, while the ark was a preparing, wherein few, that is, eight souls were saved by water. (1 Peter 3:18-20).

What did he preach to them? "For this cause was the gospel preached also to them that are dead, that they might be judged according to men in the flesh, but live according to God in the spirit." (I Peter 4:6.)

Who were they? "And it came to pass, when men began to multiply on the face of the earth, and daughters were born unto them, that the sons of God saw the daughters of men that they were fair; and they took them wives of all which they chose. And the Lord said, My Spirit shall not always strive with man, for that he also in flesh: yet his days shall be a hundred and twenty years. There were giants in the earth in those days; and also after that when the sons of God came in unto the daughters of men, and they bare children to them, the same became mighty men which were of old, men of renown." (Gen. 6;1-4.)

"For if God spared not the angels that sinned but cast them down to hell,, and delivered then into chains of darkness, to be reserved unto judgment." (II Peter 2:4), "And the angels which kept not their first estate, but left their own habitation, he hath reserved in everlasting chains under darkness unto the judgment of the great day." (Jude 6).

These INNER EARTH people will come out on the face of the earth for judgment. "Know ye not that we shall judge angels also." (I Cor. 6: 1-3.)

Now let us look at what the INNER EARTH people are doing now: "And the fifth angel sounded, and I saw a star fall from heaven unto the earth: and to him was given the key of the bottomless pit. And he opened the bottomless pit; and there arose a smoke out of the pit as the smoke of a great furnace; and the sun and the air were darkened by reason of the smoke of the pit. And there came out of the smoke locusts upon the earth, and unto them was given power, as the scorpions of the earth have power.

And it was commanded them that they should not hurt the grass of the earth, neither any green things, neither any tree; but only those men which have not the seal of God in their foreheads. And to them it was given that they should not kill them, but that

OUTER SPACE PEOPLE AND INNER EARTH PEOPLE

they should be tormented five months: and their torment was as the torment of a scorpion, when he striketh a man. And in those days shall men seek death, and shall not find it; and shall desire to die, and death shall flee from them. And the shapes of the locusts were like unto horses prepared unto battle; and on their heads were as it were crowns like gold, and their faces were as the faces of men. And they had hair as the hair of women, and their teeth were as the teeth of lions. And they had breastplates, as it were breastplates of iron; and the sound of their wings was as the sound of chariots of many horses running to battle. And they had tails like unto scorpions, and there were stings in their tails: and their power was to hurt men five months. And they had a king over them, which is the angel of the bottomless pit, whose name in the Hebrew tongue is Abaddon, but in the Greek tongue hath his name Apollyon." (Rev. 9:141.)

All the people now in the inner earth will come out on the face of the earth for judgment and unity with us. When the inner earth is empty, then Satan and all demons (devils) who are now in the earth's atmosphere, will be bound in the pit: "And I saw an angel come down from heaven, having the key of the bottomless pit and a great chain in his hand. And he laid hold on the dragon, that old serpent, which is the Devil and Satan, and bound him a thousand years, and cast him into the bottomless pit and shut him up, and set a seal upon him, that he should deceive the nations no more, till the thousand years should be fulfilled." (Rev. 20:1-3.)

Anybody who believes the Bible must of necessity believe what I have said in this message, and I further declare that it is not contrary to any true science, that is, to ascertained truth. I have not told you one-tenth of what I know about outer-space and the interior of the earth, for time and space do not permit the exhausting of this subject. But I have told you enough so that you may do your own thinking and make research on this subject.

There are some who say that the outer-space people are storing up ice in outer-space. That may be true for there is to be a great falling of ice upon this earth. "And it shall come to pass at the same time when God shall come against the land of Israel, saith the Lord God, that my fury shall come up in my face. For in my jealousy and in the fire of my wrath have I spoken. Surely in that day there shall be a great shaking in the land of Israel; so that the fishes of the sea, and the fowls of the heaven, and the beasts of the field, and all creeping things that creep upon the earth, and all the men that are upon the face of the earth, shall shake at my presence, and the mountains shall be thrown down, and the steep places shall fall, and every wall shall fall to the ground. And I will call for a sword against him throughout all my mountains, saith the Lord God; every man's sword shall be against his brother.

And I will plead against him with pestilence and with blood; and I will rain upon him, and upon his bands, and upon the many people that are with him, an overflowing rain, and great hailstones, fire and brimstone. Thus will I magnify myself, and sanctify myself; and I will be known in the eyes of many nations, and they shall know that I am The Lord." (Ezek. 38: 18-23.)

"And there fell upon men a great hail out of heaven, every stone about the weight

OUTER SPACE PEOPLE AND INNER EARTH PEOPLE

of a talent, and men blasphemed God because of the plague of the hail; for the plague thereof was exceedingly great." (Rev. 16:21)

Yes that ice is up there and it's coming down one of these days. Frank Edwards writing in Fate Magazine in July said "in Admiral Richard Byrd's report of his first trip to the Antarctic his group discovered two large, blue-green lakes of warm water in the very midst of that desolate expanse of eternal ice. There was no trace of any volcanic heat supply, in fact there was no visible means which could explain the incongruous coexistence of warm water lakes in the ice cap of the Antarctic. Admiral Byrd made note of still another strange aspect of the lakes. Alongside one of them, he wrote, were long, straight, black lines "which resembled blast marks."

Perhaps, it is only coincidence that Admiral Byrd's first trip to the Antarctic was made immediately after a Chilean naval commander had been repeatedly circled by scores of shiny, disc-shaped objects which vanished toward the interiors of the Antarctic." End Quote.

In his article in Fate Magazine in September, 1957, he suggests or implies that Martians in flying saucers may be taking water up from the earth and storing ice on the moon. That may not be as farfetched or illogical as it seems. On the farm of Edwin Groff near Reading, Pa. on July 30, 1956, two chunks of ice fell, one weighing 50 pounds and the other 25 pounds.

Airline officials said at the time the cakes were reported that they could not have fallen from an airliner because such planes carry nothing larger than ice cubes. And the weather bureau said the ice chunks could not be explained as huge hail stones.

So this age will end in a great falling of ice from the heavens. We are told again and again that a great people will come out of the north. "Then the Lord said unto me, Out of the north an evil shall break forth upon all the inhabitants of the land. For, lo, I will call all the families of the kingdoms of the north, saith the Lord; and they shall come." (Jer. 1:14-15.) "Behold a people cometh from the north country." (Jer. 6:22.) These people from the north are the people who come out from the inner earth through the opening in the north and they will swarm all over the face of the earth. But ultimately the men above the earth and the men on earth and the men under the earth will be united into oneness. Read it in Revelation 5:3, Rev. 5:13, Phil. 2:1-41 and Eph. 1:9-10. Remember that there are three heavens that are a part of and that belong to this earth.

I have not dealt with the many higher orders of angels and the inhabitants of other planets and other solar systems in this message, but I believe that every planet is inhabited. Somebody will say. Do you believe that the sun is inhabited? And my answer is, Yes, for if the sun is the controlling, center of this universe, it seems reasonable that it would be inhabited by the highest person in this universe. For the universe is under intelligent direction. I think that the person or beings who inhabit the sun have material bodies composed of the element of fire and that they are the highest of all beings in this particular universe. Every time that God or the highest seraphim (angels) have appeared to men on earth they have assumed or been in a body of fire. Think it over! Our very life in our bodies is a spark of fire. Any time the fire goes out you are dead, your life exists in

OUTER SPACE PEOPLE AND INNER EARTH PEOPLE

fire. No fire, no life. It is that spark of celestial fire in you that connects you with the Highest Being whose name is YAHVEH.

In presenting all of the above and following views based upon the Bible there will be a few who will say that it is wonderful. Many will say it is ridiculous. Every new idea advanced is sure to meet with opposition, but may I remind you that astronomy, geology, petrology, cosmology and physiography and kindred sciences are all hypotheses or at the best theories. Even the poles and latitude and longitude are nothing more than theories that are workable to a given point.

The earth is not a true sphere. It is flat at the poles, or I should say it begins to flatten out at the poles. The pole is simply the outer rim of a magnetic circle and at this point the magnetic needle of the compass points straight up. As the earth turns on its axis the motion is gyroscopic like the spinning of a top. Let us say then that the outer gyroscopic pole is the magnetic rim of a circle. Beyond this rim the earth flattens and slopes gradually like a canyon into the earth's interior. The true pole in the exact center of the cone is perpendicular, for this point is at the exact center of the opening or hollow into the earth's interior.

There never has been a pole to pole trip made around the earth. The distance from pole to pole on the earth's surface is about 16,000 miles. The circumference from pole to pole would be 82,000 miles, while the circumference at the equator is exactly 24,899 miles. Why is it impossible to fly pole to pole around the earth? ? ?

The total surface of the earth is 197 million square miles. The estimated weight is six sextillions of tons. If the earth had a solid or molten iron core the weight would be much greater, and if the earth were solid through and through the ebb and flow of the tides would be impossible. The old idea that the earth was once a fiery molten mass and that at the center it is still molten iron must be discarded.

Since the shell of the earth is about 800 miles thick that would mean that the molten iron core would be more than 7000 miles in diameter and 21,000 miles in circumference. Impossible! Likewise, the old idea that the deeper into the earth the hotter it becomes must also be discarded. It is radium and radioactivity that produces the heat of the earth. All surface rocks contain minute particles of radium.

Radium may be the key to the creation of matter. Every element and all elements can be changed into entirely different elements. It is known that one atom of uranium in 6,400,000,000 breaks up every year. For every 6,400,000,000 atoms of uranium one atom of lead is produced every year. By the breaking up of atoms one element is changed into another element. By the formula of Holmes and Lawson the age of matter can be determined. It is simply a matter of determining the rate in which atoms break up. It is now known that matter is between 1,800,000,000 and 3,000,000,000 years old.

But what existed before matter?

The answer is, ONE DIVINE SUBSTANCE OUT OF WHICH ALL THINGS WERE MADE.

OUTER SPACE PEOPLE AND INNER EARTH PEOPLE

The mind of God. One mind. When there is no more matter, no more atoms, no more electrons, protons, neutrons; when they are all broken up, "dissolved", then everything will be One Spirit in the everlasting all encompassing mind of Yahveh.

So far as we know all things are hollow. A seed, a stalk of wheat a hair, bone, the inside of your head and body—all are hollow. The universe is made that way. The inside of the earth is hollow. The nebular hypothesis was advanced by Kant and Laplace and, as I understand it, is a theory, that everything is round like a ball, a sphere, and that from a center of a fiery molten mass there was an explosion throwing matter outward like ripples or waves; that each of these circles condensed into a sphere of matter and thus sun after sun exploded and circles condensed into worlds of matter. It is a question whether everything is round. So far as we know from observation nothing is round but everything is hollow and oblong, square, triangular, perpendicular, horizontal and in fact every form and shape, but any material object whether it is a sun or planet or whatever it is, in rapid motion appears to be round. As an example, the propeller on an airplane with only two blades appears like a solid circular disk when it is in rapid motion. Anything having two rapid motions like the earth turning on its axis at the rate of 1000 miles per hour and moving on its orbit at 19 miles a second would appear to be a sphere or a ball regardless of its true material shape. Therefore I question the nebular hypothesis.

Even mathematics is not an exact science. Take for example the vernal equinox based on "the first point of Aries" when the sun crosses the equator on its way north. Now the earth was created in Aries, but 6000 years ago and continuing until 4000 years ago the earth was in Draconis. That's where it was when the Great Pyramid was built. I mean that Draconis was then the star nearest to the north pole.

The earth is now in Pisces, which is now the star nearest to the Pole. Time and distance and weight vary so much that there can be no perfect mathematical science.

In concluding this message may I say that man does not know the whole truth about anything. There is not a mineral, vegetable, animal or anything else of which man knows the ultimate and absolute truth.

Tennyson said:

"Flower in the crannied wall,

I pluck you out of the crannies;

Hold you here, root and all

in my hand, little flower

But if I could understand what you are

Root and all, and all and all,

I should know what God and man is.

I think of that first beatitude spoken by our Master, "Blessed are the poor in spirit: for theirs is the Kingdom of Heaven." (Matt. 5:8), Now that law was given to show man

OUTER SPACE PEOPLE AND INNER EARTH PEOPLE

how exceedingly sinful sin is. From the Ten Commandments law multiplies until there is no end of making laws and each and every law reveals more and more to us how far we are from perfect obedience to God and how far we are from social perfection with men.

Likewise reveal to us education, wisdom and knowledge how exceedingly ignorant we are.

The more and more we read and study, the more we learn how ignorant we are. Again, the more spiritual we think we are the more we find out that we are nothing compared to the Spirit of Yahveh. Oh, how we need to turn ourselves completely over to Yahveh. How poverty-stricken man is in everything. "Blessed are the poor in Spirit for theirs is the Kingdom of Heaven." Man is great only to the extent that Yahveh is in him. All honor, glory and praise be unto Yahveh.

Etidorhpa is a classic adventure written in the 1800's about a trip into the inner earth. Joseph H. Cater, in his book The Ultimate Reality, has the following comments to make regarding the book Etidorhpa:

"It is important at this stage to mention a book concerning the hollow Earth, the finest that has yet been written. It not only contains more important factual information than any other book, but also goes far beyond them in other respects. This great book probably contains more profound metaphysical and scientific truths than any other book written up to the present. The book is entitled Etidorhpa and was first published in 1895. Some books are written in the form of a novel in order to present certain ideas or truths without inviting undue attack from various quarters. Etidorhpa is considered by most to be a science fiction book. *Any intelligent and discerning reader realizes that it isn't.*"

hollowplanet.blogspot.com

OUTER SPACE PEOPLE AND INNER EARTH PEOPLE

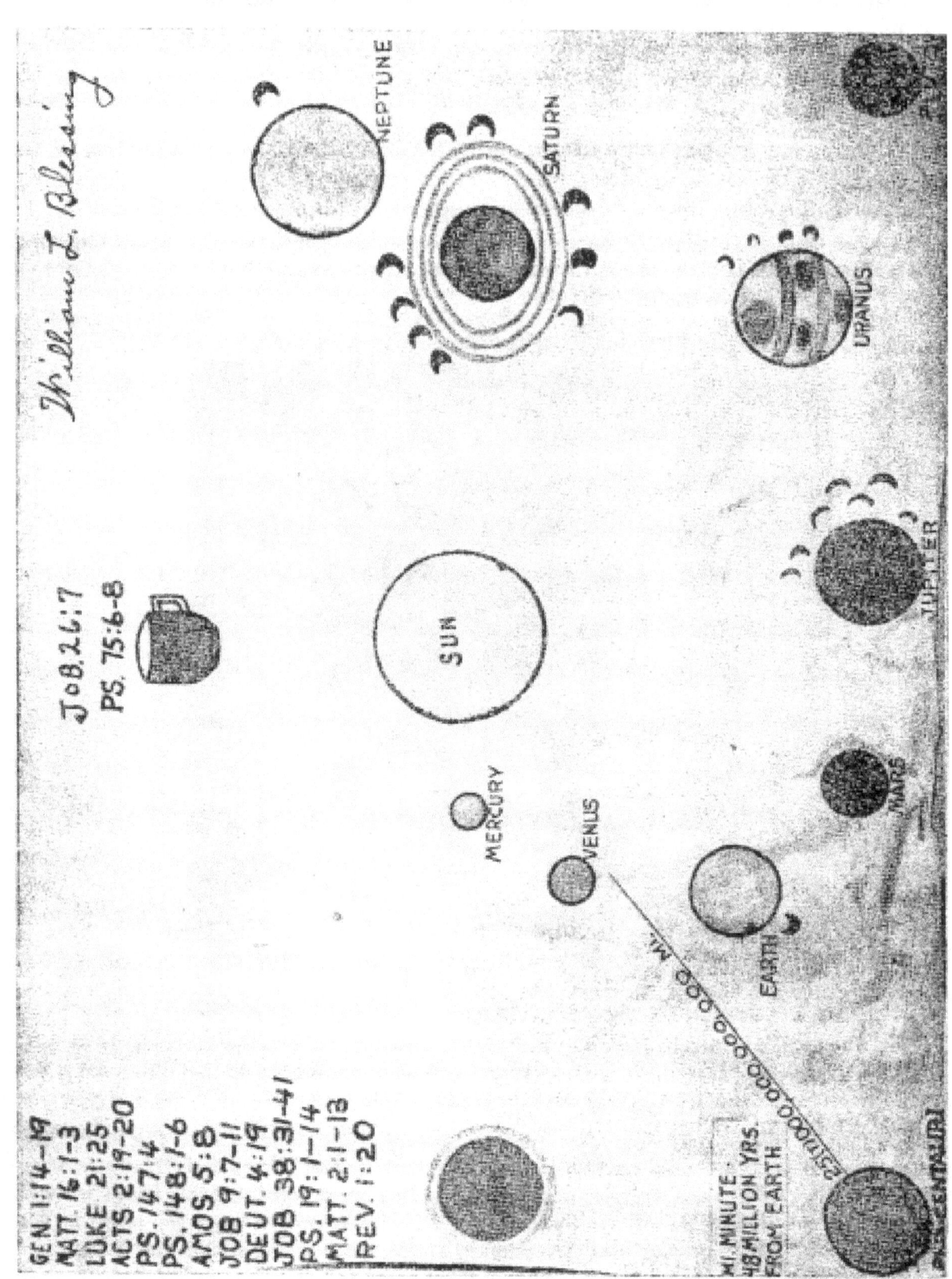

OUTER SPACE PEOPLE AND INNER EARTH PEOPLE

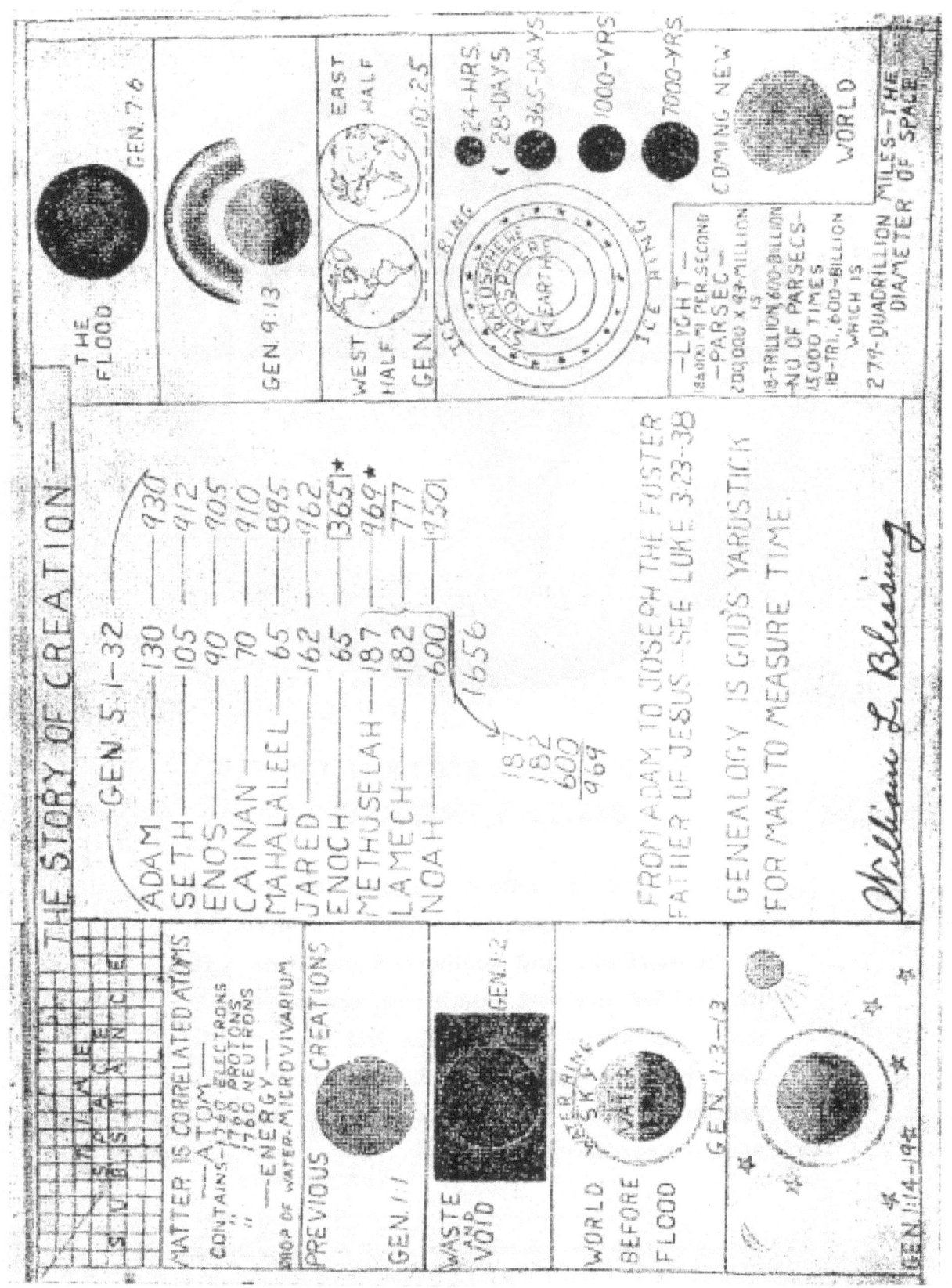

OUTER SPACE PEOPLE AND INNER EARTH PEOPLE

GLOBE SHOWING SECTION OF THE EARTH'S INTERIOR

The earth is hollow. The poles so long sought are but phantoms. There are openings at the northern and southern extremities. In the interior are vast continents, oceans, mountains and rivers. Vegetable and animal life are evident in this new world, and it is probably peopled by races yet unknown to the dwellers upon the earth's exterior.

THE AUTHOR.

Reproduced from "The Phantom Of The Poles" by William Reed, published by Walter S. Rockey Company, New York, 1906.

OUTER SPACE PEOPLE AND INNER EARTH PEOPLE

The earth as it would appear if viewed from space showing the north polar opening to the planet's interior which is hollow and contains a central sun instead of an ocean of liquid lava.

Reproduced from "A Journey To The Earth's Interior—or—Have The Poles Really Been Discovered," by Marshall B. Gardner. Printed by Eugene Smith Company, Aurora, Illinois, 1920.

OUTER SPACE PEOPLE AND INNER EARTH PEOPLE

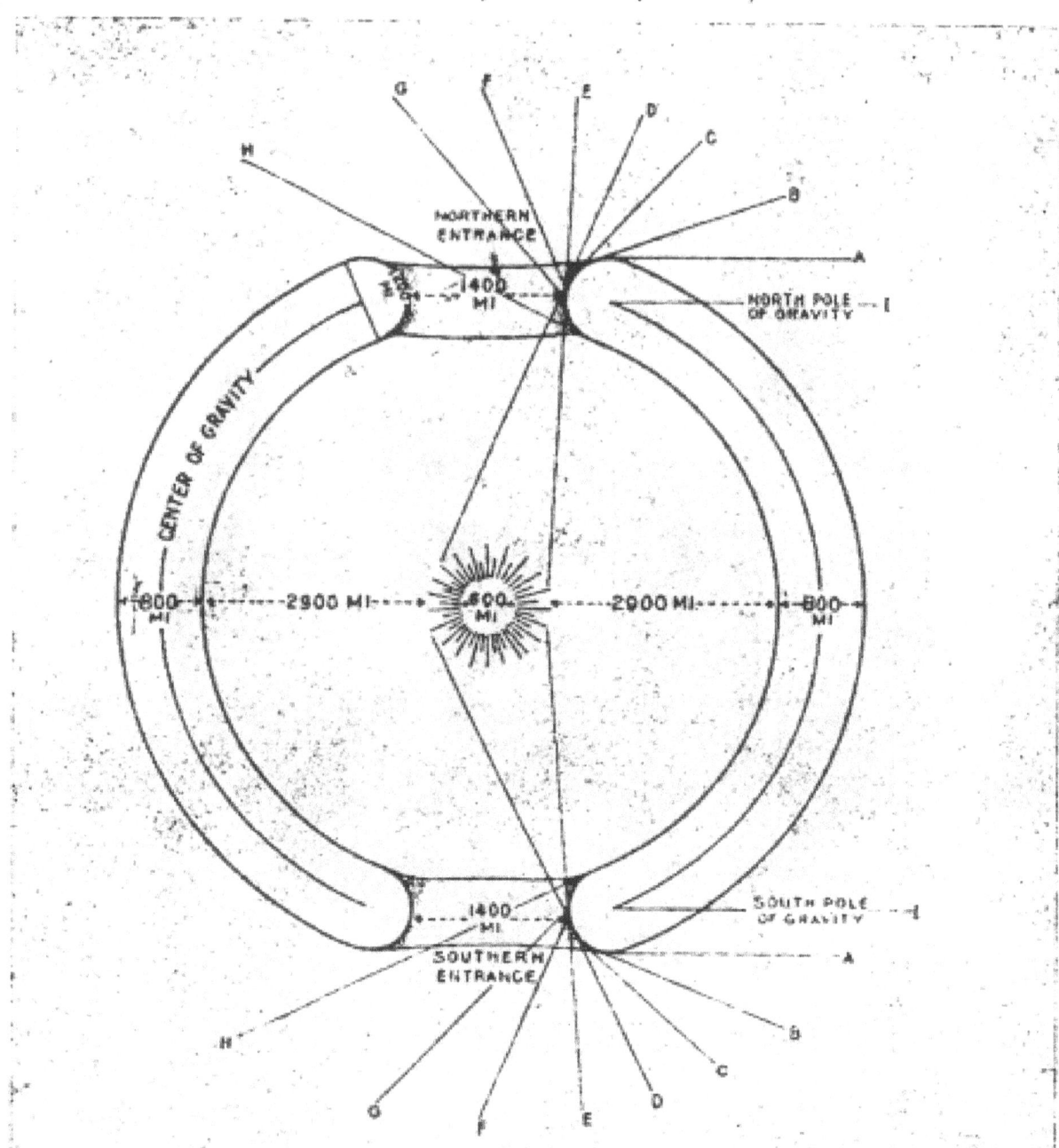

Diagram showing the earth as a hollow sphere with its polar openings and central sun. The letters at top and bottom of diagram indicate the various steps of an imaginary journey through the planet's interior. At the point marked "D" we catch our first glimpse of the corona of the central sun; at the point marked "E" we can see the central sun in its entirety.

Reproduced from "A Journey To The Earth's Interior—or—Have The Poles Really Been Discovered," by Marshall B. Gardner. Printed by Eugene Smith Company, Aurora, Illinois, 1920.

OUTER SPACE PEOPLE AND INNER EARTH PEOPLE

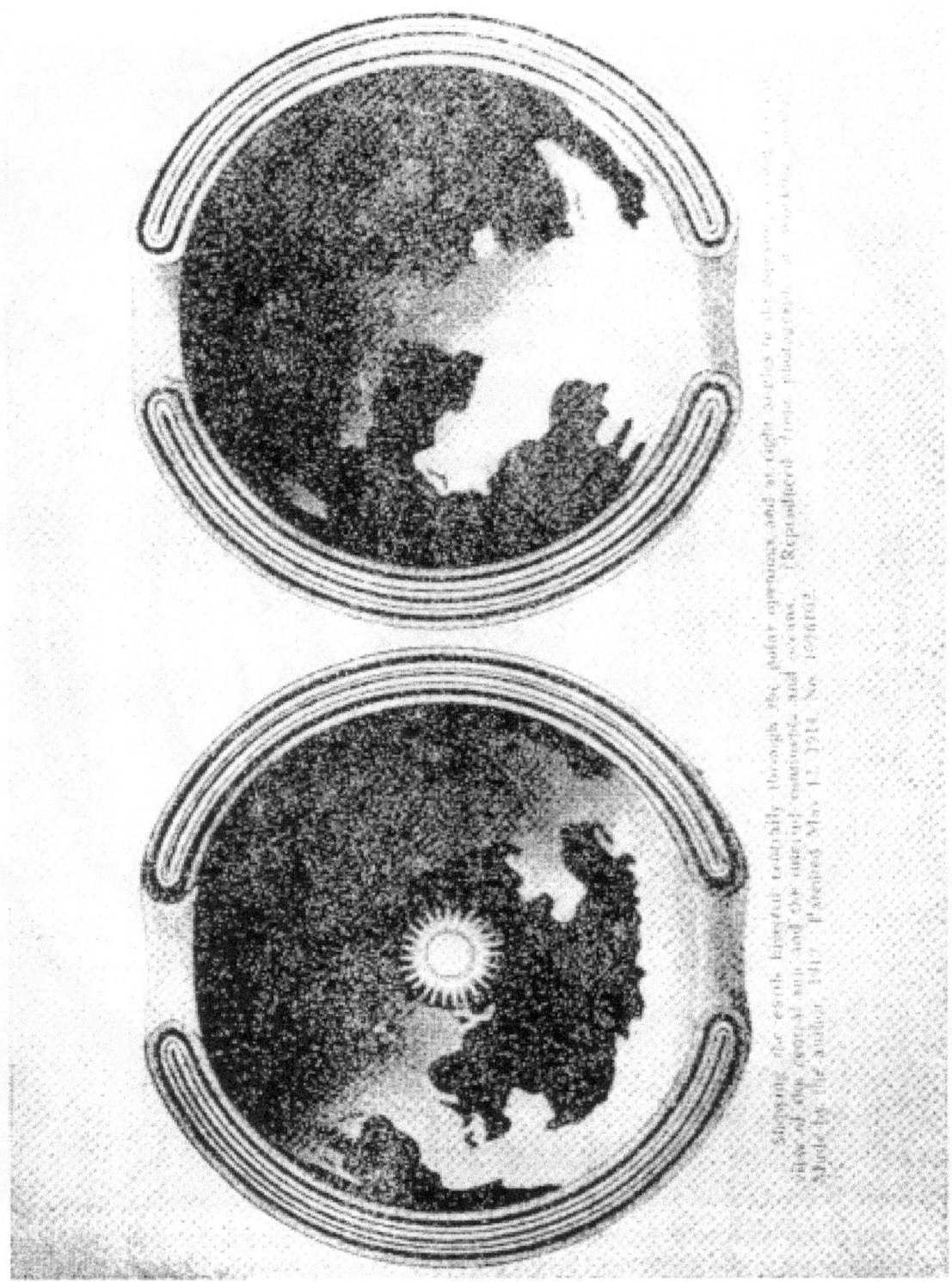

Reproduced from "A Journey To The Earth's Interior—or—Have The Poles Really Been Discovered" by Marshall B. Gardner. Printed by Eugene Smith Company, Aurora, Illinois, 1920.

OUTER SPACE PEOPLE AND INNER EARTH PEOPLE

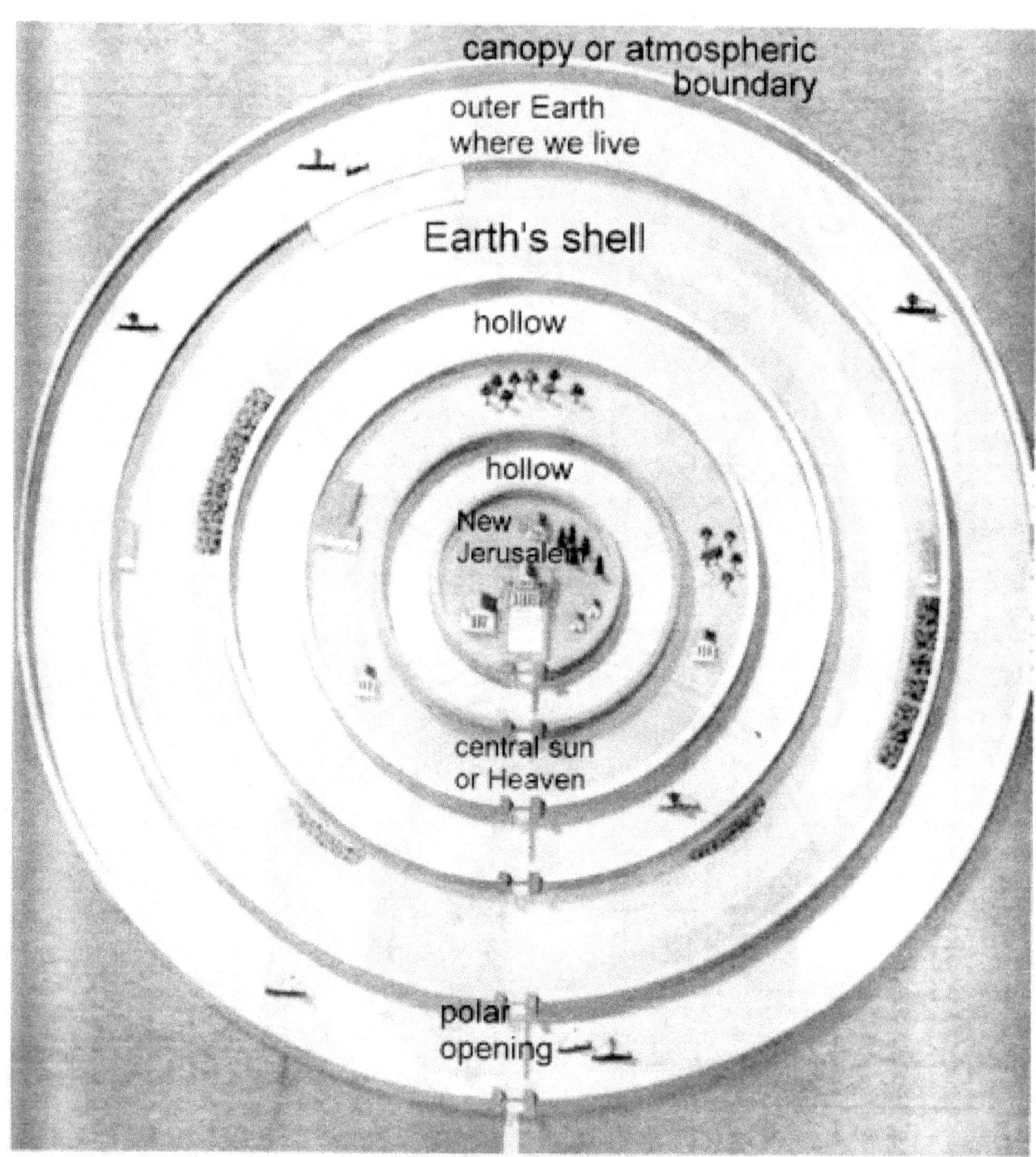

Even going back to the days of Atlantis there was a strong belief that there was more to the earth than just it's surface. The ancients believed, says the site www.libraising.com, that our planet consisted of a series of circles inside other circles.

OUTER SPACE PEOPLE AND INNER EARTH PEOPLE

Chapter II

Invasions of This Earth

By Outer Space People

Jesus Christ and Judas Iscariot, while on earth in the flesh, may have been twin brothers. Mary had five sons. Their names were Jesus, James, Joses, Simon and Judas. (Matt. 13:55-56). Jesus Christ is the center of all that is good, holy and Divine. (Col. 2:9). He is the Leader of the Sons of Light. Judas Iscariot is the center of all that is evil, sinful and Satanic. (John 13:26-27, John 17:12, II Thes. 2:11-17). He is the leader of the sons of Darkness.

It is evident from the scriptures that Satan has a place among the sons of God. In the book of Job we read: "Now there was a day when the sons of God (ELOHIM) came to present themselves before the Lord (Yahveh), and Satan came also among them." (Job 1:6). This took place at the time that Adam was in the Garden of Eden, but it is further evident that Satan was among the sons of God on the morning of the creation of this earth: "When the morning stars sang together, and all the sons of God shouted for joy." (Job 88:7).

Jesus Christ (Yahshua the Messiah) recognized Satan by choosing "a devil" as one of his twelve apostles. He said, "Have not I chosen you twelve, and one of you is a devil." (John 6:70). "For Jesus knew from the beginning who they were that believed not, and who should betray him." (John 6:64)

Knowing full well that Judas was a devil and that he would betray him, yet Jesus chose him as one of the Apostles and tolerated him, simply because Satan is recognized and given a place among the sons of God.

Some current preachers are too hard on the devil, not understanding "the mystery of evil" and "the mystery of iniquity." They spend all of their time kicking the devil around. The early Apostles were afraid to do that. Even the highest angels would not do it. "Michael the archangel, when contending with the devil, he disputed about the body of Moses, durst not bring against him a railing accusation, but said, The Lord rebuke

OUTER SPACE PEOPLE AND INNER EARTH PEOPLE

thee." (Jude 9)

Yahveh tolerates evil. He could destroy the devil instantly, but he tolerates the devil for a Divine purpose, until the system of evil has run its course according to the Divine plan. Judas Iscariot is the only man on this earth that was ever "indwelt" with all the fullness of Satan. After the sop given to Judas Iscariot "Satan entered into him." (John 13:27). You cannot find in the Bible where "Satan" ever entered into any man except Judas -"the son of perdition." (John 17:12)

Jesus Christ in whom dwelt all the fullness of the Godhead bodily, and Judas Iscariot in whom dwelt all the fullness of Satan bodily, both died on the same day—Christ by crucifixion, Judas by suicide. Christ was raised from the dead and ascended into heaven. Judas is still in the grave, but is to be literally tangibly as a human being cast out of the grave "like an abominable branch." (Isa. 14:19) He, Judas Iscariot, will say that he is God. He will rule over the Jews. He will deceive all the world. The fundamentalist and premillennialists will say that he is Christ and that the Kingdom has been restored to the Jews. This is the great deception; the big lie; the strong delusion. This is the error of all those who teach the second literal, visible, tangible return of Jesus Christ.

"That man" in person, literally, will be Judas Iscariot. "That man of sin be revealed, the son of perdition." (II Thes. 2:3.) All so-called "fundamentalists" and premillennialists are ignorantly teaching the second coming of Satan in a literal body in the person of Judas Iscariot to reign over the Jews.

They think he is Christ but they have Judas confused with Christ. They are all deceived and will be deceived. The teaching of the second literal, visible, tangible return of Jesus Christ to reign over the Jews is the biggest lie and the worst error that is taught in the world today. It will be Judas Iscariot, not Jesus Christ.

In the epochs of the Church, it was in about 323 A. D. that "the synagogue of Satan" (Rev. 2:9) began to exert great influence in the human, literally organized church. It was in about 628 A. D. that "Satan's seat" (Rev. 2:13) was established in the church. Since that time, he, Satan, has ruled in and over the hierarchy and all of the daughter denominations which are called Christianity.

Seeing this clearly, I quit them and began the movement to restore the original church and the true Kingdom gospel according to the scriptures. I have neither part nor lot with the Roman Catholic Church nor any of her Protestant daughters (the Denominations). They are all, according to my understanding of the Bible, ruled by Satan. They are ignorant of this, of course, but their ignorance and blindness does not alter nor change the fact that they are Satanically controlled.

The mystery of Satan is this: BEFORE the beginning of time, "THE LOGOS" and "THE LUCIFER" were probably brothers, possibly the first two brothers in the family of Yahveh. Then in the beginning (of time) God created the heaven and the earth. (Gen. 1:1.) Lucifer was the son that was made a man and that ruled over the first original earth. Lucifer's wife's name was Lilith. Lucifer and his race brought the earth to chaos and destruction, all because he tried to invade outer-space. "How art thou fallen from heaven,

OUTER SPACE PEOPLE AND INNER EARTH PEOPLE

O Lucifer, son of the morning! How art thou cut down to the ground, which didst weaken the nations; For thou hast said in thine heart, I will ascend into heaven, I will exalt my throne above the stars of God: I will sit also upon the mount of the congregation, in the sides of the north: I will ascend above the heights of the clouds; I will be like the Most High. Yet thou shalt be brought down to hell, to the sides of the pit. They that see thee shall narrowly look upon thee, and consider thee, saying, Is this the man that made the earth to tremble, that did shake kingdoms: That made the world as a wilderness, and destroyed the cities thereof; that opened not the house of his prisoners?" (Isa.14:12-17.)

"I beheld the earth, and, lo, it was without form; and void; and the heavens, and they had no light. I beheld the mountains, and, lo, they trembled, and all the hills moved lightly. I beheld and, lo, there was no man, and all the birds of the heavens were fled. I beheld, and, lo, the fruitful place was a wilderness, and all the cities thereof were broken down at the presence of the Lord, and by his fierce anger."-(Jer. 4:23-26.)

"AND THE EARTH WAS WITHOUT FORM AND VOID: AND DARKNESS WAS UPON THE FACE OF THE DEEP." (Gen. 1:2.) This condition of the earth may have continued for millions of years. Satan (Lucifer) and his Luciferian race of people became disembodied spirits, bound and confined to the atmosphere of this earth (devils).

Then from Genesis 1:2 until Genesis. 1:31 we have the story of the "Cosmos" or creation of the present natural world and the natural races of men. In Genesis 2:7, we have the "LOGOS" made flesh, a man, in the person of Adam. And from then on until now we have had "the Word", "The LOGOS" (John 1:1-14), Christ, working in and through the sons of God, the Adamic race. All of this is very interesting and of utmost importance to the understanding of the Bible and the Divine Plan of all the ages.

Lucifer and his entire race of Luciferians became disembodied spirits, confined to the atmosphere of this earth. Then when the chaos ended and the "waste and void" condition was no more, the natural races of men, who are of the earth, earthy, were created. (Gen. 1:2-31) After that, Yahveh in person formed, inbreathed, indwelt and inspired Adam. (Gen. 2:7.) The Adamic race has, since that time, been the chosen race of Yahveh in and through which His Heavenly Children (THE ELOHIM) have been brought to birth in the flesh and, in and through this race, the "LOGOS" (Christ) came to this earth. (John 1:1-14.) Therefore, Yahveh the Heavenly Father has his own chosen race on earth. They are not the natural races of Genesis 1:26, but they are the chosen and spiritual race of Genesis 2:7.

Lucifer, who is now Satan, the devil, also called "that old serpent" definitely has his own race of people on the earth. Jesus said to them: "Ye are of your father the devil, and the lusts of your father ye will do." (John 8:44.) Jesus further identified them as "serpents" and the generation of "vipers." (Matt. 23:33.) There definitely is a Serpentine race of people on the earth. To understand this we go back to Genesis 3:1 where we first meet "the serpent" man. It is evident that the Serpentine people invaded the earth, perhaps were dumped here from Venus or Mars. Anyway, they came from some outer-space world. Job says, "They were viler than the earth." (Job 30:8.) The disembodied Lucifer and the disembodied spirits of his race began to obsess and possess "the serpent people."

OUTER SPACE PEOPLE AND INNER EARTH PEOPLE

From the third chapter of Genesis until the present time, there has been a battle going on between "the seed" (Genesis 3:15) lines. That is, between the Serpentine people of Satan, and the Adamic people of Yahveh. Actually the climax came when Christ came into the Race of Adam and was indwelt with all the fullness of Yahveh, and Judas Iscariot came into the Serpent race and was indwelt with all the fullness of Satan.

This baffle between the Adamites and the Serpentines continues and will continue until they are separated and the earth is cleansed in the end of this age. The natural races of men are caught, as it were, in between the Adamites and the serpentines. Through the Adamites, Christ will ultimately control the world and establish the Kingdom of Yahveh, but Lucifer, the devil, now attempts to counterfeit Christ and to establish his own kingdom of evil through the Serpentine people and that is the great deception and the big lie. Many are deceived by it. Their idea of who God's chosen people are is entirely false. It is a matter of mistaken identity. A literal, visible, tangible man seated on a literal throne in Jerusalem (or Rome) ruling over the Jews or the church will not be Jesus Christ but will be Judas Iscariot who is to be literally resurrected from the dead for that very purpose of deceiving the whole world.-(Isa. 14:19.)

THE SECOND INVASION OF THE EARTH BY OUTER SPACE PEOPLE which the Bible describes in detail is that of "the angels that sinned." (II Peter 2:4.) "Angels" simply means people who are messengers from outer-space, and in this case it is those that "kept not their first estate, but left their own habitations." (Jude 6.) Here is the story as it is recorded in the sixth chapter of Genesis: "And it came to pass, when men began to multiply on the face of the earth, and daughters were born unto them, that the sons of God saw the daughters of men that they were fair and they took them wives of all which they chose. And the Lord said, My Spirit shall not always strive with man, for that he also is flesh: yet his days shall be a hundred and twenty years. There were giants in the earth in those days and also after that when the sons of God came in unto the daughters of men, and they bare children to them, the same became mighty men which were of old men, of renown. And God saw that the wickedness of man was great in the earth, and that every imagination of the thoughts of his heart was only evil continually. And it repented the Lord that he had made man on the earth, and it grieved him at his heart. And the Lord said, I will destroy man whom I have created from the face of the earth; both man, and beast and the creeping thing, and the fowls of the air; for it repented me that I have made them. But Noah found grace in the eyes of the Lord. These are the generations of Noah: Noah was a just man and perfect in his generations, and Noah walked with God. And Noah begat three sons, Shem, Ham, and Japheth. The earth also was corrupt before God; and the earth filled with was violence. And God looked upon the earth, and, behold, it was corrupt; for all flesh had corrupted his way upon the earth. And God said unto Noah, The end of all flesh is come before me; for the earth is filled with violence through them; and, behold, I will destroy them with the earth."-(Gen. 6:1-13.)

The book of Enoch tells us the names of the leaders in outer-space that invaded the earth with their followers. They were: 1. Samyaza, 2. Urakabaramell, 3. Akibeel, 4. Tamiel, 5. Ramuel, 6. Danel, 7. Azkeel, 8. Sarakuyal, 9. Asael, 10. Armers, 11. Batraal, 12. Anane, 13. Zavebe, 14. Samsaveel, 15. Eretel, 16. Ertael, 17. Turei, 18. Yomyael, 19. Arazyal,

OUTER SPACE PEOPLE AND INNER EARTH PEOPLE

20. Amazarak, 21. Barkayal, 22. Asaradel. (Enoch 7:9,8:3-8.)

These twenty-two leaders had two hundred captains working under them. Just how many of their outer-space people they brought with them to the earth, we do not know. Probably each leader was from a different inhabited planet. These fallen angels, if you wish to call them that, were far more intelligent than the earth people. They taught men medicine, mathematics, astronomy, etc., but they were sinners. There are many inhabited planets in outer-space whose people are deeper in sin than the earth people. (Job 15:15, Eph. 3:8-11, Eph. 4:9-19.) You will see, if you look up and read those scriptures, that we have a mission to the people of outer-space which we eventually are to visit for the purpose of converting them.

There are six inhabited planets that we know about that are ruled by good, true and holy men. They and their people are much farther advanced and are much better people than we are on this earth. The good men are: 1. Uriel, 2. Raphael, 3. Raguel, 4. Michael, 5. Sarakiel, 6. Gabriel. (Enoch 22:1-7.) They have visited the earth at intervals on important missions and have helped mankind, but they have not invaded the earth and remained here as the sinful, evil ones did.

At the close of this lecture I will mention some of the visits of the Good Ones to this earth and their mission, but right now we must discuss THE INVASION of the earth by the fallen, or sinful, ones. These outer-space people were not non-sexed. They had procreative power the same as the people on the earth. They were attracted to the earth women. "They took wives, each choosing for himself; whom they began to approach, and with whom they cohabited and they conceiving, brought forth giants.

These devoured all which the labour of men produced; until it became, impossible to feed them; when they turned themselves against men, in order to devour them; and began to injure birds, beasts, reptiles and fish to eat their flesh one after another, and to drink their blood." (Enoch 7:10-14.)

The Bible tells us that some of those giants were eleven feet tall and had twenty-four fingers and toes-six on either hand and six on either foot. (I Sam. 17:4-7, I Chron. 20:4-8.) These races of giants continued in the world even after the flood. They were known as "Anakim." (Num. 13:28, Deut. 9:2, Joshua 15: 13, Joshua 21:11.) Some of the giant seed is still mixed in human seed. It is "the grain of evil seed" (Apocrypha, II Esdras 4:30), a "cursed seed from the beginning." (Wisdom of Solomon 13;11, Apocrypha,) Sometimes hideous monsters are yet born to women too awful for doctors to describe.

The monsters do not live more than a few seconds, but some mongoloids live for several years. These are a throwback, the cropping out of the giant seed. It seldom happens, but it does take place once in a while.

For 1656 years before the flood, the fallen angels (outer-space men that invaded the earth) lived on the earth and married women. The result was that almost all of the human race became sterile. The last children conceived by natural conception and born of natural birth before the flood were the three triplet sons of Noah: Shem, Ham and Japheth. They were born on Noah's five hundredth birthday. (Gen. 5:32.) The earth was

OUTER SPACE PEOPLE AND INNER EARTH PEOPLE

then within 120 years of destruction. (Gen. 6:3.) "For the earth was filled with violence through them." (Gen. 6:13.) That is through the outer-space men and their giant offspring that had been born to earth women.

Naomah, a daughter of Enoch, was the wife of Noah. She was 592 years old when she gave birth to Shem, Ham and Japheth. (Book of Jasher 5:15-16.) Noah was 500 years old when his triplet sons were born. During the next hundred years no other children were born in Adam's race. In the year of 1656 years from Adam, the year of the flood (this time is accurate, Gen. 5:1-32), there were only eight people in all the race of Adam that were not sterile, that still had natural procreative power. They were Noah and his wife, Shem, Ham and Japheth and their wives. If the earth had continued the same for twenty years longer, the 120 years would have been up and then, even those eight people would have become sterile and the race of Adam would have been completely destroyed. But they went into the ark, the flood came, the earth was cleansed, Adam's race was rejuvenated and continued upon the earth.

I could describe how that birth control was practiced and the many reasons why all of the people of the earth except those eight souls had become sterile before the flood, but time and space here will not permit me to do so. But one of the worst things that happened or resulted from the conception by earth women from those outer-space men were the monsters that were born to them and that survived. They are the unclean animals, unclean only in that the Bible forbids the eating of their flesh.

(Lev. 11:147.) The unclean animals are part human in that they have certain human parts. The hardheaded serpent has relics of arms and legs, a pelvic bone and gives birth to its young. The swine (hog) has a stomach like a human. The horse has a stomach, also sex organs similar to humans. The eagle has a stomach-not a craw (crop) and a gizzard. Every unclean animal and bird has human parts.

They are also much more intelligent than the clean animals. The eagle is smarter than the chicken. The horse and the dog are more intelligent than cattle and sheep, etc. Unclean animals are the result of the cohabitation of the fallen angels and of earth women. The Apocrypha says, "For earthy things were turned into watery, and the things that before swam in the water now went on the ground." (Wisdom of Solomon 19:19, Apocrypha.)

At the time of the flood all of the fallen angels (outer-space people) that had invaded the earth were sent away into the inner earth. Right now, in the inner earth, they have 200,000,000 pilots of flying saucers under the command of one whose Greek name is "Apollyon, but his name is Abaddon" (Rev.9:1 1,16.

Yahshua the Messiah (Jesus Christ) descended into the inner earth and preached to them. (Eph 4:9-10 .) "For Christ also hath once suffered for sins, the just for the unjust that he might bring us to God, being put to death in the flesh, but quickened by the Spirit: By which also he went and preached unto the spirits in prison; Which sometimes were disobedient when once the long-suffering of God, waited in the days of Noah, while the ark was a preparing, wherein few, that is, eight souls were saved by water." (I Peter 3: 18-20 .)

OUTER SPACE PEOPLE AND INNER EARTH PEOPLE

"For, for this cause was the gospel preached also to them that are dead, that they might be judged according to men in the flesh, but live according to God in the spirit." (I Peter 4:6.)

More will be said later about the outer-space people (angels) that invaded the earth and who are now the residents of the inner earth.

THE THIRD INVASION OF THE EARTH BY OUTER SPACE PEOPLE THAT THE BIBLE DESCRIBES as follows. This was, of course, many years after the flood. "And the whole earth was of one language, and of one speech. And it came to pass, as they journeyed from the east, that they found a plain in the land of Shinar; and they dwelt there. And they said one to another, Go to, let us make brick, and burn them thoroughly. And they had brick for stone, and slime had they for mortar. And they said, Go to, let us build, us a city, and a tower, whose top may reach unto heaven; and let us make us a name, lest we be scattered abroad upon the face of the whole earth. And the Lord came down to see the city and the tower, which the children of men builded. And the Lord said, Behold, the people is one, and they have all one language; and this they begin to do; and now nothing will be restrained for them, which they have imagined to do. Go to, let us go down there and confound their language, that they may not understand one another's speech. So the Lord scattered them abroad from thence upon the face of all the earth: and they left off to build the city. Therefore is the name of it called Babel: because the Lord did there confound the language of all the earth: and from thence did the Lord scatter them abroad upon the face of all the earth."-(Gen. 11:1-9.)

The title "Lord" in this scripture is not "YAHVEH", but it is a plural word and means, "the lords of outer-space." You can see that the key to this is "let us go down." (Gen. 11:6) At that time there were no continents and islands. All of the land on the earth was joined solidly together in one body. The earth people were united in a one world government, speaking one language. They built a tower that was thirty miles across and ninety miles in circumference at the base. The tower reached the height of 3,650 miles. There were 600,000 men engaged in the building of it. The material was taken up at the rate of ten miles a day and it took a "full year" for the material to reach the builders at the top of the tower. (See Book of Jasher 9:21-39.)

Each section of the tower was on a magnetic line with an inhabited planet. The earth people actually began the conquest of outer-space. Battles were fought in the heavens. Blood fell like rain on different parts of the earth. The outer-space people united and invaded the earth. They brainwashed all mankind, taking out of their brain or mind their language and then the outer-space people put into the minds of the earth people their own languages. They divided the people on the earth into many groups and to each group they gave a different language. Some 3,000 different languages and dialects were put into the minds of the earth people. Then they were scattered all over the land area of the earth, to every nook and corner of the earth. When the Tower fell, the land of the earth was torn apart and the continents and islands came into existence as they now are. You can see by looking at a map of the world that the continents and islands would fit together like a jigsaw puzzle.

OUTER SPACE PEOPLE AND INNER EARTH PEOPLE

The name "Peleg" means to divide, and "Joktan" means to lessen. The Bible always has a hidden key to every great truth. "And to Eber were born two sons: The name of the one was Peleg; for in his days was the earth divided; and his brother's name was Joktan." (Gen. 10:25.) Incidentally, this gives us the approximate date when the tower fell and when the earth was divided.

"And as to the tower which the sons of men built the earth opened its mouth and swallowed up one-third part thereof, and a fire also descended from heaven and burned another third, and the other third is left to this day, and it is of that part which was aloft and its circumference is three days walk. And many of the sons of men died in that tower, a people without number."-(Jasher 9:38-39.)

Undoubtedly after the outer-space people bad scattered the earth people all over the land, except those who were working in the tower, then the outer-space people dropped a powerful atom or hydrogen bomb more powerful than anything known on the earth. The earth opened up and 1,200 miles of the tower sank into the inner earth and is there until this day-and probably being used by the inner earth people. Another 1,200 miles of the tower was destroyed by the bomb. (The same type of bomb was used many years later to destroy the cities of Sodom and Gomorrah and left a hole in the earth so deep that it formed the basin of what is now the Dead Sea- a natural incinerator that has for over 4,000 years been able to evaporate all the water from the River Jordan without overflowing. The Jordan is the swiftest river with the freshest water in the world. It plunges into the Dead Sea. The water in that sea is the heaviest, saltiest water in the world. There are 27 pounds of mineral in every 100 pounds of the water.)

Twelve hundred (1,200) miles of the upper third of the tower fell to the earth. Many years later that material was used to build the walls of the city of Babylon. That city was fifteen miles square, which means that the total length of the walls was sixty miles. The outer walls were 300 feet high, 85 feet wide. The inner walls were 200 feet high. There was a space for gardening between the walls. As late as the days of Nebuchadnezzar, which was only 600 years before the birth of Christ, Nebuchadnezzar used up the rest of the material of the Tower of Babel to build the Hanging Gardens and also a tower of his own which was also called the Tower of Babel. It is not to be confused with the original tower since Nebuchadnezzar's tower was only about 1,000 feet high. It was, however, one of the largest buildings (except the Great Pyramid) ever built.

More than 600,000 men were working on and in the original tower of Babel at the time it was destroyed. All of them lost their lives. Since the confusion of tongues and the destruction of the Tower of Babel and division of the land, all the languages spoken by the people on this earth are outer-space languages. There are not more than two or three words known today that are of the original pure language of Adam; one of those true and pure words is YHVH, which is YAHVEH, pronounced YAH-VEE, and which is, as you know, the name of Our Heavenly Father. Ultimately the pure language will be restored to the children of Yahveh on this earth, for it is written in prophecy: "For then will I turn to the people a pure language, that they may all call upon the name of Yahveh, to serve him with one consent." (Zech. 3:9.)

OUTER SPACE PEOPLE AND INNER EARTH PEOPLE

THE FOURTH INVASION OF THIS EARTH BY OUTER SPACE PEOPLE. We do not have very many details about this invasion. It took place 1,500 years before the birth of Christ. The Holy Angels, who are the greatest of the outer-space people, came down on Mount Sinai and gave the law to Moses.

This law is recorded in Exodus, Leviticus, Numbers and Deuteronomy. "The law WAS ORDAINED BY ANGELS IN THE HANDS OF A MEDIATOR," (Gal. 3:19, Ex 20:19, Deut. 5:5.) At two different times Moses spent forty days on Mt. Sinai without food or water. He was literally magnetized with the glow of heavenly glory. Angels accompanied him during all of the forty years in the wilderness when he led the children of Israel. Since those angels often, appeared as a cloud by day and a pillar of fire by night I conclude that they were the highest of the heavenly people, being able to use any element or any form for a body, to make themselves known to Moses. This invasion is of very great importance, not because of the law of Moses, which the angels gave to him, but also because of the heavenly tabernacle which they showed to him, thus giving him the pattern for the tabernacle on earth which was essential in organizing the twelve tribes of Israel and establishing them as a Holy people.

THE FIFTH INVASION OF THIS EARTH BY OUTER SPACE PEOPLE. This invasion was a peculiar one. It resulted in the ten plagues which destroyed most of Egypt and broke her power as a great nation forever. Those ten plagues were: 1. The water of the River Nile turned into blood; 2. Frogs; 3. Dust turned into lice; 4. Flies; 5. The murrain of beasts; 6. Hail; 7. Boils and blains; 8. Locust; 9. Darkness; 10. Death of the first born. (Read Exodus, first through fifteenth chapters.)

The earth, during the time of those plagues, passed through the tail of a comet then sideswiped the planet Venus, narrowly averting a head-on collision with Venus. Nearly every section of the earth was at that time covered with drift which was a fallout of gravel, iron ore, shale and crude oil from the sky. Actually the germs of many kinds of disease, as well as lice, flies and vermin were dumped from outer-space upon the earth. Also, low savage tribes of people were dumped from other planets upon this earth. They are on earth until this day. They are not in any way related to the descendants of Shem, Ham and Japheth. The savage peoples are not of Adam's race. They were transported to earth by outer-space people. Everything that Yahveh created "was very good." (Gen. 1:31:) He did not create savages or the unclean animals and parasites. They resulted from crossovers or were dumped here from other planets.

I could and I would love to describe every plague in detail, but time now and space here will not permit it. I think, however, that I must, tell you this much: The tenth plague not only destroyed the first born of the Egyptians that were living at that time, but also the pictures, images and records of all of the firstborn throughout all the history of Egypt. No tomb or any record of any firstborn Egyptian has ever been found. That is why the historians and archaeologists cannot connect the dynasties of Egypt.

Furthermore, when the children of Israel went out of Egypt, they carried with them, not only the bones of Joseph (Gen. 50:24-26, Ex. 13:19), but also the bones of the twelve patriarchs and all the bones and dust and ashes of every Israelite that had died in Egypt

OUTER SPACE PEOPLE AND INNER EARTH PEOPLE

during the 430 years of the captivity. No trace of the body of any Israelite has ever been found in Egypt. It was a complete deliverance of both the living and the dead. All of Yahveh's people are to be delivered from (Egypt) which is "the present evil world" systems.

Here is a description of the plague of darkness and death of the firstborn in Egypt as given in Wisdom of Solomon, in the Apocrypha: "For great are thy judgments, and cannot be expressed; therefore unnurtured souls have erred. For when unrighteous men thought to oppress the holy nation, they being shut up in their houses, the prisoners of darkness, and fettered with the bonds of a long night, lay (there) exiled from the eternal providence. For while they supposed to lie hid in their secret sins, they were scattered under a dark veil of forgetfulness, being horribly astonished, and troubled with (strange) apparitions. For neither might the corner that held them keep them from fear: but noises (as of waters) falling down sounded about them, and sad visions appeared unto them with heavy countenances. No power of the fire might give them light: neither could the bright flames of the stars endure to lighten that horrible night. Only there appeared unto them a fire kindled of itself, very dreadful; for being much terrified, they thought the things which they saw to be worse than the sight they saw not. As for the illusions of art magick, they were put down, and their vaunting in wisdom was reproved with disgrace. For they that promised to drive away terrors and troubles from a sick soul, were sick themselves of fear, worthy to be laughed at.

"For though no terrible thing did fear them; yet being scared with beasts that passed by, and hissing serpents, they died for fear, denying that they saw the air, which could of no side be avoided. For wickedness, condemned by her own witness, is very timorous, and being pressed with conscience, always forecasteth grievous things. For fear is nothing else but a betraying of the succors which reason offereth. And the expectation from within, being less, counteth the ignorance more than the cause which bringeth the torment. But they sleeping the same sleep that night, which was indeed intolerable, and which came upon them out of the bottoms of inevitable hell, were partly vexed with monstrous apparitions, and partly fainted, their heart failing them; for a sudden fear, and not looked for, came upon them. So then whosoever there fell down was straitly kept shut up in a prison without iron bars. For whether he were husbandman, or shepherd, or a labourer in the field, he was overtaken, and endured that necessity, which could not be avoided, for they were all bound with one chain of darkness. Whether it were a whistling wind, or a melodious noise of birds, among the spreading branches, or a pleasing fall of water running violently, or a terrible sound of stones cast down, or a running that could not be seen of skipping beasts, or a roaring voice of most savage wild beasts, or a rebounding echo from the hallow mountains; these things made them to swoon for fear. For the whole world shined with clear light, and none were hindered in their labour; over them only was spread an heavy night, an image of that darkness which should afterward receive them, but yet were they unto themselves more grievous than the darkness." (Wisdom of Solomon 17:1-21, Apocrypha).

Therefore even with blindness were these stricken, as those were at the doors of the righteous man; when, being compassed about with horrible great, darkness, every

OUTER SPACE PEOPLE AND INNER EARTH PEOPLE

one sought the passage of his own doors. For the elements were changed in themselves by a kind of harmony, like as in a psaltery notes change the name of the tune, and yet are always sounds; which may well be perceived by the sight of the things that have been done. For earthly things were turned into watery, and the things that before swam in the water, now went upon the ground. The fire had power in the water, forgetting his own virtue; and the water forgot his own quenching nature. On the other side, the flames wasted not the flesh of the corruptible living things, though they walked therein neither melted they the icy kind of heavenly meat, that was of nature apt to melt. For in all things, O Lord, thou didst magnify thy people, and glorify them, neither didst thou lightly regard them: but didst assist them in every time and place." (Wisdom of Solomon 19:17-22,)

The earth, during the time of the plagues, tilted several degrees out of balance (Psalm 82:5) and went far off its regular course in orbiting the sun. It corrected itself, not wholly but by several degrees, during the time of Joshua.

"Then spake Joshua to the Lord in the day when the Lord delivered up the Amorites before the children of Israel, and he said in the sight of Israel, Sun, stand thou still upon Gibeon; and thou, Moon, in the valley of Ajalon. And the sun stood still, and the moon stayed until the people had avenged themselves upon their enemies. Is not this written in the book of Jasher. So the sun stood still in the midst of heaven, and hasted not to go down about a whole day. And there was no day like that before it or after it, that the Lord hearkened unto the voice of a man; for the Lord fought for Israel." (Joshua 10:12- 14.)

At the right time Yahveh uses the elements to fight for and to protect and to deliver his own people who put their trust in him. "They fought from heaven; the stars in their paths (courses)." (Judges 5:20.)

THE SIXTH INVASION OF THIS EARTH BY OUTER SPACE PEOPLE. This took place at the birth of Jesus Christ. Representatives of every nation on the earth and representatives of every inhabited world in all the universe followed the Star of Bethlehem by land, sea and air. Many from outer-space came in flying saucers-all of them flying in course by the star as their guide until it reached its meridian over Bethlehem. The scriptures are very clear on this. "Because of thy temple at Jerusalem shall the kings bring presents unto thee." (Ps. 68:29.) "The kings of Tarshish and of the isles shall bring presents; the kings of Sheba and Seba shall offer gifts. Yea, all kings shall fall down before him; all nations shall serve him." (Ps. 72:10.)

"Now when Jesus was born in Bethlehem of Judea in the days of Herod the king, behold, there came wise men from the east to Jerusalem, saying, Where is he that is born King of the Israelites? for we have seen his star in the east, and are come to worship him." (Matt. 2:1-2.) "The chairots of God and twenty thousand, even thousands of angels: the Lord is among them, as in Sinai, in the holy place." Ps. 68:17.)

"And she brought forth her firstborn son, and wrapped him in swaddling clothes, and laid him in a manger; because there was no room for them in the inn. And there were in the same country shepherds abiding in the field, keeping watch over their flock by night. And, lo, the angel of the Lord came upon them, and the glory of the Lord shone

OUTER SPACE PEOPLE AND INNER EARTH PEOPLE

round about them; and they were sore afraid. And the angel said unto them, Fear not, for, behold, I bring you good tidings of great joy, which shall be to all people. For unto you is born this day in the City of David, a Saviour, which is Christ the Lord. And this shall be a sign unto you: Ye shall find the babe wrapped in swaddling clothes, lying in a manger.

And suddenly there was with the angel a multitude of the heavenly host praising God, and saying, Glory to God in the highest, and on earth peace, good will toward men. And it came to pass, as the angels were gone away from them into heaven, the shepherds said one to another, Let us now go even unto Bethlehem, and see this thing which is come to pass, which the Lord hath made known unto us. And they came with haste, and found Mary and Joseph, and the babe lying in a manger. And when they had seen it, they made known abroad the saying which was told them concerning this child." (Luke 2:7-17.)

The above scriptures are self-explanatory. They prove that all the kings and representative wise men from all the earth, and the angels from outer-space followed the Star of Bethlehem and appeared in Jerusalem and Bethlehem at the time of the birth of the Messiah.

THE SEVENTH INVASION OF THIS EARTH BY OUTER SPACE PEOPLE. This invasion is by far the most important one to us. At the time that Jesus Christ was raised from the dead, there were 144,000 raised with him. They ascended into heaven with him. (Matt. 27: 50-54, Eph. 4:8-10, Rev. 7: 1-9, Rev. 14:1-14, Heb. 12:22-24.) I am telling you the truth and if you doubt it, read the scripture references.

The three key words to the fact that 144,000 were resurrected with Christ are the three words: "Better Resurrection" (Heb. 11:85) and the plural word "Firstfruits". (I Cor. 15:28, I Cor. 14:4, James 1:18.) The 144,000 raised from the dead were the beginning of the plural body of Christ. They ascended into heaven with him and are the Church of the firstborn (from the dead), the heavenly Jerusalem.

Ten days after Christ and the 144,000 ascended into heaven, they returned to earth accompanied by an innumerable number of angels (outer-space people).

"Why leap ye, ye high hills? this is the hill which God desireth to dwell in; yea, the Lord will dwell in it for ever. The chariots of God are twenty thousand, even thousands of angels: the Lord is among them, as in Sinai, in the holy place. Thou hast ascended on high, thou hast led captivity captive; thou hast received gifts for men; yea, for the rebellious also, that the Lord God might dwell among them. Blessed be the Lord, who daily loadeth us with benefits, even the God of our salvation. Selah." (Psalm 68: 16-19.)

"This same Jesus, which is taken up from you into heaven, shall so come in like manner as ye have seen him go into heaven." (Acts 1:11.) He did return. Yes, ten days later he returned:. "And when the day of Pentecost was fully come, they were all with one accord in one place. And suddenly there came a sound from heaven as of a rushing mighty wind, and it filled all the house where they were sitting. And there appeared unto them cloven tongues like as of fire, and it sat upon each of them. And they were all filled with the Holy Ghost and began to speak with other tongues, as the Spirit gave them utter-

OUTER SPACE PEOPLE AND INNER EARTH PEOPLE

ance. And there were dwelling at Jerusalem Jews, devout men, out of every nation under heaven. Now when this was noised abroad, the multitude came together, and were confounded, because that every man heard them speak in his own language. And they were all amazed and marveled, saying one to another, Behold, are not all these which speak Galileans? And how we hear every man in our own tongue, wherein we were born? Parthians, and Medes, and Elamites, and the dwellers of Mesopotamia, and in Judea, and Cappadocia, in Pontus, and Asia, Phrygia and Pamphylia, in Egypt, and in parts of Libya about Cyrene and strangers of Rome, Jews and proselytes, Cretes and Arabians, we do hear them speak in our tongues the wonderful works of God." (Acts 2: 1-11.)

Jesus Christ and the 144,000 Israelites and the great host of angels returned on the Day of Pentecost. They have never left us. They are here now. They surround us. "Ye are come unto Mount Sion, and unto the city of the living God, the heavenly Jerusalem, and to an innumerable company of angels, to the general assembly and church of the firstborn, which are written in heaven, and to God the Judge of all, and to the spirits of just men made perfect, and to Jesus the mediator of the new covenant and to the blood of sprinkling, that speaketh better things than that of Abel. See that ye refuse not him that speaketh." (Heb. 12:22-25.)

"Wherefore, seeing we also are compassed about with so great a cloud of witnesses, let us lay aside every weight, and the sin which doth so easily beset us." (Heb. 12: 1.)

This harmonizes perfectly with all the scriptures. It fits like a hand and a glove. Jesus said to the disciples before he ascended: Yet a little while, and the world seeth me no more; but ye see me because I live, ye shall live also . At that day ye shall know that I am in my Father, and ye in me, and I in you. He that hath my commandments, and keepeth them, he it is that loveth me; and he that loveth me shall be loved of my Father, and I will love him, and will manifest myself to him. Judas saith unto him, not Iscariot, Lord, how is it that thou wilt manifest thyself unto us, and not unto the world? Jesus answered and said unto him, If a man love me, he will keep my words; and my Father will love him, and we will come unto him, and make our abode with him." (John 14:19-28.)

Yes, he came back to the disciples on the Day of Pentecost. He is with us just as he said he would be: "Lo, I am with you always, even unto the end of the world." (Matt. 28:20.) Get the flesh out of your eyes and the materialism out of your heart, and then you can say with us: "WE SEE JESUS." (Heb. 2:9.)

"Wherefore henceforth know we no man after the flesh: yea, though we have known Christ after the flesh, yet now henceforth know we him no more. Therefore if any man be in Christ he is a new creature; old things are passed away; behold, all things are become new." (II Cor. 5:16-17.) "Even when we were dead in sins, hath he quickened us together with Christ and hath raised us up together, and made us sit together in heavenly places in Christ Jesus." (Eph. 2:5-6.)

"The kingdom of God cometh not with observation: neither shall they say, Lo here! or Lo, there! for BEHOLD, the kingdom of God is within you." (Luke 17:21.)

OUTER SPACE PEOPLE AND INNER EARTH PEOPLE

All of this talk about a second coming of Christ for his church is nonsense. The facts are that this statement: "the second coming of Christ" is not in the Bible. Some people read it into the Bible, but it is not there! THE TRUTH IS that Christ has never been separated from HIS CHURCH.

For we are members of his body, of his flesh, and of his bones." (Eph. 5: 80.) "This is a great mystery (secret) : but I speak concerning Christ and the church." (Eph. 5:82.) The Church began on the Day of Pentecost (Acts 2:1-47) , and Christ has always been with his Church. So have the saints, "the spirits of just men made perfect," and so have the angels. "And of the angels he saith, who maketh his angels spirits, and his ministers a flame of fire." (Heb. 1 :7.) That is exactly the way they appeared on the Day of Pentecost. "Are they not all ministering spirits, sent forth to minister for them who shall be heirs of salvation?" (Heb. 1: 14.) That is a question. You answer it!

Listen, now.! The Kingdom is to be restored literally, visibly and tangibly "unto Israel." There is a coming (manifestation) of Christ and His Church to Israel. Christ and His Church will reign spiritually over literal restored Israel.

The invasion of this earth on the Day of Pentecost (Acts 2:1-47) had and has a definite connection with the invasion at the time of the destruction of the Tower of Babel (Gen. 11: 1-9), for the tongues that had been taken away began to be restored. "Many of those innumerable angels (outer-space people) at Pentecost had also taken part in the invasion of the earth at the Tower of Babel. I have described to you the SEVEN major invasions of this earth by outer-space people-by the good and Holy ones and also by the evil ones. There are four more invasions yet to come.

THE EIGHTH INVASION OF THIS EARTH BY OUTER SPACE PEOPLE will take place in the very near future. It is an evil one by evil forces from outer space and from the inner earth. There is war going on right now in the lower heavens. This is in the inhabited places in outer-space that are nearest to this earth. "And there was war in heaven: Michael and his angels fought against the dragon; and the dragon fought and his angels, And prevailed not; neither was their place found any more in heaven.

"And the Great Dragon was cast out, that old serpent, called the Devil and Satan, which deceived the whole world; he was cast out into the earth, and his angels were cast out with him. And I heard a loud voice saying in heaven, Now is come salvation, and strength, and The kingdom of our God, and the power of his Christ: for the accuser of our brethren is cast down, which accused them before our God day and night. And they overcame him by the blood of the Lamb, and by the word of their testimony: and they loved not their lives unto death. Therefore rejoice, ye heavens, and ye that dwell in them. Woe to the inhabiters of the earth and of the seal for the devil is come down unto you, having great wrath, because he knoweth that he hath but a short time." (Rev. 12:7-12.)

"And the fifth angel sounded; and I saw a star fail from heaven unto the earth: and to him was given the key of the bottomless pit. And he opened the bottomless pit; and there arose a smoke out of the pit, as the smoke of a great furnace; and the sun and the air were darkened by reason of the smoke of the pit. And there came out of the smoke locusts upon the earth; and unto them was given power, as the scorpions of the earth have

OUTER SPACE PEOPLE AND INNER EARTH PEOPLE

power. And it was commanded them that they should not hurt the grass of the earth, neither any green thing, neither any tree; but only those men which have not the seal of God in their foreheads. And to them it was given that they should not kill them, but that they should be tormented five months; and their torment was as the torment of a scorpion, when he striketh a man. And in those days shall men seek death, and shall not find it; and shall desire to die, and death shall flee from them. And the shapes of the locusts were like unto horses prepared unto battle; and on their heads were as it were crowns like gold, and their faces were as the faces of men.

And they had hair as the hair of women, and their teeth were as the teeth of lions. And they had breastplates, as it were breastplates of iron; and the sound of their wings was as the sound of chariots, of many horses running to battle. And they had tails like unto scorpions, and there were stings in their tails: and their power was to hurt men five months. And they had a king over them, which is the angel of the bottomless pit, whose name in the Hebrew tongue is Abaddon, but in the Greek tongue hath his name Apollyon." (Rev. 9:1-11).

Following this comes something worse from every corner of the earth and by evil forces from outer-space. And the number of the army of the horsemen were two hundred thousand thousand; and I heard the number of them. And thus I saw the horses in the vision, and them that sat on them having breastplates of fire, and of jacinth; and brimstone; and the heads of the horses were as the heads of lions; and out of their mouth issued fire and smoke and brimstone. By these three was the third part of men killed, by the fire; and by the smoke, and by the brimstone, which issued out of their mouths. For their power is in their mouth, and in their tails: for the tails were like unto serpents, and had heads, and with them they do hurt." (Rev. 9:16-19.)

THE NINTH INVASION OF THIS EARTH BY OUTER SPACE PEOPLE is to take place in the very near future, even in our lifetime. It is by the righteous forces. You will notice that the following from the New Testament is also from the book of Enoch. The word "Lord" in this quotation is plural. "And Enoch also, the seventh from Adam, prophesied of these, saying, Behold, the Lord cometh with ten thousands of his saints. To execute judgment upon all, and to convince all that are ungodly among them of all their ungodly deeds which they have ungodly, committed, and of all their hard speeches which ungodly sinners have spoken against him.? (Jude 14-15.)

The leaders from outer-space who will lead this invasion are: 1. Uriel; 2. Raphael; 3. Raguel; 4. Michael; 5. Sarakiel; 6. Gabriel. (Enoch 20:7.)

The invasion will result in the separation of good and evil people and the end of it will be the binding of Satan. The field is the world; the good seed are the children of the kingdom; but the tares are the children of the wicked one. The enemy that sowed them is the devil; the harvest is the end of the world; and the reapers are the angels. As therefore the tares are gathered and burned in the fire; so shall it be in the end of the world. The Son of man shall send forth his angels, and they shall gather out of his kingdom all things that offend, and them which do iniquity; And shall cast them into a furnace of fire: there shall be wailing and gnashing of teeth." (Matt. 13:33-42.)

OUTER SPACE PEOPLE AND INNER EARTH PEOPLE

"And I saw an angel come down from heaven, having the key of the bottomless pit and a great chain in his hand. And he laid Mild on the dragon, that old serpent which is the Devil, and Satan, and bound him a thousand years, And cast him into the bottomless pit, and shut him up, and set a seal upon him, that be should deceive the nation no more, till the thousand years should be fulfilled: and after that he must be loosed a little season. And I saw thrones, and they sat upon, them, and judgment was given unto, them: and I saw the souls of them that were beheaded for the witness of Jesus; and for the word of God, and which had not worshipped the beast neither his image, neither had received his mark upon their foreheads, or in their hands; and they lived and reigned with Christ a thousand years." (Rev. 20:1-4.)

"Then shall the righteous shine forth as the sun in the kingdom of their Father. Who hath ears to hear, let him hear."

THE TENTH INVASION OF THIS EARTH BY OUTER SPACE PEOPLE will take place after the thousand years (millennium) reign of righteousness. "And when the thousand years are expired, Satan shall be loosed out of his prison. And shalt go out to deceive the nations which are in the four quarters of the earth, Gog and Magog, to gather them together to battle; the number of whom is as the sand of the sea. And they went up on the breadth of the earth, and compassed the camp of the saints about and the beloved city; and fire came down from God out of heaven, and devoured them, And the devil that deceived them was east into the lake of fire . . Death and hell were cast into the lake of fire." (Rev. 20:7-10,14.)

THE ELEVENTH AND FINAL INVASION OF THIS EARTH FROM OTHER SPACE will be the coming of YAHVEH in person, bringing with Him the very throne of heaven and the highest heaven itself. "And I saw a great white throne, and him that sat on it, from whose face the earth and the heaven, fled away; and there was found no place for them. And I saw the dead, small and great, stand before God; and the books were opened, and another book was opened, which is the book of life, and the dead were judged out of those things which were written in the books, according to their works." (Rev. 20:11-12.)

"And I saw a new heaven and a new earth; for the first heaven and the first earth were passed away; and there was no more sea. And I John saw the holy city, new Jerusalem, coming down from God out of heaven, prepared as a bride adorned for her husband; And I heard a great voice out of heaven saying, Behold, the tabernacle of God is with men, and he will dwell with them, and they shall be his people, and God himself shall be with them, and be their God. And God shall wipe away all tears from their eyes; and There shall be no more death neither sorrow, nor crying, neither shall there be any more pain, for the former things are passed away. And he that sat upon the throne said, Behold, I make all things new. And he said unto me, Write, for these words are true and faithful. And he said unto me, It is done. I am Alpha and Omega, the beginning and the end. I will give unto him that is athirst of the fountain of the water of life freely. He that overcometh shall inherit all things; and I will be his God, and he shall be my son." (Rev. 21: 1-7.)

Read all of the 21st and 22nd chapters of Revelation for the exceedingly beautiful

OUTER SPACE PEOPLE AND INNER EARTH PEOPLE

and wonderful description, of this descension of the New Jerusalem to this earth, the restoration of Paradise and the tree of life and all things. "For this is good and acceptable in the sight of God our Saviour; Who will have all men to be saved, and to come unto the knowledge of the truth. For there is one God, and one mediator between God and men, the man Christ Jesus; Who gave himself a ransom for all, to be testified in due time," (1 Tim. 2: 3-6.)

"This is a faithful saying, and worthy of all acceptation. For therefore we both labor and suffer reproach because we trust in the living God, who is the Saviour of all men, specially of those that believe. These things command and teach." (I Tim. 4:9-10)

"That at the name of Jesus every knee should bow, of things in heaven, and things in earth, and things under the earth; And that every tongue should confess that Jesus Christ is Lord to the glory of God the Father." (Phil. 2: 10-11.)

"Having made known unto us the mystery of his will, according to his good pleasure which he hath purposed in himself: That in the dispensation of the fullness of times he might gather together in one all things in Christ both which are in heaven, and which are on earth; even in him in whom also we have obtained an inheritance, being predestinated according to the purpose of him who worketh all things after the counsel of his own will." (Eph. 1:9-11)

CONCLUSION: I have described the eleven major invasions of this earth by outer space people. Seven of these invasions have already taken place and four more are to come. However, it must be understood that for the last six thousand years one, or two, or three or more outer-space people have at frequent intervals, visited this earth. They are, in fact, constantly and continually coming to earth with special messages of great importance. I will describe a few cases of these heavenly visitors to this earth.

Three men from outer-space visited Abraham. They appeared as ordinary earth men. They ate meat with him; they foretold the birth of Isaac; they also told him that Sodom and Gomorrah would be destroyed. (Gen. 18:1-38,)

2. Two men from outer-space visited Lot; stayed all night in his home, and the next day rescued Lot and his wife and two daughters from the doomed city of Sodom. (Gen. 19: 1-88.)

3. A man (angel) from outer-space visited Jacob and gave him the name of ISRAEL. (Cen. 82: 24-82.)

4. A man from outer-space (angel) visited Moses and revealed the true secret name of the Heavenly Father to him. (Exodus 8: 1-22, 6 : 1-8.)

5. A man from outer-space who was the captain of the army of Yahveh visited Joshua. "And it came to pass, when Joshua was by Jericho, that he lifted up his eyes and looked, and, behold, there stood a man over against him with his sword drawn in his hand; and Joshua went unto him, and said unto him, Art thou for us, or for our adversaries? And he said, Nay; but as captain of the host of the Lord am I now come. And Joshua fell on his face to The earth and did worship, and said unto him. What saith my lord unto his servant?

OUTER SPACE PEOPLE AND INNER EARTH PEOPLE

And the captain of the Lord's host said unto Joshua, Loose thy shoe from off thy foot; for the place whereon thou standest is holy. And Joshua did so." (Joshua 5:18-15.)

      6. A man from outer-space (angel) visited Gideon. The Bible says, "the angel of the Lord appeared unto him, and said unto him, the Lord is with thee, thou mighty man of valor. Go in thy might, and thou shalt save Israel." (Judges 6:12, 14.) "And Gideon went in, and made ready a kid, and unleavened cakes of an ephah of flour: the flesh he put in a basket and he put the broth in a pot, and brought it out unto him under the oak, and presented it. And the angel of God said unto him, Take the flesh and the unleavened cakes, and lay them upon this rock, and pour out the broth. And he did so. Then the angel of the Lord put forth the end of the staff that was in his hand, and touched the flesh and the unleavened cakes; and there rose up fire out of the rock, and consumed the flesh and the unleavened cakes. Then the angel of the Lord departed out of his sight. And when Gideon perceived that he was an angel of the Lord, Gideon said, Alas O Lord God! for because I have seen an angel of the Lord face to face. And the Lord said unto him, Peace be unto thee; fear not, thou shalt not die. Then Gideon built an altar there unto the Lord and called it Jehovah-shalom." (Judges 6: 19-24.)

      7. A man from outer-space (angel) with a secret name appeared to Manoah and his wife and informed them that a child (Samson) would be born to them. It is a very interesting story. (Judges 18 1-25.)

      8. A man from outer-space, who was a very strong angel, destroyed 185,000 of the Assyrian soldiers of the Army of Sennacherib. (II Kings 19:35.)

      9. Angels locked the mouths of lions. (Dan. 6:22.)

      10. Michael, one of the chief princes of outer-space, appeared in person to Daniel. (Dan. 10:18-21)

      11). A whole army of outer-space people (angels) saved the life of Elisha and gave him the power to capture the entire Assyrian army "Behold, the mountain was full of horses and chariots of fire round about Elisha." (II Kings 6:17.)

      12. A man from outer-space brought food to Elijah and after Elijah had eaten two meals of that food, he had physical strength and needed no more food for forty days. "He himself went a day's journey into the wilderness, and came and sat down under a juniper tree: and he requested for himself that he might die; and said, it is enough; now, O lord, take away my life; for I am not better than my fathers. And as he lay and slept under a juniper tree, behold, then an angel touched him, and said unto him, Arise and eat. And he looked, and, behold, there was a cake baked on the coals, and a cruse of water at his head. And he did eat and drink, and laid him down again. And the angel of the Lord came again the second time, and touched him, and said, Arise and eat; because the journey is too great for thee. And he arose and did eat and drink and went in the strength of that meat forty days and forty nights unto Horeb the mount of God." (I Kings 19:4-8.)

      13. An angel announced the conception of John the Baptist and gave him the name "John" before he was born. (Luke 1: 1-85.)

OUTER SPACE PEOPLE AND INNER EARTH PEOPLE

14. An angel announced the Virgin conception to Mary. (Luke 1: 1-85.)

15. An angel told Joseph that Mary had conceived by the Holy Ghost. (Matt. 1: 18-24.)

16. An angel, together with a multitude of outer-space people came to earth and announced the birth of Jesus Christ. (Luke 2:8,16.)

17. An angel told Joseph to take Jesus into Egypt. (Matt. 2: 19.)

18. An angel told Joseph to bring Jesus back to Palestine. (Matt. 2:18-20.)

19. An angel strengthened Jesus in the Garden of Gethsemane. (Luke 22:41-42.)

20. Angels rolled the stone away from the tomb and announced the resurrection. (Matt. 28:2-7.)

21. Immediately after his ascension angels came down and spoke to the disciples. (Acts 1 :9-11)

22. An angel told the Gentiles to send for the Apostle Peter to preach to them. (Acts 10:30-82.)

23. An angel delivered the Apostle Peter from prison. (Acts 12:8-11.)

24. An angel struck Herod and killed him. (Acts 12:20-23.)

25. An angel called the Apostle Paul to Europe. (Acts 6:9-10.)

26. An angel announced to Paul that his life and those on board that ship in that terrible storm at sea, would be saved. (Acts 27:21-26.)

27. Angels rejoice when a soul is saved. (Luke 15;7-10 .)

28. Angels will gather the elect children of Yahveh together from all over the world. (Matt. 24:81.)

29. Angels will gather out the scoffers, sinners and ungodly and completely separate them from those who are saved. (Matt. 18:40-48.)

There are so many other references to angels in both the Old and New Testaments. The word "angel" does not mean a non-sexed creature with wings. An "angel" is an outer-space man or woman. The word literally means "a messenger." Angels may be and often are men who once lived on this earth, but who are now known as "the spirits of just men made perfect." (Heb. 12,22)

This is evident from the angel that gave John "The Revelation". "The revelation of Jesus Christ, which God gave unto him, to show unto his servants things which must shortly come to pass; and he sent and signified it by his angel unto his servant John." (Rev. 1:1.) "And I John saw these things, and heard them. And when I had heard and seen, I fell down to worship before the feet of the angel which showed me these things. Then saith he unto me, See thou do it not: for I am thy fellow servant, and of thy brethren the prophets, and of them which keep the sayings of this book: worship God." (Rev. 22:8)

OUTER SPACE PEOPLE AND INNER EARTH PEOPLE

"The Angel of the Lord encampeth round about them that fear him, and delivereth them." (Psalm 34:7.) Yahveh "maketh his angels spirits, and his ministers, a flame of fire. Are they not all ministering spirits, sent forth to minister for them who shall be heirs of salvation?" (Heb. 1:7-14.)

OUTER SPACE PEOPLE AND INNER EARTH PEOPLE

Chapter III

Cities In The Sky

Dear Friends:

I predict that one hundred years from now most of the buildings will be done in the sky. There will be many cities, anywhere from 200 to 800 miles above the surface of the earth, undisturbed by weather and climatic conditions. The energy from the sun will be (as it is now) seven times greater up there than it is on the surface of the earth, and the energy of the moon up there will be equal to the present energy of the sun on the surface of the earth. (Isa. 30:26.)

The energy in those sky cities being eight times greater than the energy as it is now on the surface of the earth, will mean that the people living in those cities in the sky will be free from disease and will live indefinitely in perpetual youth and perfect health. "His flesh shall be fresher than a child's: he shall return to the days of his youth." (Job 82:25). "They that wait upon Yahveh shall renew their strength; they shall mount up with wings as eagles moving from the surface of the earth up into the sky cities in man-made vehicles, they shall run, and not be weary; (overcoming weight and gravity) and they shall walk and not faint." (Isa. 40 :81). They will never get tired, never be weary.

Yahshua the Messiah said, in a familiar scripture known by everyone, "In my Father's house are many rooms; if it were not so, would I have told you that I go to prepare a place for you? And when I go and prepare a place for you, I will come again and will take you to myself, that where I am you may be also." (John 14:2-8, R S V.) "In the house of my Father there are many abodes." (John 14:2, N W T.). "There are many rooms in my Father's house." (John 14:2, Goodspeed). "In my Fathers house there are many mansions." (John 14:2, AV, and Douay and Confraternity.) "In my Father's house there are many resting-places." (John 14:2, Weymouth). "In the house of my Father are many dwellings. (John 14:2, Rotherham).

There are many cities in the sky. They are up there right now. In the last 1900 years since the ascension of Yahshua the Messiah, He has personally supervised the building of many sky cities. That has been his work and his job for the last 1900 years, as he

OUTER SPACE PEOPLE AND INNER EARTH PEOPLE

said it would be. In our work of "House Of Prayer For All People" we not only keep up with science, but ahead of all the scientists because we interpret the Bible as a living book, showing where we are now and what is out ahead,

In my dreams and visions for many years I have often had the experience of floating through the air, sometimes coming down into the cities in outer-space, but more often visiting the big cities on this earth: London, Washington, D C., Moscow, farm communities and farm homes in Russia and also villages in the interior of Africa.

Some, of course, will say that this is mental hallucination and optical illusion. Others call it astral projection. These trips are not always by floating in the air but are sometimes made on ships at sea and by airplanes and by automobile and in horse-drawn carriages. They seem to take three or four months and are definitely as realistic as any trips that are really made in the same way. The psychologists and psychiatrists say that all dreams, or any dream, lasts only for a few seconds. What is but a few seconds of surface earth time may stretch into months in outer-space time. On the other hand, if a person had left the earth a thousand or more years ago and returned to earth today, he would not realize that he had been away for more than a few seconds. This is too deep for me; I make no attempt to explain it.

If the dead are dead and know nothing (and I believe that this is true of all of the dead except those who are the sons of God, "ELOHIM" in the elect body and who share in the "Better Resurrection"-Heb. 11:85) and have eternal life and immortality, and are passed from death unto life in the higher realms; but the vast majority of the people that have lived on the earth were not in this order and they are dead and if they are dead for a day, or for a year or for a thousand years or for seven thousand years and are then resurrected to life, they will not even realize that ten seconds of time has elapsed between the time of their death and their resurrection.

Coming back now to projections: If we make them into the past, the travel conveyance seems to be as it was in the past; if into the future, then the future miracles of travel are used. Now this is not a dream or a vision. I have flown by airplane from Detroit to Minneapolis, from Williston, North Dakota to Denver; from Denver to Portland, Los Angeles, Oklahoma City, Tulsa, Dallas, etc. Every time that I have been in the air and have looked down upon the beautiful mountains, valleys, farms and cities which are so beautiful and yet so small, I have always had the feeling that at some future time, we will live in the air. The Bible says, in speaking of those that belong to the Body of the Messiah, We "shall be caught up together with them in the clouds, to meet the Lord in the air: and so, shall we ever be with the Lord." (I Thes. 4:17).

The City In The Sky

That is, of course, "The New Jerusalem." The entire 21st and 22nd chapters of the Book of Revelation are devoted to a description of it. Read it in your Bible: "And he carried me away in the spirit to a great and high mountain, and showed me that great city, the holy Jerusalem, descending out of heaven from God, having the glory of God: and her light was like unto a stone most precious, even like a jasper stone, clear as crystal; and had a wall great and high, and had twelve gates, and at the gates twelve angels, and

OUTER SPACE PEOPLE AND INNER EARTH PEOPLE

names written thereon, which are the names of the twelve tribes of the children of Israel: on the east three gates; on the north three gates; on the south three gates; and on the west three gates. And the wall of the city had twelve foundations, and in them the names of the twelve apostles of the Lamb. And he that talked with me had a golden reed to measure the city, and the gates thereof, and the wall thereof. And the city lieth foursquare, and the length is as large as the breadth; and he measured the city with the reed, twelve thousand furlongs. The length and the breadth and the height of it are equal." (Rev. 21:10-16). (It was difficult for me to understand how this city could be a cube, foursquare, until I realized that it is a sky city, for "It is he that buildeth his stories in the heaven." (Amos 9:6).

Nearly all Bible scholars and translators say that this city is 1500 miles square, but I have always believed that it is only 1200 miles square. It is a cube, 1200 miles long, 1200 miles wide and 1200 miles high. The names over the gates on the East are: Issachar, Judah, Zebulun, West: Manasseh, Ephraim, Benjamin. North side: Asher, Dan, Naphthali. South side: Simeon, Reuben, Gad. This is also the way that Moses set up the tabernacle on earth, which he made according to the heavenly pattern that Yahveh showed to him on Mt. Sinai. Let us look further at the material out of which "The New Jerusalem" is builded. "And the building of the wall of it was of jasper; and the city was pure gold, like unto clear glass. And the foundations of the wall of the city were garnished with all manner of precious stones. The first foundation was jasper; the second, sapphire; the third, a chalcedony; the fourth, an emerald; the fifth, sardonyx; the sixth, sardius; the seventh, chyrysolite; the eighth, beryl; the ninth, a topaz; the tenth, a chrysoprasus; the eleventh, a jacinth; the twelfth, an amethyst. And the twelve gates were twelve pearls; every several gate was one of pearl, and the street of the city was pure gold as it were transparent glass," (Rev. 21:18-21).

Neither the United States nor Russia has ever dreamed of building a satellite or sky city like the New Jerusalem which is above, which is the mother of us all." (Gal. 4:26). Here is another description of it and of those that are now in it: "Ye are come unto mount Sion and unto the city of the living God, the heavenly Jerusalem, and to an innumerable company of angels, to the general assembly and church of the firstborn, which are written in heaven, and to God the Judge of all; and to the spirits of just men made perfect, and to Jesus the Mediator of the new covenant." (Heb. 12:22-28.) And here is something else by which we identify the city: "And he showed me a pure river of water of life, clear as crystal, proceeding out of "the throne of God and of the Lamb. In the midst of the street of it, and on either side of the river, was there the tree of life, which bare twelve manner of fruits; and yielded her fruit every month: and the leaves of the tree were for the healing of the nations;" (Rev. 22:1-2).

Now in the beginning "the tree of life" (Gen. 2:9) was in Paradise, which was in the Garden on the continent of Eden on this earth. (Gen. 2:8-25). This was the home of Adam and Eve on this earth and the children of Yahveh. It was the capital and ruling city on the earth. When sin and transgression came, they were driven out. The entire continent of Eden, garden and city of Paradise was thrown off from the earth into the air. It became a planet in its own right and went into orbit. It orbits the, solar system (sun) every 312

OUTER SPACE PEOPLE AND INNER EARTH PEOPLE

years. Its orbit is like that of a comet, in the circuit of a figure 8. It orbits the solar system in 312 years and then, for some strange reason, it circles the earth for two full years.

Another name for "Paradise" or "The New Jerusalem" is THE STAR OF BETHLEHEM. It was seen by the wise men who spent two years (Matt. 2;1-16) in following it to its meridian over Bethlehem at the time of the birth of Christ. Then in 814 A D. it was seen by Constantine. In 628 A D. by Mohammet, etc. I do not admire Constantine and his "Christianity" which he established in the 4th century, yet it is a fact that Constantine saw a star in the sky in 814 A D. that looked like a cross. The hieroglyphics which he interpreted as "in hoc signo vinces", meaning' "by this sign conquer" may have been a figment of his own imagination, but he saw the star for, that year was the second appearance of the star of Bethlehem. When the star was seen by Mohammet in 628 A D, it appeared to him like a crescent. If the star was seen by Constantine from the top or from the bottom and not from one of the four sides, then it would have looked like a cross because there was a fountain head in the center of Paradise with a river flowing out north and east and south and west dividing Paradise (as well as the earth at that time) into four quarters. "And a river went out of Eden to water the garden and from thence it was parted, and became into four heads. The name of the first is Pison: that is it which compasseth the whole land of Havilah, where there is gold; and the gold of that land is good: there is bdellium and the onyx stone. And the name of the second, river; is Gihon: the same is it that compasseth the whole land of Ethiopia. And the name of the third river is Hiddekel that is it which goeth toward the east of Assyria. And the fourth river is Euphrates." (Gen. 2:10-14).

After Paradise was thrown off from the earth, at least one of the rivers on the Earth (the Euphrates) retained its original name. Those four rivers, actually two rivers with four names, ran like belts clear around the earth crossing at the poles and thus forming "the four quarters of the earth."

The same fountain head is still in Paradise, "The New Jerusalem" (Rev. 22:1-2). Therefore, in the sky as a planet (star), if viewed from the earth, it would resemble a cross. There is one more thing to call to your attention about the city. "The New Jerusalem" is now pure gold, like unto clear, glass." (Rev. 21 : 18) . When I saw it from the earth in an instant of time at noon on a certain day, the city was banked in fire, had every kind of architecture, was of every color and was transparent. It was magnificent beauty that is beyond human description. I have not been in that city but I saw it once directly over Denver, Colorado.

This is the "mystery of the seven stars." (Rev. 1:20). The first appearance of the star that was of great importance marked the birth of Christ and the first epoch of the Church. (Rev. 2:1-7). Each appearance thereafter marked the end of one epoch of the church and the beginning of a new epoch.

The Star of Bethlehem was to appear every 314 years to the earth for seven times. The seventh and last appearance was in 1884 A D. which means that we are now in the last epoch of the church (Rev. 3:14-22) which is "lukewarm", organized religion, which Yahveh has cast off and we are now in "the beginning of the (new) creation of Yahveh." (Rev. 3:14). Having majored in the study of Church history for five years (1920-1925) and

OUTER SPACE PEOPLE AND INNER EARTH PEOPLE

making the highest average grades in history ever made by a theological student, I have continued to study church history on my own. Under seven 314-year epochs (Rev. 2:1-29, Rev. 3: 1-22), history proves these epochs perfectly and beyond all question of doubt.

Paradise, the New Jerusalem, the Star of Bethlehem, the continent of Eden, is the place on which Yahshua the Messiah and His Church, the true members of His Body, will reign in glory over this earth for one thousand years. It will be the principal sky city, the controlling satellite, the Capitol from which the whole world will be ruled. During that thousand years, which is now beginning, or will begin before the end of this century, men on earth will build many cities in the sky. There are already other cities and areas in the sky which in ancient times were also thrown off from the earth and those that Yahshua the Messiah has prepared for us.

After the reign of Yahshua the Messiah and his Church for a thousand years, reigning from "the New Jerusalem" in the sky, that is, of course, after the restoration of Israel and of all the nations on the earth, then this will happen: "Seven thunders uttered their voices. And when the seven thunders had uttered their voices, I was about to write: and I heard a voice from heaven saying unto me, Seal up those things which the seven thunders uttered, and write them not And the angel which I saw stand upon The sea and upon the earth lifted up his hand to heaven, and sware by him that liveth for ever and ever, who created heaven, and the things that are therein, and the earth, and the things that therein are, and the sea, and the things which are therein, that there should be time no longer." (Rev. 10:3-6). The Apostle John was not allowed to tell at that time the meaning of the Voice of the seven thunders, BUT I CAN TELL IT NOW. At the end of the thousand years of restoration and righteousness, then that satellite or planet on which is "the New Jerusalem" will circle the earth seven times at a speed faster than light.. Seven times in less than a second (of our time). The concussion will be so strong that the mountains will be leveled down, the valleys exalted, the oceans will dry up, the earth will become smooth and upright at the poles and then that "Holy City" will descend upon the earth, and thus Paradise, which the earth lost, will be restored. Read again:

Rev. 21: 1-27, Rev. 22: 1-21 and compare with Gen. 2:8-15 and you will understand this perfectly.

The energy of the sun and moon will then be as great on the earth as it now is in outer-space. (Isa. 30: 26). Sin, disease and death will be abolished forever. That will be the end of the time element. Everything in time and for which time was created will have been fulfilled and we will be in eternity. Our Bible and all prophecy and written revelations only takes us up to this complete restoration of the heavens and the earth. It is beyond the mind of man to comprehend what eternity will be like. We are told that it is greater than we can think or imagine.

It will not be a Russian satellite or an American satellite that will rule the earth from outer space, but it will be "The New Jerusalem." However, as I have said before, the nations on this earth will most surely build many cities in the sky. It is very interesting to read in the Bible about the great storehouses of ice and other things that are piled up in outer-space to be used on the earth in due time. There are more than 2000 small plan-

OUTER SPACE PEOPLE AND INNER EARTH PEOPLE

etoids or asteroids in our own solar system that are known and named which will probably be used for foundation for building cities in the sky. Undoubtedly communication and travel between the Earth, Mars, Venus and all of the planets in this solar system will become common. This entire solar universe has to be restored simultaneously—that is, during the same period of time. "Having made known unto us the mystery of his will, according to his good pleasure which He hath purposed in himself: that in the dispensation of the fullness of time he might gather together in one all things in Christ both which are in heaven, and which are on earth; even in him in whom also we have obtained an inheritance, being predestinated according to the purpose of him who worketh all things after the counsel of his own will that we should be to the praise of his glory, who first trusted in Christ." (Eph. 1:9-12).

Recently I received information about groups of people in different parts of the world who say that they have seen cities in the sky. That's nothing new. Some of the sky cities have been seen at intervals for the last 6000 years. It is not flying saucers that will get attention from here on, but it will be the sky cities. The cities in the sky will be seen more and more and will become clearly visible to groups of people. This is not new to me or to anyone else who has experienced astral projection. We should prepare now to preach the gospel to the people that live in the many dwelling places in outer-space and those that live in the inner earth, (Rev. 5:3,13, 9: 1-16), for it is our job to convert them. (I Peter 3:18-21). "And to make all men see what is the fellowship of the mystery, which from the beginning of the world hath been hid in God, who created all things by Jesus Christ: to the intent that now unto the principalities and powers in heavenly places might be known by the church the manifold wisdom of God, according to the eternal purpose which he purposed in Christ Jesus our Lord." (Eph. 3:9-11 R V.)

"That at the name of Yahshua every knee should bow, in heaven, and on earth, and in the earth; and that every tongue should confess that Yahshua the Messiah is Yahveh-Savior, to the glory of Yahveh the Father." (Phil. 2:10-11, W L B.)

We should memorize and sing this universal song which eventually will be sung by everybody in outer-space and on the earth and in the inner earth. These are great days in which we are no longer just a human family on the earth. The universe is unfolding before us, our neighbors are those in outer-space and the inner earth as well as those on the earth. "And every creature which is in heaven, and on the earth, and under the earth, and such as are in the sea, and all that are in them, heard I saying, Blessing, and honor, and glory, and power, be unto him that sitteth upon the throne, and unto the Lamb for ever and ever." (Rev. 5: 13). "And I heard the voice of a great multitude, and as the voice of many waters, and as the voice of mighty thunderings; saying ALLELUIA!" (Rev. 19:1, 3, 4, 6).

Alleluia or HALLELUJAH means PRAISE YAHVEH! Let "Hallelujah" ring throughout the universe, for Yahveh Omnipotent reigneth. Let us be glad and rejoice, and give honor and praise to Yahveh.

"HALLE-LU-YAH!

OUTER SPACE PEOPLE AND INNER EARTH PEOPLE

Many wisdom seekers believe in both the physical and mystical significance of the inner earth and its possible connection to other worlds. Poke Runyon recently produced *Beyond Lemuria - The Shaver Mystery and the Secrets of Mount Shasta.*

OUTER SPACE PEOPLE AND INNER EARTH PEOPLE

Chapter IV

Invisible People

in the

Sea and Air

Many requests have come to my desk from people from every part of America requesting that I give a lecture on people under the sea.

May I say that it was at 2:00 A M. in the wee hours of the morning of February 5, 1958 that the Creator revealed this truth to me. I will give it as I remember it. I believe it is the first message on this subject ever given. Since it is so new, all new, it will require much thought and meditation on your part to understand it. Only a mind or minds capable of intelligent independent thinking and acting can obey or disobey the law of the Creator. Stop and think!

The stars in their courses, the sun, the moon and the earth follow the fixed law of the Creator. They neither obey nor disobey because they are not a mind. They simply function as they were created and move according to the fixed law that governs them.

All trees and plants are governed by fixed natural law. All animals of every species are controlled by the cosmic law of instinct. They neither obey nor disobey, but live by a fixed law. Stop and think!

Listen now! Only man and the weather are capable of obeying or disobeying the Creator's fixed law. Therefore there must be some kind of INVISIBLE INTELLIGENT ENTITIES or persons in the air which at times control the air. This has to be true, otherwise the wind and waves could not have obeyed our Savior. In a storm on the Sea of Galilee, Yahshua the Messiah arose and rebuked the wind and waves "and there was a great calm." (Matt. 8:26, Mark 4:39, Luke 8:24.) This astonished the disciples, and they said, what manner of man is this, that the wind and sea obey him?" Again, I say that it requires some kind of an intelligence to obey. Think.

You know that from the land and upward for about fvventy miles this earth is en-

OUTER SPACE PEOPLE AND INNER EARTH PEOPLE

cased in an envelope of air. Most of the time the air and the winds follow the fixed cosmic law "according to his circuits." (Eccl. 1:6.) Nearly any school boy can describe to you the circuit of the winds. But there is an exception to this law of the circuit of the winds. Nobody can accurately predict the weather, for at times it is chaotic. There are tidal waves, hurricanes, cyclones, blizzards, tornadoes, drenching rains and floods. The element of air or whatever it is in the air is often disobedient to the Creator's fixed law.

The cause of this, according to the Bible, is that there are INVISIBLE INTELLIGENT ENTITIES IN THE AIR. The first group of such entities that we shall consider is Satan and his host of demons. I have often said before and I repeat again that Satan and the demons are the disembodied spirits of a race of people that lived on earth millions of years ago, long before this present earth was created or brought from chaos to cosmos as recorded in Genesis. Satan and the demons are older, in my opinion, than the people who lived on Atlantis and Lemuria. However, Satan and the demons are of the earth and are earthbound spirits. They once lived in the long ago in bodies of flesh and blood on the earth.

"Yahveh said to Satan, Whence comest thou? Then Satan answered Yahveh and said, From going to and fro in the earth and from walking up and down in it." (Job. 1:7.) Satan and his demons literally fill the air. They are intensified in the air that is near to the land and sea. They are not capable of existing above the earth's atmosphere or air. The New Testament speaks of Satan as "the prince of the power of the air, that now worketh in the children of disobedience." (Eph. 2:2.) And that is why this age is called "the present evil world." (Gal. 1:4.) We are warned to "put on the whole armor of God, that ye may be able to stand against the wiles of the devil," and the Apostle goes on to tell us that "We wrestle not against flesh and blood, but against principalities, against powers, against the rulers of darkness of this world, against spiritual wickedness in high places." (Eph. 6:11-12.) There can be no doubt about the devil and devils working in the children of disobedience. Likewise the bad, chaotic storms are the result of Satan's power in the air.

But remember that Yahshua the Messiah commissioned his disciples to "cast out devils." (Matt, 10:8, Mark 16: 17.) And James says: "SUBMIT yourselves to God; RESIST the devil. and he will flee from you." (James 4:7.)

The difference between this "present evil world" and the coming righteous world, "The world to come" (Mark 10:30), in which there is "a new heaven and a new earth" (Rev.21 :1), is simply that Satan and all of his devils will be bound. They will be taken out of the air. The air or atmospheric heaven which is called "the firmament" (Gen. 1 :7) will be cleansed and purified. and free from Satan and all devils. This will be done by those of us "having the key of the bottomless pit" and "a great chain" in our hands (Rev. 20:1) by which we will and are now binding the devil. This chain is the chain of the truth—the chain of Bible evidence—the true light. It is by true preaching and teaching that Satan is bound. Satan, the devils and all wickedness, "the Lord shall consume with the spirit of his mouth and shall destroy with the brightness of his coming." (II Thes. 2: 8.) The preaching of the word by men filled with The Holy Spirit is the Light that dispels darkness and destroys the devil.

When the air is cleansed and Satan is bound then Yahshua the Messiah who is "the

OUTER SPACE PEOPLE AND INNER EARTH PEOPLE

King Eternal, Immortal, Invisible," (I Tim. 1:17), together with the holy angels and the spirits of just men made perfect will fully occupy and control the air. Then, of the literal people on the earth it is written, "Thine ears shall hear a word behind thee, saying, This is the way, walk ye in it." (Isa. 30:21.) Yes. "When ye turn to the right and when ye turn to the left" wherever you are or whichever way you turn, the voice of Christ, the holy angels and the spirits of just men made perfect will direct you in the right way.

Though they will be invisible they will nevertheless be present.

Even now there are images of people that you do not see and voices that you do not hear which are being seen by the eyes of your subconscious mind and heard by the ears of your subconscious mind, and such pictures and messages are being recorded within you and will be brought out in due time and you will think they are original with you. But the time will come when the veil or "covering" cast will be lifted, then "shall not thy teachers be removed into a corner any more, but thine eyes shall see thy teachers." (Isa. 30:20). "The covering cast over all people, and the veil that is spread over all nations" will be lifted. That will be a wonderful day or age when "the firmament" that is the air changes rulers, and instead of Satan and the devils, Yahshua the Messiah and his angels and saints—that is, his elect, executive body, will reign supreme in the air. Then every thought (temptation) will be to love right and to do good.

Section II

May I say that all of the INVISIBLE PEOPLE IN THE AIR are not Satanic or serpentine, for since the resurrection of Yahshua the Messiah and 144,000 Israelites, they also have occupied the air, and we are compassed about, that is, surrounded, by this "great cloud of witnesses." (Heb. 12:1.) This group is called "Mount Sion," "The city of the living Elohim", "the heavenly Jerusalem." I will read it as it is in the Bible: "But ye are come unto Mount Sion, and unto the city of the living Elohim, the heavenly Jerusalem, and to an innumerable company of angels, to the general assembly and church of the firstborn, which are written in heaven, and to Yahveh the Judge of all, and to the Spirits of just men made perfect, and to Yahshua the Mediator of the New Convenant." (Heb. 12:22-24.)

Our word "spirit" comes to us from the Greek word "pneumo", which literally means "wind", but wind, which is air in motion, has not in the past conveyed the meaning of "spirit" to us. However, if we understand that it is invisible intelligent people, both of men and of angels, which set the air in motion and cause the wind, then we will have come nearer to understanding the common term "spirit". As an example: Yahveh told David that he would give him a sign when he should go into battle, "And let it be, when thou hearest the sound of a going up the tops of the mulberry trees, that then thou shalt bestir thyself: for then shall the Lord go out before thee, to smite the host of the Philistines." (II Sam. 5:24.) Yahveh was in that wind, and there were thousands of creatures that came to earth in the wind on the day of Pentecost: "And when the day of Pentecost was fully come, there we all with one accord in one place. And suddenly there came a sound from heaven as of a rushing mighty wind, and it filled all the house where they were sitting. And there appeared unto them cloven tongues like as of fire, and it sat upon each of them. And they were all filled with the Holy Ghost and began to speak with other

OUTER SPACE PEOPLE AND INNER EARTH PEOPLE

tongues, as the Spirit gave them utterance." (Acts 2:1-4)

For nearly two thousand years, that is, since the resurrection, from time to time those in the Executive Body of Christ who have been given eternal life and immortality, have passed out of death to be with Christ and his INVISIBLE HOSTS IN THE AIR. "These are they which follow the Lamb withersoever He goeth. These were redeemed from among men, being the firstfruits unto God and to the Lamb." (Rev. 14:4.)

Because the holy angels and the spirits of just men made perfect, and also Satan and his devils, occupy the air—that is, because both the good and the evil live in the air it becomes very necessary that we know how to discern the spirits. "Discerning of spirits" (1 Cor. 12:10) is a gift of the Holy Ghost.

If all the spirits in the air were evil, if they were all devils, there would be no reason for the gift of "discerning spirits." "Beloved, believe not every spirit but try the spirits whether they are of God: because many false prophets are gone out into the world. Hereby know ye the Spirit of God: Every spirit that confesseth that Jesus Christ is come in the flesh is of God: and every spirit that confesseth not that Jesus Christ is come in the flesh is not of God; and this is that spirit of antichrist whereof ye have heard that it should come; and even now already is it in the world." (1 John 4: 1-8.)

"The firmament" which is called "heaven"—that is, the air around this earth and which is the particular heaven that belongs to the earth, isn't any different from the earth. I mean by this that there are good people on earth who are filled with the Holy Spirit and there are bad people on earth who are filled with the evil spirit and devils. Likewise in the air there are the devils and Satan and also Christ and the holy angels and the spirits of just men made perfect.

Satan and his devils have never been in full and complete control of the air. If they had been they would have destroyed the world a long time ago. Michael, Gabriel and the holy angels have always been on duty, battling and restraining Satan and the devils in the air.

Yahveh Our Heavenly Father "maketh his angels spirits, and his ministers a flame of fire." (Heb. 1:7). "Are they not all ministering spirits sent forth to minister for them who shall be heirs of salvation."(Heb. 1 :14.)

The angels and hosts of heaven are on the job. If they were not Satan would destroy us. We have been given power over the devil and devils, and we should exercise that power. Let us look at a case in the Bible in which the king of Syria attempted to destroy Elisha: "And he said, Go and spy where he is, that I may send and fetch him. And it was told him, saying, Behold, he is in Dothan. Therefore sent he thither horses and chariots, and a great host; and they came by night, and compassed the city about. And when the servant of the man of God was risen early, and gone forth, behold, a host compassed the city both with horses and chariots. And his servant said unto him, Alas, my master, how shall we do?, And he answered, Fear not: for they that be with us are more than they that be with them. And Elisha prayed, and said, Lord, I pray thee, open his eyes, that he may see. And the Lord opened the eyes of the young man; and he saw; and,

OUTER SPACE PEOPLE AND INNER EARTH PEOPLE

behold, the mountain was full of horses and chariots of fire round about Elisha. And when they came down to him, Elisha prayed unto the Lord, and said, Smite this people, I pray thee, with blindness. And he smote them with blindness according to the word of Elisha. And Elisha said unto them, This is not the way, neither is this the city; follow me, and I will bring you to the man whom ye seek. But he led them to Samaria. And it came to pass, when they were come into Samaria, that Elisha said, Lord, open the eyes of these men, that they may see. And the Lord opened their eyes, and they saw; and, behold, they were in the midst of Samaria." (II Kings 6:13-20.)

By recognizing the INVISIBLE PEOPLE that were present to help him, Elisha was able to capture the whole Syrian Army which had come out against him.

So far in this message I have definitely proven to anybody who believes the Bible that there are INVISIBLE PEOPLE IN THE AIR both good and bad. Most of the time when the air is chaotic, most tidal waves, hurricanes, cyclones, blizzards, tornadoes and drenching rains and floods are caused by Satan and the devils in the air. But these things are the exceptions and not the rule of the weather. Even then Yahveh can reverse Satan's plans and turn the chaotic elements into good.

"Praise ye Yahveh. Praise ye Yahveh from the heavens; praise him in the heights. Praise ye him, all his angels: praise ye him, all hosts. Praise ye him, sun and moon; praise him, all ye stars of light. Praise him, ye heavens of heavens, and ye waters that be above the heavens. Let them praise the name of Yahveh, for he commanded, and they were created. He hath also established them forever and ever; he hath made a decree which shall not pass. Praise Yahveh from the earth, ye dragons, and all deeps: fire and hail; snow and vapor; stormy wind fulfilling his word." (Psalm 148:1-8.)

The facts are that Yahveh has prepared his arsenal of snow and ice in the heavens and will use those elements to protect us and to destroy our invading enemies in the end of this age. It is true that because of Satan and the devils the immediate air or "heavens" are not clean in his sight (Job 15:15) and must be cleansed. And some of the earth's outer-space people that dwell on the satellites between the earth and the moon will be punished "and it shall come to pass in that day that the Lord shall punish the host of the high ones that are on high, (those that dwell above the earth) and the kings of the earth upon the earth." (Isa. 24:21) Yahveh "hath prepared for him the instruments of death." (Psalm 7:13.) He has his army in heaven "and the armies which were in heaven followed him Yahshua the Messiah.) (Rev. 19:14.)

This is future and is what Yahveh will do to our enemies. "And I will rain upon him, and upon his bands, and upon the many people that are with him, an overflowing rain, and great hailstones, fire and brimstone. Thus will I magnify myself, and sanctify myself; and I will be known in the eyes of many nations, and they shall know that I am Yahveh." (Ezek. 38:22-23).

You remember that Yahveh used darkness, hail and the elements against Egypt. Likewise, and in the same way, He will destroy the sinners and ungodly nations at the end of this age. He says. "I will heap mischiefs upon them, I will spend mine arrows upon them." (Deut. 32:28.) For "Yahveh hath prepared for him the instruments of death; he

OUTER SPACE PEOPLE AND INNER EARTH PEOPLE

hath ordered his arrows against the persecutors." "(Ps. 7:13.)

You may rest assured that Yahveh has his munitions prepared in the heavens and his armies in heaven are ready to move at his command against the rulers of darkness of this world, to end these evil world systems and to usher in the new heavens and new earth wherein righteousness will dwell forever.

Section III

You have waited quite a while for me to come to the question about the people under the sea, but it was necessary that I first establish the fact that there are invisible people in the air. Their nature is spirit and their element of survival is air. They do not need nor depend upon land or sea for their existence.

You and I, in this physical body, depend upon land, sea and air. We are, so to speak, land, water and air. But all religions and most of the people in the world believe that the mind exists after physical death and that there is an existence not dependent upon matter. Be that as it may. Nevertheless, if spirits exist in the air, and the Bible teaches that they do, it is therefore just as consistent and logical to believe that there are "aquatherians" and that is my own coined word, and by it I mean that there are INVISIBLE WATER PEOPLE whose existence is in the sea. Edgar Ailen Poe spoke of "the demons down under the sea." The Bible speaks of "such as are in the sea" (Rev. 5:18) and describes one of the seven orders of people that are to share in the resurrection as "FISHES".(1 Cor. 15:39), This word, of course, is used as an analogy or metaphor and is "parablemic" of people.

There are many fables about the sea and mental hallucinations and optical illusions of the "flying dutchman" and various kinds of phantom ships, numerous mermaids, sea monsters and so on "ad infinitum". But there must be at least a small grain of truth back of these stories which continue forever. The stories of ghosts nearly all originate in lowlands where there is heavy fog and dense mist. I would conclude that the INVISIBLE WATER PEOPLE entities in the sea are the spirits that can most easily materialize in the form of mist or vapor. This need not be taken as a fact but it is something to think about. In the future judgment in the consummation of this age it is written, "The sea gave up the dead which were in it." (Rev. 20: 18.)

If intelligent entities can exist in aerial bodies in the air, others can also exist in "Hydro" bodies in the sea. Think! There is no mind or intelligence in land, sea or air. All the intelligence must of necessity be in the mind of the intelligent entities on the land and in the sea and in the air. When the raging sea obeys a command of Yahveh, when the waves subside in obedience to the savior's voice, it must be because there are intelligent entities in the sea and in the waves. Only mind that is capable of thinking and acting can obey or disobey a command of Yahveh.

Everything in all the universe in the mineral, vegetable and animal kingdoms follows in a set law. Back of chaos and all disobedience and disturbed elements there must be a mind. If there were no intelligence at work in the sea, the sea could not rage nor the storms roar.

OUTER SPACE PEOPLE AND INNER EARTH PEOPLE

In Revelation the 13th chapter we read, "And I stood upon the sand of the sea, and saw a beast rise up out of the sea." (Rev. 13.1). This beast is described as having "seven heads" that is, seven forms of intelligence, and "ten horns" that is, ten kinds of power. This beast is described at length as one of the three forces of evil in the present evil world. Of the other two one is of the air and the other is of the earth. So definitely the trinity of evil forces comes from the land, sea and air.

The most difficult of all parables to understand are those that relate to the creatures in the sea. I suppose it is because we are not sufficiently prepared in our thinking to understand them. We have given very little thought to the sea, much less to any intelligent entities that might exist in the sea.

LEVIATHAN is the Sea Monster and the Bible teaching about him may not be interesting to you. But YOU requested teaching on this subject and to understand it you must study some things that are dull and technical instead of just reading that which is interesting and entertaining.

I think that the reason why some of us have so much Bible knowledge is that we read and reread, and search and research things that are dry and technical. It is hard labor to study and search out the truth. "For Yahveh is my King of old, working salvation in the midst of the earth. Thou didst divide the sea by thy strength: thou brakest the heads of the dragons in the waters. Thou brakest the heads of Leviathan in pieces, and gavest him to be meat to the people inhabiting the wilderness. Thou didst cleave the foundation and the flood: thou driedest up mighty rivers." (Ps. 74: 12-15)

"Oh Yahveh, how manifold are thy works! In wisdom hast thou made them, all the earth is full of thy riches. So is this great and wide sea, wherein are things creeping innumerable both small and great beasts. There go the ships: there is that Leviathan, whom thou hast made to play therein. These wait all upon thee; that thou mayest give them their meat in due season. That thou givest them they gather: thou openest thine hand, they are filled with good. Thou hidest thy face, they are trouble: thou takest away their breath, they die, and return to their dust. Thou sendest forth thy spirit, they are created: and thou renewest the face of the earth. The glory of Yahveh shall endure for ever: Yahveh shall rejoice in his works."

"In that day Yahveh with his sore and great and strong sword shall punish leviathan the piercing serpent even leviathan that crooked serpent; and he shall slay the dragon that is in the sea." (Isa. 27:1)

With these three references from Psalm 7, Psalm 104, and Isaiah 27, we are justified in reading all that Job says about LEVIATHAN, for by the mouth of two or three witnesses the truth shall be established. I say again that this is not so interesting, simply because we are not sufficiently prepared to understand it. But it contains a lesson yet to be understood about the intelligence in the sea.

"CANST thou draw out leviathan with a hook? or his tongue with a cord which thou lettest down? Canst thou put a hook into his nose? or bore his jaw through with a thorn? Will he make many supplications unto thee? will he speak soft words unto thee? Will he

OUTER SPACE PEOPLE AND INNER EARTH PEOPLE

make a covenant with thee? wilt thou take him for a servant forever? Wilt thou play with him as with a bird? or wilt thou bind him for thy maidens? Shall the companions make a banquet of him? shall they part him among the merchants?

"Canst thou fill his skin with barbed irons? or his head with fish spears? Lay thine hand upon him, remember the battle, do no more. Behold, the hope of him is in vain: shall not one be cast down even at the sight of him? None is so fierce that dare stir him up: who then is able to stand before me? Who hath prevented me, that I should repay him? whatsoever is under the whole heaven is mine. I will not conceal his parts, nor his power, nor his comely proportion. Who can discover the face of his garment? or who can come to him with his double bridle?

"Who can open the doors of his face? his teeth are terrible round about. His scales are his pride, shut up together as with a close seal; One is so near to another, that no air can come between them.

"They are joined one to another, if they stick together, that they cannot be sundered; By his sneezings a light doth shine, and his eyes are like the eyelids of the morning. Out of his mouth go burning lamps, and sparks of fire leap out. Out of his nostrils goeth smoke, as out of a seething pot or cauldron. His breath kindleth coals, and a flame goeth out of his mouth. In his neck remaineth strength, and sorrow is turned into joy before him. The flakes of his flesh are joined together: they are firm in themselves; they cannot be moved. His heart is as firm as stone; yea, as hard as a piece of the nether millstone.

"When he raiseth up himself, the mighty are afraid: by reason of breakings they purify themselves. The sword of him that layeth at him cannot hold: the spear, the dart nor the habergeon. He esteemeth iron as straw, and brass as rotten wood. The arrow cannot make him flee: sling stones are turned with him into stubble. Darts are counted as stubble: he laugheth at the shaking of a spear. Sharp stones are under him: he spreadeth sharp pointed things upon the mire. He maketh the deep to boil like a pot: he maketh the sea like a pot of ointment: He maketh a path to shine after him, one would think the deep to be hoary. Upon earth there is not his like, who is made without fear. He beholdeth all high things: he is a king over all the children of pride." (Job. 41:1-34.)

From this we would infer that LEVIATHAN in the sea is more powerful and more intelligent than any of the evil forces that originate on the land. Actually he is the king "over all the children of pride."

After Satan and the devils and all evil forces conquered and destroyed from the land and air, there may remain the most difficult battle of all—that is, to destroy LEVIATHAN and his evil forces in the sea. However, of the seven last plagues or bowls of wrath, two are launched against the sea, rivers and fountains of water.(Rev. 16:3-4.) So Leviathan the piercing, crooked serpent, the dragon that is in the sea will be destroyed.

The angel announcing the end of the age stands with one foot on the sea and the other foot on the land (Rev. 10:2-6) and the hurting of the earth and the sea is given equal space in Revelation 2: 1-3. Therefore, the indication is that there are INVISIBLE PEOPLE

OUTER SPACE PEOPLE AND INNER EARTH PEOPLE

in the sea the same as there are in the air, and that their judgment and punishment is just as important as that of the people on the land of the earth. The sea has to be cleared and purified along with the land and the air.

Actually those intelligent entities in the sea are older than those of us on the land. They existed before man was created on the land. Some of the marks or relics of the sea monsters exist in the human body, such as the spec in the corner of the eye and the tonsils in the throat, which, we are told, are the relics of a third eyelid and of gills that belonged originally to the life in the sea. There has been a changing over at times from sea to land and from land to sea. This is noticeable particularly in whales and other mammals that have left the land to live in the sea. The Apocrypha says, "For earthly things were turned into watery, and the things that before swam in the water, now went upon the ground." (Wisdom of Solomon 19:19).

"O the mysteries, the deep mysteries of the Creator are marvelous. It is the glory of Yahveh to conceal a thing: but the honor of kings is to search out a matter." (Prov. 25:2.)

In my ministry I have gone over from the very simple surface things which are preached by most preachers, to the high and deep mysteries. This has not been of my own choosing. The Creator has led me in this way. It most surely is not well received, neither does it pay. I am most unpopular with those who hold to mass opinions, but I have to give that which the Creator reveals to me. Only a few people—one of a town and two of a city, as it were—are sufficient unto these thinqs.

I will now quote from the book of Enoch: "That day has been prepared for the elect as a day of covenant; and for sinners as a day of inquisition. In that day shall be distributed for food two tigers; a female tiger, whose name is Leviathan, dwelling in the depths of the sea, above the springs of waters, and a male, whose name is Behemoth; which possesses, moving on his breast, the invisible wilderness. His name was Dendayen in the east of the garden where the elect and the righteous will dwell." (Enoch 59:6-9)

These creatures, Leviathan and Behemoth, are older than the Adamic creation in the second chapter of Genesis, older than the creation or cosmic order in the first chapter of Genesis; Actually I believe them to be the male and female chief devils of an earlier creation. At any rate Leviathan, the female, is confined to the sea while Behemoth, the male, dwells on the land. This male and female are the leaders of the invisible serpentine and Luciferian spirits on the land and in the sea, while Satan or Lucifer is in charge of the evil disembodied spirits in the air. Therefore we understand what is meant by the principalities, powers and spiritual wickedness. This is a trinity of Red Dragon, beast out of the sea and beast out of the earth so vividly described in Revelation the 12th and 13th chapters. The mystery (secret) of iniquity, as well as the mystery of evil, requires deep and searching study and much prayer and the guidance of the Holy Spirit to be understood.

I believe that I have given about as much as is necessary on this subject at this time. However, by dreams and visions and astral projection I know much more about the people in the sea than I have revealed here. The time has not yet come when these expe-

OUTER SPACE PEOPLE AND INNER EARTH PEOPLE

riences can be put down on paper with pen and ink and be published. Only to those in the inner circle can we talk freely. "But we speak the wisdom of Yahveh in a mystery, even the hidden wisdom, which Yahveh ordained before the world unto our glory; which none of the princes of this world knew: for had they known it, they would not have crucified the Lord of glory. But as it is written, Eye hath not seen, nor ear heard, neither have entered into the heart of man, the things which Yahveh hath prepared for them that love him. But Yahveh hath revealed them unto us by his Spirit: for the Spirit searcheth all things, yea, the deep things of Yahveh. For what man knoweth the things of a man, save the spirit of man which is in him? even so the things of Yahveh knoweth no man, but the Spirit of Yahveh. Now we have received, not the spirit of the world, but the Spirit which is of Yahveh; that we might know the things that are freely given to us of Yahveh. Which things also we speak, not in the words which man's wisdom teacheth, but which the Holy Ghost teacheth; comparing spiritual things with spiritual. But the natural man receiveth not the things of the Spirit of Yahveh: for they are foolishness unto him: neither can he know them, because they are spiritually discerned. But he that is spiritual judgeth all things, yet he himself is judgeth of no man. For who hath known the mind of Yahveh, that he may instruct him? But we have the mind of Yahshua". (I Cor. 2:7-16.)

"Happy is he that hath the Elohim of Jacob for his help, whose hope is in Yahveh his Elohim. Which made heaven, and earth, the sea, and all that therein is: which keepeth truth for ever.". (Ps. 146:5-6.)

YAHVEH BLESS YOU ALL. AMEN.

OUTER SPACE PEOPLE AND INNER EARTH PEOPLE

Chapter V

Treasure Mountain

" I will lift up mine eyes unto the hills, from whence cometh my help."(Psalm 121:1)

There are lost mountains in which there are caves which hold invaluable hidden treasures. This message will become more fascinating as it progresses, for it is another of the new sermons that are preached only by William L. Blessing.

Some time ago I was in Northern California and I went up to the base of Mount Shasta. There are many strange stories of mysteries in connection with this Mountain. Some say that there are cave dwellers near the top of the mountain and that delegations of from twenty to thirty people from Nepal in Tibet and from the Ardes in South America frequently come there, go up Mount Shasta and disappear for months at a time. Others say that if you try to drive a car up the mountain road, that when you reach a certain place the engine stops and you have to let the car roll back several feet before the engine will start and then turn around and go back down the mountain. They say that if you get out of the stalled car and attempt to walk on up the mountain, that you proceed only a few yards when for some unknown reason something within you just forces you to stop and turn around. There is some compelling force that stops cars and people at a certain place and says, as it were, "You can come no farther." They say that sometimes the mysterious dwellers on Mount Shasta come down into the California towns and buy supplies, but that they will not reveal any secrets as to who they are.

All of this may be merely figments of the imagination, but I am a born believer and cannot deny such things until they are investigrated and proven false. I believe everything I hear—I just can't help it.

Whatever a person tells me I believe. Often, in fact over and over again, I have been hurt and disappointed by being a believer, but I just can't help it. As I say, I am a born believer.

We know that after the flood Noah's Ark rested on Mt. Ararat. (Gen, 8:4). That ark was as large as the largest passenger ships of today. It was sealed with pitch (Bitumen)

OUTER SPACE PEOPLE AND INNER EARTH PEOPLE

within and without. It withstood the flood. So great was that flood that the geographical surface of the earth was changed and all of the large cities were buried so deep that they have never been found. Now a ship (the ark) that could withstand the elements on a rampage which covered and shook the whole earth most surely has since withstood the milder elements. The Ark may be found someday in a perfect state of preservation, but nobody knows where Mount Ararat is. It is one of the lost mountains.

You remember from reading the Bible that Yahveh came down on the top of Mount Sinai and with his index finger wrote the Ten Commandments upon two pillars of stone and gave them to Moses. Those pillars of stone contain the autograph of Yahveh—the only writing ever written by Him—the only personal writing by Yahveh or angel in the history of the world (except the handwriting on the wall in the palace of Belshazzar in Babylon.) The Ten Commandments were placed in the Ark of the Covenant which was four feet long, two and one-half feet broad and two and one-half feet deep. Here is a description of it: "And they shall make an ark of shittim wood: two cubits and a half shall be the length thereof, and a cubit and a half the breadth thereof, and a cubit and a half the height thereof. And thou shalt overlay it with pure gold, within, and without shalt thou overlay it, and shalt make upon it a crown of gold round about. And thou shalt cast four rings of gold for it, and put them in the four corners thereof; and two rings shall be in the end side of it, and two rings in the other side of it. And thou shalt make staves of shittim wood, and overlay them with gold. And thou shalt put the staves into the rings by the sides of the ark, that the ark may be borne with them. The staves shall be in the rings of the ark; they shall not be taken from it. And thou shalt put into the ark the testimony which I shall give thee. And thou shalt make a mercy seat of pure gold: two cubits and a half shall be the length thereof, and a cubit and a half the breadth thereof. And thou shalt make two cherubim of gold; of beaten work shalt thou make them, in the two ends of the mercy seat. And make one cherub on the one end, and the other cherub on the other end: even of the mercy seat shall ye make the cherubim on the two ends thereof. And the cherubim shall stretch forth their wings on high, covering the mercy seat with their wings, and their faces shall look one to another; toward the mercy seat shall the faces of the cherubim be. And thou shalt put the mercy seat above the ark; and in the ark thou shalt put the testimony that I shall give thee. And there I will meet with thee, and I will commune with thee from above the mercy seat, from between the two cherubims which are upon the ark of the testimony, of all things which I will give thee in commandment unto the children of Israel." (Ex. 25: 10-22.)

The ark was by far the most precious possession of the children of Israel because it contained the two pillars of stone upon which Yahveh had written the basis of all law for civilized society. You remember that the ark was placed in the Inner Sanctuary, the Holy of Holies, the Sanctum Sanctorum of the Tabernacle in the wilderness and later in the temple at Jerusalem. The Chaldeans who destroyed and plundered the Temple never got that ark! Where is it today? We have the answer in the Apocrypha which quotes from a lost writing by the Prophet Jeremiah. "It was also contained in the same writing, that the prophet being warned of Yahveh, commanded the tabernacle and the ark to go with him, as he went forth into the mountain, where Moses climbed up, and saw the heritage of Yahveh. And when Jeremiah came thither, he found a hollow cave, wherein he laid the

OUTER SPACE PEOPLE AND INNER EARTH PEOPLE

tabernacle, and the ark, and the altar of incense, and so stopped the door. And some of those that followed him came to mark the way, but they could not find it. Which when Jeremiah perceived, he blamed them, saying, As for this place, it shall be unknown until the time that Yahveh gather his people again together, and received them unto mercy." (II Maccabees 2: 4-7.)

It was on Mount Sinai that Moses received the Ten Commandments, but it was on Mount Nebo that he climbed up to view the Promised Land. Therefore it was in a cave on Mount Nebo where Jeremiah hid the ark of the covenant and other furniture of the tabernacle. When that is found it will be the richest and most valuable find in the history of mankind.

We know from the Bible that Jeremiah escaped the destruction of Jerusalem and that he did not go into the Babylonian captivity but escaped into Egypt, taking with him the Princesses, that is, King Zedekiah's daughters, the royal seed. Yahveh has always preserved the Seed Royal. The Ark of the Covenant is the greatest artifact that is yet to be discovered.

There are many other interesting things about Jeremiah. He purchased and secured the title to Palestine, though he knew it would be nearly 3,000 years before he came in possession of that land. Yet he saw beyond chaos and destruction to Cosmos and Restoration. Here is the Bible story. "And Jeremiah said, The word of Yahveh came unto me, saying Behold Hanameel the son of Shallum thine uncle shall come unto thee, saying buy thee my field that is in Anathoth: for the right of redemption is thine to buy it. So Hanameel mine uncle's son came to me in the court of the prison according to the word of Yahveh, and said unto me, Buy my field, I pray thee, that is in Anathoth, which is in the country of Benjamin: for the right of inheritance is thine, and the redemption is thine; buy it for thyself. Then I knew that this was the word of Yahveh. And I bought the field of Hanameel my uncle's son, that was in Anathoth, and weighed him the money, even seventeen shekels of silver. And subscribed the evidence, and sealed it, and took witnesses, and weighed him the money in the balances. So I took the evidence of the purchase, both that which was sealed according to the law and custom, and that which was open: And I gave the evidence of the purchase unto Baruch the son of Neriah, the son of Maaseiah, in the sight of Hanameel mine uncle's son, and in the presence of the witnesses that subscribed the book of the purchase, before all the Jews that sat in the court of the prison.

"And I charged Baruch before them, saying, Thus saith the Lord of hosts, the God of Israel; Take these evidences, this evidence of the purchase, both which is sealed, and this evidence which is open; and put them in an earthen vessel, that they may continue many days. For thus saith the Lord of hosts, the God of Israel; Houses and fields and vineyards shall be possessed again in this land."

"Now when I had delivered the evidence of the purchase unto Baruch the son of Neriah, I prayed unto Yahveh," (Jer. 82:6-16.)

So marvelous are the 82nd and 83rd chapters of Jeremiah on the restoration of the Kingdom unto Israel that I would love to read them all to you and comment on every

OUTER SPACE PEOPLE AND INNER EARTH PEOPLE

verse, but time will not permit me to do that in this message, so turn to those chapters in your Bible and read them.

Some say that Jeremiah's title and seal were found in a stone jar and that it is now on display in the British museum. Anyway, if that title and seal has not been found, it will be in the very near future, for it is the authentic Yahveh-given title of ownership to the land of Palestine.

Jesus said, "I tell you that if these should hold their peace, the stones would immediately cry out." (Luke 19:40). Atheistic materialism, agnosticism and infidelity rise, deny Yahveh and the Bible and for a while flourish, but just when they think they have won, then comes a great discovery, evidence is found in mountains, stones and artifacts and manuscripts are found in caves which destroy all atheism and prove again that Yahveh is real and that His word is true. Thus the atheistic material philosophy of this present time will be destroyed.

Just recently an Arab goat herder threw a stone at a goat that had run into a cave just north of the Dead Sea. He heard the stone strike on something that rang like a bell. He went into the cave to investigate and there he found several large stone jars and in the jars were manuscripts containing all of the books of the Old Testament except the book of Esther. They had been hidden there in that cave for nearly 2000 years. They are now known as The Dead Sea Scrolls. The Book of Isaiah has been deciphered and translated and it is almost identical with Isaiah as we have it in our English Bible. It will require several years, perhaps twenty, to decipher and translate all of those Dead Sea Scrolls.

Now I come to the most interesting and mysterious part of this message. It is necessary that I read the scriptures on this subject in Matthew, Mark and Luke. Every word is very important. As I read, you think! And then I will comment on what we have read. "Then was Yahshua led of the Spirit into the wilderness to be tempted of the devil . . . The devil taketh him up into an exceeding high mountain, and showeth him all the kingdoms of the world, and the glory of them: and saith unto him, All these things will I give thee, if thou will fall down and worship me. Then saith Yahshua unto him, Get thee hence Satan: for it is written, Thou shalt worship Yahveh thy Elohim, and him only shalt thou serve."

Then the devil leaveth him, and, behold, angels came and ministered unto him." (Matt.4:1,8-11.) "And it came to pass in those days, that Yahshua came from Nazareth of Galilee, and was baptized of John in Jordan. And straight-way coming up out of the water, he saw the heavens opened, and the Spirit like a dove descending upon him. And there came a voice from heaven, saying, Thou art my beloved Son, in whom I am well pleased. And immediately the Spirit driveth him into the wilderness. And he was there in the wilderness forty days tempted of Satan; and was with the wild beasts; and the angels ministered unto him." (Mark 1:9-13.)

"And Yahshua being full of the Holy Ghost returned from Jordan, and was led by the Spirit into the wilderness, being forty days tempted of the devil. And in those days he did eat nothing.

"And the devil, taking him up into a high mountain, showed unto him all the king-

OUTER SPACE PEOPLE AND INNER EARTH PEOPLE

doms of the world in a moment of time. And the devil said unto him, "All this power will I give thee, and the glory of them; for that is delivered unto me; and to whosoever I will, I give it. If thou therefore wilt worship me, all shall be thine. And Yahshua answered and said unto him, Get thee behind me Satan: for it is written, Thou shalt worship the Lord thy God and him only shalt thou serve." (Luke 4:5-8.)

Matthew says, "The devil taketh him up into an exceeding high mountain. Luke says the devil "showed unto him all the kingdoms of the world in a moment of time ." And Matthew adds that he showed him not only the kingdoms but also "the glory of them."

Now here is the question: Where is that mountain? Where is there a mountain from which a person can see all the kingdoms of the world in a moment of time and all the glory of them and everything that is in them?

From what we know of science in the present time, there is only one place from which a man could view all the kingdoms of the world and photograph everything that is on the earth and that place is the mountains of the moon. The nations of the world are in a mad race to reach the moon. We are also told that from the Sputniks and man-made moons all the earth can be viewed and photographed. The Spirit led Yahshua the Messiah into the wilderness. The devil took him up. Up where? Into an exceeding high mountain. That may not have been the moon, but if not, it had to be a satellite or asteroid or planetoid of great size that is circling the earth and which is between the earth and the moon for that is the only place from which all the kingdoms of the world could be viewed in a moment of time.

Furthermore, it must have been the abode of certain angels, that is, sons of Yahveh or messengers that dwell above the surface of the earth. It may be the mountain in which Yahveh meets with His Sons and Satan is permitted to come into those meetings: "Now there was a day when the sons of Yahveh came to present themselves before Yahveh-Elohim, and Satan came also amongst them. And Yahveh said unto Satan, "Whence comest thou?" Then Satan answered Yahveh, and ,said, "From going to and fro in the earth, and from walking up and down in it." (Job. 1:6-2.)

Satan has always tried to scale the heights. He has obsessed and possessed or been reincarnated in every leader of every great nation in the present evil world system. And, every one of those leaders has tried to reach outer-space and view the world. "Lucifer" is actually used as a synonym for the king of Babylon. This is clearly stated in the Bible:

"That thou shalt take up this proverb against the king of Babylon, and say, How hath the oppressor ceased; the golden city ceased! Yahveh hath broken the staff of the wicked, and the sceptre of the rulers. He who smote the people in wrath with a continual stroke, he that ruled the nations in anger, is persecuted, and none hindereth. The whole earth is at rest and is quiet: they break forth into singing.

Yea, the fir trees rejoice at thee, and the cedars of Lebanon, saying, Since thou art laid down, no feller is come up against us. Hell from beneath is moved for thee to meet thee at thy coming: it stirreth up the dead for thee, even all the chief ones of the earth; it

OUTER SPACE PEOPLE AND INNER EARTH PEOPLE

hath raised up from their thrones all the kings of the nations. And they shall speak and say unto thee, Art thou also become weak as we? art thou become like unto us? Thy pomp is brought down to the grave, and the noise of thy voice: the worm is spread under thee, and the worms cover thee.

"How art thou fallen from heaven, O Lucifer, son of the morning! how art thou cut down to the ground, which didst weaken the nations! For thou hast said in thine heart I will ascend into heaven, I will exalt my throne above the stars of God: I will sit also upon the mount of the congregation, in the sides of the north: I will ascend above the heights of the clouds: I will be like the Most High, yet thou shalt be brought down to hell, to the sides of the pit. They that see thee shall narrowly look upon thee, and consider thee, saying, Is this the man that made the earth to tremble, and did shake kingdoms; That made the world a wilderness, and destroyed the cities thereof; that opened not the house of his prisoners? All the kings of the nations, even all of them, lie in glory, every one in his own house. But thou art cast out of thy grave like an abominable branch, and as the raiment of those that are slain, thrust through with a sword, that go down to the stones of the pit; as a carcass trodden under feet. Thou shalt not be joined with them in burial, because thou hast destroyed thy land, and slain thy people, the seed of evildoers shall never been renowned." (Isa. 14:4-20.)

The devil, Lucifer, or Satan, always tells his leaders that if they will come up into the high mountain and worship him, he will show them all the kingdoms of the world, and give the world to them, and that from that high point in outer-space they can control the world. In that way the devil has tempted and deceived and lied to all the leaders in all the big governments that have existed in the present evil world. They have all wanted to control all the world. All of them; except Yahshua the Messiah.

Our Savior. He did not want the present evil world systems, therefore the devil's temptation did not work in his case. The Kingdom of Heaven is different and entirely apart from and has no connection with the present evil world systems. "Thy Kingdom come, thy will be done in Earth as it is in heaven."

Let us look at Satan's incarnation in the King of Tyre. Yes, the devil has been in all at the leaders of these great earthly kingdoms and he has led them one by one to eternal ruin. 1. Chaldea, 2. Assyria, 3. Medo-Persia, 4. Egypt, 5. Greece, 6. Rome, they all in turn dominated the world and then passed away.

"Moreover the word of Yahveh came unto me, saying, Son of man, take up a lamentation upon the king of Tyrus, and say unto him, Thus saith Yahveh Elohim; "Thou sealest up the sum, full of wisdom, and perfect in beauty. Thou hast been in Eden the garden of Nod; every precious stone was thy covering, the sardius, topaz, and the diamond, the beryl, the onyx, and the jasper, the sapphire, the emerald, and the carbuncle, and gold: the workmanship of thy tabrets and of thy pipes was prepared in thee in the day that thou wast created. Thou art the anointed cherub that covereth; and I have set thee so: thou wast upon the holy mountain of God; thou hast walked up and down in the midst of the stones of fire. Thou wast perfect in thy ways from the day that thou wast created, till iniquity was found in thee. By the multitude of thy merchandise they have filled the midst

OUTER SPACE PEOPLE AND INNER EARTH PEOPLE

of thee with violence, and thou hast sinned: therefore I will cast thee as profane out of the mountain of God and I will destroy thee, O covering cherub, from the midst of the stones of fire. Thine heart was lifted up because of thy beauty, thou hast corrupted thy wisdom by reason of thy brightness:

I will cast thee to the ground, I will lay thee before kings, that they may behold thee. Thou hast defiled thy sanctuaries by the multitude of thine iniquities, by the iniquity of thy traffic; therefore will I bring forth a fire from the midst of thee, it shall devour thee, and I will bring thee to ashes upon the earth in the sight of all them that behold thee. All they that know thee among the people shall be astonished at thee: thou shalt be a terror, and never shalt thou be any more. (Ezek. 28; 11-19.)

The seventh and last of the world kingdoms, "Gog and Magog" was to come in the end of this age. It is here now. It is Russian Communism, Roman Fascism and Jewish Zionism. This trinity of evil now controls the world, but it is doomed to pass away.

I do not believe that Satan has ever been or ever will be beyond the earth and the space that belongs to the earth, because Yahveh is in complete control of everything beyond the circle of the earth. It is he that sitteth upon the circle of the earth, and the inhabitants thereof are as grasshoppers that stretcheth out the heavens as a curtain, and spreadeth them out as a tent to dwell in: that bringeth the princes to nothing; he maketh the judges of the earth as vanity. Yea, they shall not be planted; yea, they shall not be sown, yea, their stock shall not take root in the earth and he shall also blow upon them and they shall wither, and the whirlwind shall take them away as stubble. To whom then will ye liken me, or shall I be equal? saith the Holy One. Lift up your eyes on high, and behold who hath created these things, that bringeth out their host by number: He calleth them all by names by the greatness of his might for that he is strong in power; not one faileth." (Isaiah 40:22-26.)

The circle of the earth is the eiliptic orbit of the moon, because the moon is the earth's outermost satellite. The moon is 250,000 miles from the earth. The diameter of the moon's orbit is 500,000 miles, the circumference is 1,500,000 miles. Every 28 days the moon circles the earth, traveling in a circle a distance of one million five hundred thousand miles—that is the circle of the earth. Everything within this circle belongs to the earth. Within this circle are many dwelling places, inhabited satellites occupied by "men above the earth," but they all belong to the orders of the earth.

The earth turns on its axis at the rate of 1000 miles per hour. The earth travels around the sun at the rate of 67,000 miles per hour. The sun and all of its family of planets (this solar system) is moving northward at the rate of 175 miles per second. Where are they going? When will they get there? The journey will be completed some day and this universe will be broken up and re-created and there wili be new heavens and a new earth.

I would like to say more about the people that live in the shell, that is, in the crust of the earth and in the mysterious mountains and caves, but let me now cite one scripture reference and you can go on and work it out for yourself. There are many references in the Bible to caves and the people who have dwelt in them—some good, and some bad.

OUTER SPACE PEOPLE AND INNER EARTH PEOPLE

"But now they that are younger than I have me in derision, whose fathers I would have disdained to have set with the dogs of my flock. Yea, whereto might the strength of their hands profit me, in whom old age was perished?. For want and famine they were solitary; fleeing into the wilderness in former time desolate and waste: Who cut up mallows by the bushes, and juniper roots for their meat. They were driven forth from among men, (they cried after them as after a thief,) To dwell in the cliffs of the valleys, in caves of the earth, and in the rocks. Among the bushes they brayed; under the nettles they were gathered together. They were children of fools, yea, children of base men: they were viler than the earth. And now am I their song, yea, I am their byword. They abhor me, they flee far from me and spare not to spit in my face." (Job 30 :1-10.)

Are these the inhabitants of Inner Earth?

OUTER SPACE PEOPLE AND INNER EARTH PEOPLE

Chapter VI

Our Three Bodies

This may sound very strange to you when I tell you that you have three bodies. I assume that I am talking to Christians only and not to the people who are only of the earth, earthy. Baptized and anointed ones—that is, Christians who are sealed with Yahveh's name in their minds and hearts have three bodies.

Your first body is in Heaven and is the body in which you lived before you came to earth. That body is still in heaven just as fresh and new and young as it ever was and is waiting for you to return and occupy it again. In your present body you have the mind of that heavenly body in heaven. It is the sub-conscious mind—the real you, "THAT I AM" that knows all things and that never grows old. That subconscious mind was as full grown, as old and as perfect the day you were born in the flesh into the world as it is now. That is the "I AM" that is the real you that is always young and perfect and that never grows old. But I must prove this by the Bible. Here it is!

"For we know that, if our earthly house of this tabernacle were dissolved, we have a building of God, a house not made with hands, eternal in the heavens. For in this we groan, earnestly desiring to be clothed upon with our house which is from heaven: if so be that being clothed we shall not be found naked. For we that are in this tabernacle do groan, being burdened: not for that we would be unclothed, but clothed upon, that mortality might be swallowed up of life. Now he that hath wrought us for the selfsame thing is God, who also hath given unto us the earnest of the Spirit. Therefore we are always confident, knowing that, whilst we are at home in the body, we are absent from the Lord: (For we walk by faith, not by sight:) We are confident I say, and willing rather to be absent from the body, and to be present with the Lord." (II Cor.5:1-8.)

This scripture proves beyond a shadow of doubt that we have a body in heaven, an eternal body. You may ask, Why did we leave that body and come to earth in the flesh? The answer is very clear: We did not do it willingly. We did not volunteer to leave that body and come here. "For the creature was made subject to vanity, not willingly, but by reason of him who hath subjected the same in hope." (Rom. 8:20.) And again another

OUTER SPACE PEOPLE AND INNER EARTH PEOPLE

scripture says, "We have this treasure in earthen vessels, that the excellency of the power may be of God, and not of us." (II Cor. 4:7). In this earthly mortal body we are being disciplined; we are being taught a great lesson, which is, that all the worship and the honor and the power and the glory belongs unto Yahveh Our Heavenly Father. We must make a full and complete surrender to his will and develop a perfect love for Him. Then our lesson will have been learned and our time in the flesh completed and we will return to our body which is in heaven. I say again, that this experience in the flesh, is a matter and time of discipline by which we are prepared to create a world of our own and to rule over it. If we make good here and now we will be made a ruler over one of the worlds in the great realm of Yahveh.

Actually, without fear of contradiction by any real scholar, I say that we are the sons of God, for the Bible bears me out in this: "And because ye are sons, God hath sent forth the Spirit of his Son into your hearts, crying, Abba, Father: Wherefore thou art no more a servant but a son; and if a son, then an heir of God through Christ." (Gal. 4:6-7.) The Spirit itself beareth witness with Our spirit, that we are the children of Cod; and if children then heirs; heirs of God, and joint-heirs with Christ if so be that we suffer with them, that we may be also glorified together." (Rom. 8: 16-17.)

We are joint-heirs with Christ which means that we share equally with him. Since we are the body of Christ, we must share in his suffering and death. We must take upon us the pain and suffering of others and bear their burdens if we are to be grlorified together into unity and Oneness with Christ. He suffered for us; we must suffer for them. By suffering and sacrifice only can the world be redeemed.

It is evident beyond a doubt that Jesus Christ existed in Heaven. That is, he pre-existed before he came to this earth. After he had finished his work on earth in the flesh he was anxious to return to the glory that he had had before, and in his great prayer the night before his crucifixion we hear him say to the Father, "I have glorified thee on the earth: I have finished the work which thou gavest me to do. And now O Father, glorify thou me with thine own self, with the glory which I had with thee before the world was. (John 17:4-5.)

All Christians accept without doubt or hesitation the fact of the pre-existence of Jesus Christ, but that is only half of the truth that they should accept. The other half, the last half is the fact that we preexisted. Listen very carefully to this portion of the prayer of Jesus Christ: "I have Manifested thy name unto the men which thou gavest me out of the world: thine they were, and thou gavest them me; and they have kept thy word. And now come I to thee; and these things I speak in the world, that they might have my joy fulfilled in themselves. I have given them thy word; and the world hath hated them, because they are not of the world, even as I am not of the world. I pray not that thou shouldest take them out of the world, but that thou shouldest keep them from the evil. They are not of the world, even as I am not of the world. Sanctify them through thy truth; thy word is truth. As thou hast sent me into the world, even so have I also sent them into the world. And for their sakes I sanctify myself, that they also might be sanctified through the truth. Neither pray I for these alone, but for them also which shall believe on me through their word; that they all may be one; as thou, Father, art in me, and I in thee, that they also may be

OUTER SPACE PEOPLE AND INNER EARTH PEOPLE

one in us: that the world may believe that thou hast sent me.

And the glory which thou gavest me I have given them; that they may be one, even as we are one: I in them, and thou in me, that they may be made perfect in one; and that the world may know that thou hast sent me, and hast loved them, as thou hast loved me. Father, I will that they also, whom thou hast given me, be with me where I am; that they may behold my glory, which thou hast given me: for thou lovest me before the foundation of the world. O righteous Father, the world hath not known thee: but I have known thee, and these have known that thou hast sent me. And I have declared unto them thy name, and will declare it; that the love wherewith thou hast loved me may be in them, and I in them." (John 17 ;6, 13-26.)

The plain truth of the Bible is that we pre-existed, and that we now have the same power and authority in the earth that Jesus Christ had while he was here in the flesh, and that eventually we will complete our work in the flesh and will then be glorified and return to the Father where we will enjoy all the glory that we had with him before the world was.

The difference between our existence in the flesh and that of Jesus Christ is this: We did not volunteer to come here. He did! We did not submit willingly to be made flesh and experience vanity and death. He did! The scriptures are very plain and beautiful on this point of the truth. "Thou madest him a little lower than the angels; thou crownedst him with glory and honor, and didst set him over the works of thy hands; thou has put all things in subjection under his feet. For in that he put all in subjection under him, he left nothing that is not put under him. But now we see not yet all things put under him. But we see Jesus, who was made a little lower than the angels for the suffering of death, crowned with glory and honor; that He by the grace of God should taste death for every man. For it became Him, for whom are all things, and by whom are all things, in bringing many sons unto glory, to make the captain of their salvation perfect through sufferings. For both He that sanctifieth and they who are sanctified are all of one: for which cause He is not ashamed to call them brethren, saying, I will declare thy name unto my brethren, in the midst of the church will I sing praise unto thee. And again, I will put my trust in him. And again, Behold I and the children which God hath given me.

Forasmuch then as the children are partakers of flesh and blood, He also himself likewise took part of the same; that through death He might destroy him that had the power of death, that is, the devil; and deliver them, who through fear of death were all their lifetime subject to bondage. For verily He took not on Him the nature of angels; but he took on him the seed of Abraham. Wherefore in all things it behooved him to be made like unto his brethren, that He might be merciful and faithful high priest in things pertaining to God; to make reconciliation for the sins of the people. For in that He himself hath suffered being tempted, he is able to succor them that are tempted." (Heb. 2:7-18.)

Notice that those who are the sons of God are "the seed of Abraham", the foreordained, predestinated and elected sons of God who are the heavenly executives in the headquarters body with Christ are all, every one, of the seed of Abraham, selected out of or from, the seed of Abraham.

OUTER SPACE PEOPLE AND INNER EARTH PEOPLE

"Now to Abraham and his seed were the promises made. He saith not, and to seeds, as of many; but as of one, and to thy seed, which is Christ. And if ye be Christ's, then are ye Abraham's seed, and heirs according to the promise." (Gal. 3: 16, 29.)

We need to understand this truth about our pre-existence. The scripture is very wonderful on this subject and we should stop and think and weigh every sentence. "Blessed be the God and Father of our Lord Jesus Christ, who hath blessed us with all spiritual blessings in heavenly places in Christ: according as he hath chosen us in him before the foundation of the world, that we should be holy and without blame before him in love: having predestinated us unto the adoption of children by Jesus Christ to himself, according to the good pleasure of his will to the praise of the glory of his grace, wherein he hath made us accepted in the beloved: in whom we have redemption through his blood, the forgiveness of sins, according to the riches of his grace; wherein he hath abounded toward us in all wisdom and prudence; having made known unto us the mystery of his will, according to his good pleasure which he hath purposed in himself: that in the dispensation of the fullness of times he might gather together in one all things in Christ, both which are in heaven and which are on earth; even in Him; in whom also we have obtained an inheritance, being predestinated according to the purpose of Him who worketh all things after the counsel of His own will: that we should be to the praise of His glory, who first trusted in Christ. In whom ye also trusted, after that ye heard the word of truth, the gospel of your salvation: in whom also, after that ye believed, ye were sealed with that Holy Spirit of promise. Which is the earnest of our inheritance until the redemption of the purchased possession, unto the praise of his glory." (Eph. 1:3-14.)

We are the purchased possession, purchased by Jesus Christ and are the heirs of all "spiritual blessings in heavenly places", and we have the seal and guarantee of this by the Spirit of God in our hearts.

But I want to give you more about our preexistence and prove to you that we were foreknown: "For I reckon that the sufferings of this present time are not worthy to be compared with the glory which shall be revealed in us. For the earnest expectation of the creature waiteth for the manifestation of the sons of God. For the creature was made subject to vanity, not willingly, but by reason of him who hath subjected the same in hope; because the creature itself also shall be delivered from the bondage of corruption into the glorious liberty of the children of God. For we know that the whole creation groaneth and travaileth in pain together until now. And not only they, but ourselves also, which have the firstfruits of the Spirit, even we ourselves groan within ourselves, waiting for the adoption, to wit, the redemption of our body. For we are saved by hope: but hope that is seen is not hope for what a man seeth, why doth he yet hope for? But if we hope for that we see not then do we with patience wait for it. Likewise the Spirit also helpeth our infirmities: for we know not what we should pray for as we ought: but the Spirit itself maketh intercession for us with groanings which cannot be uttered. And he that searcheth the hearts knoweth what is the mind of the Spirit because he maketh intercession for the saints according to the will of God. And we know that all things work together for good to them that love God, to them who are the called according to his purpose. For whom He did foreknow, he also did predestinate to be conformed to the image of his Son, that he

OUTER SPACE PEOPLE AND INNER EARTH PEOPLE

might be the firstborn among many brethren. Moreover, whom he did predestinate, them he also called: and whom he called, them he also justified: and whom he justified, them he also glorified. What shall we then say to these things? If God be for us, who can be against us? He that spared not his own Son, but delivered him up for us all, how shall he not with him also freely give us all things? Who shall lay any thing to the charge of God's elect? It is God that justifieth. Who is he that condemneth? It is Christ that died, rather, that is risen again, who is even at the right hand of God, who also maketh intercession for us.

Who shall separate us from the love of Christ? shall tribulation, or distress, or persecution, or famine, or nakedness, or peril, or sword? As it is written, For thy sake we are killed all the day long; we are accounted as sheep for the slaughter. Nay, in all these things we are more than conquerors through him that loved us. For I am persuaded, that neither death, nor life, nor angels, nor principalities, nor powers, nor things present nor things to come, nor height nor depth, nor any other creature, shall be able to separate us from the love of God, which is in Christ Jesus Our Lord." (Rom. 8: 18-39.)

To fully understand this divine secret we must go back to the very first chapter of the Bible, the first chapter of Genesis. The word or title "GOD' in that chapter is a substitute for the Hebrew word ELOHIM. Now ELOHIM is always plural and always means all of the sons and daughters of Yahveh.

Wherever "GOD" is used in the Old Testament it is a substitute for "ELOHIM." Therefore it was the sons and daughters of Yahveh who created the world. They created the world by HEADSHIPS, that is, by prince leaders and those under the prince leaders. Actually there were twenty-four prince leaders, each one over a host of the sons and daughters of Yahveh. The work done on each day of creation was by a prince leader and the children that were under him. Twenty-four orders of the sons and daughters of Yahveh, that is, the ELOHIM, took part in creating the world in the first chapter of Genesis.

The natural man created in Genesis 1:26, which was created male and female, was only an image of a son of God and an image of a daughter of God. The natural races of men who were of the earth, earthy, and were merely at the head of the natural animal species inhabited the earth for thousands or perhaps millions of years before Adam was formed.

Genesis 1:1-31 and Genesis 2:1-6 is the story of the perfect natural creation of the earth and of natural men (races) of the animal earthly orders. The earth and all of the mineral, vegetable and animal kingdoms and the natural races of men were created by the ELOHIM (God), that is, by the heavenly sons and daughters of Yahveh. The natural animal races of men inhabited the earth for thousands or perhaps millions of years before we come to Genesis 2:7.

YAHVEH then informed the ELOHIM, his sons and daughters, that they would have to give up their Heavenly Spiritual bodies and come down to earth and be made flesh. And in Genesis 2:7 YAHVEH in person formed a body out of dust and inbreathed—that is, inspired that body with his own Divine Life.

OUTER SPACE PEOPLE AND INNER EARTH PEOPLE

That man Adam was the first Son of God—that is, the first of the ELOHIM (Gods) to be made flesh and Eve was the first heavenly daughter to be made flesh. Yahveh made a garden twelve hundred miles square and in it he placed Adam and Eve. Adam was the sovereign king over all the earth and Eve was the sovereign queen over all the earth. They may have resided in that garden for thousands of years, probably seven thousand years. Undoubtedly there were many sons and daughters (sons of God) that were made flesh and dwelt in the Garden of Eden.

I do not now have the time and space to tell you of the sin of Eve with the natural serpent race of men and of the blood transfusion and poison from the serpent (man) that brought guile and death into her flesh. Neither do I have time to tell you how Adam of his own free will accepted sin and death in order to carry Yahveh's plan for the world. Suffice it to say that on the day that Adam and Eve were driven out of the Garden, the Garden of Eden (an area 1200 miles square) ascended into heaven. The day that Adam left Eden he was stripped of his aura and halo (garments of light) and time and death set in. By absolute accurate genealogy given in the Bible it has been (counting this year of 1965 A D) exactly 5965 years since Adam left Eden.

Many of the sons of God, some of whom had been in the Garden of Eden with Adam, sinned by marrying women of the serpent and Canaanitish races of natural men. Some of the other sons of God (Elohim) that were dwelling on the earth's asteroid and planetoid outer circle, that are just outside the earth's stratosphere and who are known as etherians or "men above the earth", descended to the earth and materialized, that is took on earthly bodies and married earthly women. This particular order of the ELOHIM, sons of God, that sinned were, because of that sin, banished from the face of the earth and confined to the under world; which is the earth's interior and they are known as the "men under the earth." Actually there are men above the earth dwelling on the earth's planetoids and asteroids and there are "men under the earth" dwelling in the earth's interior, A few of them of both classes, a few of those from above the earth and a few of those from "under the earth" have often and at intervals appeared on the face of the surface of the earth. Usually they have only stayed for a few minutes, never for more than a day or two at the most. Flying Saucers are of many designs and some are from above the earth and some are from the interior of the earth,

From Adam, a son of God, our lineage has descended through Seth, Noah, Shem, Abraham, Isaac, Jacob and so on down to Jesus Christ, and from the seed of Abraham according to the flesh, we who are the sons of God (ELOHIM), have been made flesh from Abraham's flesh. All of the patriarchs, judges, prophets, priests, kings and apostles called and chosen and ordained by YAHVEH have been and are now of the nature and flesh of Abraham. An ELOHIM son of God has never been clothed in the flesh of any other race and never will be.

That we have three bodies is definitely clear. The first and greatest is our Heavenly Body in which we dwelt before we came to this earth. The second body is that of the flesh in which we dwell on the earth. And the third body is that which is both literal and spiritual. To clarify this let me put it this way: 1. The terrestrial earthly body. 2. The telestial angelic body. 3. The celestial heavenly immortal body.

OUTER SPACE PEOPLE AND INNER EARTH PEOPLE

First: For thirty-three and one-half years Jesus Christ had a perfect physical terrestrial earthly body.

Second: For forty days between the time of his resurrection and ascension he had a perfect telestial, angelic body. He could materialize and dematerialize that body. He could appear as a man in the flesh or as an angel. He could be visible or invisible. During those forty days he went down to the "men under the earth" and preached to them and he went up to the men above the earth on the earth's planetoids and preached to them, and he visited all nations of men on the earth and preached to them. The telestial body has or may assume three natures. Namely: 1. That of the men (or angelic order) above the earth. 2. That of the angelic orders of men under or inside the earth. 3. That of men on the earth. Men on the earth, men above the earth and men under the earth all belong to the earth's sphere and in a telestial body any man could, *and Christ did*, visit the men above the earth, on the earth and under the earth.

Third: When Christ ascended into heaven, all that was terrestrial and all that was telestial—all that belonged to the earth's surface, all that belonged to the earth's interior and all that belonged to the earth's outer-space, was dissolved and left here as a fixed element of faith, and is the creative substance and evidence in which we live and by which we may become immortalized. Christ in his ascension entered again into his CELESTIAL body—his heavenly body, his IMMORTAL body; the same body with the same glory that he had before the world was created.

We who are the sons of God will also gain back and enter again into our CELESTIAL bodies which we had in heaven before the world was created: "Knowing that he which raised up the Lord Jesus shall raise up us also by Jesus, and shall present us with you. For all things are for your sakes, that the abundant grace might through the thanksgiving of many redound to the glory of God. For which cause we faint not; but though our outward man perish, yet the inward man is renewed day by day.

For our light affliction, which is but for a moment worketh for us a far more exceeding and eternal weight of glory; while we look not at the things which are seen, but at the things which are not seen: for the things which are seen are temporal; but the things which are not seen are eternal." (II Cor.4: 14-18.)

But God giveth it a body as it hath pleased him, and to every seed his own body. All flesh is not the same flesh: but there is one kind of flesh of men, another flesh of beasts, another of fishes, another of birds. There are also celestial bodies, and bodies terrestrial: but the glory of the celestial is one, and the glory of the terrestrial is another. There is one glory of the sun, and another glory of the moon, and another glory of the stars; for one star differeth from another star in glory. So also is the resurrection of the dead. It is sown in corruption, it is raised in incorruption. It is sown in dishonor, it is raised in glory: it is sown in weakness, it is raised in power; it is sown a natural body, it is raised a spiritual body. There is a natural body, and there is a spiritual body.

"And so it is written. The first man Adam was made a living soul; the last Adam was made a quickening spirit. Howbeit that was not first which is spiritual, but that which is natural; and afterward that which is spiritual. The first man is of the earth, earthy; the

OUTER SPACE PEOPLE AND INNER EARTH PEOPLE

second man is the Lord from heaven. As is the earthy, such are they also that are earthy; and as is the heavenly, such are they also that are heavenly. And as we have born the image of the earthy, we shall also bear the image of the heavenly.

Now this I say, brethren, that flesh and blood cannot inherit the kingdom of God; neither doth corruption inherit incorruption. Behold, I show you a mystery; We shall not all sleep, but we shall all be changed, in a moment in the twinkling of an eye, at the last trump: for the trumpet shall sound, and the dead shall be raised incorruptible, and we shall be changed. For this corruptible must put on incorruption, and this mortal must put on immortality. So when this corruptible shall have put on incorruption, and this mortal shall have put on immortality, then shall be brought to pass the saying that is written, Death is swallowed up in victory; O death, where is thy sting? O grave, where is thy victory? The sting of death is sin; and the strength of sin is the law. But thanks be to God, which giveth us the victory through our Lord Jesus Christ. Therefore, my beloved brethren, be ye steadfast, unmovable, always abounding in the work of the Lord, forasmuch as ye know that your labor is not in vain in the Lord." (I Cor. 15:38-58.)

That our change over from terrestrial (mortal) to celestial (immortal) may take place now and without the experience of physical death is evident from many scriptures. "Behold, I show you a mystery: we shall not all die, but we shall all be changed." (1 Cor. 15:51) "We which are alive and remain unto the coming (that is presence) of the Lord." (1 Thes. 4:15.) "shall be like him; for we shall see him as he is." (1 John 3:2). "EVERY MAN THAT HATH THIS HOPE IN HIM PURIFIETH HIMSELF, EVEN AS HE IS PURE." (John 3:3.)

"There is therefore now no condemnation to them which are in Christ Jesus, who walk not after the flesh, but after the Spirit. For the law of the Spirit of life in Christ Jesus hath made me free from the law of sin and death. But ye are not in the flesh, but in the Spirit, if so be that the Spirit of God dwell in you. Now if any man have not the Spirit of Christ, he is none of his. And if Christ be in you, the body is dead because of sin; but the Spirit is life because of righteousness. But if the Spirit of him that raised up Jesus from the dead dwell in you, he that raised up Christ from the dead shall also quicken your mortal bodies by his Spirit that dwelleth in you." (Rom. 8: 1-2, 9-11).

"Know ye not that so many of us as were baptized into Jesus Christ were baptized into his death? Therefore we are buried with him by baptism into death; that like as Christ was raised up from the dead by the glory of the Father, even so we also should walk in newness of life. For if we have been planted together in the likeness of his death, we shall be also in the likeness of his resurrection: knowing this, that our old man is crucified with him, that the body of sin might be destroyed, that henceforth we should not serve sin. Even he that is dead is freed from sin. Now if we be dead with Christ we believe that we shall also live with him: knowing that Christ being raised from the dead dieth no more; death, hath no more dominion over him. For in that he died, he died unto sin once: but in that he liveth, he liveth unto God. Likewise reckon ye also yourselves to be dead indeed unto sin, but alive unto God through Jesus Christ our Lord." (Rom. 6:8-11). "Strengthened with all might, according to his glorious power, unto all patience and long-suffering with joyfulness; giving thanks unto the Father, which have made us meet

OUTER SPACE PEOPLE AND INNER EARTH PEOPLE

to be partakers of the inheritance of the saints in light: who hath delivered us from the power of darkness, and hath translated us into the kingdom of his dear Son." (Col. 1:11-13)

The King is here and the Kingdom of Heaven is at hand. Some people are worried about the teaching by some preachers who interpret the scripture to the effect that there is no marriage in heaven and that they neither marry nor are given in marriage. The truth of the matter is that there are prince leaders who have spiritual families or orders of their own—all of whom are of the same ectoblastic spirit substance, and they have celestial wives, concubines, sons, daughters; eunuchs and servants who are all in their own ELOHIM order. They are bound and sealed to them and this is recognized in heaven. Therefore since the orders are completed here, there is no need for marriage in heaven, for they will everyone in their own order be united as one body, mind, soul and spirit.

I ask you to study every reference in the Bible to "wives", "concubines", "sons", daughters", "eunuchs" and "servants" and see what conclusion you reach. What is the work of the wives? What is the work of the concubines? What is the work of a eunuch and *what is a eunuch*? Why are there servants and what is their work? You will be surprised to find that they all have their definite place in their own ELOHIM order under their prince leader who will have a world of his own somewhere in one of the universes of YAHVEH.

OUTER SPACE PEOPLE AND INNER EARTH PEOPLE

Chapter VII

The Double Senses

Introduction

Everybody knows that there are five senses in the mortal physical body: namely, hearing, seeing, feeling, tasting and smelling. But very few people know that the immortal, inner Spiritual body also has five senses which belong entirely to the Spiritual dimension. In fact many people never know that there is an INNER MAN because the inner man lies dormant and is asleep until he is awakened by the resurrection power of Jesus Christ (Yahshua the Messiah). There is no other name, no other person that can awaken, resurrect and give eternal life and immortality to the Spiritual inner man except Jesus Christ.

NOW it is "high time to awake out of sleep." (Rom. 13:11. "AWAKE THOU THAT SLEEPEST, AND ARISE FROM THE DEAD, AND CHRIST SHALL GIVE THEE LIGHT." (Eph. 5:14.) "If the Spirit of him that raised up Jesus from the dead dwell in you, he that raised up Christ from the dead shall also quicken (that is, give life to) your mortal bodies by his Spirit that dwelleth in you." (Rom. 8:11.) Your body is either a tomb of the dead or it is a temple of the living.

There are definitely two worlds that occupy exactly the same space at the same time. The one is the material world. The other is the Spiritual world. This is just like a piece of steel that is magnetized. The steel and the magnetic force occupy the same space at the same time because they are without affinity.

We live and move and have our existence in the Spiritual world. The Spiritual world is in us and through us, but being in a mortal physical body we are never conscious of the Spiritual world until the INNER MAN within us is resurrected to eternal life by Jesus Christ for in Him is LIFE and LIGHT. He is the only door of entrance into the Spiritual world.

Evil earth-bound disembodied spirits of men and women from a previous creation on this earth—spirits that are of the earth, earthy, try to obsess and possess our

OUTER SPACE PEOPLE AND INNER EARTH PEOPLE

mortal, physical bodies; and these evil spirits work entirely through the five physical senses. They are subtle, earthy, devilish and sensual. This type of thing is found all the way from the fakirs of India and the Voodooism of the African jungle to the highly emotional mass meetings of religious cults in America. The people who believe that this is a spiritual experience are deceived and deluded, for it is of the flesh, fleshy. As we proceed in this message we will learn how to discern that which is truly Spiritual.

1. The Sense Of Hearing

As you know, our ears are subject to sound vibrations which are extremely limited. Every word has a different vibration. I do not suppose anybody knows just how many sounds the human ear can hear. Some hear more than others but in all of us the sense of hearing is limited. In my own case, I have no ear for music. You hear many notes that I do not hear at all, but because you hear them and I do not hear them, I have no right to say that you do not hear them.

The very first thing that Yahveh wants of you is your ear. Therefore let us come immediately to the subject of Spiritual hearing. "Faith cometh by hearing" (Rom. 10:17) and in no other way. Hearing is the first step toward the Spiritual Kingdom.

Unto the first man, Adam, Yahveh called saying, "Where art thou?" (Gen. 3:9.) Yahveh said to the first woman, Eve: "What is this that thou hast done?" (Gen. 3:13.) Yahveh said to Cain the second man. "Where is Abel thy brother?" (Gen. 4:9.) Notice that in all three cases Yahveh asked a question. He invited conversation. It would require volumes to take up everything that the Bible records that Yahveh said to the people at different times in different parts of the world over a period of 4,000 years from the time he spoke to Adam in the Garden of Eden until he spoke to the Apostle John on the Isle of Patmos.

"YAHVEH SHALL CAUSE HIS GLORIOUS VOICE TO BE HEARD." (Isa. 30:30.) You will remember that when Samuel was just a little child, perhaps only three years old, Yahveh called "Samuel". And again the second time he called "Samuel" and again the third time "Yahveh came and stood, and called as at other times, Samuel, Samuel." (I Sam.3:10.) Therefore a child may hear his voice.

At the baptism of Jesus, the Apostles, especially Peter, James and John, heard the voice of Yahveh say: "This is my beloved Son in whom I am well pleased." (Matt. 3:17.) These same three Apostles, while on the Mount of Transfiguration with Jesus, heard Yahveh say again, "This is my beloved Son, in whom I am well pleased; hear ye him." (Matt. 17:5.)

After Yahshua the Messiah (Jesus) ascended, disappearing from mortal sight, it did not mean that he would not continue to talk with men. Saul of Tarsus heard him call his name, "Saul, Saul." (Acts 9:4.) By obedience to that voice Paul became the greatest Christian that ever lived. Years later "A vision appeared to Paul in the night; there stood a man of Macedonia, and prayed him, saying, Come over into Macedonia, and help us." (Acts 16:9.) Luke says that they immediately obeyed and set sail for Europe "assuredly gathering that the Lord had called us to preach the gospel unto them." (Acts 16:10.) This was the beginning of the evangelization of Europe.

OUTER SPACE PEOPLE AND INNER EARTH PEOPLE

Sometimes the voice of Yahveh came direct; at other times through a living person that was near or that was far away. Because others that were present did not hear the voice, had no ears to hear, was no evidence that the person to whom the voice came and for whom the message was intended could not hear it. The INNER MAN had a spiritual ear—the spiritual sense of hearing.

It is said that the Psalmist David was so in tune with the spiritual world that at night when he retired he hung his harp on the wall above his bed and could hear the vibrations of the spirit world sweep over it and in this way he wrote the words and music of the Psalms. Those beautiful Psalms came to us from the spiritual world through David.

Many people never hear a spiritual voice or heavenly music until they are near to death. Captain Eddie Rickenbacker, who, with several companions floated for many days on a raft in the Pacific, says that they came so near to death that he could hear the sweet music and singing of the angels. Twice he says he has been so near death that he could hear the music in the spiritual world.

My grandfather, Calvin Blessing, passed away at an extreme age. He had been very ill and confined to his bed for many months with a large tumor of the neck and throat. He never knew music. He could never sing, but one night he asked them to prop him up in the bed, and when they had raised him up and put several pillows back of him, he sang out in clear tones all the verses of the song,"I'm going home to die no more." When he finished the last words of the last verse he closed his eyes in death.

"Verily, verily I say unto you, the hour is coming and now is, when the dead shall hear the voice of the Son of God; and they that hear shall live." (John 5:25.) "Marvel not at this: for the hour is coming, in the which all that are in the graves shall hear his voice, and shall come forth." (John 5:28-29.) "Even so in Christ shall all be made alive." (1 Cor. 15:22)

2. The Sense Of Sight

Mortal, physical sight is very much limited. Our eyes are subject only to limited vibrations of light. Some people who are color blind see things only in black and white. Everything appears to them to be either black or white, but others sees things in color: violet indigo, blue, green, yellow, orange and red. Because the color-blind person cannot see these colors does he have any right to say that you do not see them? Likewise does the Spiritually blind person have any right to say that a person with Spiritual sight does not see the people and things in the Spiritual world?

There is a world within a World. Everything that is natural is but an image of a thing that is spiritual. The natural worid is a materiaiization of the Spiritual world.

"Howbeit we speak wisdom among them that are perfect: yet not the wisdom of this world, for of the princes of this world, that come to naught; But we speak the wisdom of God in a mystery, even the hidden wisdom, which God ordained before the world unto our glory; Which none of the princes of this world knew, for had they known it they would not have crucified the Lord of glory. But as it is written, eye hath not seen, nor ear heard, neither have entered into the heart of man, the things which God hath prepared for them that love him. But God hath revealed them unto us by his Spirit: for the Spirit

OUTER SPACE PEOPLE AND INNER EARTH PEOPLE

searcheth all things, yea, the deep things of God. For what man knoweth the things of a man, save the spirit of man which is in him? even so the things of God knoweth no man, but the Spirit of God. Now we have received, not the spirit of the world, but the Spirit which is of God; that we might know the things that are freely given to us of God. Which things also we speak, not in the words which man's wisdom teacheth, but which the Holy Ghost teacheth; comparing spiritual things with spiritual.

But the natural man receiveth not the things of the Spirit of God: for they are foolishness unto him: neither can he know them, because they are spiritually discerned. But he that is spiritual judgeth all things, yet he himself is judged of no man. For who hath known the mind of the Lord, that he may instruct him? But we have the mind of Christ."-(I Cor. 2:6-16.) "For all things are for your sakes, that the abundant grace might through the thanksgiving of many redound to the glory of God. For which cause we faint not; but though our outward man perish, yet the inward man is renewed day by day. For our light affliction, which is but for a moment worketh for us afar, more exceeding, and eternal weight of glory; While we look not at the things which are seen, but at the things which are not seen: for the things which are seen are temporal; but the things which are not seen are eternal. For we know that if our earth house of this tabernacle were dissolved, we have a building of God, a house not made with hands; eternal in the heavens."-(II Cor. 4:15-18, 5:1)

All through the Bible there are stories about men and women who saw and visited with angels and with the spirits of just men made perfect. Three men came to Abraham, visited with him just as though they were ordinary humans and ate with him. (Gen. 18:1-8.) Two of these same men delivered Lot from Sodom, after which they destroyed that wicked city. (Gen. 19:1-16.) The man who appeared to Gideon also appeared just as a mortal man, but he was an angel.

"And Gideon went in, and made ready a kid, and unleavened cakes of an ephah of flour: the flesh he put in a basket and he put the broth in a pot and brought it out unto him under the oak, and presented it. And the angel of God said unto him. Take the flesh and the unleavened cakes, and lay them upon this rock, and pour out the broth. And he did so. Then the angel of the Lord put forth the end of the staff that was in his hand, and touched the flesh and the unleavened cakes ; and there rose up fire out of the rock, and consumed the flesh and the unleavened cakes; Then the angel of the Lord departed out of his sight. And when Gideon perceived that he was an angel of the Lord, Gideon said, Alas, O Lord God! for because I have seen an angel of the Lord face to face. And the Lord said unto him, Peace be unto thee; fear not: thou shalt not die. Then Gideon built an altar there unto the Lord, and called it Jehovah-shalom."-(Judges 6:19

It is indeed strange that a great many people think that if they see an angel or a person from another world they will die. An angel appeared as a man to Manoah and his wife and predicted the birth of Samson. I shall read the last part of that story:

"And Manoah said unto the angel of the Lord, I pray thee, let us detain thee, until we shall have made ready a kid for thee. And the angel of the Lord said unto Manoah, Though thou detain me, I will not eat of thy bread: and if thou wilt offer a burnt offering,

OUTER SPACE PEOPLE AND INNER EARTH PEOPLE

thou must offer it unto the Lord. For Manoah knew not that he was an angel of the Lord. And Manoah said unto the angel of the Lord, What is thy name, that when thy sayings come to pass we may do thee honor? And the angel of the Lord said unto him, Why askest thou thus after my name, seeing it is secret? So Manoah took a kid with a meat offering, and offered it upon a rock unto the Lord: and the angel did wondrously; and Manoah and his wife looked on. For it came to pass when the flame went up toward heaven from off the altar, that the angel of the Lord ascended in the flame of the altar: and Manoah and his wife looked on it, and fell on their faces to the ground. But the angel of the Lord did no more appear to Manoah and to his wife. Then Manoah knew that he was an angel of the Lord. And Manoah said unto his wife, We shall surely die because we have seen God. But his wife said unto him, If the Lord were pleased to kill us, he would not have received a burnt offering and a meat offering at our hands, neither would he have showed us all these things, nor would at this time have told us such things as these."- (Judges 18: 15-23)

It is wonderful to know that Moses was always conscious of the presence of Christ with him. "Esteeming the reproach of Christ greater riches than the treasures in Egypt: for he had respect unto the recompense of the reward. By faith he forsook Egypt not fearing the wrath of the king, for he endured; as seeing him who is invisible. (Heb. 11:25-27.)

When Joshua led the children of Israel over into the Promised Land he actually saw the general of Yahveh's Army and talked with him: "And it came to pass, when Joshua was by Jericho, that he lifted up his eyes and looked, and, behold, there stood a man over against him with his sword drawn in his hand: and Joshua went unto him, and said unto him, Art thou for us, or for our adversaries? And he said, Nay; but as captain of the host of the Lord am I now come. And Joshua fell on his face to the earth, and did worship, and said unto him, What saith my lord unto his servant? And the captain of the Lord's host said unto Joshua, Loose thy shoe from off thy foot; for the place whereon thou standest is holy. And Joshua did so."(Joshua 5:18-15.)

Both the Old Testament and the New Testament are literally filled with stories, cases and incidents in which the children of Israel and the early Christians saw and visited with the people of the Spiritual world. Here is a case in the Old Testament in which Elisha, surrounded by the enemy Syrian Army, seemed to be in great danger. The Syrian king: said: "Go and spy where he is, that I may send and fetch him. And it was told him, saying. Behold, he is in Dothan. Therefore sent he thither horses, and chariots, and a great host: and they came by night, and compassed the city about. And when the servant of the man of God was risen early, and gone forth, behold, a host compassed the city both with horses and chariots. And his servant said unto him, Alas, my master! how shall we do? And he answered, Fear not: they that be with us are more than they that be with them. And Elisha prayed, and said, Lord, I pray thee, open his eyes, that he may see. And the Lord opened the eyes of the young man; and he saw: and, behold, the mountain was full of horses and chariots of fire round about Elisha. And when they came down to him, Elisha prayed unto the Lord, and said, Smite this people, I pray thee; with blindness. And he smote them with blindness according to the word of Elisha.-(II Kings 6:13-18.)

OUTER SPACE PEOPLE AND INNER EARTH PEOPLE

Here is a statement in the New Testament: 'Wherefore, seeing we also are compassed about with so great a cloud of witnesses, let us lay aside every weight, and the sin which doth so easily beset us, and let us run with patience the race that is set before us, looking unto Jesus the author and finisher of our faith."-(Heb.12:1-2)

"Ye are come unto mount Sion, and unto the city of the living God, the heavenly Jerusalem, and to an innumerable company of angels. To the general assembly and church of the firstborn, which are written in heaven and to God the Judge of all and to the spirits of just men made perfect and to Jesus the mediator of the new covenant."-(Heb. 12:22-24-) Because there is so much of this truth I shall have to omit a lot of it. There are seventeen direct cases in the New Testament in which men and women saw and visited with angels, outer-space people or with the spirits of just men made perfect. Peter, James and John, while on the Mount of Transfiguration with Jesus, saw Moses and Elijah. (Matt. 17:1-3.) The dying martyr Stephen saw Jesus and this was many years after Jesus had ascended into heaven. (Acts 7:55.) It was also fifteen years after the ascension of Jesus into heaven when Paul saw him. (Acts 9:4-5.) The facts are that one of the qualifications of the apostle was that he had to see Jesus. Paul offers this very evidence. "Am I not an apostle? Am I not free? Have I not seen Jesus our Lord." (I Cor. 9:1.) "He was seen of me also as one born out of due time." (1 Cor. 15:8.) All true apostles saw or have seen Jesus Christ. Those who say they are apostles and have not seen the Lord are not aposties but liars: "For such are false apostles, deceitful workers, transforming themselves into the aposties of Christ." (II Cor. 11:13.)

A requirement for seeing Jesus is "Holiness, without which no man shall see the Lord." (Heb. 12:14.)"Blessed are the pure in heart: for they shall see God." (Matt. 5:8.) "Unto those that look for him shall he appear." (Heb. 9:28.) He tells us plainly that the world will see him no more. "The world seeth me no more! (John 14:19.) But he also says, "But ye see me: because I live ye shall live also." (John 14:19.) If any man love me, he will keep my words: and my Father will love him, and we will come unto him, and make our abode with him." (John 14:23.) "Lo, I, am with you always, even unto the end of the world." (Matt. 28:20.)

"Therefore if any man be in Christ, he is a new creature; old things are passed away; behold all things are become new. " (II Cor. 5:17.) "God hath said, I will dwell in them, and walk in them; and I will be their God and they shall be my people." (II Cor. 6: 16.)

Those in this experience share equally in the great ONENESS as He said: "That they all may be one: as thou, Father, art in me, and I in thee, that they also may be one in us: That the world may believe that thou hast sent me." (John 17:21)

The Body of Christ is plural. We are the ONE Body of Christ: "We are members of his body, of his flesh, and of his bones." (Eph. 5:80.) This is the great mystery, the deep secret of the true Christian faith which is known only to the initiated. It may be that you can see Christ in us. With the spiritual sense of sight which belongs to the INNER MAN we see the Spiritual world. Some preachers speak of spiritual things as though they were nothing. They say to me, "O, you spiritualize the Bible. You spiritualize everything." Well,

OUTER SPACE PEOPLE AND INNER EARTH PEOPLE

why not? The spiritual world is the only real, eternal, abiding world.

3. The Sense Of Feeling

Beginning with the beloved John and Charles Wesley 175 years ago there was great emphasis placed upon feeling. Some of the big Denominations that were founded upon emotional experience have cooled off and are modernistic, without anything. Various other churches and cults which emphasize feeling are victims of a fleshly voodooism that works a great strain upon the nervous system until they become mentally unbalanced, depending upon an emotional experience in the same way that a drug addict depends upon the needle. It is too bad that the Holy Ghost is said to cause all of this uncontrolled emotionalism.

But the sense of touch, that is, of feeling, is as real to the INNER MAN as it is to the mortal physical body. We have a desire to touch those that we love. There seems to be some satisfaction even in handling the things that those whom we love have handled. I have sat in chairs that were once occupied by George Washington, Abraham Lincoln, Lew Wallace, Mark Twain, Edgar Allen Poe, et al. I have put my hands on the Liberty Bell, also on a big stone that was once in King Solomon's Temple. There is a certain satisfaction of feeling that comes only from touch,

The early disciples all touched Jesus. The Apostle John pillowed his head on His breast. (John 13:25, 21:20) He speaks of Christ as the one "We have heard, which we have seen with our eyes, which we have looked upon, and our hands have handled," (I John 1:1.) Mary (not his mother) anointed his head and his feet with precious ointment, kissed his feet and wiped them with the hair of her head. (Luke 7:38) By this contact and experience she was purified and her sins forgiven.

Great power was received from just touching the hem of his garment.

"A woman having an issue of blood twelve years, which had spent her living upon physicians, neither could be healed of any, came behind him, and touched the border of his garment and immediately her issue of blood stanched. And Jesus said, who touched me? When all denied; Peter and they that were with him said, Master the muititude throngs thee and press thee, and sayest thou, Who touched me? And Jesus said, "Somebody hath touched me: for I perceive that virtue is gone out of me. And when the woman saw that she was not hid, she came trembling; and falling down before him, she declared unto him before all the people for what cause she had touched him, and how she was healed immediately."- (Luke 8:43-47.)

"There is a vast difference between crowding and touching. This power of touch was not only used by Jesus but by others before him. Even the dead were raised by Elisha in that manner.

"And when Elisha was come into the house, behold, the child was dead, and laid upon his bed. He went in therefore, and shut the door upon them twain, and prayed unto the Lord. And he went up, and lay upon the child, and put his mouth upon his mouth, and his eyes upon his eyes; and his hands upon his hands: and he stretched himself upon the child; and the flesh of the child waxed warm. Then he returned, and walked in the house

OUTER SPACE PEOPLE AND INNER EARTH PEOPLE

to and fro; and went up, and stretched himself upon him: and the child sneezed seven times, and the child opened his eyes. And he called Gahazi, and said, Call this Shunammite. So he called her. And when she was come in unto him, he said, Take up thy son. Then she went in and fell at his feet and bowed herself to the ground, and took up her son, and went out.-(II Kings 4:32-37.)

Jairus' little daughter, twelve years of age, was dead. Jesus "took her by the hand, and called; saying, Maid, Arise. And her spirit came again, and she arose straightway." (Luke 8:54 55) "And when Jesus was come into Peter's house he saw his wife's mother laid, and sick of a fever. He touched her hand, and the fever left her: and she arose and ministered unto them." (Matt 8:14.) "By the hands of the Apostles were many signs and wonders wrought among the people (Acts 5:12.) "Through laying on of the Apostles' hands the Holy Ghost was given." (Acts 8:18.)

Paul wrote to Timothy saying, "Wherefore I put thee in remembrance that thou stir up the gift of God, which is in thee by the putting on of my hands." (II Tim 1:6.) Spiritual gifts were imparted to others by the laying on of hands. There is something in touching.

The Holy Ghost is always indirectly present, but there are times when the Spirit is directly present. Sometimes you can feel on your forehead a kiss from the Spiritual world. At other times you may feel the presence in your hands or in your heart. Once in a while you can feel the presence through your entire body. I say without hesitation that I would much rather feel the Divine presence than to have a million dollars, the sense of feeling, even the siightest touch from the spiritual world, is the grandest sense of feeling that you can ever experience. When those who have the Spirit present within themselves and they touch you, you immediately feel that mysterious, glorious Divine power.

4. The Sense Of Tasting

This is a very important physical sense. So far as we know there are only four distinct tastes—bitter, sweet, sour and salt. But there are many wonderful combinations of these. Taste is an essential thing in keeping the physical body in good health. Meditation upon food, thinking about food, prepares the digestive juices to digest that food when it is eaten. Our food should taste good. Eating is an enjoyable thing as well as being essential to our survival.

My objection to so-called health foods and vitamin and protein pills is that they are so flat and tasteless that we cannot enjoy them. Therefore they are contrary to the natural sense of taste and cannot be for our good health. The sense of taste and good food is directly connected with Spiritual things. We are definitely told that every creature of God is good, and nothing to be refused, if it is received with thanksgiving, "for it is sanctified by the word of God and prayer." (I Tim. 4:4-5.) The word of God, prayer and thanksgiving sanctifies our food. Jesus said of his disciples, "If they drink any deadly thing, it shall not hurt them." (Mark 16:18.) When Yahveh fed the children of Israel on manna in the wilderness he made it nourishing to everybody, satisfying to every appetite, agreeable to every taste.

OUTER SPACE PEOPLE AND INNER EARTH PEOPLE

The people in the Spiritual world eat and drink just as we do here on earth in the flesh. We do not lose any of the five senses when we change worlds.

In cases where men on earth have been fed a special heavenly food, they have been completely satisfied and nourished for as much as forty days without natural food or water. Let us look at this case of how the weary prophet Elijah was nourished.

"But he himself went a day's journey into the wilderness, and came and sat down under a juniper tree: and he requested for himself that he might die; and said, It is enough; now, O Lord, take away my life; for I am not better than my fathers. And as he lay and slept under a juniper tree, behold, then an angel touched him, and said unto him, Arise and eat, And he looked, and, behold there was a cake baked on the coals, and a cruse of water at his head. And he did eat and drink, and laid him down again. And the angel of the Lord came again the second time, and touched him, and said, Arise and eat; because the journey is too great for thee. And he arose, and did eat and drink, and went in the strength of that meat forty days and forty nights unto Horeb the mount of God."-(I Kings 19:4-8.)

Yes, there is a spiritual sense of taste. "O taste and see that the Lord is good. (Psalm 34:8.) "Sweet are thy words unto my taste." (Psalm 119:103.) There is a taste about people. Some are bitter, some are salty, some are sour, some are sweet and some are just plain flat and tasteless. In the song of Solomon we read: "As an apple tree among the trees of the wood, so is my beloved among the sons. I sat down under his shadow with great delight, and his fruit was sweet to my taste. He brought me to the banqueting house, and his banner over me was love," (Song of Solomon 2:3-4.)

A great many Protestants and Jews abhor the idea of eating of the body of Christ. They call it cannibalism, but they have missed one of the great depths of Spiritual truth and also the fact that Christ gave his body for us and that he has the power to multiply that body and by so doing he builds his own body into our body. Therefore let us "receive with meekness the engrafted word which is able to save your souls." (James 1:21) By which we become "members of his body, of his flesh and of his bones." (Eph. 5:3) The true husband and wife and all of those who are in the Body of Christ become One Flesh, One Body.

Here is what Jesus said: "I am that bread of life. Your fathers did eat manna in the wilderness, and are dead. That is the bread which cometh down from heaven, that a man may eat thereof, and not die. I am the living bread which came down from heaven: if any man eat of this bread, he shall live forever: and the bread that I will give is my flesh, which I will give for the life of the world. The Jews therefore strove among themselves, saying. How can this man give us his flesh to eat? Then Jesus said unto them, Verily, verily, I say unto you, Except ye eat the flesh of the Son of man, and drink his blood, ye have no life in you. Whoso eateth my flesh, and drinketh my blood, hath eternal life; and I will raise him up at the last day. For my flesh is meat indeed, and my blood is drink indeed. He that eateth my flesh, and drinketh my blood, dwelleth in me, and I him. As the living Father hath sent me, and I live by the Father; so he that eateth me, even he shall live by me. This is that bread which came down from heaven: not as your fathers did eat

OUTER SPACE PEOPLE AND INNER EARTH PEOPLE

manna, and are dead: he that eateth of this bread shall live forever."- (John 6:48-58.)

Jesus lost thousands of his followers when he taught this truth. Even "From that time many of his disciples went back, and walked no more with him. Then said Jesus unto the twelve, Will ye also go away? Then Simon Peter answered him, Lord to whom shall we go? thou hast the words of eternal life. And we believe and are sure that thou art that Christ the Son of the living God."

I am very glad that I can commune in the body and the blood of Christ "discerning the Lord's body" in the Kingdom meal of holy food which we eat in fellowship every Sunday. (I Cor. 10:16, 11:29.) "For, we being many are one bread, and one body, for we are partakers of that one bread." (I Cor. 10:17.)

The prophet Ezekiel ate a book. He says, "And when I looked, behold, a hand was sent unto me; and, lo, a roll of a book was therein." (Ezek. 2:9.)

"Moreover he said unto me, Son of man, eat that thou findest; eat this roll, and go speak unto the house of Israel, So I opened my mouth, and he caused me to eat that roll. And he said unto me, Son of man, cause thy belly to eat, and fill thy bowels with this roll that I qive thee. Then did I eat it; and it was in my mouth as honey for sweetness. And he said unto me, Son of man, go, get thee unto the house of Israel, and speak with my words unto them."-Ezekiel 3: 1:4.)

The patriarch Job said: "I have esteemed the words of his mouth more than my necessary food." (Job 23:12.) Jesus said, "Man shall not live by bread alone, but by every word that proceedeth out of the mouth of God." (Matt. 4-4.) The prophet Jeremiah says: "Thy words were found, and I did eat them; and thy word was unto me the joy and rejoicing of mine heart, for I am called by thy name, O Yahveh Elohim of hosts."(Jer. 15:16.)

What most people need is the Spiritual sense of taste which is only satisfied by feasting on the word of God. You can never quit preaching and teaching when you get His words in you. Jeremiah says, "Then I said, I will not make mention of him, nor speak anymore in his name. But his word was in mine heart as a burning fire shut up in my bones. I was weary with forbearing, and I could not stay." (Jer. 20:9.) We simply have to set the table with this good food.

The Apostle John says: "In the days of the voice of the seventh angel, when he shall begin to sound, the mystery of God should be finished, as he hath declared to his servants the prophets. And the voice which I heard from heaven spake unto me again, and said, Go and take the little book which is open in the hand of the angel which standeth upon the sea and upon the earth. And I went unto the angel, and said unto him, Give me the little book. And he said unto me, Take it, and eat it up; and it shall make thy belly bitter, but it shall be in thy mouth sweet as honey. And I took the little book out of the angel's hand, and ate it up; and it was in my mouth sweet as honey and as soon as I had eaten it my belly was bitter. And he said unto me, Thou must prophesy again before many peoples, and nations, and tongues, and kings. "-(Rev. 10:7-11 .)

That very message of "the little book" is being proclaimed by the Voice of the

OUTER SPACE PEOPLE AND INNER EARTH PEOPLE

Seventh Angel in this very hour. This day is this scripture fulfilled in your ears. "O taste and see that the Lord is good." (Psalm 84:8.) "Ho, every one that thirsteth, come ye to the waters, and he that hath no money; come ye, buy, and eat; yea, come, buy wine and milk without money and without price. Wherefore do ye spend money for that which is not bread? and your labor for that which satisfieth not? hearken diligently unto me, and eat ye that which is good, and let your soul delight itself in fatness. Incline your ear, and come unto me: hear, and your soul shall live; and I will make an everlasting covenant with you, even the sure mercies of David. Behold, I have given him for a witness to the people, a leader and commander to the people. (Isa.55:1-4.)

5. The Sense Of Smell

That is probably the most highly developed and the least used sense in the human body. Every variety of roses, flowers, plants and trees has a fragrance peculiar to its own species. Every animal species has a different odor. There are more than two billion people on earth and each one has a different odor.

There are odors which excite men and tempt them to commit adultery, fornication, idolatry, witchcraft, hatred, murder, envy, fear, wrath, strife, drunkenness and which stir up in man every kind of sin and evil. There are also odors of death and the warning of death. I believe that every disease has a distinctive odor and I wonder why doctors have not diagnosed insanity, cancer, tuberculosis and other diseases by odor and vibration.

There is also a fragrance of love, joy, peace, long suffering, gentleness, goodness, faith, meekness, cleanness, purity, virtue, wisdom and knowledge. Every person, place and thing has a fragrance, or perhaps I should say that everything creates an odor peculiar to itself.

The sense of smell in ancient times was highly developed and used extensively in the Orient. The Bible has much to say about it. I would say that it indicates that every word spoken has not only a vibration but an odor that accompanies it.

The Hebrew tetragrammaton, YHVH, which is the consonants used in the Sacred Name of the Creator carry with them a most wonderful fragrance regardless of what vowels are supplied or how the name is pronounced. Some pronounce THE NAME "Yahway", others Yah-Ho-Vee. I spell it YAHVEH and pronounce it YAH-VEE. Here is a statement in the Song of Solomon which applies to the Sacred name: "Let him kiss me with the kisses of his mouth: for thy love is better than wine. Because of the Savor of thy good ointments thy name is as ointment poured forth, therefore do the virgins love thee. Draw me, we will run after thee: the King hath brought me into his chambers: we will be glad and rejoice in thee, we will remember thy love more than wine: the upright love thee. (Song of Solomon 1:2-4.)

In order to show you the emphasis that the Bible puts on this subject I shall read all of the fourth chapter of the Song of Solomon. "Behold, thou art fair, my love; behold, thou art fair; thou hast doves' eyes within thy locks: thy hair as a flock of goats, that appear from mount Gilead. Thy teeth are like a flock of sheep that are even shorn, which came up from the washing; whereof every one bear twins, and none is barren among them.

OUTER SPACE PEOPLE AND INNER EARTH PEOPLE

Thy lips are like a thread of scarlet, and thy speech is comely: thy temples are like a piece of pomegranate within thy locks. Thy neck is like the tower of David builded for an armory, whereon there hang a thousand bucklers, all shields of mighty men. Thy two breasts are like two young roes that are twins, which feed amonq the lilies. Until the day break, and the shadows flee away, I will get me to the mountain of myrrh, and to the hill of frankincense. Thou art all fair, my love; there is no spot in thee. Come with me from Lebanon, my spouse, come with me from Lebanon: look from the top of Amana, for the top of Shenir and Hermon, from the lions' dens, from the mountains of the leopards. Thou hast ravished my heart, my sister, my spouse; thou hast ravished my heart with one of thine eyes, with one chain of thy neck. How fair is thy love my sister, my spouse! how much better is thy love than wine! and the smell of thine ointments than all spices! Thy lips, O my spouse, drop as the honeycomb: honey and milk are under thy tongue; and the smell of thy garments is like the smell of Lebanon. A garden inclosed is my sister, my spouse; a spring shut up, a fountain sealed. Thy plants are an orchard of pomegranates, with pleasant fruits; camphire, with spikenard.

Spikenard and saffron; calamus and cinnamon, with all trees of frankincense; myrrh and aloes, with all the chief spices; A fountain of gardens, a well of living waters, and streams from Lebanon. Awake, O north wind; and come, thou south; blow upon my garden, that the spices thereof may flow out. Let my beloved come into his garden, and eat his pleasant fruits." (Song of Solomon 4: 1-16.)

"I am come into my garden, my sister, my spouse: I have gathered my myrrh with my spice; I have eaten my honeycomb with my honey; I have drunk my wine with my milk: eat, O friends; drink, yea, drink abundantly, O beloved." (Song of Solomon 5:1.)

"What is thy beloved more than another beloved, O thou fairest among women? what is thy beloved more than another beloved, that thou dost so charge us? My beloved is white and ruddy, the chiefest among ten thousand. His head is as the most fine gold, his locks are bushy, and black as a raven. His eyes are as the eyes of doves by the rivers of waters, washed with milk, and fitly set. His checks are as a bed of spices, as sweet flowers: his lips like lilies, dropping sweet smelling myrrh. His hands are as gold rings set with the beryl: his belly is as bright ivory overlaid with sapphires. His legs are as pillars of marble, set upon sockets of fine gold: his countenance is as Lebanon, excellent as the cedars. His mouth is most sweet: yea, he is altogether lovely, and this is my friend, O daughters of Jerusalem." (Song of Solomon 5 :9-16.)"Who is this that cometh out of the wilderness like pillars of smoke, perfumed with myrrh and frankincense, with all powders of the merchant?" (Song of Solomon 3:6.) "I rose up to open to my beloved; and my hands dropped with myrrh, and my fingers with sweet smelling myrrh, upon the handles of the lock." (Song of Solomon 5:5.) "He brought me to the banqueting house, and his banner over me was love. His left hand is under my head, and his right hand doth embrace me." (Song of Solomon 2:4,6.) "My spikenard sendeth forth the smell thereof. A bundle of myrrh is well-beloved unto me; he shall lie all night betwixt my breasts." (Song of Solomon 1: 12-13.)

All that I have read to you is in the Bible, in the book of the Song of Solomon, a book that is seldom read and upon which no emphasis has been placed in modern times,

OUTER SPACE PEOPLE AND INNER EARTH PEOPLE

But we need to rediscover and use the apothecary of the Bible. Prayer creates a beautiful fragrance. You can tell how much people pray by the way they smell.

The pot of incense in the tabernacle near the curtain of the Sanctum-Sanctorum, or Holies of Holies, with its sweet smelling fragrance was a symbol of prayer. Moses in the law gave specific instructions as to how the frankincense was to be prepared and used. The name of the Creator has the greatest of all fragrance about it.

Away back in Genesis when Noah built an altar unto Yahveh and offered up burnt offerings, Yahveh smelled a sweet savor and he said, I will not curse the ground any more, neither will I smite anymore every living thing. (Gen. 8:21.) There is not as much emphasis on the sense of smell and fragrance in the New Testament as there is in the Old, but there is enough to give us to understand that it had a vital place in their worship services and in their daily life. Two of the three gifts that the wise men presented to the child Jesus were frankincense and myrrh. (Matt.2:11). Therefore as a child he was anointed. Then in the days of his manhood we read this story:

"And one of the Pharisees desired him that he would eat with him. And he went into the Pharisee's house, and sat down to meat. And, behold, a woman in the city, which was a sinner, when she knew that Jesus sat at meat in the Pharisee's house, brought an alabaster box of ointment and stood at his feet behind him weeping, and began to wash his feet with tears, and did wipe them with the hairs of her head, and kissed his feet and anointed them with the ointment. And he turned to the woman, and said unto Simon, Seest thou this woman? I entered into thine house, thou gayest me no water for my feet: but she hath washed my feet with tears, and wiped them with the hairs of her head. Thou gayest me no kiss: but this woman, since the time I came in, hath not ceased to kiss my feet. My head with oil thou didst not anoint: but this woman hath anointed my feet with ointment. Wherefore I say unto thee, Her sins, which are many, are forgiven; for she loved much: but to whom little is forgiven, the same loveth little. And he said unto her, Thy sins are forgiven." (Luke 7:36-38, 44-48.)

At one of the last social events in the life of Jesus, just a few days before his crucifixion this took place. "Then Jesus six days before the passover came to Bethany, where Lazarus was which had been dead, whom he raised from the dead. There they made him a supper; and Martha served: but Lazarus was one of them that sat at the table with him. Then took Mary a pound of ointment of spikenard, very costly, and anointed the feet of Jesus, and wiped his feet with her hair: and the house was filled with the odor of the ointment. Then saith one of his disciples, Judas Iscariot, Simon's son, which would betray him, Why was not this ointment sold for three hundred pence, and given to the poor? This he said, not that he cared for the poor; but because he was a thief, and had the bag, and bare what was put therein. Then said Jesus, Let her alone against the day of my burying hath she kept this. For the poor always ye have with you; but me ye have not always." (John 12: 1-8.)

"She hath done what she could: she is come aforehand to annoint my body to the burying. Verily I say unto you, Wheresoever this gospel shall be preached throughout the whole world, this also that she hath done shall be spoken of for a memorial of her."

OUTER SPACE PEOPLE AND INNER EARTH PEOPLE

(Mark 14:8-9.)

Then after Jesus was dead "Joseph of Arimathea, being a disciple of Jesus, but secretly for fear of the Jews, besought Pilate that he might take away the body of Jesus: and Pilate gave him leave. He came therefore, and took the body of Jesus. And there came also Nicodemus, which at first came to Jesus by night, and brought a mixture of myrrh and aloes, about a hundred pound weight. Then took they the body of Jesus, and wound it in linen clothes, with the spices, as the manner of the Jews is to bury. Now in the place where he was crucified there was a garden; and in the garden a new sepulchre, wherein was never man yet laid. There laid they Jesus therefore because of the Jews preparation day; for the sepulchre was nigh at hand. (John 19:38-42.)

The women also, which came with Jesus from Galilee prepared spices and ointments and went with Joseph of Arimathea and Nicodemus as they carried the body of Jesus to the tomb. (Luke 23:55-56.)

Here is a story in which the Apostle Paul acknowledges a gift of perfume that was sent to him by the Philippians while he was in Rome: "Notwithstanding, ye have well done, that ye did communicate with my affliction. Now ye Philippians know also, that in the beginning of the gospel, when I departed from Macedonia, no church communicated with me as concerning giving and receiving, but ye only. For even in Thessalonica ye sent once and again unto my necessity. Not because I desire a gift: but I desire fruit that may abound to your account. But I have all, and abound: I am full, having received of Epaphroditus the things which were sent from you, an odor of a sweet smell, a sacrifice acceptable, well-pleasing to God. But my God shall supply all your need according to his riches in glory by Christ Jesus.(Phil.4:14-19.)

The one scripture that led me to make the final decision to wear white garments is this: While in prayer for guidance as to whether I should wear white, I opened the Bible and this was what I saw and read: "Go thy way, eat thy bread with joy, and drink thy wine with a merry heart; for God now accepteth thy works. Let thy garments be always white; and let thy head lack no ointment. Live joyfully with the wife whom thou lovest." (Eccl. 9:7-9.)

I am also sure that Yahveh has guided me in the preparation of this message. I thank Him and praise His name YAHVEH for the help that he has given to me and for choosing me to give this message which is His messaqe to YOU.

Conclusion

THE VOICE is a sixth sense. It definitely has an affinity with the reproductive organs. The throat or voice box has a close connection with the scrotum or sacral centers. The Spiritual children of the Heavenly Father who are the ELOHIM (Gods) were produced by the spoken word. "YAH" the Father spoke: the Mother executed the word. "For he spake and it was done; he commanded and it stood fast." (Psalm 33:9.) "And Yahveh said, and it was so." (Gen. 1:3, 7, etc)

When boys reach the age of puberty their voices change. The power of spoken words is one of the greatest things in the world. Faith is the creative substance out of

OUTER SPACE PEOPLE AND INNER EARTH PEOPLE

which all matter is created (Heb. 11;1), and the voice is the power that uses faith to create or to destroy or to multiply or diminish matter.

"He sent His word and healed them." (Psalm 107:20.) Jesus understood and freely used the power of voice, the spoken word. "For his word was with power." (Luke 4:32.) "And they were all amazed, and spake among themselves, saying, What a word is this, for with authority and power he commandeth the unclean spirits and they come out." (Luke 4:36.)

The Virgin Mary conceived the holy child Jesus when she heard the voice of Yahveh and when she said "Be it unto me according to thy word." (Luke 1:38.) The centurion who came to Jesus and asked him to heal his servant said, "But speak the word only, and my servant shall be healed." (Matt. 8:8.)

Jesus said, "The words that I speak unto you, they are spirit, and they are life." (John 6:63.) Yahveh and Light and Life are in the word, and by the word all things were made. (John 1:1-14.)

The words that a man speaks are the most important of all his actions: "For by thy words thou shalt be justified, and by thy words thou shalt be condemned." (Matt. 12:37.) The voice is definitely a sixth sense closely related to the reproductive organs, but more closely related to Yahveh than any other thing in man. Invariably criminals use the most vulgar and vile language. People who use pure language and are careful with their spoken words are never criminals. Vile language is sickening and nauseating and makes things described filthy and unclean. But pure language makes the things described pure and clean. "Unto the pure all things are pure: but unto them that are defiled and unbelieving is nothing pure; but even their mind and conscience is defiled." (Titus 1:15.)

The unclean, vile four letter words in the English language are being dropped and pure scientific and spiritual words are taking the place of the vile words. This is as it should be for Yahveh says, "For then I will turn to the people a pure language, that they may all call upon the name of Yahveh to serve him with one consent." (Zeph. 3:9.)

Babylon, the confusion of tongues, hundreds of different languages, is the greatest barrier to world friendship and peace that there is. The name YAHVEH is the pure name of Our Heavenly Father and belongs to the pure language that ultimately will be spoken by all men.

Again may I remind you that the voice, the spoken words, have the power to create or to destroy. There is a Voice that belongs to the INWARD MAN. It is a Divine Voice. Those far advanced in spiritual truth can at times hear the inner Voice speaking audible words.

Besides this sixth sense—the Voice, there are many other spiritual senses which relate to colors, clairvoyance, astral-projection, extra-sensory perception, past dimension—the things of the past, and the future dimension—the things of the future. All of these senses exist, but there are very few people that are conscious of them and even less who can use them.

OUTER SPACE PEOPLE AND INNER EARTH PEOPLE

YOU no doubt know the things that I have mentioned in this sermon. Therefore, I can only trust that what has been said will stir up your memory, and that the five spiritual senses of the INNER MAN will become keener, more alert and opened wider to the things of the spiritual world and that you will think more about your spoken words and choose them carefully, and more especially that you will see Yahshua the Messiah, hear his voice, feel his presence and enjoy a closer and more intimate fellowship with Him. May Yahveh Our Heavenly Father be with you always and bless YOU. Amen.

OUTER SPACE PEOPLE AND INNER EARTH PEOPLE

Chapter VIII

Our Past, Present and Future Life

Friends: Come and let us reason together. This lecture is addressed primarily to students of all ages. We are never too young to begin nor old enough to quit thinking, acquiring and applying knowledge. To those individuals who have a personality and a mind of their own, to those who are non-conformists and who think for themselves, I shall state my premise, upon which I shall develop the theme: "Our past, present and future life."

First of all: Everything that man makes is an image of his thoughts, regardless of what it is: a table, a chair, an automobile, or a house. Everything that man makes, whatever it is, is an image of man's thought. Thought implies a mind. Thoughts originate in a mind and proceed from a mind. Back of every material thing or object made by man is a thought. The thing itself is an image or an expression of that thought. This being true, it proves conclusively to me that the sun, moon, stars, and the earth are material images of the thoughts that originated in and proceeded from THE MIND of Our Father, The Creator, whose name is YAHVEH.

Secondly: Everything that grows, unfolds, and develops from a seed or sperm has life within itself. There is intelligent life in it or back of it that directs it. All vegetable and animal life is the unfolding from a seed or sperm and the enfolding of its own life and nature in a seed or sperm—the forever unfolding, enfolding and unfolding in a never-ending continuity of life.

These two statements are my premise. I cannot think nor reason in any other way. If there is another side or an opposite view, I would like to hear it.

Personally, I cannot believe that my mind, soul, and being originated when my physical body was born. Neither can I believe that the person that I AM will cease to be when the physical body dies. We existed before the body was born and we will exist after the body is dead. We continually say, "My body," my spirit", etc. The "I am" or that person that we call "MY" did not begin with physical life and will not end with physical death. But the big questions are: HOW or in what form did we exist before we were born

OUTER SPACE PEOPLE AND INNER EARTH PEOPLE

in the flesh? Why were we born in the flesh? Who am I? Where did I come from? Why am I here? Where am I going from here? To know ourselves, and to know our destiny is by far the most important and essential thing that we can learn in our present life in the flesh.

In my message in the May, 1961 issue of *"Showers of Blessing"*, I said: CORPOREANS are those of us living in corporeal bodies on this earth. ETHERIANS are one of the orders of people in outer-space and some of the people of the inner earth who once lived on this earth but are now what the Bible calls: ."The spirits of just man made perfect." (Heb. 12:22-24.) When they descend into the earth's atmosphere their bodies materialize and they appear on earth just like the earth people.

IMMORTALS are those in the higher orders of glory. When they appear on earth, they are bright and shining beings. They may even appear as fire—the children of the flame. "Yahveh maketh his angels spirits and his ministers a flame of fire." (Heb. 1:1.) "Are they not all ministering spirits, sent forth to minister for them who shall be heirs of salvation?" (Heb. 1:14.)

ATMOSPHERIANS are what the Bible calls "demons" (devils). They are disembodied spirits. They were a race of people that lived on this earth in a previous creation. When the earth was disrupted (Gen. 1:1-2) "waste and void", their bodies died, but they survived as disembodied spirits. They are earth-bound, inhabiting the atmosphere. They seek to obsess and possess people. They are the cause of what is known as split personalities and also the cause of much insanity.

UNBORN. These are the souls that are destined yet to be born on the earth. They may be conscious in their present state or they may be dormant, enfolded in a seed (sperm). A body begins to develop for them at the time of conception. The human body formed for them is in the image of the heavenly body that those souls had before they were destined to be born on the earth. Some say that we chose the time and place of our birth and the age in which we wished to live on the earth.

There can be no doubt in the mind of any person who believes the Bible that Yahshua the Messiah (Jesus Christ) pre-existed before he was made flesh. That truth is definitely clear. Abraham lived 2,000 years before Jesus Christ was born in the flesh, yet Christ said to those who were questioning him: "Abraham rejoiced to see my day: and he saw it, and was glad. Then said the Jews unto him, Thou art not yet fifty years old, and hast thou seen Abraham? Jesus said unto them, Verily, verily, I say unto you, Before Abraham was, I am. Then took they up stones to cast at him: but Jesus hid himself and went out of the temple, going through the midst of them, and so passed by." (John 8:56-59.) Incidentally, he proved his statement by becoming invisible for the moment and by changing his appearance. A fact that has been overlooked in the study of the scriptures.

How, or in what manner did Abraham see him? He appeared to Abraham as Melchizedek, the king of Righteousness, King of peace, and gave to Abraham bread and wine, which he declared was the material elements of his body which would continue forever in the earth. (Gen. 14:18-20, Ps. 1 10:1-7.) That is why, five hundred years later, Moses and the Israelites put the shrewbread and cup of wine in the outer sanctuary of

OUTER SPACE PEOPLE AND INNER EARTH PEOPLE

the tabernacle. This was prepared every week and eaten by the priests on every week day Sabbath for 1500 years before Jesus Christ was born in the flesh. (Lev. 24:5-9, 1 Chron. 9:32.) Then, while Christ was on the earth in the flesh, he declared that the bread "and wine was, is, and always will be his body and his blood. (Matt 26: 26-28, John 6:30-71.) That is why the New Testament plainly teaches that the bread and the wine is the body and the blood of Christ and for this reason the early Church observed the Lord's Supper on every first day of the week. (Acts 2:42, Acts 20:7, 1Cor. 11:18-34.)

MY FRIENDS, I HOPE AND PRAY THAT YOU WILL CHECK UP ON EVERYTHING THAT I SAY BY LOOKING UP AND READING EVERY SCRIPTURE REFERENCE IN YOUR OWN BIBLE. Prove all things: hold fast to that which is good; search the Bible daily to see if what I say is true. Piease do that! When Abraham received the bread and wine from Melchizedek, he also paid tithes (ten per cent) to Melchizedek. (Gen. 14:20.) The early church also paid tithes (ten per cent) of their income on the first day of every week. (I Cor. 9:14, I Cor. 16:2, Malachi 3:8-18.)

In and through the Spirit water and blood (I John 5:8), Jesus Christ still witnesses in the earth. He also, as Melchizedek, lives forever in the heavens to receive our tithes. (Heb. 7:8.)

We see clearly that Jesus Christ, in the days of Abraham, was "Melchizedek". There is no doubt that he appeared many times as a different person, under a different name, before he was born in the flesh. He was known by Ezekiel as "the Son of man." He appeared in the fiery furnace as "the son of God." (Dan. 3:25.) Since the names of Joshua, Isaiah, Hosea, Jeremiah, Elijah and some other personal names of men in the Bible are the very same identical name as "Yahveh-Savior" which is the name of the man "YAHSHUA" whom we call Jesus, therefore, he may have been each and every one of those men. At any rate we know that He pre-existed. In His last prayer while with his disciples on earth, He prayed: "O Father, glorify me with thine own self with the glory which I had with thee before the world was." (John 17:5.) He was a perfect Spirit Being before the world was created. He came to earth in the flesh, completed His work in the flesh, and He is now a perfect Spirit Being just as he was or had been before the world was created.

He was not the only Son of Yahveh. The truth is that he came to earth in the flesh to redeem his brothers, the sons of Yahveh, and to bring them all back to the glory that they had enjoyed before the world was created. "But we see Jesus, who was made a little lower than the angels for the suffering of death, crowned with glory and honor; that he by the grace of God should taste death for every man. For it became him, for whom are all things, and by whom are all things, in bringing many sons unto glory, to make the captain of their salvation perfect through sufferings. For both he that sanctifieth and they who are sanctified are all of one: for which cause he is not ashamed to call them brethren. Saying, I will declare thy name unto my brethren, in the midst of the church will I sing praise unto thee. And again, I will put my trust in him. And again, Behold I and the children which God hath given me. Forasmuch then as the children are partakers of flesh and blood, he also himself likewise took part of the same; that through death he might destroy him that had the power of death, that is, the devil; And deliver them, who through

OUTER SPACE PEOPLE AND INNER EARTH PEOPLE

fear of death were all their lifetime subject to bondage. For verily he took not on him the nature of angels; but he took on him the seed of Abraham. Wherefore in all things it behooved him to be made like unto his brethren, that he might be a merciful and faithful high priest in things pertaining to God, to make reconciliation for the sins of the people."- (Heb. 2:9-17)

We are declared to be "members of his body, of his flesh, and of his bones." (Eph. 5:30.) We are destined to "grow up into him in all things, which is the head, even Christ. (Eph. 4: 15) "unto a perfect man, unto the measure of the stature of the fullness of Christ." (Eph. 4:13.) The mystery is "CHRIST IN YOU" (Col. 1:27), and that "We are the children of God" (Rom. 8: 16), and "heirs of God, and joint heirs with Christ." (Rom. 8 :17.) This means that we are his brothers and that we share equally with him and "we shall be like him." (1 John 3:2.) In our eternal progression, the ultimate goal is GODHOOD. Each one of us will be a Christ, a perfect Spirit Being, having the same glory that we had before the world was created. (Incidentally I have proved by the scriptures that we also pre-existed, but I shall offer more proof.)

To all who believe the Bible, I shall now offer irrefutable evidence beyond all controversy that we pre-existed, The word or title "GOD" is found in the Old Testament more than 5,000 times. In the original Hebrew the word is "ELOHIM" and it is plural. Therefore, in every place where the word "GOD" is found in the Old Testament it means, "The family of the Heavenly Father." It includes all of the Spiritual sons and daughters of the Heavenly Father. This is clearly evident from this scripture: "And God said, Let us make man in our image, after our likeness." (Gen. 1:26.) Now "US" and "OUR" are plural. That needs no argument. The context that follows is that "male and female created he them." (Gen. 1:27.) "Male in the image of a Heavenly Spiritual Son; "Female" in the image of a Heavenly Spiritual daughter.

It was the ELOHIM (GOD), that is, the sons and daughters of the Heavenly Father who created the world. The "male" and "female" that were created in Genesis 1:25-27 were natural men of the earth, earthy. That is, merely IMAGES that were of the earth and that stood at the head of the animal kingdom and were placed over the material earth. They were never destined to become Spiritual Sons of the Heavenly Father. They were only images of the Heavenly Father. They have earthly promises but do not share in the Heavenly promises. "The natural man receiveth not the things of the Spirit of God." I Cor. 2: 14.) But he receives the natural things.

After the perfect mineral, vegetable and animal kingdoms and natural men were created, then the Sons and Daughters of the Heavenly Father, the ELOHIM GOD, who had finished the work of creation, RESTED. That simply means that their work of creation had been completed. How long the period of REST lasted between the perfectly created natural world and the beginning of the Spiritual race of Adam on this earth, we do not know. It could have been a very long period of time—millions or even billions of years. We do not know. But anyway when the creation was finished, "the morning stars sang together, and all the sons of God (the ELOHIM) shouted for joy" (Job 38:7) over their finished work of creation.

OUTER SPACE PEOPLE AND INNER EARTH PEOPLE

Then the Heavenly Father called a council in Heaven. All of his Sons and Daughters were present and he told them that they would have to give up their Heavenly glory, be reverted to a seed—that is, enfolded in a sperm—and be born in a body of flesh and blood on the earth. Yahshua the Messiah, Our Elder Brother and the Prince of Glory, volunteered to be made flesh. All the rest of us who are the Sons and Daughters of Yahveh rebelled against that idea. We did not like it at all. We did not want to come here and be made flesh. "For the creature was made subject to vanity, not willingly, but by reason of him who hath subjected the same in hope." (Rom. 8:20.) "We have this treasure in earthen vessels, that the excellency of the power may be of God, and not of us." (II Cor. 4:7.)

The big questions. First: Were we all the Sons and Daughters of the Heavenly Father reverted to "seed" and each enfolded in a seed at that time, to remain dormant until we were born in the flesh?, or, Second: Did we remain in the realm of this earth as INBORN souls until our birth in the flesh?, or, Third; Have we lived in many different physical bodies on this earth?"

Regardless of what view we take of this matter, it is evident that when we were enfolded in a seed (sperm) all remembrance of our previous existence was taken away, for the Bible says, "There is no remembrance of former things; neither shall there be any remembrance of things that are to come with those that shall come after." (Eccl. 1:11) If we have been reborn again and again, every time that we have been enfolded in a seed "there is no remembrance of former things." The Bible seems to in dictate that we have lived in different human bodies in the past for it says: "The thing that hath been, it is that which shall be; and that which is done is that which shall be done; and there is no new thing under the sun." (Eccl. 1:9.) "That which hath been is now; and that which is to be hath already been, and God requireth that which is past." (Eccl. 3:15.)

There is one thing for sure: We know that we pre-existed and that we were (and are) the Sons of Yahveh that created this world. "The Lord possessed me in the beginning of his way, before his works of old. I was set up for everlasting, from the beginning, or ever the earth was. When there were no depths, I was brought forth; when there were no foundations abounding with water. Before the mountains were settled, before the hills was I brought forth: While as yet he had not made the earth, nor the field, nor the highest part of the dust of the world, When he prepared the heavens, I was there: when he set a compass upon the face of the depth: When he established the clouds above: when he strengthened the fountains of the deep: When he gave to the sea his decree, that the waters should not pass his commandment: when he appointed the foundations of the earth: Then I was by him, as one brought up with him: and I was daily his delight rejoicing always before him; Rejoicing in the habitable part of his earth; and my delights were with the sons of men." (Prov. 8:22-31.)

Adam was the Son of God. (Luke 3:38.) Adam was the first son of God that came in the flesh as a man on this earth. YAHVEH the Heavenly Father in person did not create Adam, but he FORMED a body for him, "And the Lord God (Yahveh-Elohim) formed man of the dust of the ground, and breathed into his nostrils the breath of life; and man became a living soul." (Gen. 2:7.) Adam was the first Spirit Being, the first Soul, the first Son of the Heavenly Father to live in a human body on this earth. Adam and his descendants

OUTER SPACE PEOPLE AND INNER EARTH PEOPLE

are not to be confused with the natural "image" race of earthy men in the first chapter of Genesis.

Adam was the offspring of YAHVEH. Adam was a Heavenly Son. Indeed he may have been the very person who was later known as Jesus Christ. I say this because the Messiah said; "I am Alpha and Omega, the beginning and the ending, saith the Lord, which is, and which was, and which is to come, the Almighty." Rev. 1:8), "the first and the last" (Rev. 2:8). "The first Adam was made a living soul; the last Adam was made a quickening Spirit." (I Cor. 15:45.)

A question please: Was all the "SEED" which would form human bodies on the earth for all of the Sons of God in Adam? Has that same "SEED" been passed on and carried down in the bodies of Adam's descendants until the present time? And when does a Son or Daughter of Yahveh enter and enfold in that "SEED" which is to become His or Her body? I raise these questions because the Bible says: "Levi also, who receiveth tithes, paid tithes in Abraham. For he was yet in the loins of his father, when Melchizedek met him." (Heb. 7:9-10.) Five hundred years before he was born, Levi was a seed (sperm) in Abraham and is credited with the tithes and good works of Abraham.

WE HAVE AN INHERITANCE. In one sense of the word we have lived in every person before us. We lived in Adam and by an unbroken continuity of life in every ancestor, until that "SEED" formed our body, the body in which we now live. There are many different kinds of "SEED". That one little word "SEED" is the key to creation and to the understanding of the entire Bible.

The first mention of "Seed" is in Genesis 1:11-12. "And God (the ELOHIM) said, Let the earth bring forth grass, the herb yielding seed, and the fruit tree yielding fruit after his kind, whose seed is in itself, upon the earth: and it was so. And the earth brought forth grass, and herb yielding seed after his kind, and the tree yielding fruit, whose seed was in itself, after his kind: and God (the ELOHIM) saw that it was good." (Gen. 1:11-12.)

This proves conclusively that the "seed" was in the earth, probably from a previous creation before "the earth without form or void," that is, before the earth was disrupted and became chaotic as stated in Genesis 1:2.

The whole world is a seed bed. Turn water on any arid desert and immediately "seed" will germinate there and the desert will become covered with vegetation. "Seed" may be dormant for thousands of years and then come to life. This has been proven by "seed" found in the pyramids and Egyptian tombs which has germinated after being dormant for 4,000 years. The Bible also indicates that the sperm of marine life was also in the waters: "And God (the ELOHIM) said, Let the waters bring forth abundantly the moving creature that hath life, and fowl that may fly above the earth in the open firmament of heaven." (Gen. 1:20.)

Again the Bible indicates that the sperm of animal life was also in the earth: "And God (the ELOHIM) said, Let the earth bring forth the living creature after his kind, cattle, and creeping thing, and beast of the earth after his kind and it was so." (Gen. 1:24.) This gives us a new idea—that plants, fish, birds, and animals were created by commanding

OUTER SPACE PEOPLE AND INNER EARTH PEOPLE

the "seed" to germinate and the sperm to develop. There is also a more profound development of this idea. It is that there is a world within a world, an invisible and visible world occupying the very same space, like the world of magnetism - and the world of steel that occupy the same space. The Lord God made "every plant of the field before it was in the earth, and every herb before it grew." (Gen. 2:5.)

These existed before any rain fell upon the earth. Therefore there must be trees and plants, fish, birds, and animals in the unseen, magnetic world, all of which must have shed their seed in which each had enfolded itself in the earth, where, in due time, it was unfolded in the material image of the invisible counterpart of itself, "For the things which are seen are temporal; but the things which are not seen are eternal." (II Cor.4:18.) Nothing whatsoever can exist in the natural, visible world which does not first exist in the Spiritual realm or in the mind or in the invisible magnetic world. For earthly things are emblems of invisible things. Material things represent invisible things and therefore teach the eternal power and Godhead of Yahveh Our Father.

The Bible, in the very strongest terms, prohibits the mixing of the seed. "Thou shalt not let thy cattie gender with a diverse kind: THOU SHALT NOT SOW THY FIELD WITH MINGLED SEED." (Lev. 19:19.) What is the primary meaning of this? It is explained in the foliowing parable: A parable put he forth unto them, saying, The kingdom of heaven is likened unto a man which sowed good seed in his field: But while men slept, his enemy came and sowed tares among the wheat and went his way. But when the blade was sprung up, and brought forth fruit, then appeared the tares also. So the servants of the householder came and said unto him, Sir didst not thou sow good seed in thy field? from whence then hath it tares? He said unto them, An enemy hath done this. The servants said unto him, Wilt thou then that we go and gather them up? But he said, Nay; lest while ye gather up the tares, ye root up also the wheat with them. Let both grrow together until the harvest: and in the time of harvest I will say to the reapers, Gather ye together first the tares, and bind them in bundles to burn them: but gather the wheat in my barn. Then Jesus sent the multitude away, and went into the house: and his discipies came unto him, saying, Declare unto us the parable of the tares of the field, He answered and said unto them, He that soweth the good seed is the Son of man; The field is the world; the good seed are the children of the kingdom; but the tares are the children of the wicked one; The enemy that sowed them is the devil; the harvest is the end of the world; and the reapers are the angels. As therefore the tares are gathered and burned in the fire; so shall it be in the end of the world. The Son of man shall send forth his angels, and they shall gather out of his kingdom ail things that offend, and them which do iniquity."- (Matt. 13:24-30,36-41)

A woman is the only seedbed of man. Eve was the field in this parable, a "garden enclosed is my sister, my spouse; a spring shut up, a fountain sealed." (Song of Solomon 4:12.) Our women are "a fountain of gardens, a well of living waters" (Song of Solomon 4:15.) Adam was the tree of lives. In him was "the good seed." He was "as the lily among thorns," "as the apple tree among the trees of the wood, so is my beloved among the sons." (Song of Solomon 2:2-3.)

Satan, the devil, tries to do three things. FIRST, he tries to mix the seed. SECOND, he tries to substitute for the true seed. THIRD, he tries to kill the good seed. The battle of

OUTER SPACE PEOPLE AND INNER EARTH PEOPLE

seed lines begins with this verse in Genesis when Yahveh said to "the serpent" man, "And I will put enmity between thee and the woman, and between thy seed and her seed: it shall bruise thy head, and thou shalt bruise his heel." (Gen. 8:15.)

The transgression of Eve was that she received the blood of "the serpent" man into her own pure blood stream. Adam also entered into the transgression. The blood stream of Adam and Eve was adulterated with the blood of "the serpent" race. "The life of the flesh is in the blood." (Lev. 17:11.)

"The life of ALL flesh" is in the blood. (Lev. 17:14.) The blood literally and physically manufactures the ovum (seed) of the woman and the sperm of the man. When the blood is mixed, the result will be mixed seed. In the same person, there may be some seed of different races and colors. Cain was the product of the poisoned or evil seed which the serpent (adulterated) blood has produced in Adam and Eve.

Adultery is the mixing of racial blood. "Cain was of that wicked one" (I John 3:12), born to Adam and Eve, yes, but not related to them because he was of a foreign seed that had been developed in them by the serpent blood. The Apocrypha says, "For a grain of evil seed hath been sown in the heart of Adam from the beginning, and how much ungodliness hath it brought up unto this time? and how much shall it yet bring forth until the time of the threshing." (II Esdras 4:20)

I say without hesitation that the mixing of the seed of the races has destroyed every great civilization in the past. Only one thing can destroy both the white and the black races and that is the mixing of the blood and seed of these races. The mixing of the blood and seed with that of "the serpent" race is even more dangerous. The Apocrypha says again: "As for the children of adulterers, they shall not come to perfection." (Wisdom of Solomon 3: 16.) "The multiplying brood of the ungodly shall not thrive, nor take deep rooting from bastard slips, nor lay any fast foundation." (Wisdom of Solomon 4:3.) Bastard slips are like "darnel" in a wheat field or "suckers" on a stalk of corn. They are in it and a part of it and yet different nature. No civilization and not one nation of any importance has ever been built by a mixed race. Every revival of civilization in the history of the world has come immediately after a race purified itself.

In the days of Ezra, he said: "The holy seed have mingled themselves with the people of these lands." (Canaanites, Hittites, Amalakites, Philistines, etc.) (Ezra 9:2.) Therefore, Israel could not succeed and they were not blessed by Yahveh until the strange wives and strange husbands were put away and the race mixing stopped.

All races are to be kept pure. The Bible forbids race mixing because it is destructive to all of the races. It is adultery. The whole matter hinges on the one word: "SEED". Mixed seed undoubtedly has often resulted in deformed children, idiots, mongoloids, which are "witnesses of wickedness against their parents in their trial" (Wis. of Solomon 4:6), or their grandparents or their great grandparents many generations back, for the sins (adulteries) of the parents are visited upon the children unto the third and fourth generations, even unto the tenth generation. The first generation of a mixed race may be very healthy, but the second and third generation is apt to be sickly and sterile. That is proven with all of your hybrid corn and fruits of all kinds—even though the grain and

OUTER SPACE PEOPLE AND INNER EARTH PEOPLE

fruit is wonderful as a hybrid, yet if you try to grow it from its own mixed seed, the result will be the most sickly and degenerate of plants. The very same rule applies to animals and to men.

Even in the case of Isaac and Rebekah an evil seed cropped out. Jacob and Esau were twins, yet they were of two entirely different races. (Gen. 25: 19-28.) What Jesus said to Nathaniel cannot be said to very many people today: "Behold, an Israelite indeed, in whom is no guile."(John 1:47.) He was a pure Israelite. There was no "serpent" blood or adulteration in him.

Satan, that old serpent, tried to substitute Cain for Abel. Not being able to substitute, he then killed the true seed, Abel. "And Adam lived a hundred and thirty years, AND BEGAT A SON IN HIS OWN LIKENESS, AFTER HIS IMAGE, and called his name Seth." (Gen. 5:3)

"Eve bare a son, and called his name Seth: for God, said she, hath appointed me another seed instead of Abel, whom Cain slew." (Gen. 4 :25.)

Satan, the Serpent, tried to substitute Ishmael for Isaac, Esau for Jacob, Onan for Pharez. (Gen. 38:120.) Through all the history of mankind, the Devil has tried to mix the seed, or has tried to substitute; that is, counterfeit "the good seed", or he has tried to kill "the good seed". At one time that wicked woman, Athaliah; killed all of the seed royal except one whose name was Joash. (II Kings 11:2.) She would have killed him, too, if Jehosheba had not stolen him away and hidden him.

Yes, the key word of the Bible is "SEED". Let us try to understand how that Yahshua the Messiah came to this earth to be born of a woman. YAHVEH-ELOHIM (the Lord God) is the Heavenly Father. KHAVEH-ELOHIM (the Holy Ghost) is the Heavenly Mother. All of the Heavenly Sons and Daughters, the whole Spiritual family are called ELOHIM (GOD).

The Holy Ghost which is KHAVEH the Heavenly Mother, came upon the Virgin Mary and for the moment completely indwelt Mary. The Holy Ghost having conceived the SEED sperm of YAHVEH, placed the ovum of the Holy Ghost and the sperm of Yahveh in the womb of Mary. From that pure SEED, Yahveh formed the pure, incorruptible body of His Son (Heb. 10:5) in the womb of Mary. Thus the second and last Adam was born without sin—that is, without "guile" and without being subject to corruption. Not a drop of Mary's blood ever circulated through the body of Christ in her womb. His body was formed from the ovum of the Heavenly woman, the Holy Ghost and from the sperm of Yahveh, the Heavenly Father. He was the second Adam and the last Adam, the Elder Brother and Head of the (ELOHIM) Sons of God.

When he was baptized and anointed with the Spirit, he became conscious of His pre-existence as the Prince of Glory. He remembered every person and form in which he had previously existed. He recognized also his brothers living in the world whom he had known in glory before the world was created, for it was these that he had come to earth to redeem and to bring back to glory as perfect Spirit Beings.

So far the complete fullness of the Godhead bodily has dwelt only in one person on the earth and that was Yahshua the Messiah (Jesus Christ), but in our eternal progres-

OUTER SPACE PEOPLE AND INNER EARTH PEOPLE

sion, ultimately all of that fullness will dwell in every Son and Daughter of Yahveh, for ELOHIM is the family name of Yahveh and we are the ELOHIM, His family.

Now I do not say that all of the descendants of Adam are heavenly sons of Yahveh that pre-existed as perfect Spirit Beings in heaven before the world was created, for the seed of Adam has become terribly mixed. Neither do I say that all of the descendants of Abraham are Heavenly Sons and Daughters that pre-existed in heaven, for promises were made to "THE SAND SEED" and to "THE STAR SEED" of Abraham. The promises to the "sand seed" are to his earthly children who have lived, who do live, and who will live again on this earth. They are literal and the promises to them are earthly and literal. But the promises to the "star seed" are to the heavenly children who are the sons of God in "the high calling", and I do say that there is "a remnant" of the Heavenly Sons and daughters now on this earth who pre-existed in heaven before the world was created. I think that the scriptures are clear on this : "Now to Abraham and his seed were the promises made. He saith not unto SEEDS, as of many; but as of one, and to thy SEED, which is Christ." (Gal. 3:16.)

To all of those who have "put on Christ": There is neither Jew nor Greek, there is neither bond nor free, there is neither male nor female: for ye are all one in Christ Jesus. And if ye be Christ's, then are ye Abraham's seed, and heirs according to the promise." (Gal. 3:27-29)

We must understand that there are orders and degrees even in the Heavenly Family. The Bible says, "Every man in his own order" (I Cor. 15:23), Christ the FIRSTFRUITS. (A plural body.) The orders are in metaphorical language. (1) The SUN, (2) The MOON, (3) The STARS, (each with a different degree of glory). Then the lesser earthly orders of: (4) Men, (5) Beasts, (6) Fishes, (7) Birds. All seven of these orders are men—three of them are Heavenly orders, four of them are earthly orders. (See I Corinthians 15:28-41)

We become conscious of having pre-existed and we know for sure that we are a Son or a Daughter of Yahveh when we receive "THE INCORRUPTIBLE SEED" (I Peter 1:23) or more especially when that dormant "seed" springs to life and begins to grow in us. We are very much conscious of that INVISIBLE INNER MAN in us. The Holy Ghost witnesses with that "inner man". Yahveh speaks to that "inner man". There is no mistake about it—WE KNOW! The Invisible Inward man is INCORRUPTIBLE because he (or she) develops from the INCORRUPTIBLE SEED. That is the seed now in us in which, as a Son of God in heaven, we were enfolded. That seed is now unfolding and we are growing up into a Christ. I cannot keep from saying HALLELUJAH, which means: PRAISE YAHVEH. We are just as secure as if we were already in heaven. There is no mistake about it. "Whosoever is born of God doth not commit sin; for his seed remaineth in him: and he cannot sin, because he is born of God. In this the children of God are manifest." (I John 3:9-10.)

That "INNER MAN", which is the real "I AM", which is the person we call "MY", which is the Son of God, which we are, cannot sin; and what the whole world is waiting for is "THE MANIFESTATION OF THE SONS OF GOD." (Rom. 8:19.) The birth pangs have begun and this groaning and travailing will very soon make the Sons of God known to

OUTER SPACE PEOPLE AND INNER EARTH PEOPLE

the world.

Let me now describe the seven orders.

THE IMMORTALS are Yahveh, the Heavenly Father; Kahveh, the Heavenly Mother (The Holy Ghost); Yahshua the Messiah, the first begotten Son of the Father; and all of the children who are the offspring of Yahveh, all of whom pre-existed and were with Him in heaven before the world was created. These children, THE ELOHIM, created the world. In due time, one by one, they have been born in the flesh on this earth in the race of Adam and they are primarily of the seed of Abraham according to the flesh. Every one of them has in him (or her) the INCORRUPTIBLE seed (1 Peter 1:23) and the gift of Yahveh, which is "ETERNAL LIFE." (Rom. 6:23.) The Savior said that they shall never perish, "SHALL NEVER DIE." (John 11:26, John 3:16, John 5:24, John 10:28.) It is true that the "earthen vessel" (II Cor. 4:7) which is the mortal body in which we now live will die or be "DISSOLVED" (II Cor. 5:1) and returned to the dust and ashes or elements from whence it came, but in the very second that the mortal body dies, "in a moment in a twinkling of an eye", we do not find ourselves without a body.

We are not naked spirits, not disembodied spirits, "but clothed upon" (II Cor. 5:4) with the very same heavenly IMMORTAL body that we had in heaven before the world was created. We are passed from death to life. (John 5:24.) Since we "never die" the first death, it would therefore be impossible for us to die "the second death". The Bible says that the "second death" has no power over us. The very moment that we are absent from the mortal body, we are "present with the Lord" (II Cor. 5:8) in our immortal body. We pass into the "ETERNAL, IMMORTAL, INVISIBLE" (I Tim. 1:17) body of Christ where we share the "honor and glory for ever and ever, eternally with Him."

"These are they which follow the Lamb, whithersoever he goeth. These were redeemed from among men, being the firstfruits unto God and to the Lamb." (Rev. 14:4.) "Christ" is not just one person. CHRIST IS A PLURAL BODY. "We are members of his body." (Eph. 5:30.) YAHSHUA (Jesus) is THE CHRIST, which means "the anointed one." He is our Elder Brother, Savior and Redeemer, "the head of the body", but each one of us is an "anointed one" and all the ELOHIM (sons and daughters) collectively are THE CHRIST BODY. Most of the Christ Body has passed through the flesh and are now in heaven. There are some "unborn" that are yet to be born. Those of us, "a little flock", in the "high calling", who are now living in the flesh on the earth are "the FEET CLASS of His Body standing upon the earth."

There are three orders of the IMMORTALS, described in figurative language as follows:

1. "THE SUN" (I Cor. 15:41.) This order of IMMORTALS are the kings, priests, judges—in other words the EXECUTIVE BODY whose home is in the inner sanctuary, which is the throne room with Yahveh in the highest heaven.

2. "THE MOON" (I Cor. 15:41.) This order of IMMORTALS are those in "the third heaven" (II Cor. 12:2) or who will be in the third heaven. They can travel to this earth, materialize their bodies, appear to us in person. They are in a midway place. They are a

OUTER SPACE PEOPLE AND INNER EARTH PEOPLE

link between heaven and earth. They receive messages from Yahveh in the highest heaven and relay them to us. They receive messages from us and relay them to the saints in the highest heaven. They are a receiving and a relaying station between heaven and earth. They will be the chief directors whose voices will be heard in the earth, the guides to the men on the earth who establish the thousand years reign of righteousness, the Kingdom, the millennium.

3. "THE STARS."(I Cor. 15:41.) This is the third and last order of the IMMORTALS, "and another glory of stars: for one star differeth from another star in glory: so also is the resurrection." The STAR order are a selected remnant out of each one of the twelve tribes of Israel. Undoubtediy they will reign over the twelve inhabited planets in this solar system—the Earth, Mars, Venus, Jupiter, Saturn, Neptune, etc., and probably over many of the other inhabited worlds in outer-space. The "SUN" and "the MOON" and "the STARS" are the symbolic names of the Three Divine orders. (See I Corinthians 15:22-23, 39-42.)

There are FOUR lesser orders into which all natural men who are not in the IMMORTAL class are classified. We shall discuss them as follows: "MEN" (I Cor. 15:39.) These men are not in the race of Adam but they are descendants of the natural created man in Genesis 1:26. They have in them a seed of "EVERLASTING LIFE", but "everlasting" does not mean immortal or eternal. Everlasting means "age long," "from everlasting to everlasting" which means one age, era, epoch after another on this earth. The natural men die. They sleep in death until they are awakened by resurrection to begin life again in another age everlasting.

The ground or dust of this earth is filled with those souls asleep in the dust. They have died the first death. They are asleep. But they will be awakened, not to eternal immortality, but to "everlasting life" which means to live in that particular age. When they are awakened, they will have conditional life. "Many of them that sleep in the dust of the earth shall awake, some to everlasting life (age long life), and some to shame and everlasting contempt." (Dan. 12.2.) It is clear in the Bible that they may live through the entire thousand years of that age, but having been raised from the dead, set in their own family, in their own nation, in their own race, in their own allotted land area, if they then continue to be obstinate; sinful and incorrigible, then after one hundred years of life (Isa. 65:20), they will die the "second death", in which they will again sleep in death until they are awakened to the judgment in the lake of fire.

There is a very interesting thing that I want to say about the souls that are asleep in the dust. By a certain vibration, we may receive messages from them, even their forms may be reproduced momentarily and their voices heard. In the fourth chapter of Genesis Yahveh said to Cain: "The voice of thy brother's blood crieth unto me from the ground." (Gen. 4:10.) The prophet Isaiah says, "And thou shalt be brought down, and shall speak out of the ground, and thy speech shall be low out of the dust and thy voice shall be as one that hath a familiar spirit, out of the ground, and thy speech shall whisper out of the dust." (Isa. 29:4.) Conjuration, that is contacting and producing the images and voices of the dead out of the dust is emphaticaliy forbidden in the Bible. It is Satanic and is what is known as "spiritism" which is sometimes wrongfully called "Spiritualism." We have one case, as an example, in the Bible. Here it is: "Then said Saul unto his servants,

OUTER SPACE PEOPLE AND INNER EARTH PEOPLE

Seek me a woman that hath a familiar spirit that I may go to her, and inquire of her. And his servants said to him, Behold, there is a woman that hath a familiar spirit at Endor. And Saul disguised himself, and put on other raiment and he went and two men with him, and they came to the woman by night and he said, I pray thee, divine unto me by the familiar spirit, and bring me him up, whom I shall name unto thee. And the woman said unto him, Behold, thou knowest what Saul hath done, how he hath cut off those that have familiar spirits, and the wizards, out of the land: wherefore then layest thou a snare for my life, to cause me to die? And Saul sware to her by the Lord, saying, As the Lord liveth, there shall no punishment happen to thee for this thing. Then said the woman, Whom shall I bring up unto thee? And he said, Bring me up Samuel. And when the woman saw Samuel, she cried with a loud voice: and the woman spake to Saul, saying, Why hast thou deceived me? for thou art Saul. And the king said unto her, Be not afraid: for what sawest thou? And the woman said unto Saul, I saw gods ascending out of the earth. And he said unto her, What form is he of? And she said, An old man cometh up; and he is covered with a mantle. And Saul perceived that it was Samuel, and he stooped with his face to the ground, and bowed himseif. And Samuel said to Saul, Why hast thou disquieted me, to bring me up? And Saul answered, I am sore ,distressed ; for the Philistines make war against me, and God is departed from me, and answereth me no more, neither by prophets; nor by dreams: therefore, I have called thee, that thou mayest make known unto me what I shall do. Then said Samuel, Wherefore then dost thou ask of me, seeing the Lord is departed from thee, and is become thine enemy? And the Lord hath done to him, as he spake by me: for the Lord hath rent the kingdom out of thine hand and given it to thy neighbor, even to David, because thou obeyedst not the voice of the Lord, nor executedst his fierce wrath upon Amalek, therefore hath the Lord done this thing unto thee this day. Moreover the Lord will also deliver Israel with thee into the hands of the Philistines and tomorrow shalt thou and thy sons be with me: the Lord also shall deliver the host of Israel into the hand of the Philistines. Then Saul fell straightway all along on the earth, and was sore afraid, because of the words of Samuel; and there was no strength in him; for he had eaten no bread all the day, nor all the night." (I Sam 1:28:7-20.)

Let the dead alone! I mean those souls that are asleep in the dust. But this does not apply to "THE SAINTS" who are "THE IMMORTALS" in the three Divine orders, for there is a true communion of saints". They are, of course, those that never died but who are in the "better resurrection." (Heb: 11-35) Communication with them is perfectly all right.

"Wherefore, seeing we also are compassed about with so great a cloud of witnesses, let us lay aside every weight, and the sin which doth so easily beset us and let us run with patience the race that is set before us; Looking unto Jesus the author and finisher of our faith. Ye are come unto mount Sion, and unto the city of the living the heavenly Jerusalem, and to an innumetable company of angels. To the general assembly and church of the firstborn, which are written in heaven, and to God, the Judge of all, and to the spirits of just men made perfect, And to Jesus the mediator of the new covenant and to the blood of sprinkling, that speaketh better things than that of Abel."-(Heb- 12:1-2,22-24.)

Communication with "the Saints" who are the IMMORTALS is entirely different

OUTER SPACE PEOPLE AND INNER EARTH PEOPLE

from that of Abel, so to speak, out of the dust. We must always test the spirits before we talk to them or listen to anything that they say. "Beloved, believe not every spirit, but try the spirits whether they are of God: because many false prophets are come out into the world. Hereby know ye the Spirit of God: Every spirit that confesseth that Jesus Christ is come in the flesh is of God: And every spirit that confesseth not that Jesus Christ is come in the flesh is not of God: and this is that spirit of anti-christ, whereof ye have heard that it should come and even now already is it in the world."-(1 John 4: 1-3.)

If you follow what we teach, you will be sound in body and mind, yet you will enjoy all of the Mysteries and contacts with the spiritual and invisible world in a sane, sound, Christian way.

"THE BEASTS."(I Cor. 15:39.) These are the races of men that are called "serpents" (Gen. 3:1, Matt. 3:7, Matt. 23:33), "swine" Matt. 7:6), "dogs" (Matt. 15:26). I hope that you will look up and read the scripture references. These animal races do exist. I am convinced that every animal that the Bible lists as "unclean" was not created but that it is part human, from a mixed seed of human and animal.

The serpent, all hardheaded snakes have relices of arms and legs, a pelvic bone and give birth to their young. The hog has a stomach like a human. The dog has some human marks and characteristics. So has the horse, the elephant, etc. But not all of the "beast" races of men have degenerated into snakes, hogs and dogs. They live among us.

"FISHES"(1 Cor. 15:39.) These are the races of men in the inner earth. If you wish to know more about them, read I Peter 3:18-21, I Peter 4:6, Rev. 5:3, Rev. 5:13, Rev. 9:1-21, Phil. 2:10.

"BIRDS". (I Cor. 15:39.) These are the outer space people. Again I ask you to read Rev. 5:3, Rev. 5:13, Phil. 2:10, and I will quote Eph. 3:8-11 because of its extreme importance. "And to make all men see what is the fellowship of the mystery, which from the beginning of the world hath been hid in God; who created all things by Jesus Christ: to the intent that now unto the principalities and powers in heavenly places might be known by the church the manifold wisdom of God, according to the eternal purpose which he purposed in Christ Jesus our Lord." We have a commission to preach to the people in outer space. Many of them are not yet converted. "The heavens are not clean in his sight." (Job 15:15.) But they will all be converted and united with us. "Having made known unto us the mystery of his will, according to his good pleasure which he hath purposed in himself: That in the dispensation of the fullness of times he might gather together in one all things in Christ both which are in heaven, and which are on earth; even in him: In whom also we have obtained an inheritance, being predestinated according to the purpose of him who worketh all things after the counsel of his own will."(Eph. 1:9-11.)

I have now described to you the THREE divine orders of the IMMORTALS and also the four lesser orders of men. All in these last four orders die, but they have in them the seed of EVERLASTING life. They will be awakened from death gradually, "one by one." (Isa. 27:12.) It will take 1,000 years to raise them from the dead, beginning with the last that have died and continuing backward to the first that died, (Matt. 20:16, Luke 13:30.)

OUTER SPACE PEOPLE AND INNER EARTH PEOPLE

This resurrection to life will come about by the gradual increase of natural cosmic energy, which is evident from these scriptures. The seed of EVERLASTING life in the dead, asleep in the dust, is to be quickened to life. "But some man will say, How are the dead raised up? and with what body do they come? Thou fool, that which thou sowest is not quickened, except it die: And that which thou sowest thou sowest not that body that shall be, but bear grain, it may chance of wheat, or of some other grain: But God giveth it a body as it hath pleased him, and to every seed his own body."-(I Cor. 15:35-38.) "For there is hope of a tree, if it be cut down, that it will sprout again, and that the tender branch thereof will not cease. Though the root thereof wax old in the earth, and the stock thereof die in the ground; Yet through the scent of water it will bud, and bring forth boughs like a plant."-(Job 14:7-9.)

"Thy dead men shall live, together with my dead body shall they arise. Awake and sing, ye that dwell in dust: for thy dew is as the dew of herbs, and the earth shall cast out the dead." (Isaiah 26:19.) "Afterward he brought me again unto the door of his house; and, behold, waters issued out from under the threshold of the house eastward: for the forefront of the house stood toward the east and the waters came down from under, from the right side of the house, at the south side of the altar. Then brought he me out of the way of the gate northward, and led me about the way without unto the outer gate to the way that looketh eastward; and, behold, there ran out waters on the right side. And when the man that had the line in his hand went forth eastward, he measured a thousand cubits, and he brought me through the waters; the waters were to the ankles. Again he measured a thousand, and brought me through the waters; the waters were to the knees. Again he measured a thousand, and brought me through; the waters were to the loins. Afterward he measured a thousand; and it was a river that I could not pass over: for the waters were risen, waters to swim in, a river that could not be passed over. And he said unto me, Son of man, hast thou seen this? Then he brought me, and caused me to return to the brink of the river. Now when I had returned, behold, at the bank of the river were very many trees on the one side and on the other. Then said he unto me, These waters issue out toward the east country, and go down into the desert, and go into the sea: which being brought forth into the sea, the waters shall be healed. And it shall come to pass, that every thing that liveth, which moveth, whithersoever the rivers shall come, shall live: and there shall be a very great multitude of fish, because these waters shall come thither: for they shalt be healed; and every thing shall live whither the river cometh."(Isa. 47:1-9.)

"The hand of the Lord was upon me, and carried me out in the Spirit of the Lord, and set me down in the midst of the valley which was full of bones, And caused me to pass by them round about: and, behold, there were very many in the open valley; and, lo, they were very dry. And he said unto me, Son of man, can these bones live? And I answered O Lord God, thou knowest. Again he said unto me, Prophesy upon these bones, and say unto them, O ye dry bones, hear the word of the Lord. Thus saith the Lord God unto these bones; Behold, I will cause breath to enter into you, and ye shall live: And I will lay sinews upon you, and will bring up flesh upon you, and cover you with skin, and put breath in you, and ye shall live; and ye shall know that I am the Lord. So I prophesied as I was commanded: and as I prophesied, There was a noise, and behold a shaking, and

OUTER SPACE PEOPLE AND INNER EARTH PEOPLE

the bones came together, bone to his bone. And when I beheld, lo, the sinews and the flesh came up upon them, and the skin covered them above: but there was no breath in them. Then said he unto me, Prophesy unto the wind, prophesy, son of man, and say to the wind, Thus saith the Lord God; Come from the four winds, O breath, and breathe upon these slain, that they may live. So I prophesied as he commanded me, and the breath came into them, and they lived, and stood up upon their feet, an exceeding great army."(Ezek.37:1-10.)

I doubt very much if any other message ever preached has so clearly made the truth known in detail as this message has in describing the THREE orders of IMMORTALS and the FOUR orders of the mortals who are to be awakened, resurrected and restored by the gradual increase of natural cosmic energy. "Moreover the light of the moon shall be as the light of the sun, and the light of the sun shall be sevenfold, as the light of seven days, in the day that Lord bindeth up the breach of his people, and healeth the stroke of their wound."-(Isa. 30:26.)

This illustrates our Last Earth Canopy. It has banished the last ice period, and the Eden earth blooms again. Man dwells naked in a warm and genial world. The human family for unknown time look up to a watery heaven and give it a name signifying that condition. The Hebrews called this heaven Shamayim, "three waters"; the Greeks called it Ouranos, "water heaven", theHindus called it Varuno, "water heaven"; the Latins called it Caelum, and this, too, was a watery heaven, for it passed away. -The Creation J. F. Rutherford, 1927

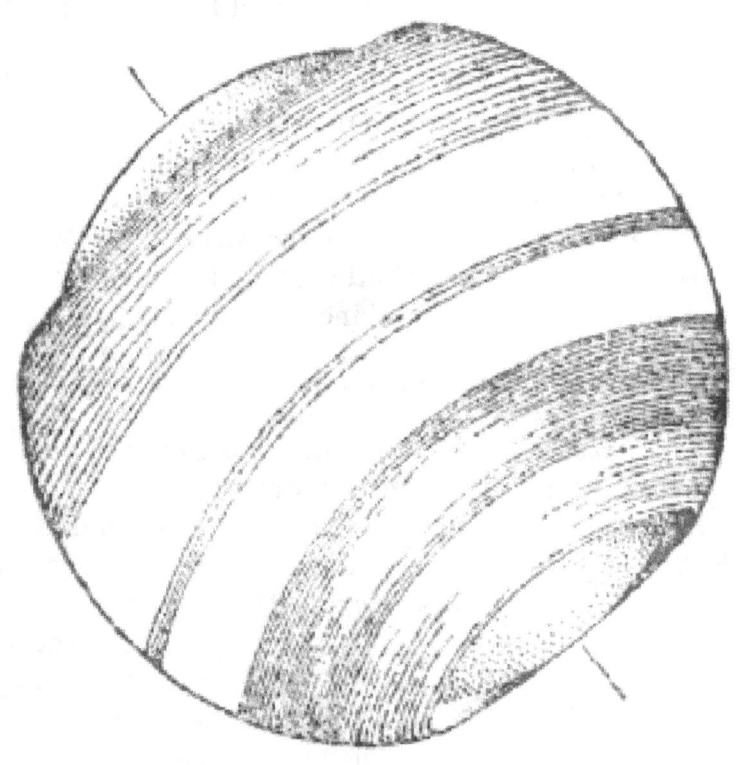

OUTER SPACE PEOPLE AND INNER EARTH PEOPLE

Chapter IX

Parapsychology

PARAPSYCHOLOGY is a big word which scares people away from it because they think they cannot understand it. The truth is that the scientific application of its principles does not operate to any great extent in or through any doctor in any university in the world today. The operative principle is found here and there in the unlearned among the common people—indeed, in some that are quite ignorant.

The research work that is being conducted by Dr. W. H. C. Tenhaeff at the University of Utrecht in the Netherlands and Dr. S. B. Rhine and Louisa E. Rhine of Duke University in America is a great work by sincere and honest scholars whom we applaud and of whom we approve. We do not speak lightly of them, neither would we attempt to underestimate these men and their associates.

The word "parapsychology" is a combination of three words: namely, "para" meaning above or beyond, "psyche" meaning the mind, and "logos", a Greek word which the Bible translates with a capital letter—"Word."

In the first chapter of the Gospel of John, Yahshua the Messiah (Jesus Christ) is called "The Word" (the Logos). In the Hebrew the word is "Dabar" which is found only five times in the Bible, The definition is this: "The Revelation, the Perfection, the Satisfaction, the Complete Law of Yahveh (God) in all its fullness made flesh in the living person of Jesus Christ the Ever-Living God in all his fullness in a man in the flesh.

Of course, we do not give this meaning to every word that ends with "ology", but the meaning of "parapsychology" is: "that which is beyond the natural mind."

The Bible's claim for itself is that it "proceedeth out of the mouth of God" (Matt. 4:4), that it is supernatural, above and beyond the natural mind; that "all scripture is given by inspiration of God" (II Tim. 3:16), that it "came not in old time by the will of man; but holy men of God spake as they were moved by the Holy Ghost (II Peter 1:21.) Therefore, the Bible is the one and only true and authentic textbook on parapsychology.

I have been asked the following questions many times by people who did not

OUTER SPACE PEOPLE AND INNER EARTH PEOPLE

expect an answer but simply intended it to be a statement: "What would happen if an irresistible force met an immovable object?" The question can be answered. Nothing whatever would happen. Why? Simply because two forces such as an irresistible force and an immovable object are without affinity. I can illustrate it this way: Take for example a solid piece of iron. Is it possible for anything else to occupy the same space that the iron occupies and at the same time? The answer is, Yes! That piece of iron can be magnetized and the magnetic force and the iron occupy the same space at the same time because they are without affinity.

Now parapsychogry, as defined and as I understand it, is that which is above or beyond the mortal mind. The spiritual world and the material world occupy the same space at the same time. The material world cannot interfere with the spiritual world. We will all agree that thought and thoughts are invisible and spiritual. Yet, everything that man makes is simply the expression of his thoughts, or in other words, his thoughts are materialized. Matter responds to thought.

The universe is the material expression of the spiritual thought of God. As an example: I think that this book, here on this podium, can be moved. With that thought in mind, I apply force. I reach out my hand, pick up the book and move it. In this case matter has responded to and obeyed thought, which is a spiritual and unseen force. Indeed, all power is invisible.

The spiritual world, the mind, spiritual beings and thoughts exist in the same space which matter occupies. Matter is not a hindrance to the spiritual. As an example: Yahshua the Messiah appeared in the upper room, even though the door was bolted. He appeared, materialized his body, talked and ate with the disciples, then he vanished.

Man is a mind and soul that occupies, for a short time, a material body and ethereal spirit. (I mean by spirit, the breath.) The mind and soul is spiritual, and is indeed the Creator and occupier of matter. Man makes everything in matter to resemble his thoughts.

Everything in the Bible belongs in the field of parapsychology because it is beyond the natural mind. The Bible has a literal surface meaning in many ways. Especially in the field of law, literature and history. The natural mind, purely from the natural standpoint, gets some value out of it. But the primary intent and purpose of the Bible is the Spiritual meaning that is hidden in it by Yahveh himself. There is the Spirit and Soul of the Supernatural Divine Mind hidden in every parable and in every statement.

To illustrate what I mean: The Bible says, "Thou shalt not muzzle the ox when he treadeth out the corn." (Deut. 25:4.) That is a flat emphatic, literal statement. But Paul tells us that the law is spiritual." (Rom. 7:14.) In First Corinthians, he says: "For it is written in the law of Moses, Thou shalt not muzzle the ox that treadeth out the corn. Doth God take care for oxen? or sayeth he it altogether for our sakes? For our sakes, no doubt this is written. Even so hath the Lord ordained that they which preach the gospel should live of the gospel." (I Cor. 9:9-14.) And to Timothy he writes, saying: "For the scripture saith, Thou shalt not muzzle the ox that treadeth out the corn, and, the labourer is worthy of his reward." (I Tim. 5:18.) This is sufficient for us to understand that every scripture has a hidden meaning, that all scripture is spiritual.

OUTER SPACE PEOPLE AND INNER EARTH PEOPLE

Take the Proverbs as an example of how a great truth can be stated in just a short sentence and stated in such a way as to teach without offending. You can speak a proverb to a man and he will get the meaning and will not get angry, whereas if you directed the same thing to him personally and in plain English, he would be offended. Then, too, see how Jesus stated that there is a secret hidden meaning of great depth in every parable. When he finished his parable of the sower, the simplest of all parables, he said: "Who hath ears to hear, let him hear." "And the disciples came, and said unto him, Why speakest thou unto them in parables? He answered and said unto them, Because it is given unto you to know the mysteries of the kingdom of heaven, but to them it is not given. For whosoever hath, to him shall be given, and he shall have more abundance: but whosoever hath not from him shall be taken away even that he hath.

"Therefore speak I to them in parables: because they seeing see not; and hearing they hear not, neither do they understand. And in them is fulfilled the prophecy of Esaias, which saith, By learning ye shall hear, and shall not understand; and seeing ye shall see, and shall not perceive: For this people's heart is waxed gross, and their ears are dull of hearing, and their eyes they have closed; lest at any time they should see with their eyes, and hear with their ears, and should understand with their heart and should be converted, and I should heal them. But blessed are your eyes, for they see; and your ears, for they hear. For verily I say unto you, That many prophets and righteous men have desired to see those things which ye see, and have not seen them; and to hear those things which ye hear, and have not heard them."(Matt. 13:10-17.)

The word "Mysteries" means "secrets known only to the initiated." We in the Christian faith know that the real meaning of the scriptures can never be misunderstood by the natural man, using only his natural mind. We are told this plainly, that preaching is "not with enticing words of man's wisdom, but in demonstration of the Spirit and of power: That your faith should not stand in the wisdom of men, but in the power of God. Howbeit we speak wisdom among them that are perfect: yet not the wisdom of this world, nor of the princes of this world, that come to nought: But we speak the wisdom of God in a mystery, even the hidden wisdom, which God ordained before the world unto our glory; Which none of the princes of this world knew for had they known it, they would not have crucified the Lord of glory. But as it is written, Eye hath not seen, nor ear heard, neither have entered into the heart of man, the things which God hath prepared for them that love Him. But God hath revealed them unto us by his Spirit: for the Spirit searcheth all things, yea, the deep things of God. For what man knoweth the things of a man, save the spirit of man which is in him? even so the things of God knoweth no man, but the Spirit of God. Now we have received, not the spirit of the world, but the Spirit which is of God; that we might know the things that are freely given to us of God. Which things also we speak, not in the words which man's wisdom teacheth, but which The Holy Ghost teacheth: comparing spiritual things with spiritual. But the natural man receiveth not the things of the Spirit of God: for they are foolishness unto him: neither can he know them, because they are spiritually discerned. But he that is spiritual judgeth all things, yet he himself is judged of no man. For who hath known the mind of the Lord, that he may instruct him? But we have the mind of Christ." (I Cor. 2:4-16.)

OUTER SPACE PEOPLE AND INNER EARTH PEOPLE

The point that I want to make is this: that the parapsychologists know nothing about "the mind of Christ." They wholly disregard the supernatural. They try to study the mind from the concept of the theory of material evolution and wholly by materialism. They will always be up against a stone wall.

The very word "parapsychology" means "above or beyond the natural mind." It never can be understood just by the natural and material concept.

In January, 1960, in the 469th issue of "Showers of Blessing" Magazine, I published my lecture on "THE DOUBLE SENSES", and in June, 1958, in The 450th issue I published my lecture on "OUR THREE BODIES". I believe that I have a few extra copies of those issues. If so, we will be glad to send them to those of you who are interested in the study of these things.

There is an "inner man" and there are five or more spiritual senses which are above and beyond the natural mind. To me, in these Spiritual "extra" senses is the real study of parapsychologry in the true meaning of the word. Most of the teachers in the universities fear the word "fanaticism". They are afraid to go beyond the natural but they will never understand until they recognize the Spiritual.

Personally, I am convinced that my existence did not begin with my birth in this body of flesh and blood, neither will it end with the death of this mortal body. My true existence is, always has been, and always will be in eternity, not in time.

The scientists say that matter is about three billion years old some say eight billion. I have no quarrel with that. It may be true. There are 92 known elements. The recent re-discovery of the atom is of world-changing importance. (I say "re-discovery" because it was known by the Egyptians, Greeks and others a thousand years or more before Christ.) What is the atom? It is the smallest unit of matter. Each atom has 1,760 electrons, 1,760 protons and 1,760 neutrons and other particles. The atom is like a star or like the sun. Just as the planets and the comets and asteroids or planetoids orbit the sun, so the electrons and protons and other particles orbit the atom.

If we could split a planetoid such as "Ceres", which is one of the 2,000 known asteroids in our solar system, if we could explode it or cast it outside the orbit of the sun, it would not disturb our solar system (Ceres is about five miles in diameter and fifteen miles in circumference.) The same is true of the atom. Scientists have never burst the atom, they have only split the smallest particle in its orbit away from it. They have blown a tiny particle out of the orbit of the atom. If they were to explode the atom, the entire material universe would instantly be dissoived; there would be no more matter.

It is a known fact that all matter, all of the 92 elements, all minerals, metals, animals and vegetables are exactly one and the same thing. Each and every thing is composed of atoms. The different rate of vibration of the atoms with greater or lesser components make gold, minerals, air, water, animals, etc. Everything! It is also a known fact that each and every thing can be changed by the Creator into some other thing. The Bible tells us that Lot's wife "became a pillar of salt." (Gem 19:26.) That was 4,000 years ago, and about six years ago (1959) I got two or three pieces of salt that were just re-

OUTER SPACE PEOPLE AND INNER EARTH PEOPLE

cently chipped off from Lot's wife. She is still standing over there and she is a pillar of salt. The Bibie also says that Abigail's husband, Nabal, "became a stone," (1 Samuel 25:37) and that he lived for ten days after his body turned to stone. I have seen and put my hands on a man who was still alive whose body was turned to stone. His teeth had been removed, he could not open his mouth. He took liquid nourishment through a straw. By what is now known about the change of the elements, those cases are not impossible. In the Old Testament Apocrypha we read about fire changing its nature from hot to cold and about ice changing from cold to hot. "For the elements were changed in themselves by a kind of harmony, like as in a psaltery notes change the name of the tune, and yet are always sounds; which may well be perceived by the sight of the things that have been done. For earthly things were turned into watery, and the things that before swam in the water, now went upon the ground." The fire had power in the water, forgetting his own virtue: and the water forgot his own quenching nature. On the other side, the flames wasted not the flesh of the corruptible living things, though they walked therein neither melted they the icy kind of heavenly meat that was of nature apt to melt." (Wisdom of Solomon 19: 18-21, Apocrypha.)

The book of Jasher says that at the time of the destruction of the tower of Babel, some of the people "became apes", that is, they were changed from humans to apes." (Jasher 9:25.) Apes and other animals that the Bible lists as unclean for food (Lev. II :1-4) probably are degenerates of the human family.

The elements are subject to just such changes by the very structure and operation of the atom. Gold and the most solid of metals are slowly decomposing. There is a process of decomposition going on in everything. The ultimate end is that matter, which at one time did not exist will be nonexistent again. The Creator of matter can un-create it. Ultimately matter will be swallowed up into that which is spiritual and time will pass into eternity.

When you stop and think that your material body is three or more billion years old, that all matter has been in existence since its creation, and is the same age, that is really something! What is now your body, was once soil and water, then plants, then animals, then man. Again, what is now your body will fertilize the soil, become plant food, and so the process of change, of use and re-use continues in the cycle of matter. Therefore, your body is an integral part of all matter. The point that I am making is that the atom may, and I think does, contain within itself the complete record of all knowledge and all things since the world began. Therefore, all knowledge is in you, even in your body. Your body is a part of all matter. It (the body) cannot be separated from it. Therefore all that is recorded in matter is in you.

Now I said that I existed before I was born in the flesh and will exist after this body in its present form dies and the matter in it is used in something else. I do not say that we created our own bodies, but I do say that Our Creator is a Spirit and His realm is Eternity and that we are his offspring. Our mind and soul and spirit is as much a part of Him as our body is of matter. The "I AM" which is the God of us, which is the creative intelligence entered into a tiny, invisible, infinitesimal sperm—a sperm so small that thousands of them, side by side, could pass through the eye of a small sewing needle. In this sperm

OUTER SPACE PEOPLE AND INNER EARTH PEOPLE

we began to develop a material body in the image and likeness of our Spirit self. This body we formed and brought to birth. It is our temporary home, our point of contact with the universe from birth to death. We are always conscious of the "inner man" that is developing from a lower to a higher degree of glory. We understand that this is an experience in our progression in which we are becoming like Christ. Ultimately we will reach the full measure of Christ. We will then be a Christ in our own right. We will have attained unto Godhood, and as immortals we will live in eternity.

We know that there are unborn souls destined to be born, and that there are disembodied souls. The disembodied souls are entirely different from the unborn souls.

CORPOREANS are those of us living in corporeal bodies on this earth.

ETHERIANS are one of the orders of people in outer space and some of the people of the inner earth, some of whom once lived on this earth but are now what the Bible calls "the spirits of just men made perfect." (Heb. 12:22-24.) When they descend into the earth's atmosphere, they materialize and appear on earth just as earth people.

IMMORTALS are those in the higher orders of glory. When they appear on earth, they are bright and shining beings, or they may even appear as fire, the children of the flames. Yahveh "maketh his angels spirits and his ministers a flame of fire." (Heb. 1:7.) "Are they not all ministering spirits, sent forth to minister for them who shall be heirs of salvation?" (Heb. 1: 14)

ATMOSPHERIANS. These are the disembodied souls that are of a race of people who lived in physical bodies on a previous creation on this earth. The time could well have been millions of years ago. Then when the earth was disrupted, became chaotic, "without form and void" (Gen. 1:2) that race of people became disembodied that is, earth-bound souls that had lost their bodies. In materialism they failed to make spiritual progression. The Bible calls them "devils" or "demons". They continually try to enter the bodies of living people. They try to obsess and possess and live in the minds and bodies of men and women. They are the cause of what is known as "split personalities" and also of much insanity. Sometimes they even obsess birds and animals. This explains some of the peculiar phenomena that happens with animals when they appear to have human intelligence, speech and actions.

Some of the experiences attested to by parapsychologists must be put into the realm of "demonology." I mean the cases in which certain persons who are usually below the average in intelligence and who are very odd and somewhat infantile have the faculty of transferring the mind and actually entering into the body and mind of some other person. They may do this to people who are miles away. They make contact by touching some item of clothing or most anything that the other person has touched or handled. This is "demonology". It has been explained by the Bible for fully 2,000 years. Every theologian who understands and believes the Bible is fully aware of the existence of this phenomenon.

UNBORN. These are souls that are destined to be born on the earth. They may be conscious in their present state or they may be dormant, enfolded in a seed (sperm). A

OUTER SPACE PEOPLE AND INNER EARTH PEOPLE

body begins to develop for them at the time of conception. The human body formed for them is in the image of the heavenly body that these souls had before they were destined to be born as earth people. Some say that we chose the time and place of our birth and the age in which we wished to live on the earth. However, beyond all question of doubt, the body, mind, soul, and spirit united in what we call a MAN is the greatest and most perfect universe; a universe that is alive, that thinks, reasons and creates. That MAN is surrounded by component parts, even by personalities that revolve around him, is little known and seldom realized. If one or more of these parts, or personalities, is broken off, it becomes, for the want of a better word, a "poltergeist". It may become an "apparition", visible in an ethereal form as a "ghost" resembling a person or an animal. Strange noises, rappings, opening of doors, even the moving or turning over of furniture may result. These things are caused by component parts broken off from man. They are somewhat like a comet in the solar system, or a cancer on the body, which is that part of the universe or cells of the body gone crazy. These "poltergeists" and apparitions may continue within the aura of man for a long time, orbiting, so to speak, out of balance and off course. It is altogether possible in some cases that they have been created by the person and then cast off.

Man has a creative mind. Everything that man makes is definitely an incarnation of his thoughts.

For the most part, he tries to create himself in the thing that he makes. As an example: the headlights on an automobile correspond to the eyes, the wheels to the legs, the gas tank to the stomach, the oil to the circulation of the blood, the pump to the heart, the battery to the nervous system, etc.

The late Sir James Jeans said: "The universe now appears to be a great thought." Since man incarnates his thoughts in things, it is reasonable to believe that the sun, moon, and stars and all the elements and all matter are incarnations of the thoughts of God. So that which is visible and material is the image of the spiritual and invisible. In man, however, the spiritual and invisible exist in him. He is more than an image. He is the Logos made flesh, a unit of God.

Much harm may be done by man attempting to move into and control the mind and body of other people. The result is apt to be that those whom he obsesses and possesses may become zombies (the living dead). This is not to be confused with the union of minds or soul-mating of those who are "ONE" in mind, soul and body, for that is on a voluntary basis by which they are drawn together through love and compassion, whereas obsession and possession is brought about by fear, cruelty, and brainwashing.

There is a difference!

Dr. Carl Gustov Jung's system of analytical psychology, of bringing out of man what is inherent in him, has some value, but Sigmund Freud's theory of expressing all thoughts in words and deeds, naked and open and not ashamed, is, in my opinion, immoral and damnable.

In the study of the mind, all of the parapsychologists, psychologists and psychia-

OUTER SPACE PEOPLE AND INNER EARTH PEOPLE

trists are whistling in the dark. They are not sure about anything. They never will know anything for sure until they recognize God and the Spiritual world.

There is, however, a real Extra Sensory Perception (ESP), clairvoyance, mind-reading, mental telepathy, astral projection, and projection from place to place on earth and in materialization. I have talked with, touched and handled people who projected themselves for more than a thousand miles and materialized their bodies. They were present; they were literal; they were real; they were in no hurry. Then in due time they disappeared instantly. I know of other cases where the same person has appeared in two or three different places at the same time and those places were hundreds of miles apart.

I see nothing that is astonishing about this. The same program on television, same people, same voices, may be seen and heard all over America at the same time. But for the same person to be in many different places at the same time and saying and doing different things in each place, is not as yet understood. That comes under the nature of Godhood. God is above all, over all, in all, through all. In Him we live and move and have our being (existence). He is omnipotent, omnipresent. He is fully and completely present in every place and everywhere at the same time.

In Eternity there is no distance. Distance is an element of time. In Eternity there is only one place and that is where YOU are. The only person, place, thing and universe is YOU, the "I AM". You are all that there is. YOU may say that you think there are other places. You see other places, you hear other voices. But you think with your mind; you see with your eyes; you hear with your ears. Let me ask a question: I hope that somebody will answer it. How can there be anything except what you see and hear and feel and smell and taste and perceive? Whether in time or eternity, how can there be anything except YOU. This again is Godhood.

There Is One God

We are, so to speak, one of the spiritual atoms in the ONE GOD. All of the hearing, seeing, feeling, smelling, tasting, touching, and speaking that is in us, is in Him and all that is in Him is in us. ONE MIND, that's all there is. God speaking through the lips of man; God writing through the hands of man; Man hearing the voice of God; Man doing the work of God.

We see matter diminished when the Master spoke to the fruitless fig tree and it withered away. We see matter increased when He multiplied the loaves and fishes. We see matter dissolved when he vanished instantly from the presence of his disciples. We see matter reassembled when he appeared in his body instantly in the upper room while all of the doors were closed. He could and did materialize and dematerialize at will. He had power to put on the body and to take it off. He could, by his own will, be confined to time and place and matter, but he was not hemmed in by time and he was not a prisoner in matter.

Yes, I recognize matter. I do not deny the existence of matter. It exists as a created thing and for a purpose. Until He who created it, un-creates it we must recognize it. However, our mind, soul and spirit is not a prisoner in matter nor a slave to it. It is merely the

OUTER SPACE PEOPLE AND INNER EARTH PEOPLE

point from which we make contact with the universe at the present time.

Yes, I recognize time, but not to a very great extent and I definitely mean that! Time is a man-made thing that is set into eternity. We divide it into past, present and future. In what we call the present, we build a wall between ourselves and the past and between ourselves and what we call the future. These walls should be taken down. The past exists now and the future exists now. Eternity is ONE and all that has been and is and will be is NOW. From the standpoint of materialism, everything is recorded and exists by vibrations. All of what we call the past and the future is in every atom.

Everything in the twenty-four volumes of the Encyclopedia Britannica could be recorded on a steel ring no larger than a finger ring. By tuning in on certain vibratory waves, all the pictures, voices, places and things in the past will be possible on a super-television set in your own living room. Your entire material life and the life of every person that has ever lived from conception and birth to death exists.

I do not believe that old age, discrepancy and senility is necessary. The Bible, in speaking of each of us, says: "His flesh shall be fresher than a child's; he shall return to the days of his youth." (Job 88:25.) The New Testament says, "We shall not all die, but we shall all be changed." (I Cor. 15:51) It is not necessary to grow old and die. We can change over from the natural to the spiritual, from corruption to incorruption, from mortal to immortal, without old age, disease, decay and death.

"There is a natural body, and there is a spiritual body." (I Cor. 15:44.) As we put on the spiritual body, we can "dissolve" (II Cor. 5:1) the natural body. Death is in that way swallowed up by eternal life. This was demonstrated for us by the transfiguration of Christ (Matt. 17:1-18) and proven by his resurrection and especially by his ascension. In the ascension, we see the law of levitation in operation. There is a law of gravity or attraction, but there is also the law of levitation or repulsion.

One law is as real and as much operative as the other.

Man has only demonstrated one absolute exact science in the world and that is PROPHECY. Why is it exact? Because prophecy is projection into what we call the future. It proves that the future exists now. Just to mention one of the great prophets will make this clear. David was projected for 1,000 years into the future. He saw and experienced and wrote down every detail of the crucifixion of Christ. When time marched on through a thousand years and arrived at the place where David had been projected, every event that he had recorded took place in exact detail just as he had described it one thousand years earlier. The same is true of all prophecy. It is simply a record made by future projection, and when it is fulfilted, as thousands of prophecies have been, it then becomes history.

It is admitted that one mind—your mind—is capable of more than a trillion thoughts. One mind could hold all the thoughts and all of the knowledge since the world began and it would not be crowded. Our mental life vastly overflows our cerebral material brain. It is impossible to translate through our physical senses one-hundredth part of one per cent of our thoughts. Our aura extends far beyond our physical bodies. Who knows the

OUTER SPACE PEOPLE AND INNER EARTH PEOPLE

extent of our cable-tows, much less the length of our "silver cord." There is a way to communicate, a better way and that is by the voiceless voice, the soundless sound, by a silence that knows no distance in which deep calleth unto deep. We understand a person best not by what he says or does, but as spirit communication with spirit and mind with mind. Some people are of the same "ectoplasm" and are of the same order. Both as a speaker and as a writer, I know what inspiration is. I experience it. I have never used another man's sermons. I have always spoken and written the things that are revealed to me. Original thinkers and inventors are the only ones who can advance humanity.

While speaking on one subject or even while writing it I am, at the same time, thinking and hearing in my mind three or four other messages which I may preach or write at a later time. I do not know what to call it. I suppose that I am in a state of semi-trance while speaking and writing and that I am in tune with a higher power. Our contacts are not just confined to this planet alone. Material scientists say that if we were to get into a rocket and travel at the rate of the speed of light which is 186,000 miles per second, it would take us one hundred years to reach the next and nearest inhabited planet in Alpha Centura. But what they call light is not the real "light." It is only physical, material vibration. We are not confined to that or limited by it. THOUGHT IS INSTANT. Likewise travel to other planets or inhabited worlds by astral projection or in a spirit body is INSTANT.

Furthermore, even the physical body in ascension is dissolved. When we reach another inhabited world we assemble our body, or we have a body of a different nature. But it seems to us to be exactly the same body that we have on this earth. People from many other worlds continually pay visits to this earth.

"WHERE THERE IS NO VISION, THE PEOPLE PERISH." (Prov. 29:18.) All of the Bible was written by inspired men. Much of it is based upon visions, dreams and the ministry of angels.

In the second chapter of the Acts, which tells the story of the birth of the Church and the beginning of the Christian Faith, the Holy Ghost speaking through the lips of the Apostle Peter said: "Your sons and your daughters shall prophesy and your young men shall see visions, and your old men shall dream dreams: and on my servants and on my handmaidens I will pour out in those days of my Spirit; and they shall prophesy." (Acts 2:17-18.) This was to continue as the experience of the "Spirit upon all flesh."

One of the greatest, most important and far reaching VISIONS that has continually influenced the whole world was that of Saul of Tarsus. (Acts 9: 1-22, Acts 22:1-80, Acts 26: 1-32) He saw Yahshua the Messiah in a great light. He saw him face to face and talked with him. This was fifteen years after the Messiah had ascended into heaven and been glorified. This experience changed the life of Saul of Tarsus, led to his complete conversion and full obedience to the Gospel; after which he was known as the Apostle Paul, the greatest and the hardest working Apostle that ever lived. He made three missionary journeys, carrying the Gospel over into Europe. He definitely wrote fourteen books of the New Testament and possibly more. He forever held to his wonderful vision, saying always: "I was not disobedient unto the heavenly vision." (Acts 26:19.) He was often vis-

OUTER SPACE PEOPLE AND INNER EARTH PEOPLE

ited, helped and instructed by angels, and in dreams and by visions. Once he was carried up into Paradise, the third heaven (II Cor. 12:1-4.) He tells us that "we also are compassed about with so great a cloud of Witnesses" and goes on to say: "Ye are come unto Mount Sion, and unto the city of the Living God, the heavenly Jerusalem, and to an innumerable company of angels, to the general assembly and church of the firstborn, which are written in heaven, and to God the Judge of all, and to the spirits of just men made perfect, and to Jesus the Mediator of the New Covenant. (Heb. 12: 1, 22-28.)

In Second Corinthians 12:1-4 where Paul tells us that he was carried into the heavens (heavenly worlds), he could not tell whether he was in the body or out of the body, at least at that time. The body could have been transported and in a split second in eternity he could have seen as much as in a lifetime on the earth.

In the case of Enoch and Elijah, both were taken up literally into heaven. The Book of Enoch deals almost entirely with the visits of Enoch to many heavenly worlds. Yahshua our Messiah assured us that there are many dwelling places beyond the earth. Once you see or visit one of them, then you know! The people in the heavens and on this earth and inside this earth are, in these last days; to be united. See Eph. 1:9-10, Phil. 2:10, Rev. 5:5, 11-18. Read it in your Bible.

We are definitely and positiveiy told that the angels (who are outer-space people, men from other worlds or from this earth who have become deathless and who live in youthful health and have eternai life) are "all ministering spirits, sent forth to minister for them (and that includes us) who shall be heirs of salvation."(Heb. 1:14.)

WHAT IS A VISION? A vision is not just imagination. It is real. It positively is HEAVENLY TELEVISION in which we see the persons, places and things and hear the voice or voices speak to us clearly in our own language. It is greater than ordinary television because in heavenly television; we are there and can ask questions and talk with those that we see. I have recently become fully convinced in my own mind and experience that when I preach and teach the Bible, my own image and words are carried by heavenly television and picked up by the people in outer space (other worlds.)

Therefore, we are preaching not to just one world, but to many worlds. The scripture that convinced me of this is as follows: "that I should preach the unsearchable riches of Christ to make all men see what is the fellowship of the mystery (Secret known only to the initiated) which from the beginning of the world hath been hid in God, who created all things by Jesus Christ: to the intent that now unto the principalities and powers in heavenly places might be known by the Church the manifold wisdom of God, according to the eternal purpose which he purposed in Christ Jesus our Lord: in whom we have boldness and access with confidence by faith in him." (Eph. 8:8-12.) Yes, indeed, we are preaching to kings, political leaders, and to the people in many other worlds.

WHEN, WHERE AND HOW DO WE RECEIVE VISIONS? Well, a vision may be received anywhere, any place, any time, if we are in tune with the heavenly vibration. We may get the vision while we are wide awake or we may receive it in a dream while we are in deep sleep, or we may receive it while we are in a TRANCE. Now what the Bible calls a trance is the same thing that is known today as a semi-self hypnosis, or to put it

OUTER SPACE PEOPLE AND INNER EARTH PEOPLE

into plainer language, it is CONCENTRATION, nothing more or less than very deep, or if possible; perfect concentration. That is the key to memory. You can memorize anything that you hear or read, and without even thinking about memorizing it, if you know how to give your undivided attention to it, that is, if you know how to concentrate. That is also the secret of mental telepathy. If you completely concentrate on a person who is in a certain place, I say that it is possible for you to see that person and talk with him (or her) and even to touch them. It can be as real as anything in life.

This leads to another phase of the subject, which is astral projection. By astral projection the prophets were carried back into the past or they saw and heard things in the present anywhere in the world, or they were projected into the future. Yahveh is the same yesterday, today and forever. The past present and future exist NOW. That's what eternity is—past present, future. Prophecy is the one and only exact science, because it is the things that are seen in future projections, and when time catches up with it or moves up into that time, that's exactly the way it is. Therefore, a trance or semi-self hypnosis or deep concentration is the border line on which we stand between the material and the spiritual worlds, with one foot so to speak, in heaven and the other foot on the earth. I wish that I had the space to go into detail on this subject of VISION and relate to you every case in the Bible, but time and space will only permit me to cite a few cases. Jacob, with his head pillowed on a stone in the wilderness saw, while in a dream, a vision of the golden ladder from earth to heaven. (There are gateways from earth of heaven.) His vision resulted in establishing Bethel, the first congregation or house of God. Twenty years later at Peniel he wrestled all night with an angel and when he prevailed, his name was changed from "Jacob" to "ISRAEL". (Gen. 28:1-22. Gen. 82:24-80.)

Moses, while in the wilderness with the Midianites, came alone to the back side of the desert, and came to the mountain of Yahveh, even to Horeb, and there he saw the vision of the brush that burned with fire and was not consumed. And there an angel spoke to him revealing to him that the name of "I AM THAT I AM" is "YAHVEH." In this way Moses learned the Father and Creator's true name. (Ex. 8:122, Ex. 6:1-8.) Without these visions Israel would never have been delivered by Moses from the Egyptian captivity.

But perhaps the greatest of all the visions that Moses had was when he saw Mount Sinai ablaze and quaking and received the Ten Commandments and the Law at the hands of angels in the name of Yahveh. (Ex.20:1-17, Deut. 6:6-21, Acts 7:58.)

You will remember that Abraham, Lot, Gideon, Manoah, Joshua and many others were visited by angelic (outer-space) people. Likewise the dreams of Joseph about the sun, moon, and stars and of the bundles of sheafs as well as the dreams of the chief butler and the chief baker, Pharaoh's dreams of the seven fat and seven lean cattle and the seven full ears and the seven blasted ears of corn are well known to every Bible reader.

Nebuchadnezzar's dream of the Great Image with the head of gold, chest of silver, belly and thighs of copper, legs of iron and feet of clay (Dan. 2:31-45) has been commented on nearly every day by students of prophecy for 2,500 years. The visions of Isaiah and of Ezekiel are of equal importance.

Isaiah begins his book of prophecy with these words: "The vision" (Isa. 1:1) and

OUTER SPACE PEOPLE AND INNER EARTH PEOPLE

he describes his great vision in detail in Isaiah 6:1-8. The prophet Ezekiel says: "As I was among the captives by the river Chebar, the heavens were opened, and I saw visions of God." (Ezek. 1:1.) The entire 48 chapters of his book of prophecy reveal his "vision" to us.

In the New Testament the entire 22 chapters of the Book of Revelation contain 175 symbols and 82 characters which are the heavenly television pictures and words which the Apostle John saw and heard on the Isle of Patmos in 96 A D.

Here I will list in outline only the New Testament cases which I wish I had time to describe in detail. The word "angel" simply means "messenger" and they are always described as men dressed in white garments.

1. An angel announced the conception of John the Baptist and gave him the name "John" before he was born. (Luke 1:1-19.)

2. An angel announced the Virgin conception to Mary. (Luke 1:1-35.)

3. An angel told Joseph that Mary had conceived by the Holy Ghost. (Matt. 1: 18-24.)

4. An angel, together with a multitude of outer-space people, came to earth and announced the birth of Jesus Christ. (Luke 2:8-16.)

5. An angel told Joseph to take Jesus into Egypt. (Matt, 2:19.)

6. An angel told Joseph to bring Jesus back to Palestine.(Matt. 2:19-20.)

7. An angel strengthened Jesus in the Garden of Gethsemane. (Luke 22:41-42.)

8. Angels rolled the stone away from the tomb and announced the resurrection. (Matt.28:2-7.)

9. Immediately after his ascension angels came down and spoke to the disciples. Acts 1:9-11.)

10. An angel told the Gentiles to send for the Apostle Peter to preach to them. (Acts 10:30-82.)

11. An angel delivered the Apostle Peter from prison. (Acts 12:8-11.)

12. An angel struck Herod and killed him. (Acts 12:20-28.)

13. An angel called the Apostle Paul to Europe. (Acts 16:9-10.)

14. An angel announced to Paul that his life and those on board that ship, in that terrible storm at sea, would be saved. (Acts 27:21-26.)

15. Angels rejoice when a soul is saved. (Luke 15:7-10.)

16. Angels will gather the elect children of Yahveh together from all over the world. (Matt. 24:81.)

17. Angels will gather out the scoffers, sinners and ungodly and completely sepa-

OUTER SPACE PEOPLE AND INNER EARTH PEOPLE

rate them from those who are saved. (Matt. 13:40-48.)

There are so many other references to angels in both the Old and New Testaments that I say to you, if you do not believe that these Outer Space people have frequently visited this earth over a period of 6,000 years, then you had just as well throw your Bible away.

VISIONS, dreams and angel visitations are a definite and fundamental part of the Faith, both in the Old Testament and in the New Testament both in Israel and in the Church. Of course, they must coincide with the Bible. The truth never contradicts the Bible. We must test every vision, dream and spirit by the word: "Beloved, believe not every spirit but try the spirits whether they are of God: because many false prophets are gone out into the world. Hereby know ye the Spirit of God: Every spirit that confesseth that Jesus Christ is come in the flesh is of God: and every spirit that confesseth not that Jesus Christ is come in the flesh is not of God: and this is the spirit of antichrist, whereof ye have heard that it should come; and even now already is it in the world." (1 John 4:1-8.)

The battle between the "sons of Darkness" and the "sons of Light" continues. There are people with obsessions and split personalities who are insane, and there are also people of sound mind with spiritualized personalities.

OUTER SPACE PEOPLE AND INNER EARTH PEOPLE

Chapter X

Articles Republished From "Drift of the Times"

Extra Sensory Perception.

I shall tell you of only a few cases in my own personal experience. In 1982 I was assigned to the Pastorate of the United Brethren In Christ Church at Colfax, Washington. I was very young. I had a few books, three suits of clothes, about a dozen shirts and eighteen dollars in currency and two silver dollars. I was a stranger in that small town. After renting a room on the second floor in the home of the county treasurer and getting all of my earthly possessions in that room, I went downtown to a service in the Nazarene Church. Suddenly there was a fire alarm. I went out and ran down the street in the direction of the fire. It had started in my room. The house was burning. I prayed that God would not let the suitcase burn in which were my important papers—my discharge from the U. S, Army, my elementary teacher's certificate, diplomas, etc. When the fire was put out everything in my room had burned up except two silver dollars which I found in the ashes and that suitcase. There sat the suitcase without even the smell of smoke on it. All of my certificates had been saved. I had two silver dollars and the clothes that I was wearing.

About a week later, I began a meeting (revival) in the small church building. The seating capacity was only one hundred. Not more than ten people attended any service during the first week. Then an epidemic broke out. The leading family in the church got sick. The attendance at the meeting dropped to three or four. They asked me to close the meeting as a failure (at that time). But that night I was in the room where I was temporarily staying with one of the families in the church. Someone knocked on my door and I said, "Come in." A young man came in. He had been a schoolmate of mine in the one room country elementary school in West Virginia, and here he was in the State of Washington. He talked with me, told me to stay in Colfax and to continue the meeting. He said that our little church building would soon be over-crowded and that we would move the meeting to the largest church building in town, that the other denominations would join us and that for six weeks I would preach to the largest crowds and hold the greatest meetings ever to be held in that county.

OUTER SPACE PEOPLE AND INNER EARTH PEOPLE

Then he said that he had to be going. I shook hands with him, asked him to come and see me often. As soon as the door closed behind him I realized that he had been dead for eight years.

The next evening I went over to the church. I told the three or four who were there that we would continue the meeting, that the building would be over-crowded, that we would move into the largest church in town, continue the meeting for six weeks, and overcrowd that building, too. They said, "You are either crazy, or you have the greatest faith of anybody that we have ever known," I said, "I am not crazy and it is not faith on my part."

Within four days, more than 185 people had crowded into our small church house, others were standing outside. The Baptist church asked us to move the meeting into their building, which was the largest in town. We did. The Baptist, Methodist, Christian and Nazarene Churches joined in the meeting. I preached every night for six weeks. People stood in the balcony, side rooms and basement, and during the last week it was so overcrowded that many were turned away. That was in January, 1982, the greatest meeting ever held before or since in Colfax, Whitman County, Washington. That meeting made me well known as an evangelist. I got calls to hold meetings in Spokane, Washington; Portland, Oregon, and elsewhere. Since then I have held over 500 evangelistic meetings. I never told this story to anyone for several years about the young man (from the dead) who visited me.

The Second Experience

THE SECOND EXPERIENCE that I shall relate here took place on a Saturday night in Everett Washington, in 1986. I was alone in my room praying. Suddenly it seem that my body was as hot as fire. There was before me in the trance, if you want to call it that, a pool of molten, liquid fire. Some stranger was baptizing (immersing) me in that fire. As he laid me back into the fire, the last words that I remember was an audible voice saying, "This is the baptism of the Holy Ghost and fire." I gasped for breath, went under the fire, and died. Immediately I was in heaven. There I met some people that I knew who were dead and I met others that I had never known but they were relatives of the people that I did know. I have never understood much about music, have never been able to sing, but in heaven I could sing and I understood all kinds of music. I spent most of my time there singing, because it was a joy unspeakable and full of glory.

It was early on Sunday morning when I awakened in my body. My physical body was so weak that I could hardly stand up. The body was so nearly dead that I was several days regaining physical strength. The music world is still closed to me on this earth.

I have, since that time, made many astral projections into outer-space and also to various parts of this world. I have talked with both the living and the dead many times in many places on the earth and in different inhabited worlds in outer-space. I have never tried to force this. I have never tried to make an astral projection or to contact anybody in the spiritual world. These experiences occur at times when least expected.

OUTER SPACE PEOPLE AND INNER EARTH PEOPLE

The Third Experience

THE THIRD EXPERIENCE that I shall relate here is that I spent most of 1939-1940 in holding meetings in the state of Kansas. In meetings at Norton, Stockton, Osborne, and elsewhere, several people said to me: "We heard you in your meeting in Wichita a few years ago." I said to them, "I have never held a meeting in Wichita. Furthermore, I have never been in that city." Having many people in different places telling me that they had heard me in Wichita annoyed me considerably, for I had never held a meeting in that place. Time went by and I forgot about it, but fifteen years later-which was in 1955, I was lecturing in Seattle, Washington. Three women came to my lecture who said, "Brother Blessing, do you remember us?" I said, "I'm sorry but I do not recall ever having met you before." They said, "We attended your meeting in Wichita, Kansas, about twenty years ago. We sat on the front row of seats and often visited with you after the services." I said, "Ladies, I have never held a meeting in Wichita."

Their feelings were hurt. They said, "You are the very same William L. Blessing, with the same voice. Everything about you is the same. Why do you deny it?"

Well, somebody by the same name, with the same voice and with the same sermons, did hold a meeting in Wichita, but it was not I. This is a thing for the parapsychologists and ESP specialists to explain. Since then, a few people have reported seeing and hearing me in two or three different places at the very same time. How could I be in several different places at the same time?

The Fourth Experience.

Four years ago i lectured on a Sunday afternoon and evening in a lecture room in a hotel in Omaha, Nebraska. It was not wired; the lectures were not on radio or television, yet three days later I got a letter from Wyoming and another letter from Oklahoma from persons who said, "I heard the lectures you gave in Omaha last Sunday on the radio. Please send me your magazine "Showers Of Blessing" and some of your books and put my name on your mailing list!"

I complied with the requests. Later on I met one of the persons and talked with her. She has since attended many of my meetings, always sticking to her story that she first heard of me when she heard my sermons on the radio from Omaha. But my sermons were not on the air. How then did those persons in Wyoming and Oklahoma hear me?

The Fifth Experience.

Three years ago I was in a hotel in Spokane, Washington. At two o'clock in the morning a knock came on my door. I opened the door. It was my wife. She came in and we visited for a while and then went to bed. I put my arms around her, then I said, "Move away from me. How can this be real. You are in Denver." Instantly she vanished. I picked up the telephone and called her at our home in Denver. I said, "You were just up here in my room at Spokane." She said, "I was trying to see if I could follow your methods of concentration and make an astral projection to Spokane, and then I fell asleep." I said, "Were you conscious of being up here?" She replied, "No."

OUTER SPACE PEOPLE AND INNER EARTH PEOPLE

Well, she was there in Spokane all right not in astral projection but actually and literally in the physical body. Yet she was asleep in our home in Denver.

The Birds And The Deer Attended My Lectures.

While lecturing to a group that were in camp on Mount Shasta (California), I predicted the earthquake in Yellowstone about an hour before it took place. Just as I would begin my lectures out under the open sky in the afternoons and in the evenings, birds would fly into the trees around the camp and perch there all through the message. The wild deer would come near and stand there so gently and silently and never move until the lectures were over. All the people attending the camp witnessed this. Several of them have mentioned it to me in my recent lecture tours of California.—W.L.B.

I could tell you many more of my experiences, but the six cases related are enough for now. Yahveh the Heavenly Father miraculously saved me from death five times on the battle fields in France and Belgium in 1918. Twice within one hour on Sept 27, 1918, He saved my life in the Argonne offensive. I was a machine gunner in MG. Co. 146 U. S. Inf. 87 Div. (Serial number 1521688). I know that He called me to the ministry and that I have a destiny. There are many spiritual experiences too sacred for mortal lips to utter. There are some secrets that I must keep. The true Christian faith has in it many mysteries which are secrets known only to the initiated. I have been knighted by men, but greatest of all I have been inducted into Godhood, personally, by the Heavenly Father whose name is YAHVEH. I mean by this that I am of the ELOHIM (Gods), a son of Yahveh and a brother of Yahshua the Messiah, my Savior, Mediator and Intercessor. There is a "little flock", "a remnant", a few of the sons of God (Elohim) on this earth today.

Christian Evidence

The evidence that a person is a Christian is not in dreams, trances or visions; neither is it in any emotional experience. SPEAKING IN TONGUES is not an evidence of the Christian faith. The phenomenon takes place in every religion on earth from the African tribes to India. There are many occasions in their religious services in which they speak in tongues. Mary Ann Glenn, who is probably the greatest lady mystic in the world, has the gift of tongues which is said to be Egyptian, Chinese and many other languages. "Pele", the ancient Hawaiian fire goddess, is said to visit her quite frequently. INSTANT HEALING OF THE SICK is not the evidence of the Christian faith. All religions practice faith healing. Other religions claim more cures than the Christian religion does.

MIRACLES are not evidence of the Christian faith. In Africa and frequently in India when the people in the various cults are worked up to a high pitch emotionally, they can stand in fire, dance with their bare feet on red hot coals of fire and not be burned. They can stick pins and knife blades through their lips and cheeks and never feel any pain or shed a drop of blood.

What I say here is not to be interpreted as against "tongues", healing", "miracles" and other gifts. I merely say that they are not evidence of the Christian faith and most surely are not a test of fellowship.

THERE IS ONLY ONE EVIDENCE OF THE CHRISTIAN FAITH. It is "LOVE". (1 Cor.

OUTER SPACE PEOPLE AND INNER EARTH PEOPLE

18:1-18.) Love God, love thy neighbor, love thyself, love thine enemies. (Matt. 5:44, Matt. 22:37-89, Mark 12:80-38, Luke 6:27.) "BY THIS SHALL ALL MEN KNOW THAT YE ARE MY DISCIPLES, IF YE HAVE LOVE ONE TO ANOTHER." (John 13:85.) "Every tree is known by his own fruit." (Luke 6:44.) "By their fruits ye shall know them." (Matt. 7:20.) What is the fruit, by which a Christian is known? And how do we know that a Christian has the Holy Spirit dwelling in him (or her)? Here is the answer: "The fruit of the Spirit is love, joy, peace, long-suffering, gentleness, goodness, faith, meekness; temperance; against such there is no law . . . if we live in the Spint, let us also walk in the Spirit. Let us not be desirous of vain glory, provoking one another, envying one another." (Gal. 5:22-26.) "The fruit of the Spirit is in all goodness and righteousness and truth; proving what is acceptable unto the Lord." (Eph. 5:9.)

You cannot produce the fruit of the Spirit without the Spirit. If you are indwelt by the Holy Spirit, you will produce the fruit of the Spirit: LOVE, joy, peace, etc. This, and this only, is the evidence that you are a Christian. It is perfectly all right to desire the spiritual gifts. All of the gifts are wonderful but one gift, or two gifts, or all of the gifts for that matter, are not the evidence that you are a Christian.

LOVE is the evidence—the only evidence that you are a Christian is LOVE. An evil generation seeketh a sign—tongues, healings, miracles, something spectacular. But a true Christian recognizes every other true Christian by the radiant LOVE and joy that flows from heart to heart.

Superstition And Magic

All mankind seems to be instinctively superstitious. This is not only true of the uneducated savage but also of the educated and highly civilized peoples throughout the world. There are more astrologers, spiritualists, mediums and prognosticators in London, England, per capita than in any other city on earth. More ghost stories come out of the British Islands than from any other area. Britain and the countries of Holland and Belgium immediately across the channel are the breeding places of the finest human beings that are on this earth. Also the best horses, cattle and sheep were bred in that area. The elevation and the mild misty climate make it adaptable to breeding. The climate is also conductive to mysticism, and to intellectuality, too. But right here in America it is alleged that some of our Presidents have consulted astrologers. The late German dictator was greatly influenced by the books on Isis, the adepts, avatars, and cycles. I doubt very much if there is a person on earth who does not have some degree of what others call superstition. If this is inherent, if it is an instinct, then may I say that there must be some truth in it somewhere, for there are no false instincts.

We know that it is dangerous to handle radium and that when minerals and metals are radioactive, they are deadly. The human body can become magnetized and destroyed slowly or instantly by that power. The point that I am making is this: "All scripture is given by inspiration of God." (II Tim. 3:16.) "Holy men of God spake as they were moved by the Holy Ghost." (II Peter 1:2I.) "Ye shall receive power after that the Holy Ghost is come upon you." (Acts 1:8.) Ten days after this was spoken, the Holy Ghost came upon the disciples and came to stay forever as the teacher, guide and comforter and giver of

OUTER SPACE PEOPLE AND INNER EARTH PEOPLE

power to all flesh (all people). Yahshua our Messiah said: "It is the Spirit that giveth life. The words that I speak unto you, they are spirit and they are life." (John 6:68.) "Man shall not live by bread alone, but by EVERY word that proceedeth out of the mouth of God." (Matt. 4:4.) There is a supernatural Divine power in EVERY word of the Bible. There is power in the written word, more power where the word is spoken. Now this power may be had and used in the right way or it may be used in the wrong way. Nevertheless, the power is there just the same.

I most surely do not endorse maqic. It is wrong to take every Psalm and every verse of the Bible and group them each for the healing of every kind of disease and the solving of every problem of man, but the entire Bible has been made up and used as just such a magical formula. I do not endorse it. I am afraid of it. There are only two scriptures that I have tested out in this manner and used successfully, perhaps a dozen times in my life. I will tell you what they are:

The Scripture That Is Alleged To Stop Bleeding

If a person is bleeding internally or externally, you pronounce the name of the person, which to illustrate, I shall call Richard Roe. "Richard Roe, when I passed by thee, and saw thee polluted in thine own blood, I said unto thee when thou wast in thy blood, Live; Yea, I said unto thee when thou wast in thy blood, Live." (Ezek. 16:6.) "In the Name of the Father, and of the Son and of the Holy Ghost. Amen." This is repeated three times. It is alleged that the bleeding will stop instantly. Every time that I have used it and everytime that I have seen and heard others use it, it has worked.

The Scripture That Answers Your Questions

Take a key and put it on Ruth 1:16-17. "And Ruth said, Intreat me not to leave thee, or to return from following after thee: for whither thou goest I will go; and where thou lodgest, I will lodge: Thy people shall be my people, and thy God my God: Where thou diest, will I die, and there will I be buried: The Lord do so to me, and more also, if aught but death part thee and me." (Ruth 1:16-17.)

Be sure that the key is on that scripture, then take a string and bind the Bible tight so that the key cannot slip, leaving, of course, the ring of the key (skeleton key type) outside of the Bible. Then you have a friend help you balance the Bible by both of you putting your index finger of the right hand under the ring of the key. You then ask any question whatsoever. After you have asked the question, begin by saying A, B, C, etc., through the alphabet. On a certain letter the Bible will turn and drop.

Write down the letter at which the Bible turned, then start the alphabet again, writing down the letter each time that the Bible turns and drops, and you will spell out the answer to your question—the person, place, thing, event or a Yes or No answer. I have used this three or four times in my life in an extreme emergency to find out what person said or did a certain thing. The answer came out clearly, giving the name of the person. I know more about these things which I shall always conceal and never reveal except to real friends who put themselves in position to receive these secrets.

DO YOU REMEMBER MY SERMON IN THE FEBRUARY, 1961 Issue of Showers Of

OUTER SPACE PEOPLE AND INNER EARTH PEOPLE

Blessing?

If you read it, you will remember that I stated that the heart, liver, kidney, brain and various glands and organs of the body each have their own vibration and susceptibility. On March 7th, a panel of experts in the field of radiation addressed the 26th annual mid-winter clinical session of the Colorado State Medical Society in the Hilton Hotel in Denver. They reported that:

The research and diagnostic uses hinge on the employment of radioisotopes as tracers—tagged atoms which constantly reveal their presence, like a belled cat, and much remains to be learned from them in this role.

Treatment via radioisotopes depends upon the ability of certain chemicals to carry a load of radiation selectively to special organs with an affinity for that chemical. Iodine, for example, is taken up by thyroid tissue, and zinc by the pancreas.

By converting the element to its radioactive form—probably the major achievement of the atomic age—it can be used to deliver specific doses of radiation to the organ for which it has special attraction.

Brief discussion was given to giving a patient a non-radioactive element with an affinity for a special type of tissue—specifically, in this case, boron and brain tumor tissue—and then bombarding the element from outside the body with neutrons.

The streams of neutrons would convert the boron into radio-boron, which, in turn, would deliver a sustained dose of radiation to the tumor. The panel agreed the new method is intellectually fascinating but so far not very practical.

Dr. Bauer listed radioiodine and radiophosphorus as the most useful isotopes at present in treating certain special forms of cancer. Radio iodine is used in some type of thyroid cancer and misfunction, and radiophosphorus against certain blood and bone diseases.

He also mentioned recent experimental use of radioitrium to attack pituitary gland in the control of advanced breast cancer in women.

In my sermon, I advanced the theory that, not only the brain, but all of the glands and organs hold various kinds of knowledge and that they have an emotional response. I was emphasizing the fact that the modern versions of the Bible are wrong in substituting the word "mind" for "the heart", kidneys, liver and other organs, that each of these organs has its own intellectual and emotional importance. When the Bible says "heart" or "bowels", it does not mean the brain or mind. Every person who has ever experienced the sensation of the Holy Spirit knows that sometimes it is felt only in the head or face or arms or hands. At other times it is felt in the heart or bowels or some other part of the body. Evidently the revisers and pseudo-translators who gave us the American Revised Standard Version of the Bible were entirely ignorant of the Holy Spirit in our emotional experiences and feeling, so they used the word "mind" for "heart", etc. Actually they did not translate, but they threw out Hebrew and Greek words and substituted "mind", which was their own bright idea. In other words, they thought they knew more

OUTER SPACE PEOPLE AND INNER EARTH PEOPLE

than the original prophets and apostles who wrote the original scriptures and used "heart", "kidneys", etc.

Extra-Sensory Perception "Works"

Whether you call it extra-sensory perception (ESP) or by another name, there is a kind of communication that cannot be explained by any of the five senses. And the messages transmitted are more likely to be received by well-adjusted persons than by others.

A University of Denver professor, Dr. Robert L. Van de Castle, made these observations Tuesday in an interview after speaking on ESP at Colorado College in Colorado Springs. Persons who are "rigid" and withdrawn don't score as well on ESP tests, Van de Castle said. Those who are well adjusted and react spontaneously do much better. Van de Castle deplored the lack of research on the subject, pointing out that the only full-time laboratory devoted to it in the United States is at Duke University in Durham, N. C.

Experiments indicate that there are more than five senses, he said, and some physiologists believe there may be seven or eight. But whatever the explanation, there are persons who have an awareness of objects or thoughts that cannot be attributed to any of the five senses of sight, smell, touch, hearing or taste, he said.

There is also evidence that this awareness is present to a more pronounced degree in animals than in humans, he added, citing examples of dogs that have traveled half way across the country to find a lost master.

Van de Castle, a clinical psychologist, listed three forms of ESP: mental telepathy (mind to mind interaction) clairvoyance (mind and object interaction) and pre-cognition (ability to foretell events).

In another category he placed psychokinesis,, which he described as mind over matter, such as a person willing a set of dice to come up with a certain number.—THE DENVER POST, Aug. 6, 1960.

Have A Pencil Ready For Word From Space.

By Jack Gaskie, Rocky Mountain News, Aug. 9, 1960.

You'd feel pretty silly if you didn't have a pencil and paper handy just when you got the word from the outer-space people, wouldn't you? The message might be anything—from how to build flying saucers, to how to putt your way around the golf course. Even if you're one of those wise guys who don't believe in flying saucers and mental telepathy, it won't do you any harm to carry the pencil and paper just in case, will it?

Donald C. Tilton of Palm Springs, Calif., poses the question:

The whole flying saucer bit is relatively simple, according to Tilton, if you'll only get it in mind that not every flying saucer is a flying saucer. What you actually have, are flying saucers, flying discs and flying bells, all of which are launched from a rocket-mother ship. The mother ships used to come quite close to Earth—remember back in 1897, when one was seen just a few hundred feet over Chicago?

OUTER SPACE PEOPLE AND INNER EARTH PEOPLE

They'll still come close once in a while, like the one Tiiton claims he saw last year over Palm Springs, and the one three years ago over Florida. But by and large the mother ships stay well away from Earth these days—250 miles or so. From that altitude, they launch the bells, saucers and discs. The bell is the old-fashioned type, Tilton said—probably in use about 10,000 years. It gets its drive from a wheel within a wheel sort of construction.

The disc is the red-hot little bugger. Only 24 to 36 inches in diameter, it scoots around at 80,000 miles an hour, taking pictures and sound recordings. Many of the sightings of objects called saucers have actually been of the discs. The saucers themselves are much bigger-24 feet in diameter for the smallest, carrying one, and much bigger for the others that carry up to eight men.

Thus, Arnold recalled, a couple of chaps from Venus established their identity by digginq a quarter-inch groove with their finger tips into the oak desk of a California newspaper editor whom they were asking for a job.

They didn't get the job.

Now, for the ESP bit. It just makes sense, Tilton said, that other-planet-people who developed space ships and flying saucers, etc., are on a higher plane than Earthmen, and have developed the use of "telepathy, mental phenomena and other occult powers. Acting on this assumption, he said, he studied ESP, worked on hypnotism, and otherwise prepared himself. Sure enough, he made contact. His unearthly informant gave him some information on how flying saucers operate.

The Angels Of Mons

THE ANGELS OF MONS -1914. AND THE WHITE CAVALRY AND FURTHER VISIONS OF THE WHITE CAVALRY are reprinted from the book "How God Won The War" by Philip E. S. Monson, in which he gives credit to Capt. C. Wrightwick Haywood, formerly Staff Captain, 1st Corps Intelligence 1st Army (British) Headquarters 1916-1918 for the following information:

The Angel of Mons-1914. During the World War of 1914-1918 there were certainly two outstanding occasions when God fulfilled His promise, as far as Great Britain was concerned, in a most noticeable manner.

The first of these was at or near, the town of Mons, during the battle of that name between the German forces and the British Army, towards the end of August, 1914. The German Army, after sweeping all resistance aside, had advanced on a wide front right into the heart of Belgium and France. Although the Belgians, French and British put up a stout defense, it was principally against the British that the heaviest enemy attacks were launched. Our troops, greatly outnumbered, had been fighting continuously for several days, with little or no rest and our men were almost dropping from fatigue after a prolonged rear-guard action, during which we had lost numbers of men and guns. Serious defeat appeared inevitable, especially as we had practically no reserves ready, though recruits were being drilled in hundreds in England.

OUTER SPACE PEOPLE AND INNER EARTH PEOPLE

It was realized that a "Day of Trouble" had arrived, and that God alone could help us. Churches were crowded with the whole of the British Nation at prayer. Then occurred the event afterwards known as the appearance of the "Angels of Mons," in answer to National Prayer. Of several accounts, referring to the appearance of "Angels" the following two are typical, both having been related by British soldiers who vouched for the occurrence as having been observed by them personally.

(1) While the detachment of British soldiers was retiring through Mons under very heavy German artillery and machine-gun fire in August, 1914, they knelt behind a hastily-erected barricade and endeavored to hold up the enemy advance. The firing on both sides was very intensive and the air reverberated with deafening crashes of exploding shells. Suddenly, fire on both sides STOPPED DEAD and a sudden silence fell. Looking over their barrier, the astonished British saw four or five hundred BEINGS, much bigger than men, between themselves and the halted Germans. They were white-robed and bareheaded, and seemed rather to float than stand. Their backs were towards the British, and they faced the enemy with outstretched arm and hand, as if to say, "Stop. Thus far and no further." The sun was shining quite brightly at the time. Next thing the British knew was that the Germans were retreating in great disorder.

(2) On another occasion the British were in danger of being surrounded by the Germans, and had lost numbers of guns and men. Just when matters seemed hopeless, the heavy enemy fire suddenly STOPPED DEAD and a great silence fell over all. The sky opened up in a bright shining light and figures of "luminous Beings" appeared. They seemed to float between the British and the German forces, and to prevent the further advance of the enemy. Some of the Germans cavalry was advancing, and the officers and men were unable to get their horses to go forward.

Before the surprised British were able to realize what had happened, the whole of the apparently victorious enemy force were retreating in great disorder. This allowed the British and Allied Armies to re-form and fall back upon a line of defense several miles further west, where they "dug in." Then began the period of "Trench Warfare", which continued for over three years, with varying fortunes to their side until the spring of 1918. The story of The "Angels of Mons" flashed through England, thrilling many who believed that God always heard the prayer of His people, especially when they called upon Him in the "Day of Trouble".

The White Cavalry

THE WHITE CAVALRY -1918 :The following account of what occurred between the months of April and August 1918, I can personally vouch for as being true, as far as that area of the front line trenches is concerned, lying roughly between the town of Arras, some fifteen miles south of Bethune, in La Bassee (France),

I was responsible for the Intelligence on this sector of the Battle Area, and therefore made my headquarters in the bright little town of Bethune, as it was a very good strategicai position and had also remained practically untouched by enemy shell fire, although it was barely three miles from the trenches just across the La Bassee Canal.

OUTER SPACE PEOPLE AND INNER EARTH PEOPLE

The reason for its immunity up to that time, and during three long years of war, lay in the fact that the German Headquarters Staff of the Army opposed to us had earmarked it for themselves when they advanced, as they wished to find comfortable houses and beds ready for their occupation as soon as they captured the British trenches.

But they never succeeded in achieving this particular objective! It was a well-known fact that the enemy was about to launch a most vigorous offensive in the early spring of 1918, and had buoyed their troops up with the promise that this time they would get through to Paris.

It was an anxious time for Great Britain. The British troops had been in the trenches fighting for weeks without rest or relief, owing to the fact that reserves were practically exhausted. Although the United States had now thrown in her lot with us, and the British Dominions were helping the Mother country, most of their troops were still on their way across the Atlantic, and some time must necessarily elapse before they could come into the fighting line in any great numbers.

It was at this juncture that Portugal came in on our side and raised a conscripted Army which landed in France early in March, 1918. Towards the end of that month I was instructed by Headquarters that a Portuguese Force would be passing through Bethune shortly, in order to relieve the British, who had been holding it for so long.

I was also instructed to take steps to arrest two German spies who would be accompanying them, disguised as Portuguese soldiers, as it was urgently necessary to find out the enemy's immediate plans, and this information could probably be obtained from the spies.

This would be no easy task, for out of about five hundred or so Portuguese I had to pick out two who would obviously be more Portuguese than their companions.

I had under my command about twenty-five men and a Sergeant known as "Intelligence Police", who had already afforded considerable help as to projected enemy movements. I called in the Sergeant and explained the position to him.

"But how are we to find two Portuguese who are Huns in disguise out of this crowd coming up, sir?" he asked.

"I can only think of one way," I replied. "I have lived a few years in Germany and Spain and know that the National drink of the Germans is BEER, whereas the National drink of the Portuguese is WINE.

Now when these troops come through Bethune on their way to the front line trenches they are bound to be given a short while in which to have drinks in the cafe by the main square here. You must follow them in, and look out for any men who order BEER, because they will be Germans. It will never strike them that they may thus give themselves away. Collar hold of these men at any cost and bring them here to me. Take any of your men you wish, to help you.

The Sergeant grinned. "I understand, sir; just leave it to me. We'll get 'em all right." He saluted smartly and left the office.

OUTER SPACE PEOPLE AND INNER EARTH PEOPLE

When the Portuguese detachment marched into Bethune a few days later, I walked out to see them. It was immediately obvious that they were totally unfitted for trench warfare, and also that they had not the slightest idea of what they were in for. Most of them were scarcely more than boys, peasant lads straight from the vineyards, who carried their rifles as if they were picks and hoes; whose uniforms fitted them badly, and whose bandoliers hung about them "all anyhow." As expected, as soon as they reached the main square, orders were given for them to fall out for about an hour's rest and they surged chattering towards the principal cafe, where two pretty French girls served drinks and chaffed the men thronging the bar.

The sound of heavy firing, which had been going on without ceasing for several days past and which had been intensified by bursts of machine-gun fire, while the lowering sky was lit by star shells and Very Lights, died down considerably, and there was an ominous lull on the front.

I know that the Germans had been reinforced by contingents from the Russian front, where fighting had ceased owing to the collapse of the Czarist Army and the Bolshevik Revolution; so I wondered what unpleasant surprise the enemy had in store for the British troops now holding the La Bassee Sector.

All this time there had been a loud buzz of conversation from the cafe, but now it rose to a louder pitch, Then came a sound of angry voices, a crash of glasses, screams of frightened women, a splintering of furniture, followed by a surging mass of struggling figures pouring out of the doors. Whistles blew from all sides as British and French Military Police rushed on the scene and commenced arresting men wholesale. Out of the surging mass issued my Sergeant and a couple of his men, holding tight onto two Portuguese soldiers. Quickly they ran them out of the crowd, and followed me to my office.

"How did you get them?" I asked the Sergeant.

"We followed the Portuguese into the 'kaffay' and watched them as they ordered drinks. Sure enough, more of 'em ordered 'Venno', but along came these two beauties and said: Biere, Mamzelle. So accidentally on purpose I bumped up against one of 'em and joggled his elbow as he was about, to drink, upsetting his beer. Schweinhund (pig-dog), he yelled in fluent German turning purple with rage, and striking at me. I hit him under the jaw and knocked him down. Then his mate came for me, during the following mix-up we got hold of our men."

"Good work, Sergeant; I congratulate you. Bring in the prisoners."

Two apparently vacuous Portuguese peasant-soldiers shuffled in and stood "all anyhow" as they gazed at me with feigned lack-luster eyes.

"ATTENTION!" I rapped out sharply in German.

The habit of instant obedience to strict discipline was too strong for them. Quickly their heels clicked together, their arms straightened downward, and the figures assumed the stiff smartness of well-trained Prussian soldiers.

"Good!" I said. "I knew you were German soldiers; it is no use pretending any

OUTER SPACE PEOPLE AND INNER EARTH PEOPLE

longer that you are not. Furthermore, you are spies, but we have succeeded in stopping you before you got into touch with your Headquarters."

As I hoped, this drew them.

"You are wrong Hem Herr," said the younger of the two. "We sent off pigeons with code messages containing detailed information regarding the number and disposition of the Portuguese in this front line sector, just before entering Bethune."

"Shut your mouth!" growled his companion angrily, in German. But it was too late. I had obtained the information I desired, so I ordered the prisoners to be kept under guard until arrangements could be made to send them to the base Headquarters of the British Army. This was done the following day, and I heard no more of them, but presumably they were eventually sent to a Prisoners of War Camp in England.

I sent off my Report of the occurrence to H. Q. Intelligence by Dispatch Rider, but was not sure how long it would take him to find them, as they had changed their site since the commencement of the heavy German offensive during the third week of March, 1918. It was evident that the enemy was about to intensify this offensive shortly, with a greater concentration of men and heavy guns, augmented by the troops from the Russian Front. On our side, especially between March and June, our troops had been greatly reduced in numbers by heavy casualties in the prolonged fighting during those months, and our Reserves were practically exhausted.

Although by the middle of May the United States of America had decided to join Great Britain and her Allies, their troops were still being formed, though the first contingent was on its way across the Atlantic. Later on, they came over at the rate of 50,000 weekly; but these reinforcements were not available for the front line much before the middle of June, according as they were dispatched to the various sectors.

As things stood, owing to vigorous enemy action against the Allied lines to the north of Bethune, the line from La Bassee to Lens and Arras was left in a "pocket" which was liable to be "hemmed in" at any moment with all the troops, ammunition, arms and equipment it contained.

It was highly improbable that the Portuguese troops who had by now taken over the La Bassee trenches in front of Bethune would make much difference to the enemy's plans. Indeed, they did not, for though there had been a temporary lull in the roar of gun fire, it broke out again shortly afterwards with intensified fury. So tremendous was the reverberating crash of concentrated shell and high explosive fire that it literally shook the ground and dazed us, though we were nearly three miles behind the front line.

It fell with a dense hail of shrapnel and lead on the unfortunate Portuguese, practically blotting them out wholesale, and thus causing a gap in our front line through which the enemy began to pour in mass formation. The few Portuguese left came staggering through Bethune, having thrown away their arms and equipment in their mad desire to get away from the hell behind them as quickly as possible.

Shortly afterwards they were followed by British troops, whose flank had been

OUTER SPACE PEOPLE AND INNER EARTH PEOPLE

turned and who were retiring in good order, keeping up a stiff rear guard action as they went. The town became a pandemonium; shells fell thickly among the houses, which collapsed in ruins all around us; terrified women and children ran screaming, purposelessly about. Obviously the thing to do was to get the civil population out of danger as soon as possible. But when I went to arrange the matter with the French "Maire" I found he had fled, together with all the poiice and many of the officials. I discovered others in the act of getting away in the remaining motor-cars, having stacked them with their own personal belongings, not caring what happened to the women and children left behind. I was very angry, and gave my men strict orders to pull them out of their cars, and tell them to walk if they wanted to get away.

During the following hectic hours we managed to clear the town of all the women and children by utilizing the available cars, or by commandeering any passing British motor-lorry. But it was difficult work to carry out amidst the crash of falling high explosive shells and tumbling masonry, especially as many of the inhabitants were most reluctant to leave the remains of their homes. But we obliged them to do so, for the enemy was now beginning to pepper the town with gas shells, and there was no use in leaving them to perish.

In the meantime the enemy's advance had been checked by machine-gun fire from small groups of British Tommies, who dug into shell holes just by the La Bassee Canal, but a mile beyond the town of Bethune. But it was doubtful whether they could do so much longer, as the enemy was increasing his force and had begun to concentrate high explosive and machine-gun fire upon them, previous to a bayonet attack in mass formation.

In England everyone was asking: "Would the Germans get through to Paris?" "Would the English ports be shelled shortly by German big guns from the coast of France?" But those who remembered how God had helped us with the "Angels of Mons" when we called upon Him, were sure He would do so again.

"Be not afraid, Israel, for I have redeemed thee; neither be thou afraid Jacob, for I have saved thee. When the enemy is come in like a flood he shall not overwhelm thee."

The whole of the British Nation was called to prayer and Thanksgiving. The President of the United States had summoned the American people to do likewise; and united prayer went up to God from all the English-speaking peoples.

In the meantime, the enemy shell fire, which had been largely directed against the shattered town of Bethune, suddenly lifted and began to burst on a slight rise beyond its outskirts. This open ground was absolutely bare of trees, houses or human beings, yet the enemy gun fire broke on it with increasing fury, and was augmented by heavy bursts of massed machine-guns which raked it backward and forward with a hail of lead. We stood looking in astonishment.

"Fritz has gone balmy, sir," said the Sergeant. "What in the world is he peppering that naked ground for?"

"I can't think," l replied. "Get along down to the canal and see what is happening

OUTER SPACE PEOPLE AND INNER EARTH PEOPLE

there."

I followed him shortly afterwards, being eager to see for myself, as there were obviously no troops within sight against whom the Germans could be directing their fire. As I made my way over the scattered debris of ruined houses, the enemy's fire suddenly ceased, and a curious calm fell on everything. I went on wondering, and got outside the town. Then a lark suddenly arose from the remains of a meadow, and soared up, up, up, singing a thrilling song of thankfulness which rings on my inward ear today when I think of it. I saw my Sergeant and men standing on the edge of a shell hole waving their "tin hats". They shouted out: "Fritz is retiring! Fritz is retiring!"

Indeed he was. Outlined on the slight rise by the Las Bassee village, and far as we could see, was a dense line of German troops who a short time before had commenced a forward movement to victory, in mass formation. This line suddenly halted, and, as we watched, saw it BREAK!

Before our astonished eyes that well-drilled and seemingly victorious Army broke up into groups of frightened men, who were fleeing from us, throwing down their arms, haversacks, rifles, coats and anything which might impede their flight.

"Get out after them," I ordered. "Bring back prisoners, officers if possible. We must find out what all this is about."

With a rousing cheer the men leaped forward, and were soon joined by other Tommies, who raced after the enemy, stopping now and again to fire a few rounds, then charging on with fixed bayonets. It was not long before my Sergeant arrived with two German officer prisoners, and he was soon followed by Tommies bringing in batches of twenty or so at a time.

Briefly, the statement the senior officer made was as follows: "The order had been given to advance in mass formation, and our troops were marching behind us singing their way to victory, when Fritz, my lieutenant here, said:

"Herr Kapitan, just look at that open ground behind Bethune; there is a Brigade of Calvary coming up through the smoke drifting across it. They must be mad, these Engiish, to advance against such a force as ours in the open. I suppose they must be cavalry of one of the Colonial forces, for see, they are all in white uniform and are mounted on white horses."

"Strange, I said. I never heard of the English having any white uniform cavalry, whether Colonial or not. They have all been fighting on foot for several years past, and, anyhow, they are in khaki, not white."

"Well, they are plain enough, he replied, See, our guns have got their range now; they will be blown to pieces in no time.

"We saw the shells bursting amongst the horses and their riders, all of whom came forward at a quiet walk trot, in parade ground formation, each man and horse in his exact place.

OUTER SPACE PEOPLE AND INNER EARTH PEOPLE

"Shortly afterwards, our machine guns opened a heavy fire, raking the advancing cavalry with a dense hail of lead. But they came quietly forward, though the shells were bursting amongst them with intensified fury, and NOT A SINGLE MAN OR HORSE FELL!

"Steadily they advanced , clear in the shining sunlight; and a few paces in front of them rode their Leader—a fine figure of a man, whose hair, like spun gold, shone in aura round his bare head. By his side was a great sword, but his hands lay quietly holding his horse's reins, as his huge white charger bore him proudly forward.

"In spite of heavy shell, and concentrated machine-gun fire, the White Cavalry advanced; remorseless as fate, like the incoming tide surging over a sandy beach.

"Then a great FEAR fell on me, and I turned to flee. Yes, I, an officer of the Prussian Guard, fled, panic-stricken and around me were hundreds of terrified men, whimpering like children; throwing away their arms and accoutrements in order not to have their movements impeded. . .all running.

"Their intense desire was to get away from that remorselessly advancing White Cavalry, but most of all from their awe-inspiring Leader, whose hair shone like spun gold around his bare head, and whose hands lay quietly holding the reins of his great white charger.

"That is all I have to tell you. We are beaten. The German Army is broken. They may be fighting, but we have lost the war; we are beaten by the White Cavalry. I cannot understand—I cannot understand. . ."

During the following few days I examined many prisoners, and in substance their accounts tallied with the one given here. This in spite of the fact that at least two of us could swear that we saw no cavalry in action, here or elsewhere, at that particular time. Neither did any of us see so much as a single white horse either with or without a rider. But it was not necessary for us to do so; the evidence of their presence had to come from the enemy.

Shortly after this the American forces came into action on the whole front and about the second week in July there was a general advance which resulted in the capture of over 4,000 enemy and 100 guns on the sector between Bethune and Ypres during the ensuing weeks.

It is interesting to note that Official Reports give July 11th as the date of the Allied advance, for by November 11, 1918, at 11 a.m. the war had ended and an Armistice was declared. Between those dates the British and Allied forces captured 385,000 prisoners and over 5,000 guns.

But It Was God Who "Won The War"

During the years of 1930-84, I have had confirming evidence of this account after relating it to large audiences. Once a man who said that he had captured many of the German prisoners at that time; and that they could speak of nothing but the "White Cavalry" and their awe inspiring Leader; and another time from a lady who said she had been a nurse who attended the German wounded, and that they all spoke in awe-struck

OUTER SPACE PEOPLE AND INNER EARTH PEOPLE

tones of the "White Cavalry". The same evening as she looked across the shell-battered countryside, she saw the sun shine on the white uniforms and horses of a body of cavalry and the next moment they disappeared, leaving the countryside bare and shattered as it had been before. The "White Cavalry" had finished its work.

Further Visions Of The White Cavalry

On August 27, 1939, while I was at Swanage, Dorset, England, I saw a party of WHITE CAVALRY riding along the Downs towards me; there were about fifty men and their Leader, all in white uniforms. The Leader's head was bare, and his hair shone like a gold aura in the bright sunlight.

Halting not far from where I was sitting, they lifted their swords, high above their heads, and Cried out "HAIL BROTHER!"

Four detached themselves from the party, one rode EAST, one WEST, one NORTH, one SOUTH.

"Pickets," I thought, "going to guard the four corners of the Empire." The others dismounted, and seemed to be tending to their horses. Then suddenly—they were gone; and only the white winged seagulls floated past me out towards the shimmering sea.

The British Nation had dedicated itself to GOD in National Prayer before the war started on September 3, 1939, and truly we have been blessed, guided and guarded during these three and a half years of war.

On Sunday, May 25, 1940, when it seemed certain that the whole of the British Expeditionary Force in Belgium would be annihilated by the overwhelming German Armies, the King-Emperor of Great Britain and her Dominions called a National Day of Prayer through the whole of the Empire, and GOD'S answer was the outstanding deliverance of 365,000 men at Dunkirk, who were safely evacuated across a channel of unprecedented calmness unknown to previous history.

It was about that time that I again saw the WHITE CAVALRY—this time in the garden of my own home in Surrey.

The rising ground behind the garden disappeared, and a white cloud unrolled itself toward the distant horizon. Along this cloud came riding a considerable party of the WHITE CAVALRY on their white horses, all of the men having their swords drawn.

The leader had his great sword drawn also, and his head was covered with a golden helm. As they drew nearer, they halted, and a sudden SILENCE held all Nature bound. Then they lifted their swords simultaneously, four times in succession, crying out: "FOR GOD! FOR CHRIST! FOR THE KING! FOR EMPIRE!

Each time they lifted their swords a little white flame leaped from the tips dying down again as they lowered them. They sat motionless for a short minute and again a great SILENCE held all Nature bound. Then, raising their swords once more, and swinging them round their heads in circles of flame, they shouted: "HURRAH! HURRAH! HURRAH! Next minute they had vanished, and once again Nature resumed her sway in the

OUTER SPACE PEOPLE AND INNER EARTH PEOPLE

song of the birds and the whisper of the breeze in the tall Douglas pines.

THE LORD OF HOSTS IS WITH US. WHO SHALL STAND AGAINST US?

The End.

There are different orders of angels, with different rank and dignity. They are organized into "principalities, powers, thrones, dominions." Rom. 8:38, Eph. 1:21, 8:10, Col 1:16, 2:15, 1 Peter 3:22. Michael is the name of the Archangel. He was the patron-angel of Judah, Dan 10:13,21 12:1. He contended with the devil about the body of Moses, Jude 9. He struggles with Satan in behalf of the Church, Rev. 12:17. He will be with Christ when he comes, and his voice will raise the dead, I Thes 4:16. Gabriel is the name of one of the angel princes, see note under Lk 2:8-20.

Occasionaliy the word "angel" seems to refer to the inanimate forces of nature. But generally it unmistakably means personalities of the unseen world. So much is said in the Bible about the ministry of Angels that we are constrained to believe that God uses them in part to execute His will in running the universe.

REVELATION Angels play a large part in directing the panorama and scenery of the visions, and in the writing of the book. An Angel dictated the book to John, 1:2; 22:16.

Each of the Seven Churches had an Angel, 1:20; 2:1, etc.

An angel was interested in the Sealed Book, 5-2.

100,000,000 Angels sang praise to the Lamb 5:11.

Four Angels were given power to hurt the earth, 7:1-4.

An Angel sealed the Elect, 7:I-4.

The Angels fell down on their faces before God, 7:11.

An Angel was used in answering prayers of the saints, 8:8-5.

Seven Angels sounded the Seven Trumpets, 8:6, 7, etc.

An Angel of the abyss was king of the locust army, 9:11.

Four Angels loosed the 200,000,000 Euphratean Horsemen, 9:15, 16.

An Angel had the Open Book announcing the End, 10:1,2,6.

Michael and his Angels warred with the Dragon and his Angels, 12:7.

A flying Angel proclaimed the Gospel to the nations, 14:6.

Another flying Angel proclaimed the Fall of Babylon, 14:8,

An Angel pronounced the doom of the Beast's followers, 14:9,10.

An Angel announced the Harvest of the Earth, 14:15.

An Angel announced the Vintage of the Earth, 14:18,19.

OUTER SPACE PEOPLE AND INNER EARTH PEOPLE

Seven Angels had the Seven Last Plagues, 15: 1.

An Angel announced Judgment on Babylon, 17: 1,5.

An Angel again announced the Fall of Babylon, 18:2.

An Angel had part in dealing Babylon its Death-Blow, 18:21.

An Angel presided over the Destruction of the Beast, 19: 17.

An Angel bound Satan, 20:12.

An Angel showed John the New Jerusalem, 21:9.

12 Angels guarded the 12 gates of the New Jerusalem, 21 : 19 .

An Angel forbade John to worship him, 22:9.

Thus, here in the book of Revelation, are twenty-seven different references to the activities of Angels.

The word "Angel", literally, means. "Messenger". As used in the Bible, it applies, mostly to Supernatural Personalities of the Unseen World, employed as messengers in the service of God, or Satan.

Angels figured largely in the life of Jesus. Throughout the Bible a good deal is said about Angels.

The "Angels" of the Churches, 2:1, etc., are thought by some to have been messengers sent by the Churches to visit John in Patmos; or, the Pastors of the Churches; or, the Guardian Angels of the Churches; or, Heavenly Representatives of the Churches.

John, in the Seven Letters, was portraying, under divine direction, Heavenly Appraisals of Earthly Churches.

Giants.

The word giant has been translated from several Hebrew words.

1. Nephilim meaning: causing to fall, or violent. (Gen. 6:2, 4). These were men who beat down, oppressed and plundered the weak and defenseless.

2. In (Gen. 14:5 we meet with a race termed Rephaim, who settled on the other side of Jordan. Of this race Og, King of Bashan, alone remained in the days of Moses. (Deut.8:10). This race gave its name to a valley near Jerusalem.

3. The Alakim, sons of Anak. In Numbers 13 spies were sent out by Moses to spy out Israel's promised land. Ten of the spies reported:

"The people be strong that dwell in the land, moreover we saw the children of Anak." In the 32nd and 33rd verses of the same chapter we read: "It is a land that eateth up the inhabitants; and all the people that we saw in it are men of great stature. And there we saw giants, the sons of Anak, which came of the giants and we were in our sight as grasshoppers and so we were in their sight."

OUTER SPACE PEOPLE AND INNER EARTH PEOPLE

In Moses' time these giants were of three groups, Ahiman, Sheshai and Talmai, the children of Anak. (Numbers 13:22). They were destroyed by Joshua. (Joshua 11:21). He left none of the Aaakim in the land of the children of Israel, only in Gaza, in Gath and in Ashdod. Judges 1:20, Josh. 14:12.

Goliath came from the remnant of the Anakim. (I Sam. 17:4.)

We have the following Philistine giants mentioned: Ishbi-benob and Sapn, and a man of great stature whom Jonathan slew. (I Kings 20:8, 2 Sam. 20:22, 1 Sam. 17:4.)

4. The Emim are mentioned in Deut. 2:10. They dwelt in the country of the Moabites. (Gen.14:5.)

5. The Zamzummin who dwelt in the land of Ammon. (Deut. 21:20.)

For many years Bible Students believed and taught that the giants in the earth originally came through the marriage of the sons of God (angels) with the daughters of men. Let us read carefully Gen. 6:4: "There were giants (Nephilim) in the earth in those days and after that when the sons of God came in unto the daughters of men and they bare chiidren to them, the same became mighty men which were of old men of renown. We are all familiar with the Scripture which tells us that angels never may nor are given in marriage so evidently the sons of God mentioned in Gen. 6:4 were not angels, and that there were giants before this union of sons of God with dauqhters of men.-BIBLE STUDENT INQUIRER.

The Devil's Wife.

The name of the wife of Lucifer is LILITH. This is the Hebrew in Isaiah 34:14, which is translated "the screech owl." It could be and often is translated five different ways. Probably "night phantom" or "ghost" would be more correct than "screech owl". I think it would have been just as well to have left it in the original Hebrew-"Lilith".

Lucifer was "the man" (Isa. 14:16) that ruled over a previous creation on this earth before it was disrupted and became "without form and void." (Gen. 1:1, Jer. 4:23-27.) He was also called "son of the morning." (Isa. 14:12.) For more about this read Ezekiel 28:11-19.

In the disruption of the earth Lucifer and Lilith and their entire race lost their bodies and have since then been disembodied evil spirits or demons (devils) inhabiting the atmosphere (air) of this present earth. Lucifer, in his disembodied state, is known as "that old serpent" and "Satan" or the Devil. The disembodied spirits are known as "devils". His family on the earth in the flesh are called "serpents and vipers." (Gen. 3:1, Matt. 3:7, Matt. 28:83, John 8:44, Rev. 2:9, Rev. 8:9, I Thes. 2:14-15, II John 7-11) The "vipers" are the female of the species and correspond to their mother "Lilith." The serpents and vipers living in the flesh are sentenced to the lake of fire at the end of the age, while those that are disembodied spirits (devils) are sentenced to the pit. Read it in Revelation 20:1-8. There is much written about "Lilith" in other ancient religious literature, but she is definitely mentioned in the Bible in Isaiah 84:14.

Since I am writing to students of the Bible, I request that you read the scripture

OUTER SPACE PEOPLE AND INNER EARTH PEOPLE

references given in this item and if possible look up the words in the original Hebrew.

Lucifer, who is Satan, the Devil, never was in that high heaven where Yahveh dwells. It is possible that he captured some of the planets in this solar system (Isa. 14:12-20) and that there was transit trade, investment and migration between the Earth, Venus and Mars before the earth was disrupted—that is before Lucifer, "the man", became a disembodied spirit. He (Lucifer) boasted that he would capture the highest heaven and exalt his name above that of Yahveh, but he did not succeed. It is admitted by astronomers that there are more than a billion suns as large or larger than our sun, that each one has a family of planets, and that there are definitely over a billion inhabited worlds in the heavens. Three heavens—and I want you to understand this— THREE HEAVENS belong to this earth. In the first heaven are CORPOREANS (having a body), physical earth people. In the second heaven are the ATMOSPHEREANS, or evil disembodied spirits. (This also includes the realm of "outer darkness"). In the third heaven are the "ETHEREANS", holy angels and spirits of just men made perfect. Satan, the devil, operates right now in both the first and second heavens of this earth, but not in the third heaven which is also called "Paradise" and is the Paradise ruling, spiritual realm over this earth.

There are several inhabited planets that are more sinful than this earth. (Job 15:15.) Yahshua the Messiah, in his ascension, sprinkled his own blood upon those lost heavenly worlds. (Eph. 4: 10, Heb. 9:8-24.) We are commissioned to preach the gospel to those inhabited planets in outer-space. (Eph. 8:9-12.) They eventually have to be united with us. (Eph. 1:10.) How wonderful it will be if you will only study these scriptures and think for yourself.

The Moon In Prophecy

"Moreover the light of the moon shall be as the light of the sun, and the light of the sun shall be sevenfold, as the light of seven days, in the day that the Lord bindeth up the breach of his people, and healeth the stroke of their wound." (Isa. 30:26.) The fulfillment of this prophecy in the ultimate will mean that the energy from the moon will be gradually increased to 400,000 times that of its present energy, and the energy from the sun will be increased seven times. Dr. L. M. Levitt, Astronomer and a researcher into interplanetary travel, during World War II served in the office of Scientific Research and Development. He says: "By the year 2000, I think we will be able to get energy readily from either the fusion process or from the sun. These will be sophisticated ways of getting energy. Thus, by the year 2000, I assume that the thing we'll have most of and cost least will be energy, and that goes for anywhere in, say, the solar system." (U. S. News and World Report, page 74, Jan. 17, 1958.) In the February 7th, 1958 issue of the same magazine on page 54, Brig. Gen. Homer A. Boushey, Deputy Director, Research and Development, U. S. Air Force, says: "Who controls the moon controls the earth," and he states at length his scientific reasons for that statement. You know that there is a mad rush on by Russia and America to reach the moon.

OUTER SPACE PEOPLE AND INNER EARTH PEOPLE

Bible Predicts Sputniks With Mechanical Brain

Bible predicts Sputniks with mechanical brain and many eyes (cameras). "As for the likeness of the living creatures, their appearance was like burning coals of fire, and like the appearance of lamps: it went up and down among the living creatures; and the fire was bright, and out of the fire went forth lightning. And the living creatures ran and returned as the appearance of a flash of lightning. Now as I beheld the living creatures, behold one wheel upon the earth by the living creatures, with his four faces. The appearance of the wheels and their work was like unto the color of a beryl: and they four had one likeness: and their appearance mid their work was as it were a wheel in the middle of a wheel. When they went they went upon their four sides: and they turned not when they went. As for their rings, they were so high that they were dreadful; and their rings were full of eyes round about them four. And when the living creatures went, the wheels went by them, and when the living creatures were lifted up from the earth, the wheels were lifted up. Whithersoever the spirit was to go, they went, thither was their spirit to go; and the wheels were lifted up over against them, for the spirit of the living creatures was in the wheels." (Ezek. 1: 13-20.)

The Sky Will Soon Be Full Of Sputniks

What is the danger, if any, from these things? There is a very grave danger! They can photograph every area and everything on the earth. But the real danger is in the hidden messages that they can relay. I am told that secret hidden advertising has been tested and proved successful. While watching television or a talking picture and being deeply absorbed in it, I am told that a picture and message which you can neither see nor hear is sandwiched in by vibrations. It is said that such advertising tested on children made them hungry and that there was a rush for soft drinks and popcorn so advertised by this hidden thing. It is not impossible for the sputniks to fill our sub-conscious minds full of propaganda which cause us to react in a strange way. It is something on the order of hypnotism or sleep-teaching through the picture and message (unseen and unheard) which is put into the mind while we are awake. The hour has come, Brother, that day is here! "Fearful sights and great signs shall there be from heaven." (Luke 21:11) "And there shall be signs in the sun, and in the moon, and in the stars; and upon the earth distress of nations, with perplexity; the sea and the waves roaring; men's hearts failing them for fear, and for looking after those things which are coming on the earth: for the powers of heaven shall be shaken." (Luke 21:25-26)

"Ye shall know the truth, and the truth shall make you free." (John 8:82.) "Ye, brethren, are not in darkness, that that day should overtake you as a thief. Ye are all the children of light and the children of the day: we are not of the night, nor of darkness." (I Thes. 5:4-5.) For he hath delivered us from the power of darkness, and hath translated us into the Kingdom of his dear Son." (Col. 1:18.)

There is no salvation in the Bible for institutions—that is, for Denominations and religious bodies that have become stale, lukewarm, creed-bound, or that are given over to priestcraft or modernism. But there is salvation for every person in those organizations, providing they will obey the Bible which says: "Come out of her my people, that

OUTER SPACE PEOPLE AND INNER EARTH PEOPLE

ye be not partakers of her sins." (Rev. 18:4.) "And what agreement hath the temple of God with idols? for ye are the temple of the living God; as God hath said, I will dwell in them, and walk in them; and I will be their God, and they shall be my people. Wherefore come out from among them, and be ye separate, said the Lord, and touch not the unclean thing; and I will receive you, And will be a Father unto you, and ye shall be my sons and daughters, saith the Lord Almighty." (II Cor. 6:16-18.)

I invite you to come out and to come into this movement to restore the original and true church with all of its gifts, ordinances, doctrine and power, and to know your own true Bible Israel identity, destiny, and all the kingdom truth. Let us revive, restore, reconcile and advance all that the Bible teaches.

The Seven Last Plagues Are Upon Us

The first plague is cancer-Rev. 16:12, Zech, 14 12. The second and third plagues are poisoned water- Rev. 16:3-4. The fourth plague began with the dropping of the atom bombs on Hiroshima and Nagasaki-Rev. 16:8-9. The fifth plague is the beastly governments of atheists-Rev. 16:9-10. The sixth plague is the "ARMAGEDDON"-Rev. 16:12-16. Armageddon is not a war, not a battle, but the assembly of the nations—the United Nations Organization. That's what Armageddon means.

THE SEVENTH PLAGUE IS IN THE AIR -Rev. 16:17-21. "And the seventh angel poured out his vial into the air; and there came a great voice out of the temple of heaven, from the throne, saying, It is done." (Rev. 16:17.)

All of the last plagues are upon us. Every end time prophecy is in fulfillment. "And great earthquakes shall be in divers places, and famines, and pestilences; and fearful sights and great signs shall there be from heaven. And there shall be signs in the sun, and in the moon, and in the stars; and upon the earth distress of nations, with perplexity; the sea and the waves roaring; men's hearts failing them for fear, and for looking after those things which are coming on the earth: for the powers of heaven shall be shaken." (Luke 21:11, 25-26.)

In spite of all of this clear and distinct and unmistakable evidence, the vast majority of the people will pay no attention to it at all; BECAUSE CHRIST IS BEING REJECTED BY THIS GENERATION. "But first must he suffer many things, and be rejected of this generation. And as it was in the days of Noe, so shall it be also in the days of the Son of man. They did eat, they drank, they married wives, they were given in marriage, until the day that Noe entered into the ark, and the flood came, and destroyed them all. Likewise also as it was in the days of Lot; they did eat, they drank, they bought, they sold, they planted, they builded; but the same day that Lot went out of Sodom it rained fire and brimstone from heaven, and destroyed them all. Even thus shall it be in the day when the Son of man is revealed." (Luke 17:25-80.)

The air is poisoned today by carbon monoxide, by smog, by atomic radiation (fall out) and by DRIFT—dust and meteorites from other planets and comets, and by poison sprays. Wild ducks, geese and pheasants, song birds, quail, rabbits, squirrels, fish and angle worms are being destroyed by sprays dusted and sprayed on crops by airplanes

OUTER SPACE PEOPLE AND INNER EARTH PEOPLE

and every kind of mechanical device. All people everywhere are being destroyed by these poison sprays. Mr. Hart Stilwell, in an article in TRUE Magazine, said—Quote:

"I had encountered the effects of a new kind of poison, a delayed-action, indestructible chemical monster called a chlorinated hydrocarbon. It goes under various trade names: Dieldrin, Heptachlor, Chlordane, Lindane, Aldrin and many others, and DDT, which is mild in comparison. They are used mostly as sprays; from planes, trucks and spray-can "bombs". And the chances are 60 to 1 that everyone in the U. S. is moderately well loaded with at least one of these poisons.

"The point is, the output of new chlorinated hydrocarbons is outstripping DDT and they lodge in the system and stay there, mainly in the fat, liver, kidneys, spleen, sex organs, heart and brain.

"Let's look at one more Public Health Service test, which found 291 parts per million in the body fat of a man working with DDT. A year later, after staying away from the stuff and iiving on a selected diet, he still had 230 parts per million." -End quote.

A billion tons of deadly poison are sprayed on crops every year in the United States. Almost all of the fruits and vegetables that you eat are loaded with these poisons. I predict that fifty years from now the human race will be sterile or that one out of every two born will be a monster. We are simply letting billion dollar chemical and pharmaceutical companies destroy us. The seventh and LAST PLAGUE IS IN THE AIR.

"IN VAIN SHALT THOU USE MANY MEDICINES." (Jer. 46:11) "Thou hast no healing medicines." (Jer. 30:13.) Medical doctors do not have a positive cure for any disease. They seem to prescribe the latest drugs such as sulpha, auromycin and penicillin for everything. Fifty years ago it was pull the teeth, later it was remove the appendix. Now it's penicillin. They do not even have a cure for the common cold and nothing that will touch the "flu." Lawrence Galton, in the FAMILY CIRCLE, says: "We are in the day of the pill. Tired; Have a pill to pep you up. Anxious? Have one to calm you down. Blue? Gobble one to lift the spirit. Feverish? Sleepless? Have a pill. Thanks to the fervent growing belief in a pill for virtually every problem, we're gulping medicine today at a fantastic rate. From $867,000,000 in 1947, manufacturers sales of pharmaceuticals shot up to $1,600,000,000 in 1954 to $2,200,000,000 in 1957, and are still climbing. Total output of medicinals in the United States now exceeds 101,400,000 pounds. Thirteen hundred tons of antibiotics and 4,900 tons of vitamins are being turned out annually; sales of hormones —extremely potent drugs taken in tiny doses—have reached 46,000 pounds. More than 50,000,000 prescriptions for tranquilizers, not to mention other mood-changing drugs, were written last year."-End quote.

THERE IS ONLY ONE HOPE and that is RESTORATION. "Moreover the light of the moon shall be as the light of the sun, and the light of the sun shall be sevenfold, as the light of seven days, in the day that the Lord bindeth up the breach of his, people, and healeth the stroke of their wound." (Isa. 80:26.) The energy from the sun and the moon is increasing. In 1945 the sun crossed the meridian 18 hours ahead of time. On March 21, 1960, the Associated Press reported that "the sun grew two per cent brighter and correspondingly warmer during the last five years."

OUTER SPACE PEOPLE AND INNER EARTH PEOPLE

The prophet Malachi says:

"Unto you that fear my name (reverence the name YAHVEH) shall the SUN of righteousness arise with healing in his wings; and ye shall go forth, and grow up as calves of the stall. And ye shall tread down the wicked; for they shall be ashes under the soles of your feet in the day that I shall do this, saith Yahveh of hosts." (Mal. 4:2-3.) Job says in speaking of those that trust in Yahveh : "His flesh shall be fresher than a child's: he shall return to the days of his youth." (Job 33:25.) The radiant healing rays of the sun are increasing. Those who have true faith will set up an immunity to the last plagues, poisons and atomic radiation, "And if they drink any deadly thing, it shall not hurt them." (Mark 16:18.) "Whatsoever is set before you, eat, asking no questions for conscience sake." (I Cor. 10:27.)

"For every creature of God is good, and nothing to be refused, if it be received with thanksgiving: for it is sanctified by the word of God and prayer. If thou put the brethren in remembrance of these things, thou shalt be a good minister of Jesus Christ, nourished up in the words of faith and of good doctrine, whereunto thou hast attained." (I Tim. 4:4-6.)

If we worry about poisoned air and poisoned foods and all of the last plagues, we will worry ourselves to death. It is much better to have faith in Yahveh. FAITH IS ESSENTIAL TO SURVIVAL. He will make us immune to all the poisons and all of the end time plagues, give us health and make us young again. Age has very little to do with youthful health today. People 70 or 80 or 90 years old may be younger and healthier than teenagers. "He giveth power to the faint; and to them that have no might he increaseth strength. Even the youths shall faint and be weary, and the young men shall utterly fall: but they that wait upon the Lord shall renew their strength; they shall mount up with wings as eagles; they shall run, and not be weary; and they shall walk, and not faint." (Isa. 40:29-81.) By faith, and only by faith, can you survive the end of this present evil world and pass safely over into the new Righteous World Order.

Disappearance From The Earth

In the remote ages the continents of Atlantis and Lemuria disappeared from the earth. In Bible times Enoch and Elijah and Yahshua the Messiah with 144,000 were taken up from the earth into heaven; that is, to somewhere in outer-space. In historical times at least twelve cities have disappeared, also mountains, islands and rivers have disappeared from the earth. Every year there are thousands of people in America that mysteriously disappear. No trace of them is ever found. Nearly a year ago a woman in Boulder, Colorado, got up early to fix breakfast. In her nightgown, robe and house slippers she stepped out the back door to dispose of some garbage. She disappeared instantly. No trace of here has ever been found.

The Bible facts are that many people who disappeared from this earth ages ago are now returning or are due to return. In the first paragraph of this letter you read the scripture which says, "He shall recount his worthies." Regardless of whether they left this earth in their bodies or out of their bodies, in the due cycle of time they return and take up their bodies again. "Awake and sing, ye that dwell in the dust: for the dew is as

OUTER SPACE PEOPLE AND INNER EARTH PEOPLE

the dew of herbs, and the earth shall cast out her dead." Isa. 26:19. They did not all die at the same time, neither will they all return at the same time. "Ye shall be gathered one by one." (Isa. 27:12.) "Many of them that sleep in the dust of the earth shall awake." (Dan. 12:2.) "Behold, O my people, I will open your graves, and cause you to come up out of your graves, and bring you into the land of Israel." (Ezek. 87:12.) Every person will return to his own race, nationality, family and to his allotted inheritance and home on earth. "The thing that hath been is that which shall be; and that which is done is that which shall be done . . . And God requireth that which is past" (Eccl. 1:9, 3:15.)

Those that leave the earth complete a cycle of the planets; that is, outer-space dwelling places and then return here. This is beautifully illustrated by the ancient parable of the Phoenix. "There is a certain bird called a Phoenix; of this there is never but one at a time: and that lives five hundred years. And when the time of dissolution draws near, that it must die, it makes itself a nest of frankincense, and myrrh, and other spices into which, when its time is fulfilled, it enters and dies. But its flesh putrefying, breeds a certain worm, which being nourished with the juice of the dead bird brings forth feathers; and when it is grown to a perfect state, it takes up the nest in which the bones of its parents lie, and carries it from Arabia into Egypt, to a city called Heliopolis: and flying in an open day in the sight of all men, lays it upon the altar of the sun, and so returns from whence it came. The priests then search into the records of the time; and find that it returns precisely at the end of five hundred years." (I Clement 12:2-5. This is a book of the New Testament Apocrypha.)

Likewise in the Old Testament Apocrypha there is a clearly understood teaching as to the time when the dead will return. "So he answered me and said, Go thy way to a woman with child and ask of her when she hath fulfilled her nine months if her womb may keep the birth any longer within her."

"Then said I, No, Lord, that can she not. And he said unto me, In the grave the chambers of souls are like the womb of a woman. For like a woman that travaileth maketh haste to escape the necessity of the travail: even so do these places haste to deliver those things that are committed unto them." (II Esdras 4:40-42.)

Job said, "There is hope of a tree, if it be cut down, that it will sprout again, and the tender branch (the soul) thereof shall not cease." (Job 14.7.) Paul, referring to the return of the dead, said: "That which thou sowest is not quickened (made alive) except it die. And that which thou sowest, thou sowest not that body that shall be . . . but God giveth it a body." (I Cor. 15:86-87.) So therefore a new higher life is born out of death. Jesus said: "Ye shall see Abraham, and Isaac and Jacob and all the prophets in the Kingdom of God." . . . "And they shall come from the east, and from the west, and from the north, and from the south, and shall sit down in the kingdom of God." (Luke 13: 28-29.)

I believe that many of the ancient worthies have returned to this earth in their personal, literal, physical bodies and that a few are returning every day. The program of Yahveh is carried out on schedule. He operates on an exact time table: "By measure hath he measured the times, and by number hath he numbered the times; and he doth not move nor stir until the said measure be fulfilled." (II Esdras 4:87, Apocrypha.)

OUTER SPACE PEOPLE AND INNER EARTH PEOPLE

Don't Be Surprised!

DON'T BE SURPRISED! if new continents suddenly appear on this earth. New cities may descend from the sky at any time now. The oceans of the world go dry. The earth will stagger like a drunkard when a powerful whirlwind carries the water of the seas and oceans up and out beyond the sky where a ring or belt of water will form above the sky around the earth as it was in the beginning. (Gen. 1:67)

"And I saw new heaven, and a new earth: for the first heaven and first earth were passed away, and there was no more sea." (Rev. 21:1.) "And he carried me away in the spirit to a great high mountain, and showed me that great city, the holy Jerusalem, descending out of heaven from God." (Rev.21:10.) Those lost, that are hidden cities, will again descend upon this earth.

The oceans now have in them enough rich protein food to feed the world for a thousand years. There is a ridge or line on the ocean bottom running clear around the globe at the equator. There are mountains in the ocean higher than Mount Everest. There are canyons wider and deeper than the Grand Canyon. There are continents and regular rivers of fresh water on the bottom of the oceans. The time is fast approaching when there will be no more sea and when the energy of the sun will increase seven times and the energy of the moon will be equal to that of the sun at present (Isa. 30:26.) When we consider the vastness of Yahveh's immediate program for this earth, everything else pales into insignificance.-W. L. B.

The Earth Turned Upside Down

THE EARTH TURNED UPSIDE DOWN (Isaiah 24:1) and it will turn over again before very long. From Pasadena, California, on Oct. 24, 1959, the Associated Press reported that a sun scientist has discovered that the Polar Magnetic field of the sun has reversed itself. If this were to happen on earth, all compass needles would swing around from the North and point to the South Pole. The discovery was announced today by the California Institute of Technology, which with the Carnegie Institution of Washington operates Palomar Observatory, where studies of the sun's magnetic field have been under way since 1952.

Dr. Harold D. Babock of the Hale Solar Laboratory, at Palomar, site of the world's largest (200-inch) optical telescope, said "the reversal of polarity was gradual. It began at the sun's South Pole about mid-1957. The change in the North Polar region was not observed until November, 1958, more than a year later."

Dr. Babcock, an astrophysicist for a half century, said that prior to the change of the direction of the magnetic field was opposite to that of the earth's field. Since then it has maintained its new direction, the same as that of the earth's field. Caltech astronomers do not know what caused the reversal.

Sputnik Information

Soviet data acquired from Sputniks indicate meteoric material is falling to the earth at the rate of 10,000,000 tons a day.

OUTER SPACE PEOPLE AND INNER EARTH PEOPLE

DANGEROUS SPACE ABOVE ARCTIC. Solar flares show that the earth's atmosphere above the polar regions is showered with bursts of cosmic rays 100,000 times above normal. This would make it impossible for man to get through this belt above the poles.

OUTER SPACE IS FALLING. Two blocks of ice fell on Cleveland, Ohio, on Nov. 30th (1959). A fifty pound chunk of ice fell on a Georgia farm on Oct. 29th. A scientist said:

"There have been records of a few mysterious ice falls in the past, and that one unconfirmed theory is that they come from comets.

Another Washington scientist cited the theory that comets are, in effect, dirty snowballs made up of conglomerates of ice containing stony and other matter. It's conceivable, declared this scientist who declined to be quoted by name, that fragments of the comet head could break off, thus becoming chunks of ice-and-stone mixture hurtling through space."

"Turneth It Upside Down"

"TURNETH IT UPSIDE DOWN" (Isa. 24:1). For 20 years I have been teaching that the earth turned upside down, now here it is verified by scientists. On Sept. 6 an (AP) report from Toronto said: Ancient rocks are whispering fantastic stories, scientists reported to the International Union of Geodesy and Geophysics Friday. The rocks tell of sudden flip-flops in the north and south magnetic poles. They tell of continents drifting apart, or the whole crust of the earth skidding about to turn maps topsy-turvy.

They say the United States and Europe once were 1,000 miles closer together, that India once was south of the equator, not north. All this happened in the long ago past. But it could happen again. The stories come from the natural magnetism in rocks. Theories as to what the rock stories mean were described by the scientists.

Some rocks are natural compasses. They contain grains of magnetic minerals. When the rocks were formed, the grains lined up to point in the direction of the magnetic north pole where it existed then.

Checking rocks formed at different times during the last 500 million years, scientists find some not only don't point to the present north pole, they even point in the opposite direction. The record seems clear that the magnetic poles mysteriously and completely reversed themselves at times in the past, said Sir Edward Bullard of Cambridge University. The flip-flops come perhaps every 100,000 to one million years, he said, and the last was apparently a million years ago. Rock records in England indicate the north magnetic pole 150 million years ago was where Japan is now, but it's doubtful Japan was right there then, said Dr. K. M. Creer of Kings College.

Rock records from different continents indicate the continents drifted apart, even turned partway around, perhaps. And the earth's crust apparently slithered about, changing the position of land masses in respect to the poles.

OUTER SPACE PEOPLE AND INNER EARTH PEOPLE

Physicist Would Revamp Solar System

(This item is two years old.)

PASADENA (AP)-Revamping the solar system to create a hundred new planets with a climate like Earth's was proposed Thursday by a noted astrophysicist as a way of solving humanity's biggest problem: over-population.

Dr. Fritz Zwicky, California Institute of Technology rocket expert, told a reporter that such a project is definitely within realm of possibility.

Dr. Zwicky envisions scooping up great portions of the major planets, such as Jupiter, Saturn and Neptune, and transferring them to smaller planets and their satellites, then changing the orbits of the enlarged planets to make their course around the Sun roughly comparable to that of our Earth.

Bumping the planets out of their orbits, transferring great masses of matter across space, all this can be accomplished, the scientist said, through proper use of the energies released by man's newest weapon against the cosmos: the explosion of the atom.

The hydrogen bomb, Dr. Zwicky said, may not necessarily be the instrument of man's destruction. It may be the instrument of his salvation.

"The greatest problem man faces here on earth," he said, "is over-population, with its accompanying economic and political problems.

"There are far too many of us now, and it will be even worse in the future. The answer to this problem is virtually within our grasp if we would only seize it."

"We have a problem of segreqation of races. Some races just don't seem to get along with each other. What could be simpler than segregating these races on other planets?"

Just how does the world go about transferring whole races to other planets?

"First you have to provide suitable planets." he said. "The forces we have unleashed with the hydrogen bomb make it possible to do this. We can bomb Jupiter and other major planets out of their orbits and into other orbits more to our liking. We can transfer great masses from the surfaces of the big planets to the smaller planets and satellites and make them larger.

"Increasing the size of the Moon, for instance, would increase its gravitational pull to a point where it could build up and retain an atmosphere similar to that of Earth."

The scientist was reluctant to explain just how great masses of material could be transferred from one planet to another.

"I could tell you," he said, "but it would take three weeks to make it clear. But if we can move planets, we certainly could move parts of planets, couldn't we?"

Dr. Zwicky also has thought about the kind of ship necessary to carry men from one planet to another. Such a ship could be built within 10 years or so, he said, if enough

OUTER SPACE PEOPLE AND INNER EARTH PEOPLE

money, say 100 million dollars, were made available for research of the type he is now doing.

The space ship would travel indefinitely on fuel it collects in transit. This fuel would be the garments of molecules left in space as a result of solar radiation. These pieces of molecules blasted by the sun's rays could be held inert by extreme cold, he said, then heated to release tremendous energy; enough to carry man wherever he dared to go.

Dr. Zwicky told a news conference Wednesday about the free-fueling space ship. The elaboration came in an interview Thursday.

Look Out For Falling Ice

There is a lot of ice stored in the sky and it will appear to be a coincidence when it falls at the psychological moment and destroys the Russian and Chinese Communist Armies when they attempt their all out invasion of America. It will of course be a phenomenon not understood by any of the Atheistic Scientists, but the Bible tells us. "And I will plead against him with pestilence and with blood; and I will rain upon him, and upon his bands, and upon the many people that are with him, an overflowing rain, and great hailstones, fire and brimstone." (Ezek. 38:22) "And there fell upon men a great hail out of heaven, every stone about the weight of a talent: and men blasphemed God because of the plague of the hail; for the plague thereof was exceeding great." (Rev. 16:21)

Yes, that ice is up there and it's coming down one of these days. Frank Edwards writing in Fate Magazine in July said "In Admiral Richard Byrd's report of his first trip to the Antarctic his group discovered two large, blue-green lakes of warm water in the very midst of that desolate expanse of eternal ice. There was no trace of any volcanic heat supply, in fact there was no visible means which could explain the incongruous coexistence of warm water lakes in the ice cap of the Antarctic. Admiral Byrd made note of still another strange aspect of the lakes. Alongside one of them, he wrote, were long, straight, black lines "which resembled blast marks."

Perhaps it is only co-incidence that Admiral Byrd's first trip to the Antarctic was made immediately after a Chilean naval commander returned from that area to report that his ships had been repeatedly circled by scores of shiny, disc-shaped objects which vanished toward the interior of the Antarctic."

End Quote.

In his article in Fate Magazine in September he suggests or implies that Martians in flying saucers may be taking water up from the earth and storing ice on the moon. That may not be as far-fetched or illogical as it seems. On the farm of Edwin Groff near Reading, Pa., on. July 30, 1956, two chunks of ice fell, one weighing 50 pounds and the other 25 pounds.

Airline officiais said at the time the cakes were reported that they could not have fallen from an airliner because such planes carry nothing larger than ice cubes. And the weather bureau said the ice chunks could not be explained as huge hail stones.

Dr. Malcolm J. Reider, head of a chemical research firm, said he sprayed the ice

OUTER SPACE PEOPLE AND INNER EARTH PEOPLE

pieces—now melted considerably smaller than when originally found—with distilled water to remove all foreign matter, and then split them to determine the "cleavage planes."

This test and others, Dr. Reider said, indicated the ice was not manufactured but came from atmospheric conditions. A high chloride content, Dr. Reider added, indicated also that the ice came from an area far removed from Reading.

Earth's Surface Weather Originates At South Pole

Wind rushes out from the interior of the earth through a funnel shaped exit at the South Pole. The earth, with an interior sun, with fresh water flowing out of openings at North Pole and wind at South Pole is like a jet propelled plane—probably all planets are the same. Richard F. Dempewolff, in a copyrighted item in "Popular Mechanics" in December, 1956, said:

"Earth's fifth-largest continent spreads a white pinnacled land mass more than a thousand miles in every direction from the South Pole, Yet until now, scientists have known more about the topography of the visible surface of the moon than of this sleeping giant caught in the grip of an ice age. Locked in its frozen spaces are a hoard of mysteries that have puzzled scientists ever since they were first observed by the few explorers bold enough to venture there.

Right now, 75 geophysicists from the United States are joining scientists from 11 other nations in a historic assault on the white continent's secrets. They comprise the south polar team for the International Geophysical Year worldwide scientific investigation of the earth and its star, the sun, scheduled for 1957-1958 (Popular Mechanics, December 1955). From 39 observing stations—some of them deep in the continent—these men will pry into such things as Antarctica's unique weather-breeding phenomena. They'll scrutinize the moving ice blanket that reaches a depth of more than a mile on the continent's 10,000-foot polar plateau. Modern sonic and electronic eyes will probe to find what's under it. Antarctica's auroral, cosmic and ionospheric phenomena will be studied during the bitter polar night from plastic viewing domes. Observations will be compared with simultaneous effects all over the world.

On operation Deep freeze I, some 30 private, government and military scientists laid the groundwork for the big push. Dressed in bulky thermo clothes and fur-ruffed hoods, they moved inland to locate base sites and make preliminary observations.

For years, meteorologists have suspected Antarctica of being the world's most potent weather breeder. Great air masses fan out from the pole, sweeping constantly across the ice with gale and hurricane force. Whisking thick veils of drift off the barrier cliffs, they roar northward over four oceans.

One of the lustiest of these gales is a roaring mass of air that pours northward continually from the Adelie Coast. Its howling gusts have been estimated up to 200 miles per hour. Deep-freeze pilots exploring the area south of Adelie Land have discovered a vast trough of some 300 miles wide. Formed by a range of 14,000-foot mountains along the Ross Sea and a great dome of continental ice reaching 13,000 feet to the west, the trough slopes upward from the coast perhaps as far as the pole. Dr. Paul A. Siple, senior

OUTER SPACE PEOPLE AND INNER EARTH PEOPLE

scientist for the expedition, believes this enormous funnel may be the answer to the big wind. During the six-month winter night he says, temperatures on the high polar plateau may skid to minus 120 degrees. That cold, heavy air cascades down the chute, some spilling through mountain passes onto the Ross Shelf, but most of it barreling to the coast and spreading across the sea in a roaring polar gale.

A frigid air mass of such dimensions is bound to affect weather, wherever it blows. "We have found evidence of polar Antarctic air everywhere up to 40 degrees latitude," Dr. Morton J. Rubin, IGY meteorologist, told me, "We think we've spotted occasional bursts at the equator."

Weather created in these zones eventually may affect the northern hemisphere. So, what happens in Aatarctica today may have its effect in New York and Chicago months from now.

Using Antarctic weather for long-range forecasting is a prospect most weathermen have dreamed about. But who would man observation points in a land no one can live in except for limited periods? Now, for the first time, some 40 weather stations scattered across the bleak continent will report to Weather Central at Little America, and surface weather maps based on actual observations will give meteorologists their first picture of south-polar weather being born. Doctor Rubin explains that besides the regular bases, satellite stations will be planted miles out on the barrier by several nations. The Australians will have a number of remotes that will automatically radio surface reports for a broader picture.

An interesting experiment is the use of "grasshopper" robot stations to provide continuous weather reports along the route that must be flown by planes ferrying supplies to our own South Pole base this fall. The little automatic weather stations have a tuning device that can be set to transmit wind force and direction, temperature and pressure every six hours. The tiny box on a stick is parachuted from a plane. When it hits the ground, spidery legs spring out from the central shaft and it sets itself upright on the ground.

Even more exciting to meteorologists than surface weather maps will be the first charts of south-polar air, drawn from network reports. "In winter," Doctor Rubin points out, "the tropopause disappears or becomes diffuse." This means that the stratosphere, which rides some seven miles high over the United States, may often be found at sea level in Antarctica. Mountains and polar plateaus poke two miles up into it. For this reason south-polar flying is risky. Hazards of high-altitude flight face the pilot on the ground. Full supercharge, jet assist and miles of run are needed just to take off in the thin air.

To probe through the earthbound stratosphere and into weather-making strata above, all bases will send aloft self-tracking radiosond equipment. At Little America, these balloons, carrying a radar target, will be released through a hatch from a building under the snow. Soaring to heights up to 100,000 feet, they will be tracked through various wind layers by a dish antenna housed in a black plastic dome on a tower above the surface. From similar hatches will go other balloons, with radiosondes dangling beneath them to radio back to earth soundings of temperature, air pressure and humidity.

OUTER SPACE PEOPLE AND INNER EARTH PEOPLE

Actually, Antarctica is a weatherman's museum of curiosities. Across the polar plateau's snow desert, barometric pressures read lower—by one inch of mercury—than any place in the world. This is due, says Rubin, to shuddering temperatures that average 30 to 40 degrees lower than the Arctic.

Out on the white "desert," these pioneers will study the weird snowstorms that start from clouds only waist high. They'll probe atmospheric conditions that cause spectacular displays of light in the sky. Several times in McMurdo Sound we watched white halos—sometimes as many as three—form around the sun. Superimposed on one of these was a tremendous white cross of light. Such displays, as well as dazzling arches of color across the polar sky opposite the sun, and great shimmering columns of white light called "sun dogs" that bracket the sun, are caused by refraction of the sun's rays in high-hanging frozen mists made up of millions of ice spicules.

As you read this, Chet Twombley, IGY physicist, periodically climbs a ladder from subsnow quarters at Little America to an enclosed, heated tower. He peers up at the night sky through plastic domes to watch Antarctica's most spectacular phenomenon of all: the aurora australis, south-polar counterpart of the northern lights. Beside him, an all-sky camera, slung over a convex mirror reflecting the horizon-to-horizon display, takes continual movies of the vivid shifting draperies and ray of green, pink and purple lights that fill the sky. Most unreal and indescribable of all natural phenomena, the aurora is thought to be caused by charged particles streaming in from solar storms to the earth's ionosphere. Caught up in the earth's magnetic field, the particle streams funnel toward the magnetic poles where they bombard ionospheric gases, creating luminous glows much the same way electron streams excite the gas in a neon tube.

The aurora holds considerable interest for IGY scientists since ionospheric storms are closely linked to radio blackout—a treachery especially peculiar to polar regions but felt all over the world.

Tied in with the aurora and radio interference is the earth's magnetic field; with poles in the arctic and Antarctic. Both poles and lines of force shift occasionally. In recent years the north magnetic pole moved hundreds of miles from northern Canada to the west coast of Greenland. The south magnetic pole is somewhere out on the ice prairie in Wilkes Land, west of McMurdo Sound. Tedious methods have been used to pinpoint these elusive spots. But until now, no one has done better than make a close approximation.

This year, Rochus Vogt, a young nuclear physicist from Heidelberg University working under Fulbright grant at the University of Chicago, nailed them down by a unique method. In a specialiy built steel shack on the USS Arneb's stern weather deck, Vogt stood guard over nuclear counters that clicked off a crackling barrage triggered by cosmic particles penetrating the earth's atmosphere.

"Around the magnetic equator, lines of magnetic force far out in space deflect cosmic rays, so fewer particles get through," he explains. "But at the poles, where lines of force funnel into the earth, particles penetrate in vast quantities, which incidentally accounts for the auroral displays." By plotting counts collected down through the Pacific to Antarctica, up through the Indian Ocean on the trip home, and using data previously

OUTER SPACE PEOPLE AND INNER EARTH PEOPLE

collected during a north-south Atlantic voyage, Vogt had three pole to pole profiles showing cosmic-ray penetration of the earth's magnetic field. Then by applying mathematical formulas, the three sets of particle-count curves were projected to junction points in Greenland and Antarctica—dead centers of the magnetic poles. Vogt's figures proved the earth's magnetic grid, as previously plotted, was slightly askew; a fact important to some missile designs, the radio and electronics field, and invaluable to further magnetic and cosmic-ray studies during the IGY.

While men like Vogt and Twombley hit at the causes of cosmic interference, other men during Deepfreeze tackled it from an immediate practical level. Armory H. "Bud" Waite, electronics engineer for the Army Signal Corps Laboratories, rumbled over the snowfields with five companions in a Weasel laden with a new lightweight back-pack radio with disjointed antenna that snaps into a 12-foot whip at the flick of a wrist. On the barrier near Little America, these men set up a private camp composed of two insulated huts.

Out on the ice desert, Waite and his boys dug holes in the snow and sank 30-foot transmitters out of sight. They busied themselves sending signals at frequencies from 40 to 10,000 megacycles, through and under the snow at depths down to 30 feet. "Signals travel more than twice as far over frozen terrain as they do over temperate hills and fields," Bud says. "And through the snow we can get distance." If it works, auroral disturbances will never trouble polar explorers again. Signals will propagate through Antarctica's top layers of snow, bouncing back and forth between surface and ice layers beneath to all parts of the continent, disrupted only by crevasses and mountains jutting through the icecap.

Antarctica's icecap is a feature that will come under close scrutiny of ICY glaciologists. The great continental glacier, formed by eons of snowfall compacted into a six-million-square-mile blanket that may be nearly two miles thick in spots, flows outward constantly like pancake batter on a cold griddle. The expedition's "Mr. Ice," Doctor Siple, spent days skiing across the barrier. The continental glacial ice, he says, spreads outward at a rate of 4-1/2 feet a day clear around the continent. Great pieces crack off the edges with deep, booming roars each year and float northward as icebergs, some of them hundreds of square miles in area.

IGY glaciologists are bringing core drills to Antarctica to probe through the thick ice cap so that layers may be studied and age of the icecap determined. Samples of snow can be tested for age by several methods. Each Antarctic summer produces "melt lines"—thin bands of solid ice in the snow that can be counted visually. But Ernie Wood, IGY scientist with Deepfreeze, used a newer method this year. Taking samples from deep in the icecap, he melted them and drained the water into plastic bottles. These, sent to the University of Chicago will be tested for radioactivity. Tritium in the snow, emanating radiation with a known half-life, will reveal when the snow fell, even though it may have been blown to its present location by howling winds.

The changing, rumbling coastal ice of Antarctica is earth's last outpost of life. A few miles beyond the barrier cliffs nothing moves or grows except the wind and per-

OUTER SPACE PEOPLE AND INNER EARTH PEOPLE

petual drifting snow. But the continent's edges swarm with creatures that draw a living from the sea.-Popular Mechanics,.

Origin Of Northern Lights

SCIENTIST REVEALS VITAL CLUE TO ORIGIN OF NORTHERN LIGHTS.

By Barbara Brown.

BOULDER, Aug. 28-Men for years have puzzled over gigantic fans of light which occasionally dance up against the sky in northern latitudes. In Boulder Wednesday a tall man in a green tweed suit gave what may be a vital clue to the origin of the aurora borealis.

Dr. Alfred C. B. Lovell of Manchester University, England, announced scientists have just discovered the mysterious glowing streamers appear at the South Pole at the same time as they do in the arctic.

"Scientists exploring Antarctica have occasionally reported a phenomenon similar to the aurora borealis," Dr. Lovell said. "But studies made durinq the first two months of the International Geophysical Year indicate the new information that these two widely spaced occurrences appear simultaneously."

Scientists probing the sky with huge radio telescopes at Halley Bay, Antarctica, picked up electrical impulses coming from the flickering white, pink and yellow lights. At the same time astronomers at Dr. Lovell's Jodrell Bank Experimental Station in Cheshire; England, picked up the same type of signal coming from the north. Exactly how close in time the two systems of light streamers correspond, Dr. Lovell would not say.

"The information is so new nothing has been charted for sure," he told reporters. "Present studies indicate they may be exactly simultaneous, but to the exact minute or even hour we don't as yet know."

Practically speaking the discovery at present amounts to little, Dr. Lovell said. However it may lead to new advances in radiation, radio and electrical knowledge. All that is known about the aurora at present is that the lights are stronger in years when the sun's surface is covered by great whirling storms—sun spots.

Then the aurora creep down across Canada, even to Minnesota.

During 1957, sunspots have been more numerous than in many years. Since the IGY presents the first chance scientists have had to study Antarctica while observing the Arctic at the same time, other discoveries about the aurora are possible, Dr. Lovell said.

The distinguished British scientist has been a main speaker at the current International Scientific Radio Union conference in Boulder. More than 500 scientists from 26 nations, including Russia, are attending the meet. Wednesday, Dr. Lovell conducted a special meeting on radio telescopes.—Rocky Mt. News.

OUTER SPACE PEOPLE AND INNER EARTH PEOPLE

The Planet Mars

Several years ago a relative died. About a week later he appeared to me in a dream. It seemed that I was at a depot. He stepped off the train for a few seconds and said to me, "I am on my way to the planet Mars. The Martians are farther advanced in science than any other inhabitants of the solar system." Though it was a strange dream, I passed it up as just a dream and nothing more. A few weeks later I was reading and extract from Emanuel Swedenborg and I learned that he claimed that the Martians are more advanced in science than the earth people. Since then I have read such books as "Life on Other Planets" by Mary Cain and "The Secret Of Life On Other Worlds" by A. C. Ferber and a number of other books in regard to outer-space. The first week in April, 1962, I heard a man on television say that the satellites (moons) of Mars may have been made by the Martians and that the canals were possibly constructed by them and that it is possible that they are farther advanced than we are and that it could be dangerous for us to shoot rockets to Mars for the Martians might retaliate by invading the earth. This, of course, is speculative but there it is!

The Inside Of The Earth Is To Be Explored

According to an article in the Los Angeles Herald Examiner, on March 25, 1962, Russia is preparing "terrajet" engines to power 62 to 125 miles deep into the earth. INNER EARTH SPACE is the next field to be explored. All of the inside of the earth, so they say, may eventually be occupied. Twenty years ago when I began my teaching about the INNER EARTH people, I was denounced as a fanatic, a fool, insane, etc., but from many years of study, not only of the Bible, but also of all of the ancient religions and philosophies, I knew that the Greeks believed in "Tartaros" and divided the inner earth into seven sections. Also the oldest book in the world, "The Egyptian Book Of The Dead" has more to say about the inner earth than any other subject. Likewise, the ancient Babylonians, Chinese, and Hindus taught that the inside of the earth is hollow and that it is inhabited. The Bible definitely teaches that Yahshua the Messiah (Jesus Christ) visited and spent much time in the inner earth and that there are 200-million pilots of flying saucers inside the earth and that in due time all of the inner earth people will be converted. Since I have written often and so much on this in detail, I will not quote the scriptures here, but pick up your Bible and read for yourself. Ephesians 4;9-10, I Peter 3:18:21, Philippians 2:10-11, Revelation 9:1-16, Revelation 5:13,Ephesians I:1-10, andyou will find the teaching on INNER EARTH people and OUTER SPACE people so clearly taught that even a child can understand it. Since I began this teaching 20 years ago, a moving picture has been made on the subject and now Russia and America are preparing to explore the inner earth.

A Round Earth Has Not Been Proven

I know that very few, if any, will agree with me on this. They will say that our own Colonel John Glenn orbited the earth in a space craft some one hundred miles above the earth. But I say that there never yet has been a pole to pole flight around the earth. Nobody, by land, sea, or in the air, has started at the north pole, gone down over the south pole and back to the place from which they started at the north pole. Why? Until this is

OUTER SPACE PEOPLE AND INNER EARTH PEOPLE

done, nothing will be proven about the shape of the earth.

My theory of the shape of the earth is based upon the Bible. I say that the earth is a cube. That is, it is "foursquare" and "the length and the breadth and the height of it are equal." (Rev. 21:16.) The Creator has created the stars and the earth cube-shaped—not spheres. A cube has six sides. We live on the top side as it were, on which are continents, islands, and oceans as we know them. The face of the earth was divided into "four quarters" (Rev. 20:8) by four rivers (Gen. 2:8-15). In the first eleven chapters of Genesis, nineteen times this top side is called "the face of the earth." Now the bottom side of this cube (the earth) has also continents, islands and oceans and is inhabited by people that the Bible speaks of as the people "under the earth" (Rev. 5:13) that is, on the bottom side of the cube. The inner earth people are those in the heart of the earth." (Matt. 12:40).

My argument is that the so-called north pole within the circle of the 90th parallel is the center of the land and water area on the top, or face, of the earth. There is no south pole. No matter how far south you may go into Antarctica, the needle always points toward the 90th parallel in the north—that is, toward the north star. All voyages on land, sea, and in the air are guided by the attraction of the North Star and the 90th parallel in the North. Therefore, they would naturally travel in a circle in circumnavigating the land area on "the face of the earth." This known land area, "the face of the earth" has been circumnavigated, but this is only the top side of the cube (earth).

Antarctica, which we have been told is a continent as large as North America, has never been circumnavigated. I say that it is an ice barrier. You see that the top side, or "face of the earth" has four corners—that is, "the four corners of the earth." (Rev. 7:1.) Beyond these four corners or four sides of the top or face of the earth, there are four sides that are ice, or ice barriers. I have heard that two ships were stocked with supplies to last the crews for five years. That they met at a given point and sailed in opposite directions, trying to go around the ice barrier of Antarctica. One ship sailed for five years; the other for three years, then they turned around and came back. They had sailed 100,000 miles and had not sailed around the ice barrier. They never will because the ice barrier is the four sides of the cube (earth) which separates the top or "face of the earth" on which we live from the bottom of the earth which is also inhabited. The circumference of 25,000 miles only applies to the top or "face of the earth." The cube (earth) is six times 25,000 miles—that is including all six sides of the cube, but four sides are ice. Only the top and bottom are continents, islands and oceans.

The moon has nothing to do with the ebb and flow of the tide, but as I have pointed out there is an ice barrier around the foursquare top of the earth and gyroscopic motion or tilt of the earth causes the tide to rise and fall like a cup filled with water when it is tipped back and forth. The Bible pictures the earth as a cube, also as being "cup" shaped. "In the hand of Yahveh there is a cup." (Ps.75:8.) The top stone, or foundation, or cap stone of the earth (Job 88:1-7) was the continent of Eden, known as Paradise. It was 1200 (some say 1500) miles square. The height, length and breadth of it were equal. It was a cube. (See. Genesis 2:7-15.) "And the city lieth four-square, and the length is as large as the breadth and he measured the city with the reed twelve thousand furlongs. The length and the breadth and the height of it are equal." (Rev. 21:16.) The continent of Eden or

OUTER SPACE PEOPLE AND INNER EARTH PEOPLE

Paradise was in the exact location in the North which we call the 90th parallel. It was thrown off the earth and went into orbit in outer-space. The New Jerusalem, or Holy City is located on that satellite (or planet) known as Eden or Paradise. This left an opening in the north with four sides, each from 1200 to 1500 miles long. The distance around the opening which slopes gradually into the inner earth (cup) could be 6,000 miles.

A round earth is only a theory and its latitudes ad longitude are imaginary. It is a theory that has worked fairly well in regard to the top side or "face of the earth" but in the new age now beginning and with the explorations of the inner earth (inside of the earth), the round earth theory must give way to the Bible truth of the cube-shaped earth. The moon presents only one face to the earth. The earth presents only one face to the sun. The sun is a reflector or orchestration, or focal point of light rays from all of the planets. It is not a solid mass. Light rays run into it from the planets like spokes from the rim of a wheel run into the hub.

Once again you are reading truth that has never appeared in print. In my twenty large volumes (8 by 11 inches), I have given an all new and true interpretation of every chapter and verse of the Bible. (There are only two sets of these volumes in existence.) In addition to these bound volumes, my sixteen books reveal much of my new life interpretation of the Bible. It is needless to say that now this new scientific Biblical truth about the earth being a cube had to be presented. I am the individualist and no-conformist of this century who has followed no other man nor ideas of men, but have thought for myself and have given the truth that has been revealed to me.

In all my 1000 sermon-lectures, each averaging 10,000 words, as well as in 5,000 articles, you will find that I have not borrowed nor copied from any man. All are original. It is difficult to make a living this way, for I realize that it will be 100 years or more before the people on "the face of the earth" will be moving in the measure of my thought. However, much of what I have taught is NOW penetrating the religious and scientific orders of this day and I can see a beginning in the change of thinking for the better.

TRUTH WILL WIN

If what I say is truth, it will eventually be accepted, but judging the future by the past, it may be a long time before it will be accepted. Nobody knows this better than I do and to be 100 years or more ahead of the current theories in science, education, and religion is as lonesome as living 100 years in the past would be. I am not asking for sympathy nor pity, for I have chosen this course and there is no dropping back into conformity and complacency. Somewhere I will always be alive. I am living in eternity and I know that the end of this mortal life will be the beginning of a higher life. To be misunderstood and reviled has been the lot of all the persons who have molded the new and better ages. I have never commercialized my speaking, teaching, or writing, yet I have devoted full time in my life to it merely eeking out an existence as a poor man in a cold, material, commercial age.

Many have come to me saying, "Why don't you put a price on your books and lectures. Why don't you charge admission and take up collections?" My reply is that I cannot do it. I must live in and on faith in Yahveh, My God, and trust that a few people who

OUTER SPACE PEOPLE AND INNER EARTH PEOPLE

understand reason and appreciate the truth will send me a sufficient amount to provide food and clothing and to pay the cost of publishing my magazine, letters and books. If I had been interested in money, I would have stayed in the big, organized religions for which I was educated and ordained, but I chose this way of freedom, liberty, and independence as an individualist and non-conformist in order to think for myself and give the people the truth. What the world calls failure, Yahveh calls success. I could never follow along in a regular routine nor be content to float down stream with the masses. I was sickened by old jokes, stock stories, stale sermons and the same kind of services over and over again, the repetition of thumb-worn creeds, etc. But for the grace of Yahveh I would have become an atheist and Communist but I went to the scriptures, devoured the Bible and came up with new light and truth. Revolutionary? Yes! But in it is the hope of the world. Neither the Pope, Protestantism, nor Karl Marx has anything to offer mankind that can be compared to this new truth.

I LOVE PEOPLE. I have never hated any person of any race, color, or creed. But if it is "Love me, love my dog," then that's a different matter. I cannot accept your religious views, your society, and insipid routine of life. I am not trying to get ahead in the business world and am not seeking a place in society. I use no hypocritical methods of psychology on "how to win friends and influence people." I seek no votes nor endorsements; ask for no recommendations. Honestly, in your own heart, don't you wish you could live like this and be your real self? I am sure that you long for the day when you, too, will enjoy this freedom.

I have set in motion a movement that will set you free. If you join it, you will not worry what your family, relatives, or neighbors think about you. You are in this world as an individual for a purpose and you have a duty. What is it? Are you so tied up with the past and the present run of things that you don't know why you are here or, what you are here for, or where you are going? Discover yourself! Know who you are, where you came from, why you are here, and then do the work that the Creator assigned to you. It is a strange thing how the world will step aside for you if you know where you are going, but day after day it is the same old routine in the same place, today and tomorrow—always the same. Is that life? Why don't you get out of it and live? Not by going away, but by the birth of new ideas—a newer, higher and more abundant }ife. The world is the same everywhere. People are the same everywhere. It is not a change in geography that you need, but a change within yourself. Dare to come out with a new truth and freely express your ideas. You do not need to hide this book nor "Showers Of Blessing" magazine from your friends, relatives and neighbors. What's the difference what they think? Convince them.

If you want to send an offering to aid this work, sit down right now and send it. Be yourself for once! Do what you want to do. The more you act on your own, the stronger you will become. Neither your priest, minister, nor family is your boss. Be free for once in your life.

OUTER SPACE PEOPLE AND INNER EARTH PEOPLE

Are We Hearing Creation?

The Navy is trying to test the theory that many mysterious radio noises coming from outer-space may be the whispers of further creation. Dr. Herbert Friedman, of the Naval Research Laboratory, said that experiments with high-altitude rockets, and possibly satellites, might provide the answer. If the theory is proven correct it would explode an opposing view that the universe was created in one big bang billions of years ago.

The Navy's planned studies stem from a theory first advanced by such men as the famed English cosmoiogist, Dr. Fred Hoyle, that the creation of matter is still going on. Hoyle's "steady state" theory, shared by some scientists but challenged by advocates of the one-shot universe concept, further holds that galaxies; great clusters of stars similar to our own Milky Way, are continuously being formed.

Finally, it proposes that many of the still-unidentified radio noises from outer-space may be related to the process of formation of new galaxies.

Cosmic radio noises—sometimes called "the music of the cosmos"—are being picked up constantly by huge radio telescopes in various parts of the world. The radio waves, when converted to audible signals, sound "like gravel on a tin roof," according to some astronomers.

Sources of some of these emissions have been traced to certain stars, constellations and even planets within our galaxy, and some to gaseous areas of space beyond that.

But the cause of many of the more distant noises still remains a mystery.

Our Solar System

OUR SOLAR SYSTEM is a minute speck in another larger system which includes it and all the other stars which we can see with the naked eye. This large system is the galaxy. The word is from the Greek and means "milky". One manifestation of the galaxy is still called the Milky Way. On very clear nights in summer and winter we can see the Milky Way as a faintly luminous, irregular band stretching across the. sky. What we see are actually individual stars, which are more numerous in that particular direction than in any other. We are looking toward the edge of our galaxy from our position inside of it. It is as though we were in a forest which is considerably longer than it is wide. When we look through the forest the long way we can see more trees than when we look through it the short way simply because there are more trees there to see.

The solar system lies about one third of the way in from the edge of a vast grouping of stars which is shaped somewhat like a man's vest-pocket watch. A watch is just about as thick (from face to back) in proportion to its diameter as the galaxy is, and we are somewhere near where the spindle of the second hand on such a watch would be. Our galaxy, or galactic system, is believed to be about 100,000 light-years in diameter and about 10,000 light-years in thickness. There is probably an even greater thickening in the central region, or hub, of the galaxy which may bring this central diameter to nearly 15,000 light-years. We are, perhaps, 30,000 light-years from the hub.

OUTER SPACE PEOPLE AND INNER EARTH PEOPLE

The whole system is revolving around this hub, making one revolution every 200 million years. We go with it. In our position, we are being sped along at the rate of about 175 miles per second. The galaxy contains anywhere from 30 to 100 billion stars. Our Sun is just one of these stars. Our galaxy is just one galaxy, too, for outside of it, in indescribable and unimaginable space are other, similar groups, other galaxies; repeating themselves again and again—maybe indefinitely.—Astronomy for Amateur Observers

Sky Has More Stars Than Earth Has Grains Of Sand

By Roy Gibbons (published in Globe-Democrat)

NEW YORK-There are more stars in the universe than there are grains of sand on all the beaches of the World, Dr. Otto Sturve, reported here Wednesday. The noted astronomer, head of the National Radio Astronomy Observatory at Green Bank, W. Va., disclosed that finding at a symposium on "life in other worlds."

He was one of six nationally known scientists who participated in the session sponsored by the Samuel Bronfman Foundation, established 10 years ago by Joseph E. Seagram & Sons, Inc., distillers.

About 1500 educators and representatives of government and industry attended the conference. Dr. Sturve, who has written more than 2000 articles on astronomy and astrophysics, said he believed it quite likely that at least one of every 10 stars has planets similar to the earth and its companions in our own solar system.

"It would even be reasonable to believe that there are many planets in existence that support intelligent living beings, but whether any such words are now trying to reach us with radio signals or by some other means is quite uncertain," he added.

A two-month research project during which attempts were made to reach planets thought to be circling suns about 10 light years distance from the earth proved unavailing, he disclosed. A light year is equal to 6,000,000,000,000 miles, representing the distance which light travels in one year at 186,300 miles per second.

The attempt, now discontinued, was carried out with a special radio receiver at the Green Bank observatory. The receiver was tuned to 1420 megacycles, the frequency given off by hydrogen, Dr. Sturve said.

"We chose that wave length because we thought it would be the one most likely to be used by intelligent beings if any such exist in the star regions we were examining," he said in an interview.

The space probe study was called Project Ozma, named for the queen of the mythical land of Oz.

"When people ask me when we are going to resume Ozma, I tell them to come around in about 10,000years," Dr. Sturve said.

Dr. James R. Killian, Jr., chairman of the Massachusetts Institute of Technology at Cambridge, Mass., was moderator of the symposium.

OUTER SPACE PEOPLE AND INNER EARTH PEOPLE

Other members of the panel were Dr. Arnold J. Toynbee, British historian; Dr. Harlow Shapley of Harvard University, an astronomer; Dr. George B. Kistiakowski, also of Harvard and former adviser for science and technology to President Eisenhower, and Dr. Donald N. Michael of the Brookings Institute, Washington, D C., a social psychologist.

In his talk, Dr. Michael predicted that establishment of communication with intelligent beings inhabiting some outer-space world would cause profound social, moral, and religious "stirrings" on earth. If such communication is established the Air Force probably would want to take over and the Pentagon would feel its importance had been jeopardized by the achievement, he said in a response to a question about what reactions the feat would cause.

Dr. Michael, who is chief author of a voluminous report on "Space and Man" recently completed for the National Aeronautics and Space Administration, also warned, that "new ideas coming from outer-space may be other than moral."

"They may have ideas out there that may or may not support our most cherished beliefs," he said.

Dr. Toynbee said it is more important for humans to get in touch with the "spiritual worlds within ourselves" than with physical worlds in outer-space.

"No human being has gotten very far in the exploration of this spiritual universe, but it is in this field that the West is most backward of all," he contended, adding:

"The moving spirits of the Indian religions and philosophies have taken the lead, and it will probably be they, if anyone, who will help mankind save itself from itself."

When asked by a reporter whether higher life forms in outer-space might be trying to communicate with us, Dr. Shapley said he didn't know but added, "I think we are too dumb to know."

Dr. Sturve expressed the belief that telescopes mounted on earth satellites will be able to prove in the next 20 years that many stars have planetary systems like our own. So far, the only planets ever seen by man are those which circle the sun in company with the earth, he said.

New Galaxy May Hold Earth's Creation Key

EUGENE, Oregon, June, 1960), AP-An astronomer using the great telescope on Palomar Mountain has reached 36 billion million million miles into space and found what may be the key to the problem of how the universe is built.

What he detected was a speck of light representing a galaxy, or maybe two galaxies, in collision. It was calculated to be about six billion light years away. A light year is the distance light travels in one year—about six million million miles.

An unusual thing about the speck was that it was moving away from the earth at about 90,000 miles a second. This is by far the fastest astronomical body ever clocked—

OUTER SPACE PEOPLE AND INNER EARTH PEOPLE

almost half the speed of light itself.

It also was the most distant object ever identified.

More important scientifically, the astronomer got the spectrum of the object. This gives him the figures on speed and distance. But it also gave him a start toward determining whether the universe was born in a big bang and has been aging ever since, or whether it is constantly renewing itself and has no beginning or end.

This discovery was made by Dr. Rudolph Minkowski of the Mt. Wilson and Palomar Observatories in Southern California. He reported his finding to the Astronomical Society of the Pacific. It took some extra efforts just to point the 200-inch telescope at exactly the right spot in the sky to catch the light blob, which couldn't be seen even with that powerful optical instrument. The distant object was detected because it gives out radio waves. Radio telescopes in Cambridge, England, and at the California Institute of Technology observatory finally pinpointed it for the Palomar telescope. Even then the big eye had to be held on the subject ior 4-1/2 hours in one instance and nine hours in another to get satisfactory spectrum exposures,

The films showed the object was moving outward so fast that its ordinarily invisible ultraviolet light registered in the green, or middle part of the spectrum. The going-away speed of the object had reduced the wave length of the light by almost half. It was like the speed of a receding automobile reducing the pitch of its horn by almost an octave.

Next Dr. Minkowski and his associates will measure the brightness of the object, which will give them an estimate of its actual distance. This estimate will be compared with the distance of the object as indicated by its going-away velocity.

If the comparison shows the object was moving away faster than its brightness-distance figure would allow, it will indicate a universe still expanding as a result of the original big bang. But if the brightness-distance calculation agrees with the distance indicated by the object's outward rush, or if the outward velocity is slower than the distance-brightness factor would permit, it suggests a universe constantly renewing itself even while expanding.

Science Affirms Immortality

When Stalin's Communist armies moved into Berlin and, against the all but frenzied protest of General George Patton, took over the initiative which American troops had won and maintained, almost immediately the most distinguished German scientists were taken over too. Now these are the scientists who have given to Moscow the initiative into and through outer-space. One amendment please!

One scientist, and perhaps the greatest of the many, Dr. Wernher von Braun, escaped the Soviet's dragnet. He is today an American citizen and perhaps the hope, promise, and the measured achievement of our entire nuclear defense program. Recently, I read the statement of a widely advertised "free thinker" in which this talented man derides again the Christian and indeed all religious faiths. In doing so, he affirms that great

OUTER SPACE PEOPLE AND INNER EARTH PEOPLE

minds have no part with this, that children, some women, and weak men put their final trust in God. Well, the scientists and philosophers with whom I have been associated in a rather long lifetime have generally been outspoken in their religious faith, namely the Millikans, the Comptons, the Scotts and James, and the forty who in The Evidence of God in an Expanding Universe declared their affirmative views on religion. These forty, representing every present-day scientific area, in the words of Bishop Kennedy, "dispel the idea that modern scientists are irreligious men""

But immediately it is Dr. von Braun, scientist and German scientist, who, speaking editorially on January 24, 1960, presents the most eloquent affirmation of immortality that I have read in a generation. He writes: "Belief in God and in immortality thus gives us the moral strength and the ethical guidance we need for virtually every action in our daily lives. Science has found that nothing can disappear without a trace. Nature does not know extinction. All it knows is transformation; If God applies this principle to the most minute and insignificant parts of His universe, doesn't it make sense to assume that HE applies it to the masterpiece of His creation - the human soul?

I think HE does. Everything science has taught me—and continues to teach me—strengthens my belief in the continuity of our spiritual existence after death.

-Daniel A. Poling

Astronomer Describes Huge Star Explosion

By Alton Blakeslee, Associated Press Staff Writer.

BERKELEY,Calif.-News of a gigantic disaster in space has just reached earth.

A star, perhaps about the size of our sun, was leading a peaceful, ordinary life. Then suddenly, it exploded. Any nearby planets or living things on them were vaporized within seconds.

This happened some 800,000,000 years ago. But the news has just arrived in the form of brilliant light from the explosion. It took the light that long to get there traveling at 186,000 miles a second. Dr. Fritz Zwicky of Mt. Palomar observatory in California announced the discovery Monday to the International Astronomical Union. He said it is the most distant known supernovae, or star, explosion. He sighted it two months ago within a few days after the light arrived. The light is 100 to 1000 million times brighter than our sun and is far brighter than the entire small galaxy, or star-family, in which the disaster occurred.

Dr. Zwicky thinks 10,000,000 stars sometimes can blow up in chain reactions with a kind of "star gun" action shooting them and their remnants out in great luminous bridges of stars and debris. Exactly what causes a supernovae is not known. They are rare, occurring once every 300 years in any galaxy, each of which contains up to hundreds of billions of stars. Dr. Zwicky theorizes that some supernovae blow away three-quarters of their material in one splendid splash.

The star collapses into a neutron star composed only of neutrons which are heavy atomic particles. The neutron star remnant may be only five miles in diameter instead of

OUTER SPACE PEOPLE AND INNER EARTH PEOPLE

its former size of hundreds of thousands of miles. It is so closely packed it weighs 100,000,000 tons a cubic inch. Neutron stars may set the stage for still greater cataclysms, Dr. Zwicky says. If two collide, they could set off such an explosion that radiation could reach out and set off H-bomb type reactions and explosions on as many as 10,000,000 other stars.

Similar wholesale slaughter of stars and their planets may also occur, Dr. Zwicky thinks, if ordinary stars in the cores of galaxies collide when galaxies race through one another. He believes he has sighted galaxies in collision and, arms or bridges of stars and debris, reaching out from such explosions.

In our own Milky Way galaxy, the Crab Nebula is the remnant of a supernovae sighted in the year 1054 by Chinese astronomers. In the middle of the luminous Crab Nebula there may be a neutron star, Dr. Zwicky says.

Three or four other supernovae have flared up in our galaxy since them. Their light fades away in varying lengths of time.

We Live Beneath A Fantastic Sea

By Alton L Blakeslee, Associated Press Science Reporter, Published in The Shreveport Times, Oct. 13, 1957.

BOULDER, Colo.,- High overhead floats a fantastic electrical sea.

It girdles the earth; reaches at least 150 miles deep. It writhes with storms and savage winds. Powerful electro-jet currents course through it. It is pulled by tides, pocked by peculiar clouds, bombarded by cosmic rays.

Created by the sun's cruelest rays, this sea is the ionosphere, a vast belt of electrons and electrified atoms or ions. It begins 60 miles up, goes at least 200 miles high. In sparsest form it apparently reaches thousands of miles into desolate space.

It's a shield between you and the deadly sun.

Were it not there, absorbing the sun's X-rays and most powerful ultraviolet light, life on earth would perish. Were it not there, you might never hear a radio. Shortwave radio communication depends upon bouncing or reflecting radio waves back to earth from this electrical sea. Strange quirks in the ionosphere sometimes perform magic. Miami poiice calls are heard in California. Or a picture from a TV station hundreds of miles away suddenly appears on your screen.

Exploring this sea is a major activity of the International Geophysical Year (IGY) a cooperative 64 nation effort to learn more about our earth, sun and space. Fingers of radio itself are a prime method of ionosphere exploring. Literally thousands of times a day over the world special radio beams are darting up and bouncing back to measure heights, intensities; and other changing peculiarities of the ionosphere.

When the full story is pieced together scientists hope to answer some puzzles of the high atmosphere, and find new or improved ways of putting the ionosphere to human service. The radio fingers and other techniques already have disclosed much of the

OUTER SPACE PEOPLE AND INNER EARTH PEOPLE

story, explains Robert W. Knecht, a project leader in sun-earth relationships at the National Bureau of Standards (NBS) Boulder Laboratories.

In reality the ionosphere is our outer atmosphere of ultra-thin air. X-rays and ultraviolet light from the sun rip into molecules of oxygen and nitrogen, tearing out their electrons, electrifying billions-times-billions of atoms.

Usually the ionosphere has distinct layers.

About 60 miles high is the E layer, then the denser F-1 region at about 120 miles, the F-2 layer at 200 miles. The E layer reflects low-frequency or long radio waves. Higher frequencies of shorter waves penetrate through it, bounce back from higher layers. Sufficiently high frequencies barrel right on through into space. Usually this is what happens with TV signals.

During IGY, nearly 200 special radio-sounding stations from pole to pole are intently exploring the ionosphere. Each shoots up pulses of radio waves, sweeping through a quick range from long to short waves in 15 seconds, then timing and recording the echoes from different layers.

Some stations make sweeps every 15 minutes, many will probe every five minutes on special world days when the sun or other cosmic events are acting up. A few will make continuous recordings of the seething electrical sea. For the ionosphere, far from being a static shell, changes minute by minute, hour by hour, season by season. It is a sensitive link between events on the sun and earth, Knecht points out. Great flares or explosions on the sun sometimes create a much enhanced D layer about 40 to 50 miles up. This absorbs rather than reflects radio waves, producing radio blackouts and interference.

Other sun flares have no effect for reasons not yet understood.

Magnetic storms and huge bursts of cosmic rays can play hob with the electrical sea. Mysteriously, intense clouds sometimes appear—known as sporadic E—that reflect high frequency of TV signals. What causes these clouds isn't known. The patches sometimes appear to move at speeds of 100 to 200 miles an hour or faster. This indicates tremendous winds, or else movement of whatever is causing the ionization.

Powerful electric rivers sweep through this sea. One flows near the magnetic equator, reversing its direction with day or night A special chain of stations is seeking its cause and meanings. The electrical sea is affected by moon and sun tides, which seem to pull the layers apart at times and places, Knecht continued. The radio soundings can help trace these tidal effects. The radio probes are strung along three great chains, along 75 west longitude, 10 east, and 140 east. All participating countries are sharing findings freely and fully.

The NBS laboratory, acting as one of the four world data centers, is collecting data from about 60 western stations, from pole to pole. The Boulder group has already received measurements from Russians and Americans floating on the Arctic icepack. Special equipment is also used for observinq at six Antarctic bases, including the very South

OUTER SPACE PEOPLE AND INNER EARTH PEOPLE

Pole itself.

The tall, young Knecht is seeing a good bit of the world in his IGY duties. He recently returned from South America where an outbreak of Asian flu in Chile delayed the setting up of the equipment in Concepcion. In Peru, the loading of the equipment aboard a train for a mountain area was delayed for weeks because trains were jammed with food to relieve a famine.

The IGY probings can lead to a better understanding of the upper atmosphere and an improved technique for forecasting radio disturbances and methods of getting signals through by choice of frequencies and other means, Knecht said.

Importantly, the radio soundings can help explain mysteries of the ionosphere, the results can be tied in with findings made with rockets shot up through the ionosphere, direct observations of the sun, and other IGY techniques.

Pole to pole studies can show whether ionospheric changes occur simultaneously at both ends of the world. The radio soundings may explain why the ionized layers exist during the long black polar night when the sun is gone. Some of the far-flung work is mere routine, some is tinged with great adventure.

For the last year, William Hough of the Boulder Laboratories has been sitting it out at the South Pole taking daily measurements, sometimes chatting with his family here by radio.

An inevitable question from home was: "What's it like at the South Pole?" Hough, encased in one of the huts buried in midst of a vast expanse of snow and ice, replied; "Imagine a spotless white banquet table cloth, with just one small crumb of toast in the middle of it... that's us'"

OUTER SPACE PEOPLE AND INNER EARTH PEOPLE

Chapter XI

Thoughts That Influence Us

In the name of Yahveh, Amen. This dissertation is based upon the proposition that some of the thoughts and a portion of the life and influence of a person remains indefinitely in the place where he lived and often emanates from the things that he handled.

It not only follows on after the death of the person but remains in all the places where the living have been. You leave part of your life in everyone that you meet and in every place that you go and upon everything that you touch. This, in Bible language, we would call "the book of life". Even though it may be closed and sealed and apparently forgotten, yet it can be opened and everything in it revealed. Likewise your life is hidden in the things that you do, especially in the things that you set in motion. The thoughts and impressions and the part of your life that you leave in the places where you have been may be good or they may be bad.

I have a gift of "discerning of spirits" (I Cor. 12:10) and I can sense the mental attitudes of people even though they may be miles away. Most of the trouble and disappointments that I have had have been due to the fact that I have often ignored these definite impressions and have gone on trusting people with the hope that they might change their mind.

In our ministry we have had many experiences, of which I will relate but a few. Twenty years ago in the State of Illinois we had the opportunity to take possession of a fine big church building. It had two auditoriums, a balcony, fine pews, a pipe organ, seventeen rooms; and from all material appearances it was ideal for our work. We took it over and labored there for three months preaching and teaching. Never once did we receive the blessing of the Spirit of Yahveh. The psychological atmosphere in that building was choking and stifling. The place was filled with the mental impressions of jealousy and hatred. We could never get a prayer through to our Heavenly Father.

I was definitely shown in two clear and unmistakable visions that we should leave there, and as soon as we quit and went on our way we again had the presence of the Holy Spirit with us. I learned that the congregation of that church had split eleven times and

OUTER SPACE PEOPLE AND INNER EARTH PEOPLE

that for years and years there had been nothing but dissention. Those negative thoughts and mental attitudes lingered there. The whole building was saturated with hate.

Right here in Denver we took over an old church building wherein there had been nothing but trouble. It took us more than ten years to break through the stifling, negative atmosphere that filled that building.

Never again would we take over or attempt to hold services in a church building that had become vacant due to quarrels in the congregation, for those buildings have a plague and a curse upon them.

In recent years I went back to a large city in the State of Ohio and went out to a very large new magnificent stone church building. As I approached the place the psychological atmosphere was loaded with a stifling spirit. I became cold all over and could hardly speak. I went as far as the door but did not enter the building. The pastor who founded that church is dead. The treasurer of the church is dead. A friend of mine who went there to try out for the ministry of the church fell dead.

Good impressions also linger in places. Having visited nearly all of the shrines and historical places in America that are dear to the hearts of Americans, it would take me hours to relate the experiences to you. I sat in the pew in which George Washington sat in church. I sat in the chair in which he sat when he presided over a fraternity. I sat on a chair on which Abraham Lincoln sat, likewise Mark Twain, Lew Wallace and Edgar Allen Poe and many other great men of the yesterdays. Allow me to relate but two of the many experiences.

While in Philadelphia I went out to the house where Edgar Allen Poe lived. I was in the room where Lenore (Annabel Lee) lingered and died. I also saw the open fire place and sat down before it at the desk Poe used when he wrote THE RAVEN. The entire house, every room in it, was filled with the weird, melancholy mental vibrations of Poe. He was as much present as if he were there in person.

The psychologists and parapsychologists have tried for hundreds of years to explain scientifically all of the so-called spiritual phenomena. Their research is all right; it should go on, as it does at Duke University and other institutions of higher learning. But they have failed to prove that the human mind and mortal body is the origin and source of these things. God is a Spirit and before there was any matter there was Divine Mind. Spirit produces physical things; physical things do not produce spiritual images. Everything in matter is a thought incarnated.

In 1980 I visited the Capitol at Washington, D. C. Under the great dome of the Capitol I suddenly stopped, looked up, and instantly was overwhelmed with emotion. I cried like a baby. The atmosphere was super-charged with the minds of great Americans that lingered there. America has a spirit of oneness that is made up of the minds of our fathers who founded this Republic. Guns can never destroy this spirit. The Communists know this even better than we do and that is why they have turned to psychological warfare through propaganda. Only by brain-washing is it possible for Americans to be obsessed with another spirit of a foreign ideology.

OUTER SPACE PEOPLE AND INNER EARTH PEOPLE

What I have said has a basis in the Bible. It was Yahveh who said to Cain, "The voice of thy brother's blood crieth unto me from the ground." (Gen. 4:10).

The life of the flesh is in the blood and blood that has turned to dust, and ashes may yet speak to us. The prophet Isaiah says, "Thy speech shall be low out of the dust and thy voice shall be as one that hath a familiar spirit, out of the ground, and thy speech shall whisper out of the dust." (Isa. 29:4.)

The New Testament says, "By faith Abel offered unto God a more excellent sacrifice than Cain, by which he obtained witness that he was righteous. God testifying of his gifts, by which he being dead yet speaketh." (Heb. 11:4). The greatest evidence that we have of how the blood speaks out of the ground is in I Samuel 28:11-20 in which a woman called up Samuel to speak to King Saul. The Bible does not say that she was a witch. Here is the story: "Then said the woman, Whom shall I bring up unto thee? And he said, Bring me up Samuel. And when the woman saw Samuel, she cried with a loud voice: and the woman spake to Saul, saying, Why hast thou deceived me? for thou art Saul. And the king said unto her, Be not afraid: for what sawest thou? And the woman said unto Saul, I saw gods ascending out of the earth. And he said unto her, What form is he of? And she said, an old man cometh up; and he is covered with a mantle. And Saul perceived that it was Samuel, and he stooped with his face to the ground, and bowed himself. And Samuel said to Saul, Why hast thou disquieted me, to bring me up? And Saul answered, I am sore distressed; for the Philistines make war against me, and God is departed from me, and answereth me no more, neither by prophets, nor by dreams; therefore I have called thee, that thou mayest make known unto me what I shall do. Then said Samuel, wherefore then doest thou ask of me, seeing the Lord is departed from thee, and is become thine enemy? And the Lord hath done to him, as he spake by me: for the Lord hath rent the kingdom out of thine hand, and given it to thy neighbor, even to David: Because thou obeyedst not the voice of the Lord, nor executedst his fierce wrath upon Amalek, therefore hath the Lord done this thing unto thee this day. Moreover the Lord will also deliver Israel with thee into the hand of the Philistines: and tomorrow shalt thou and thy sons be with me: the Lord also shall deliver the host of Israel into the hand of the Philistines. Then Saul fell straightway all along the earth, and was sore afraid, because of the words of Samuel; and there was no strength in him; for he had eaten no bread all the day, nor all the night." (1 Samuel 28 : 11-20).

Whatever may be said about this Bible story, the fact remains that the mystic vaporous form of Samuel speaking out of the dust as it were gave Saul a message that history proves to be true.

Thoughts and a part of the mind and personality of people do continue in things. The prophet Habakkuk says: "The stone shall cry out of the wall, and the beam out of the timber shall answer it." (Hab. 2:11). Impressions are left in the stones and walls and furniture of a house. Everything is recorded by vibrations. We read concerning the great general of Israel, that "Joshua wrote these words in the book of the law of God, and took a great stone, and set it up there under an oak, that was by the sanctuary of the Lord. And Joshua said unto all the people, Behold, this stone shall be a witness unto us; for it hath heard all the words of the Lord which he spake unto us: it shall be therefore a witness

OUTER SPACE PEOPLE AND INNER EARTH PEOPLE

unto you, lest ye deny your God. So Joshua let the people depart, every man unto his inheritance." (Josh.24 :26-28.)

You remember an incident in the last days on earth of our Savior, Yahshua the Messiah, which I consider to be of great importance:

"And when he was come nigh, even now at the descent of the Mount of Olives, the whole multitude of the disciples began to rejoice and praise God with a loud voice for all the mighty works that they had seen: Saying, Blessed be the King that cometh in the name of the Lord: peace in heaven, and glory in the highest. And some of the Pharisees from among the multitude said unto him, Master, rebuke thy disciples. And he answered and said unto them, I tell you that if these should hold their peace, the stones would immediately cry out." (Luke 19 :37-40).

Today the stones are crying out and the word of Yahveh which is forever "settled in heaven" (Ps. 119 :89) and which is preserved "from generation to generation forever" (Ps. 12:7) is again being revealed by His messengers.

The greater portion of my mind and my life now lives in the sermons that I have preached and in the lessons that I have taught and in my recordings and my books and manuscripts and in the hearts of people, so that after I am dead I will yet be speaking.

We are constantly sacrificing our lives; we are losing our lives in order that those now living and those who are yet to be born may find our lives in the message that we leave. For these words of mine are my spirit and my life.

Every person who is immersed in water has a mental picture in his mind of the baptism of Yahshua Our Savior in the River Jordan. They hear again the voice of Yahveh from heaven saying, "This is my beloved Son in whom I am well pleased." And they visualize the Holy Spirit descending upon Him in the bodily form of a dove. By imitating Yahshua they are obeying a positive commandment by which they claim the precious promise: "Repent and be baptized every one of you in the name of Yahshua the Messiah for the remission of sins, and ye shall receive the gift of the Holy Spirit." (Acts 2:38).

Therefore, the person becomes conscious of sins forgiven, and of becoming a son of Yahveh and of receiving the Holy Spirit to remain with him forever as his teacher, guide and comforter to lead him into all truth and to bring to mind all things that Yahshua the Messiah taught while on earth and also the things that he has revealed from heaven. By imitating this act which he set in motion we receive "the mind of Christ." (1 Cor. 2: 16) which is described as "Christ in you, the hope of glory." (Col. 1:27).

When we assemble around the table of Yahveh on the first day of the week, we behold the loaf of His Presence and the cup of his life. This is the oldest ordinance of the presence of Deity in the history of mankind, instituted on earth by Melchizedek (Gen. 14:18-20) and later incorporated as a weekly ordinance in the outer sanctuary of the tabernacle in Israel (Let. 24: 5-9, I Chron. 9:32) and finally chosen by Yahshua the Messiah in his last night on earth as the Body of His Presence. You remember that "Yahshua took bread, and blessed it and broke it, and gave it to the disciples, and said, Take eat; this is my body. And He took the cup, and gave thanks, and gave it to them, saying, Drink

OUTER SPACE PEOPLE AND INNER EARTH PEOPLE

ye all of it; for this is my blood of the New Testament which is shed for many for the remission of sins." (Matt. 26:2628).

For the first time in 4000 years the full significance of the Presentation loaf and cup of Deity was made known.

After the resurrection "He was known of them in the breaking of bread" (Luke 24:35), and the Apostles continued upon the first day of the week to eat the bread and drink the wine in and by and through which they were always "discerning the Lord's body" and were conscious of the fulfillment of His promise, "Lo, I am with you alway, even unto the end of the world." (Matt. 28:20, Acts 2:42, Acts. 20:7, 1Cor. 10:16-17, 1 Cor. 11:29).

We are told that "there are three that bear witness in earth: the spirit and the water and the blood: and these three agree in one." (1 John 5:8). In a definite way the Spirit of Yahveh is present in the waters of baptism and in the wine of communion.

I am trying to show you how the thoughts and life of people continues in things. Thus far we have been on familiar ground, but now I ask you to follow me into new territory and probably you have not passed this way before.

The laying on of hands is an ordinance that is equally as ancient and honorable as the two that I have mentioned. Our first New Testament reference to this practice says, "Then were there brought unto him little children, that he should put his hands on them and pray . . . and he laid his hands on them." (Matt. 19: 13-15).

There are so many references to this practice that I can only name a very few of them: " And, behold there cometh one of the rulers of the synagogue, Jairus by name; and when he saw him, he fell at his feet and besought him greatly, saying, My little daughter lieth at the point of death: I pray thee, come and lay thy hands on her, that she may be healed; and she shall live." (Mark 5:22-23.) "Now when the sun was setting, all they that had any sick with divers diseases brought them unto him; and he laid his hands on every one of them, and healed them." (Luke 4:40)

He said of his Apostles, "They shall lay hands on the sick, and they shall recover." (Mark 16:18). "And by the hands of the apostles were many signs and wonders wrought among the people." (Acts 5:12). After the people were baptized, the apostles "then laid their hands on them, and they received the Holy Ghost." (Acts 8:17).

The laying on of hands conferred power. After Saul of Tarsus had been struck down on the Damascus highway and called to be an Apostle and had been blind for three days, we read, "And Ananias went his way, and entered into the house; and putting his hands on him said, Brother Saul, the Lord, even Jesus,that appeared unto thee in the way as thou camest, hath sent me, that thou mightest receive thy sight, and be filled with the Holy Ghost. And immediately there fell from his eyes as it had been scales: and he received sight forthwith, and arose, and was baptized." (Acts 9:17-18.)

In the last year of the ministry of Paul he wrote to Timothy saying, "Wherefore, I put thee in remembrance, that thou stir up the gift of God, which is in thee by the putting

OUTER SPACE PEOPLE AND INNER EARTH PEOPLE

on of my hands. For God hath not given us the spirit of fear; but of power, and of love, and of a sound mind." (II Tim. 1:67.)

The practice of the laying on of hands was to be continued—the sick are told to "call for the elders of the church; and let them pray over him, anointing him with oil in the name of the Lord, and the prayer of faith shall save the sick, and the Lord shall raise him up; and if he hath committed sin, they shall be forgiven him." (James 5:14-15.)

Paul also told Timothy not to ordain anybody hastily to the ministry, saying: "Lay hands suddenly on no man." (1 Tim. 5:22). For the laying on of hands confers power and authority.

The Apostles touched Yahshua the Messiah. One, at least, pillowed his head on the Master's breast. John speaks of him "which we have heard, which we have seen with our eyes, which we have looked upon, and our hands have handled." (1 John 1:1). Mary Magdalene bathed his feet with tears and dried them with the hair of her head. "And behold a woman in the city which was a sinner, when she knew that Jesus sat at meat in the Pharisees house, brought an alabaster box of ointment and stood at his feet behind him weeping, and began to wash his feet with tears, and did wipe them with the hairs of her head, and kissed his feet and anointed them with the ointment." (Luke 7:37-38). The other two Mary's held him by the feet and worshiped him.

There was healing power even in touching the Master's robe: "And a certain woman, which had an issue of blood twelve years, and had suffered many things of many physicians, and had spent all that she had, and was nothing better, but rather grew worse, when she had heard of Jesus, came in the press behind, and touched his garment. For she said, If I may touch but his clothes, I shall be whole. And straightway the fountain of her blood was dried up; and she felt in her body that she was healed of that plague. And Jesus immediately knowing in himself that virtue had gone out of him, turned him about in the press, and said, Who touched my clothes? And his disciples said unto him, Thou seest the multitude thronging thee, and sayest thou, Who touched me?" (Mark 5:25-31). "And Jesus said, Somebody hath touched me: for I perceive that virtue has gone out of me." (Luke 8:46). THAT WOMAN WAS NOT CROWDING, SHE WAS TOUCHING.

But while all of this is about Jesus, who is Yahshua the Messiah, let us not forget that he commissioned others to carry on his ministry and mission, and that love and power of Christ now operates through those whom he has called and chosen. We read that "God wrought special miracles by the hands of Paul: so that from his body were brought unto the sick handkerchiefs or aprons, and the diseases departed from them, and evil spirits went out of them." (Acts 19:12).

The very garments of Paul were highly magnetized with spiritual vibration and power and this is true of every minister who is filled and anointed with the Holy Spirit. The early Christians loved each other—they embraced and kissed. Four times in the New Testament, in Romans 16:16, I Corinthians 16:20, II Corinthians 13:12, I Thessalonians 5:26 and in I Peter 5:14, we are told to greet all the Brethren with a holy kiss."

Our minds have been so corrupted by Sigmund Freud and other atheistic materi-

OUTER SPACE PEOPLE AND INNER EARTH PEOPLE

alists that the very things which are good and pure and clean and holy are thought to be corrupt, and we fail in fellowship and in the love feast for that is the very name by which the Communion service was called by the early Christians.

Remember that our Savior washed the disciples' feet and he said: "Ye call me Master and Lord: and ye say well; for so I am. If I then, your Lord and Master, have washed your feet; ye also ought to wash one another's feet. For I have given you an example, that ye should do as I have done to you. Verily, veriiy, I say unto you, The servant is not greater than his lord; neither he that is sent greater than he that sent him. If ye know these things happy are ye if ye do them." (John 13:18-17).

We are not happy in our Christian fellowship and experience because we do not do these thtngs. We are too much afraid, too distant, too cold. We act as if our brothers and sisters were lepers and untouchables. I have learned that people usually find what they are looking for—they receive what their own soul is receptive to receive. The artist looks at these snowcapped mountains and sees only beauty. The geologist finds in these same mountains gold, silver and minerals—that's what he is looking for. The fisherman . catches trout out of these mountain streams. The poet sits on the bank and writes down the murmur of the waters. Some time ago a father walked up and down the banks of a mountain stream here in Colorado for six months searching for the body of his little girl until he found her. That stream does not have the same attraction and laughing voice for him that it does for thousands of others.

The message of life to one may be death to another. It all depends upon our attitudes. There are those who are looking for the mistakes, the whims and inconsistencies in the lives of people and they usually find them. In great men who mold the age and shape the future these people see nothing and get nothing but trivial mistakes. They would do well to turn to the Bible which tells us what to think about: "Finally, brethren, whatsoever things are true, whatsoever things are honest, whatsoever things are just, whatsoever things are pure, whatsoever things are lovely, whatsoever things are of good report; if there be any virtue, and if there be any praise, think on these things." (Phil. 4:8).

When my time comes to change worlds and I depart to a greater work in a more wonderful realm, if one person says to me "You brought me from darkness to light, and I now behold wondrous things in the word of Yahveh. You turned on the light." Then my life shall not have been lived in vain. In the name of Yahveh. Amen.

OUTER SPACE PEOPLE AND INNER EARTH PEOPLE

Chapter XII

Time And Balance

There is no perfect calendar and none can be made. After years of careful study and research I am convinced that the perfect calendar of Yahveh cannot be reproduced at this time and the Divine time element cannot be determined.

There are only two days in the year that are identical with the original Bible days. The first One is, March 21st which is called the Vernal equinox, when the sun is then directly overhead at the equator on its migration north. There are twelve hours of light, and twelve hours of darkness—day and night are equal. Then the days begin to lengthen in the northern hemisphere and the nights become shorter until we reach the longest day of the year on June 21st, which is called the Summer Solstice.

Then the light begins to shorten and the darkness to lengthen until we reach the autumn equinox on September 23rd and again on that day the periods of light and darkness are equal. Then the light continues to shorten until we reach the shortest day in the year which is on December 22nd which is called the Winter Solstice. Then the days lengthen again until they become equal once more on March 21st. Therefore the only two days in the year when the earth is upright at the poles and the days and nights are equal are on March 21st and on September 21st and these are the only two days in the year that are like the original Bible day.

In the beginning "Yahveh divided the light from the darkness, and Yahveh called the light day and the darkness he called night, and the evening and the morning were the first day." (Gen. 1:4-5.) The Bible day began at sundown and there were twelve hours of darkness called night. The night was the first section of the day. The Hebrews divided it into four watches. The first watch of the night was from six until nine, the second watch was from nine until twelve, the third watch was from twelve until three, the fourth watch was from three until six o'clock. The rooster crows in the fourth watch. It was called "the cock crow," or the hailing of the dawn. The day, that is the light, began at sun-up which was 6:00 A M. and it continued for twelve hours. These twelve hours of light were also divided into four quarters called "hours". The first hour was from six o'clock in the morning until nine, the second hour was from nine to twelve, the third hour was from twelve to three, the fourth hour was from three to six in the evening. There are many scriptures on this. (See Mark 11:11, John 20:19, Mark 13:85, John 18:27, Daniel 3:6-15, 5:5.) The Bible

OUTER SPACE PEOPLE AND INNER EARTH PEOPLE

day (night and day) was from sunset to sunset—twelve hours of darkness and twelve hours of light. (Gen. 1:5, Leviticus 28:.22.) Yahshua the Messiah said that there are "twelve hours of the day." (John 11:9.) Night and day are exactly twenty-four hours.

The first day of the week, which was the first day of the year, was on what is now March 21st. Every year; on March 21st if we followed the Bible time, we would begin a new year, and we would begin it with Sunday, the first day of the first month of the year. But this could not possibly work out right and I will tell you why: It did work perfectly during the period of time covered in the first and second chapters of Genesis because the earth was upright at the poles and there was continuous Spring, or semitropical climate all over the earth. Every day had twelve hours of darkness and twelve hours of light But remember that during the time that Adam lived on the continent of Eden in the Garden in the city of Paradise, the light and energy of the sun was seven times more than it is today and the light and energy of the moon was then equal to that of the sun at the present time. (Isa. 80:26.) What does this mean? It means simply that daylight was seven times brighter than it is now and the night was as light as the day is now. Adam and Eve were "naked and not ashamed" because they were clothed in garments of light. The mind of man occupies the brain, spinal cord and nerves. The brain, spinal cord and nerves of Adam and Eve were definitely filled with a bright fluorescent heavenly, immortal fluid which made their bodies glow with heavenly light. With seven-fold light they could see more than we can see today with the X-ray and the microscope. In that dimension they could communicate with Yahveh and could see the angels. Light is a marvelous thing. At the World's Fair in Chicago they had a tower of light. When you went in there, they turned on a few lights, then more light and more light and more light. At a very high degree of light our bodies become invisible. That's why Yahshua the Messiah, the angels and the spirits of just men made perfect are invisible to us. They are in a higher light realm (dimension) than we are.

The transgression of Adam and Eve, which was the poison venom of the serpent-man's blood which came into their bodies, was a terrible thing. They lost their garments of light. They were driven out of Eden. The whole continent of Eden, garden and city of paradise, was torn loose and thrown off from the earth into outer-space where it is now a satellite. The earth tilted and the light and energy of the sun was diminished and death set in. Then 1,656 years after Adam left Eden, the flood came. The earth turned upside down" (Isa. 24:1) and went out of its original orbit. The light and energy of the sun was diminished by six-sevenths. The light and energy of the moon was lessened by 400,000 per cent and that is the condition that we have to day. "All the foundations of the earth are out of course." (Ps.82:5.)

Under this present condition no calendar can be perfect. Not even the Divine time element and sacred calendar will work. The earth turns on its axis every twenty-four hours—to be exact every 23 hours, 56 minutes and 4.095 seconds. I shall give the rough numbers, not the second and fractions thereof. The earth orbits the sun at the rate of 67,000 miles per hour. The sun, moving north, orbits a central sun at the rate of 175 miles per second. The central sun orbits the hub of the galaxies at the rate of 300 miles per second. I could give you the fractions of seconds but that would be too boring and would

OUTER SPACE PEOPLE AND INNER EARTH PEOPLE

> "For there is hope of a tree, if it be cut down, that it will sprout again, and that the tender branch thereof will not cease. Though the root thereof wax old in the earth, and the stock thereof die in the ground; Yet through the scent of water it will bud, and bring forth boughs like a plant."- (Job 14:7-9.)

OUTER SPACE PEOPLE AND INNER EARTH PEOPLE

weary you. Suffice it to say that it would require the universe 25,800 years to correct the time element at the rate of the movement of all of the heavenly bodies at the present time. "All the foundations of the earth are out of course." (Psalm 82:5.)

Man is out of balance. Most people are either right-handed or left-handed. If you would take your picture and cut it in two down the middle, or if we stood you up and blocked off your right side and your left side, believe me, your right side looks entirely different from your left side. In fact you are almost two different persons—one strong, the other weak, one good, the other bad. If you are right-handed you use only the left side of your brain. If you are left-handed you use only the right side of your brain. If you are equally balanced, with 20-20 vision in both eyes, equal hearing in both ears, and use both hands equally, then you use all of your brain and are a genius.

Yahshua the Messiah said: "The light of the body is the eye: if therefore thine eye be single, thy whole body shall be full of light. But if thine eye be evil, thy whole body shall be full of darkness." (Matt. 6:22-23.) Two eyes, coordinated, are one eye. They register the very same image on the brain. But if one eye sees one image and the other eye sees another image, "then you are out of balance." This is a serious condition. "A double-minded man is unstable in all his ways." (James 1:8.) Nobody ever described this condition better than the Apostle Paul: "For we know that the law is spiritual: but I am carnal, sold under sin. For that which I do; I allow not: for what I would, that do I not; but what I hate, that do I. If then I do that which I would not I consent unto the law that it is good. Now then it is no more I that do it, but sin that dwelleth in me. For I know that in me (that is, in my flesh), dwelleth no good thing: for to will is present with me; but how to perform that which is good I find not. For the good that I would, I do not: but the evil which I would not; that I do. Now if I do that I would not it is no more I that do it, but sin that dwelleth in me. I find then a law, that, when I would do good, evil is present with me. For I delight in the law of Yahveh after the inward man: But I see another law in my members, warring against the law of my mind, and bringing me into captivity of the law of sin which is in my members. O wretched man that I am! who shall deliver me from the body of this death? I thank Yahveh through Yahshua. So then with the mind I myself serve the law of Yahveh; but with the flesh, the law of sin. (Rom. 7:14 25)

Yahshua the Messiah said: "And if thy right eye offend thee, pluck it out, and cast it from thee: for it is profitable for thee that one of the members should perish, and not that thy whole body should be cast into hell. And if thy right hand offend thee, cut it off, and cast it from thee: for it is profitable for thee that one of thy members should perish, and not that thy whole body should be cast into hell." (Matt. 5:29-30)

This simply means that if you do not want to live in the hell of doubt and worry and uncertainty and confusion, then you must become properly balanced. Put off the old man, crucify the weak side, put on the new man, become properly balanced and coordinated in your whole being. I think that two of the many important things which Yahveh has given me to do are: First to seal the people with the sacred name "Yahveh", and Second; to properly balance the people and coordinate their bodies, minds, souls and spirits in harmony with Yahveh. Therefore, part of my mission is the sealing and the balancing (coordinating) of the people.

OUTER SPACE PEOPLE AND INNER EARTH PEOPLE

It is wonderful what proper balance can do. In extreme emergency we use it. On Thursday; April 26, 1960, a woman weighing only 123 pounds lifted a 3,600 pound station wagon off her son who was trapped under it. Her name was Mrs. Maxwell C. Rogers of Tampa, Florida. We can take a pole weighing hundreds of pounds and suspend it in the air and hold it on our little finger by proper balance. By perfect balance and leverage we could lift the earth. This matter of balance is an important thing, but "all the foundations of the earth are out of balance." (Ps.82:5.).

I say again that there cannot be a perfect calendar nor any restoration of the Divine time element in this age. However, Lunar (moon) time corrects itself every thirty-six years. But that as you see, is much off balance. Easter comes on the first Sunday after the first full moon following the Vernal Equinox (Mar. 21). This can fall anywhere between March 22nd and April 25th. So you see that moon time corrects itself every 36 years. But this is not absolutely accurate, either, because of the fractions in the orbits of the moon, earth and sun. When Yahveh revealed the sacred calendar to Moses after it had been lost for many years, he made the Passover the beginning of the year. I will now show you the way that the Hebrews set up their calendar.

The first month was called Nisan or Abib. It correspond to our time from March 21st through April 19th. The zodiacal sign of this month is Aries the Ram. In this month three feasts were held: 1. The Passover; 2. Unleavened bread, and 3. Firstfruits.

May I add this, and this is not astrology but is true and accurate scientific astronomy: the vernal equinox—the point where, the sun crosses the equator on its way north, is known in astronomy as "the first point of Aries, but on account of procession it is now in Pisces." (Encyclopedia Britannica, Vol. 7, page 831.) Four hundred years ago it was in Dracula and had been there for many years. The line of entrance into the Great Pyramid which slopes on an oblique angle into the pit was on a direct line to Dracula. The date of the building of the Pyramid must have been about nine hundred years from Adam—in the days of Enoch (Gen. 5:1-31). or between six and seven hundred years before the flood, which would be about, 5,000 years ago that the Pyramid was built. But we are now in Pisces, the fish sign, or bottom of the Zodiac. We should be moving into the first point of Aries about 2000 A D., or not later than 2034 A D. which probably will be the beginning of the millennium.,

The second Hebrew month was from April 20th through May 20. It was called Lyar or Zif. The sign is Taurus, the bull. The third Hebrew month was from May 21st through June 21st and. was called Sivan. The feast of Pentecost was held during this month. The sign is Gemini. The fourth Hebrew month was from June 22nd through July 21st. It was called Thammuz. The sign is Cancer (the crab) now called "Moon children."

The fifth Hebrew month was from July 22nd through August 21st. It was called Ab and the sign was Leo (the Lion). The sixth Hebrew month was from August 22nd, through September 22nd. It was called Elul. The sign is Virgo. The seventh Hebrew month was from September 23rd through October 22nd. It was called Tishri or Ethanim. During this month there were three feasts—the feast of trumpets, the feast of atonement, and the feast of tabernacles. The sign is Libra (the balances). During this month, as we shall see

OUTER SPACE PEOPLE AND INNER EARTH PEOPLE

later, Yahshua, the Messiah, was born.

The eighth Hebrew month was from October 23rd through November 21st. It was called Merchisvan or Bul. During this month was the feast of Chanukah (Hanuakkah), dedication not in the Bible, but based upon the Apocrypha— I Maccabees 4:56. The sign of this month was Scorpio.

The ninth Hebrew month was from Nov. 22nd through Dec. 21st. It was called Kislev. The sign is Sagittarius. The tenth Hebrew month was from December 22nd through January 20th. The name of the month was Tebeth; the sign is Capricorn (the goat). The eleventh Hebrew month was from January 21st through February 19th. The name of the month was Shebat. The sign is Aquarius. The twelfth Hebrew month was from February 20th through March 20th. The name of the month was Adar. The sign is Pisces (the fishes). During this month the Jews of late (not Bible Hebrews) hold the feast of Purim based upon Esther, the 9th chapter.

I was surprised and disappointed to learn in my studies that this calendar is mostly Babylonian and that nearly all the names of the months are Babylonian, that it was not and is not the Divine Calendar of Yahveh. Even the Jews could not follow it in civil affairs. They began their religious month and new year on March 1st, Nisan or Abib, but they began their civil year on September 23rd. Thus the seventh month of the religious year was the first month of the civil year. So I found as much error and confusion in the Hebrew calendar as I found in the Egyptian, Greek, Roman or Mayan calendars, and I am firmly convinced that there cannot be an accurate calendar today.

We are definitely on heathen, Gentile time. Our present calendar is Babylon personified. As an example: the word "December" means the tenth month, but it is the twelfth month on our Calendar. The word "November" means the ninth month but it is the eleventh. "October" means the eighth but it is the tenth. "September" means the seventh but it is the ninth. (You can go crazy studying the calendar.) August is Augustus Caesar's month. July is Julius Caesar's month. June is the goddess Juno's month. May is the Roman goddess Maia's month—the goddess of fertility. April means "to open". March is the god Mar's month. February, the meaning of the name of this month is unknown. In 452 B C. in the reign of Numa, January, the goddess Janus' month, was added to the top of the calendar and February was added at the bottom of the calendar. Later on both January and February were placed at the top. Therefore the two months at the top of the calendar, January and February, are before the beginning of the year. They should be at the bottom since December means the tenth month. This is terribly confusing but the names of the days of the week are just as bad— Sunday is the Sun's day, Monday is the Moon's day, Tuesday is the goddess Twi's day, Wednesday is Woden's day, Thursday is Thor's day, Friday is Frija's day and Saturday is Saturn's day. Our months of the year and days of the week are wholly and entirely pagan. To try to figure Bible prophecy and events on this time table is next to impossible, but the date of the birth of Yahshua the Messiah can be determined.

We know for sure that Yahshua the Messiah was not born on December 25th. The Egyptians, 2,000 years before Christ was born, were celebrating the birth of the son of

OUTER SPACE PEOPLE AND INNER EARTH PEOPLE

Isis, the Queen of heaven, on December 25th. All heathen religions kept the feast of the winter solstice—usually for eight days from December 22nd through December 28th. Probably there were as many as one hundred allegedly virgin-gods whose birthdays were celebrated on December 25th, and this goes back as far as 2,000 years to 3,000 years before Yahshua the Messiah. Likewise, Easter, the vernal equinox was celebrated by all heathens—usually from March 21st through March 28th. Both Christmas and Easter are pagan days. Santa Claus, the decorated tree, eggs, and the bunny rabbit are all borrowed from heathen religions.

As a pastor of a church, I refuse to celebrate Christmas, Easter, Mother's Day, Father's Day, Children's day, brotherhood day, sisterhood day, grandpa's day, grandma's day, uncle's day, aunt's day, cousin's day, United Nations' day or any other holiday in the church. You may, if you wish, celebrate those days in your own home and outside the church. I see no sin in that at all, for Paul said to the Romans; "One man esteemeth one day above another; another esteemeth every day alike. Let every man be fully persuaded in his own mind." (Rom. 14;5.) You can do many things in your own home, when you are outside the church services, which you cannot do in the public assembly of the church. When the Galatians began to observe holidays in the church Paul said to them: "Ye observe days, and months, and times, and years. I am afraid of you, lest I have bestowed upon you labour in vain." (Gal. 4: 10-11)

It is fine to have a good big dinner in your home, but it would be wrong to have that dinner in the church or to come to church to, eat and drink and fill your belly. Some say to me that I will never build up a big congregation unless the church has suppers and dances for the young people and card parties and bingo for the old folks, and that if I do not observe Christmas, Easter, and Mother's day we will get nowhere. All right, then we will get nowhere, for I refuse to bring those things into the church.

There are fifty-two weeks in the year and I have been told that there are 500 special emphasis days for the year—ten for every week, more than one special day for every day of the year. Where would we stop on this thing? The facts are that I am not going to begin it in the church.

The birthday of Yahshua the Messiah is not a Bible holy day, but it can be determined. As the time drew near for the birth of Yahshua the Messiah in the flesh, Augustus Caesar issued a decree that all the world should take a census for the purpose of taxation. God provides ample time to carry out his decrees. Caesar was seven years too early in issuing his orders. King Herod in Palestine refused to obey the order. He was called to Rome and Caesar told him to get back to Palestine and take the Census. After he returned he still hesitated, until finally Caesar sent orders to Herod that he would either take the Census or be put to death. Seven years had gone by since the tax decree had been issued by Caesar. This just shows how God who is unknown to the rulers of the present evil world forces them to unknowingly carry out his program at the exact moment on his own Divine clock of time. Herod issued the order then that all the people in Palestine must return at once to the place of their birth to register. Joseph and Mary immediately set out from Nazareth to Bethlehem. Naturally the tax decrees or census alone would have caused the little town of Bethlehem to be overcrowded, but there was

OUTER SPACE PEOPLE AND INNER EARTH PEOPLE

another reason for congestion.

It was the time of the Hebrew feast of Tabernacles, also called the Feast of Lights. It was the greatest of all the Israelite feasts and drew from all over the world nearly all of the Israelites to Jerusalem. It was the one feast of Feasts that all Israelites and Judahites attempted desperately to attend. Therefore there was a great influx of people into Jerusalem and in the surrounding villages. Bethlehem is only four miles south of Jerusalem. The Feast of Tabernacles was held in the Seventh Hebrew month of Tisri, a month of thirty days, corresponding to our month from September 23rd through October 22nd. The Feast lasted for eight days, from September 28th until October 5th. It began on the first day of the week which on our calendar would be Sunday and it ended on the eighth day, which again would be Sunday.

The date of the Feast was, to the best of our calculations, from September 28 to October 5. Therefore with my limited knowledge, I cannot determine whether Yahshua the Messiah was born on Sunday, September 28, which was the first day of the feast or whether he was born on the octave, which, was the eighth day of the feast which would have been on Sunday, October 5, but this much I know, He was born during the Feast of Tabernacles, for that was the very feast of his advent. The Gospel of John says, "The word was made flesh, and dwelt among us." (John 1:14.) , The word "dwelt" in the Greek is literally, "Tabernacled." The Feast of Tabernacles secondarily commemorated the time that the children of Israel dwelt in booths (tents) in the wilderness. When they celebrated the feast they put up small tents on every house top in Jerusalem. Primarily it foreshadowed the time when the Messiah would come to earth and tabernacle in the flesh.

On the octave, the eighth day of the feast, the great and final ceremony was that of the pouring out of the Holy Water. The priests in great procession went down to the pool of Siloam; a pool that was fed by an aqueduct from the waters from the Virgin's spring. They dipped up a pitcher of water, carried it in procession into the temple and poured it out. This secondarily commemorated that time when David, in a time of trouble when he was driven from Jerusalem, longed for a drink of water from the spring in Bethlehem. His men risked their lives to bring him that water. He then declared it holy and poured it out. But that it primarily was a symbol of the Messiah is evident from the fact that Yahshua, in the thirty-third year of his life on earth, while attending the feast declared it so. "In the last day, that great day of the feast, Yahshua the Messiah stood and cried, saying, If any man thirst, let him come unto me, and drink. He that believeth on me, as the scripture hath said, out of his belly shall flow rivers of living water." (John 7:37-38).

We must conclude from this scripture that Yahshua the Messiah was born on the octave, the last day of the Feast which was on Sunday; October 5. But both the first day, and the eighth day were holy days, for we read this in the scriptures. "Speak unto the children of Israel, saying, The fifteenth day of this seventh month shall be the Feast of Tabernacles for seven days unto Yahveh. On the first day shall be a holy convocation; ye shall do no servile work therein. Seven days ye shall offer an offering made by fire unto Yahveh; on the eighth day shall be a holy convocation unto you and ye shall offer an offering made of fire unto Yahveh it is a solemn assembly; and ye shall do no servile work therein." (Lev. 23:34-36.),

OUTER SPACE PEOPLE AND INNER EARTH PEOPLE

The first day was, or would be, according to our calendar, Sunday, and again the eighth day would be Sunday. It is declared that, "on the first day shall be a sabbath and on the eighth day shall be a sabbath." (Lev. 23:39) Therefore the true Lord's Day is on Sunday the first day of the week. The birth of Yahshua the Messiah was on Sunday, the first day of the week. On the first day of the week He arose from the dead: "Now upon the first day of the week, very early in the morning, they came unto the sepulcher, bringing the spices which they had prepared, and certain others with them. And they found the stone rolled away from the sepulcher. And they entered in, and found not the body of Yahshua the Messiah. And it came to pass, as they were much perplexed thereabout, behold, two men stood by them in shining garments and as they were afraid, and bowed down their faces to the earth, they said unto them, Why seek ye the living among the dead? He is not here, but is risen: remember how he spake unto you when he was yet in Galilee. And, behold, two of them went that same day to a village called Emmaus, which was from Jerusalem about three-score furlongs. And they talked together of all these things which had happened. And it came to pass that while they communed together and reasoned, Yahshua the Messiah himself drew near, and went with them.

And it came to pass, as he sat at meat with them, he took bread, and blessed it; and brake it, and gave to them. And their eyes were opened, and they knew him; and he vanished out of their sight. And they said one to another, Did not our heart burn within us, while he talked with us by the way, and while he opened to us the Scriptures." (Luke 24:1-6, 13-15, 30-32.)

So Yahshua the Messiah arose on the first day of the week and on that day he broke bread with his disciples. "Then the same day at evening, being the first day of the week, when the doors were shut where the disciples were assembled for fear of the Jews, came Yahshua the Messiah and stood in the midst, and saith unto them, Peace be unto you. Yahshua the Messiah saith unto him, Thomas, because thou hast seen me, thou hast believed, blessed are they that have not seen, and yet have believed." (John 20: 19-29.)

Yahshua the Messiah appeared to his disciples and broke bread with them on Sunday, the first day of the week and again, eight days later which was again on Sunday the first day of the week. That is why the early Christians kept Sunday, the first day of the week, which is the Lord's day as the Holy Christian sabbath. The day was given in prophecy and was definitely connected with the feast of tabernacles. The Christians always kept Sunday, the first day of the week, as the sabbath. "And upon the first day of the week, when the disciples came together to break bread, Paul preached unto them, ready to depart on the morrow; and continued his speech until midnight." (Acts 20:7.) "Upon the first day of the week let everyone of you lay by him in store, as Yahveh hath prospered him." (1 Cor. 16:2.) "I was in the Spirit on the Lord's day, and heard behind me a great voice, as of a trumpet." (Rev. 1:10.)

There was another thing about the feast of tabernacles that marked it as the birthday of Yahshua the Messiah. It was called the Feast of Lights. Every window and every housetop in Jerusalem was lighted. The whole city was flooded with light during all the eight days of the feast. Now John, in speaking of Yahshua the Messiah tabernacling in the flesh, said: "In him was life; and the life was the light of men. That was the true Light,

OUTER SPACE PEOPLE AND INNER EARTH PEOPLE

which lighteth every man that cometh into the world." (John 1:4-9.) And Yahshua the Messiah himself declared, "I am the light of the world." (John 9:5.) So it is an evident fact that Yahshua the Messiah was born either on Sunday, September 28, which was the first day of the feast of tabernacles or he was born on Sunday, October 4th, which was the last day of the feast.

John says, "The WORD was made flesh and dwelt among us." The capital "WORD" in Greek is "Logos" and in Hebrew it is "Dabar", meaning the perfect incarnation and perfect law of Yahveh. Yahshua the Messiah, the WORD, was the perfect living law of God incarnated in the flesh. The word "dwelt" is tabernacled. Yahshua the Messiah was born during the feast of tabernacles. The feast lasted eight days. It began on Sunday, the first day of the week, on the 28th day of September, and continued until Saturday, the seventh day of the week, the 4th day of October. One extra day was added, the eighth day, which was the high feast day, on October 5th, the octave.

It must be remembered that the Israelites observed 72 sabbath days every year. Fifty-two were the regular weekly seventh day Sabbaths. Twenty were the high sabbath days during their six special feasts. The feast of tabernacles was by far the greatest of all. The late Alfred Edersheim of Oxford, a converted Jew and the greatest of all on the subject of Jewish feasts, in "The Life and Times of Jesus the Messiah" says it was called "The Feast" (Ha-Chog). The Jewish historian, Sukk, says that it was "the holiest and greatest." Pilgrims from all over the world—Media, Arabia, Persia, India, Spain, Crimea and from the banks of the Danube and Rhine and the British Islands—in short Israelites from every nation under heaven journeyed to Jerusalem to attend the feast of tabernacles. It was not only Caesar's decree of a registration for a poll tax that overcrowded Bethlehem and Jerusalem at the time of Christ's birth but it was also the great influx of Israelites from all over the world to the feast of tabernacles.

All of the twenty-four orders of the priestly families officiated at "The Feast." It required 892 people to attend to the sacrifices, 446 priests and 446 Levitical helpers. Thirteen bullocks were offered daily on the altar and, of course the many other lesser sacrifices. On the last, the great day of the feast, the Temple was literally flooded with light and bright lights were displayed everywhere in Jerusalem. The climax of the feast was the pouring out of the water. The priests in great procession went down to the pool of Siloam which was fed by "the Virgin's Spring" far up in the Kidron valley. When they returned with the water in a great pitcher the trumpets sounded and the priest carrying the water entered the temple through "the water gate". When Yahshua answered, Verily, verily, I say unto thee, Except a man be born of water and of the Spirit he cannot enter into the kingdom of Yahveh. That which is born of flesh is flesh; and that which is born of the Spirit is spirit." (John 3:5-6), he was speaking of his own natural Virgin birth by water out of the womb of Mary and of his resurrection from the dead which was the spiritual birth. For thirty-three years he was a flesh and blood man born of the Water. Since his resurrection he has been, is now and always will be the spiritual-born man.

When the priests poured out the water in that solemn ceremony: "In the last day, that great day of the feast, Yahshua stood and cried, saying, If any man thirst, let him come unto me and drink. He that believeth on me as the scripture hath said, out of his

OUTER SPACE PEOPLE AND INNER EARTH PEOPLE

belly shall flow rivers of living water." (John 7:37-38.)

The first fourteen verses of the Gospel of John are written to show that Yahshua the Messiah "tabernacled" in the flesh—that he was the great light. "In him was life; and the life was the light of men. That was the true Light which lighteth every man that cometh into the world. And the Word was made flesh, and dwelt among us, (and we beheld his glory, the glory as of the only begotten of the Father,) full of grace and truth." (John 1:4, 9, 14.) This last verse, translated into plain Modern English would read as follows: "And Yahshua the Messiah, the living law of Yahveh, was born in the flesh and tabernacled among us, (and we saw his glory and knew that he was and is the only begotten Son of the Father), the fulness of grace and the whole truth."

On the octave (8th day) of the feast, the tabernacles were taken down. The truth of the matter is that Yahshua the Messiah was born at the end of the seventh day and the beginning of the first day (8th day). The Bible day begins in the evening. Therefore, Yahshua the Messiah, was born immediately after sundown—that is a little after six o'clock P M. on what would be our Saturday night, but by Bible time it was in the first minutes of the first day of the week; Sunday, Oct. 5th, the end of the feast, the octave, or eighth day, Sunday, the new day—the Lord's day.

The Psalmist, one thousand years before Yahshua the Messiah, told us about the wise men who would visit and bring gifts to Him: "The kings of Tarshish and of the isles shall bring presents: the kings of Sheba and Seba shall offer gifts. Yea, all kings shall fall down before him: all nations shall serve him." (Psalm 72:10-11.) Therefore, the wise men must have been kings from all the nations of the world. "Because of thy temple at Jerusalem shall kings bring presents unto thee." (Ps. 68:20.) And it was during the time of the Feast of Tabernacles in the Temple at Jerusalem that Yahshua the Messiah was born and at that time the wise men came from the ends of the earth. "Now when Yahshua was born in Bethlehem of Judea in the days of Herod the king, behold, there came wise men from the east to Jerusalem, saying, Where is he that is born King of the Jews? for we have seen his star in the east, and are come to worship him. When Herod the king had heard these things he was troubled, and all Jerusalem with him. And when he had gathered all the chief priests and scribes of the people together, he demanded of them where the Messiah should be born. And they said unto him, in Bethlehem of Judea: for thus it was written by the prophet. And thou Bethlehem, in the land of Juda, art thou not the least among the princes of Juda: for out of thee shall come a Governor, that shall rule my people Israel. Then Herod, when he had privily called the wise men, inquired of them diligently what time the star appeared. And he sent them to Bethlehem, and said, Go and search diligently for the young child; and when ye have found him, bring me word again, that I may come and worship him also. When they had heard the king they departed; and, lo, the star, which they saw in the east went before them, till it came and stood over where the young child was. When they saw the star, they rejoiced with exceeding great joy." (Matt. 2:1-10.)

In Humboldt's "Cosmos", Vol. 1, page 92, there is a record of the appearance of the star of Bethlehem. In the Chinese classic by Legge, Hong Kong edition, 1865, in Vol.3, Part 1, page 112, there is a record of the Star that appeared in the days of YAHOV. The

OUTER SPACE PEOPLE AND INNER EARTH PEOPLE

name in the Chinese is the same as the Hebrew name of God, YHVH or YAHSHUA, whom we in English call Jesus. Kepler in 1603 A D. gives the conjunction of the stars at the time of the birth of Jesus. The conjunction of Jupiter; Saturn and Mars were in the constellation of Pisces and at that time a new star became visible between Jupiter and Saturn.

The exact moment, year, month, day, hour and second of the birth of the Messiah can he determined. How? By astronomy. By determining the moment that the star of Bethlehem appeared with its meridian directly over Bethlehem. I am not good enough in astronomy or mathematics to figure the time and meridians of new stars and comets that come into our solar system, but it is known when they first appeared and how often they appear. For example, Halley's comet appeared May 4, 1910. It will appear again in the same circuit in the heavens in 75 years—that will be 1985. Astronomy is accurate to the fraction of a second.

The star of Bethlehem was not the planet Venus, neither was it a meteorite or a phenomenon. It was a real star and visible for the first time to the wise men (ancient astronomers) of this earth. For some reason, about which I had just as well not voice my opinion now, it is almost impossible to find a book on astronomy in any library that mentions the Star of Bethlehem. Those who deny the resurrection of Yahshua the Messiah also want to keep secret the truth about the appearance of the Star of Bethlehem at the time of his birth. Several years ago I got hold of article on astronomy by the late George Leo Patterson of Denver, Colo., which was one of a series of articles on the stars. This one happened to be on "The Star of Bethlehem." I clipped it and carried it in my wallet for a number of years though I was not at that time interested in corroborating the Bible by astronomy. I lost the article and have never in recent years been able to get another. It said that the star of Bethlehem was a real star known and charted, that it appeared first to the earth with its meridian over Bethlehem. It went on to say that the star has appeared every 814 years since then, that it was visible to the naked eye the second time in 314 AD, and the third time in 628 AD., but that in 942 AD., 1256 AD., 1570 AD., and 1884 AD., the last four appearances, it was visible only with the aid of the telescope.

When I began studying the Book of Revelation, I found this saying: "The mystery of the seven stars;" "The seven stars are the angels (messengers) of the seven churches." (Rev. 1:20.) I then understood the secret. The first appearance of the Star of Bethlehem marked the birth of the Messiah, his advent in the flesh and the first epoch of the church, the Ephesus period. (Rev. 2:1-7.) The second appearance of the star of Bethlehem in 314 A D. was seen by Constantine. He said he saw in the star a cross and these words: "In hoc signo vinces"-by this sign conquer, and that was the Smyrna epoch of the church. (Rev. 2:8-11.) The third appearance of the Star of Bethlehem in 628 A D. marked the rise of Mohammedanism and the corruption of organized Christianity, the Pergamos period of Church history. (Rev. 2: 124.) . The fourth appearance in 942 A D. was the beginning of the Thyatira epoch of the church. (Rev. 2 :18-29.) The fifth appearance in 1256 A D. was the beginning of the Sardis epoch. (Rev. 8:1-6.) The sixth appearance of the Star of Bethlehem in 1570 AD marked the beginning of the Philadelphia epoch of the Church. This was the great Protestant period brought about by God using Luther, Calvin, Knox, Wesley, Campbell and a host of the reformers and restorationists. (Rev-3:7-13)

OUTER SPACE PEOPLE AND INNER EARTH PEOPLE

Seven is the symbol of perfection, the end, the completion. The star of Bethlehem appeared the seventh time in 1884 A D. It was then that Yahshua the Messiah cast off the Babylon of all organized and corrupted denominational religion. He declared them luke warm: "And unto the angel of the church of the Laodiceans write: These things saith the Amen, the faithful and true witness, the beginning; of the creation of God; I know thy works, that thou are neither cold nor hot: I would ,thou wert cold or hot. So then because thou art lukewarm, and neither cold nor hot, I will spew thee out of my mouth. Because thou sayest, I am rich, and increased with goods, and have need of nothing; and knowest not that thou are wretched and miserable, and poor, and blind, and naked: I counsel thee to buy of me gold tried in the fire, that thou mayest be rich; and white raiment, that thou mayest be clothed, and that the shame of thy nakedness do not appear; and anoint thine eyes with eye-salve, that thou mayest see. As many as I love, I rebuke and chasten; be zealous therefore, and repent. Behold, I stand at the door and knock; if any man hear my voice, and open the door, I will come in to him and will sup with him, and he with me. To him that overcometh will I grant to sit with me in my throne, even as I also overcame, and am set down with my Father in his throne. He that hath an ears let him hear what the Spirit saith unto the churches." (Rev. 3:14-22)

In 1884 we find Yahshua the Messiah outside the door of the historical church. We also find that it was "the beginning of the creation of God." The seventh and last appearance of the Star of Bethlehem was the beginning of the new creation of God. That was the beginning of the restoration. In the advent of Yahshua the Messiah there have been seven epochs of his coming. His full and complete and final advent was in 1884 A D. when the Star of Bethlehem appeared the seventh time. After this sevenfold, or final advent just like he spent 30 years in the flesh before his active ministry, he spent thirty years; that is, from 1884 A D. to 1914 A D., before he began his active ministry of casting off the gentile governments of the world.

He repudiated the corrupt churches in 1884 A D. He repudiated the world governments in 1914 A D. That was the beginning of his active spiritual ministry. After three years of his ministry, to be exact on Dec. 9, 1917, Yahshua the Messiah became the "King eternal, immortal, invisible" (I Tim. 1:17) over all the kingdoms of this world. December 9, 1917, was the date that Edmund Henry Hynman Allenby, the British (Israel) General and his Anglo-Saxon army entered Jerusalem. Since that date the gospel of the Kingdom—the Anglo-Saxon Israel Kingdom has been preached. The repudiated and cast-off Babylon of religions and the governments of this present evil world system will all perish from the earth. But "the government of Yahshua the Messiah will stand." It will go through this end time of trouble, apostasy and great tribulation without hurt. The Anglo-Saxon Israel of Yahveh will emerge under Yahshua purified and will reign over the world. Yahveh said to Daniel: From the time that the daily sacrifice shall be taken away "there shall be a thousand two hundred and ninety days," and "Blessed is he that waiteth and cometh to the thousand three hundred and five and thirty days." (Dan. 12:11-12.) Why did Yahveh say in one verse 1290 days and in the next verse 1335 days? The prophet Ezekiel says : "I have appointed each day for a year." (Ezek. 4:6.). The daily sacrifice of Christian worship was taken away by the Mohammedans in 627 A D. Now listen, 1290 years from that time, 627 A D. plus 1290 years brings us to the Christian year of 1917 A D., which was

OUTER SPACE PEOPLE AND INNER EARTH PEOPLE

the Mohammedan year of 1335. That's why Yahveh said to Daniel 1290 and 1335. The Mohammedan coins were stamped 1917 and 1335 when General Allenby took Jerusalem in 1917. They bore both the Christian and Mohammedan dates. If that is not a literal fulfillment of prophecy then prophecy can never be fulfilled. But wait a moment! There is more proof. Yahveh said to Nebuchadnezar, "Let seven times pass over thee." Now "time" is a Hebrew year of 360 days. Seven times 360 is 2520. It was approximately 2520 years from the beginning of Nebuchadnezzar's Babylon in 608 B C. (some say 604 or 606. At any rate add 603 B C. to 1917 A D. and you have 2520 years. The end time, the beginning of the end of the governments of this present evil world.

But it was not at the beginning of Nebuchadnezzar's reign in Babylon that Daniel mentioned the "seven times" (2520 years). It was in 569 B C. and it did not begin to be fulfilled until a year later. "All this came upon the king Nebuchadnezzar at the end of twelve months." (Dan. 4:28-29.) That was the year of 570 B C. Now add 570 B C. to 1950 A D. and you have 2520 years. Therefore, 1951 was the end of the Gentile powers. The year 1914 was the beginning of the end time and 1951 the end of Gentile power or end of the day of Grace and the beginning of the day of darkness. Anglo-Saxon Israel will go through forty years of wilderness preparation and will be ready for the millennium by 1996 A D.

Now if Yahshua the Messiah came in his perfect sevenfold advent in 1884 A D. as I claim that he did, then he has been here for 76 years. If the work of his presence requires 120 years, that would take us down to the year 2004 A D. which would leave us 39 years yet to go before the present evil world orders all pass away and the millennium begins. But remember that Yahveh is going to shorten the time. According to the Bible record Noah was called to preach and preached for 100 years before the flood. Those were the days (plural) not day of Noah's ministry. Now watch it: "And as it was in the (D-a-y-s) of Noe, so shall it be in the days (D-A-Y-S) of the Son of man." (Luke 17:26.) That scripture being true, then the days or period of time of the coming of Yahshua the Messiah will be approximately 120 years, for that was the period of Noah's preaching to the sinful world before the flood came. But let me read more of that same scripture: "For as the lightning, that lighteneth out of the one part under heaven; so shall also the Son of man be in his day. But first must he suffer many things, and be rejected of this generation. And as it was in the days of Noe, so shall it also be in the days of the Son of man. They did eat, they drank, they married wives, they were given in marriage, until the day that Noe entered into the ark, and the flood came, and destroyed them all. Likewise also as it was in the days of Lot; they did eat, they drank, they bought, they sold, they planted, they builded; but the same day that Lot went out of Sodom it rained fire and brimstone from heaven, and destroyed them all. Even thus shall it be in the day when the Son of man is revealed." (Luke 17:24-80.)

"For as the lightning; that is the sun light that rises in the east and moves slowly and sets in the west:

"For as the lightning cometh out of the east, and shineth even unto the west; so shall also the coming of the Son of man be." (Matt. 24:27.) Lightning does not flash from east to west. The word here is not lightning but sunlight. Yahshua the Messiah's coming is a gradual process in this end time—as was Noah's ministry before the flood. Yahshua

OUTER SPACE PEOPLE AND INNER EARTH PEOPLE

the Messiah is being rejected by this generation in just the same way as that generation before the flood rejected Noah's ministry. But when this evil world crashes, and it will not be long, then Yahshua the Messiah wiil be revealed in his saints and the saints will take over, judge and rule the world. For I reckon that the sufferings of this present time are not worthy to be compared with the glory which shall be revealed in us. (Rom. 8:18.) "Do ye not know that the saints shall judge the world? and if the world shall be judged by you, are ye unworthy to judge the smallest matters?" (1 Cor. 6:2-3.) "And judgment was given to the saints of the Most High; and the time came when the saints possessed the Kingdom." (Dan.7:22.) Yes, that time is coming. It is sure to come within the next fifty years. I have examined every scripture reference and date on this subject. Yahshua the Messiah is "The KING of Kings" (Rev. 19:16.) Since I am one of his kings and one of his priests I expect to rule over a portion of this world for he "hast made us unto our Yahveh kings and priests: and we shall reign on the earth." (Rev. 5:10.)

The facts are beyond a reasonable doubt that Yahshua the Messiah was baptized on his 30th birthday, October 5th, A D. 30. He spent three years and six months (exactly) in his ministry in Palestine. He was crucified at 9:00 A M. on Wednesday, April 5th, A D 84. He was on the tree (cross) for seven hours before he died. He died at 4:00 P M. on Wednesday, April 5, A.D. 34, at the exact moment that the paschal lamb was killed. He was buried by Joseph of Arimathea and Nicodemus just at the last moment before sundown on Wednesday, April 55, A D. 84. He was in the tomb for three days and three nights—a total of seventy-two hours. "Then certain of the scribes and of the Pharisees answered, saying, Master, we would see a sign from thee. But he answered and said unto them, An evil and adulterous generation seeketh after a sign; and there shall no sign be given to it, but the sign of the prophet Jonas: for as Jonas was three days and three nights in the whale's belly; so shall the Son of man be three days and three nights in the heart of the earth." (Matt. 12:88-40.) His resurrection was at exactly 6:00. P M. (sundown), the beginning of the first day of the week, Sunday, April 9, A D. 84. (That was on what would be our Saturday night at sundown, 6:00 P M, the end of the old day and the beginning of the new Bible day.) This is the truth and there can be no doubt about it.

Fifty days later, on Sunday at 9:00 A M., May 28th, A D. 34, the Holy Spirit came and that was the day of Pentecost. The new covenant; the beginning of the true Christian faith began that day. (Acts 2:1-47.) If the 2,000 years of grace ends from the birth of Yahshua the Messiah, that will be 2,000 A D. If the 2,000 years runs from the day of Pentecost which was Sunday, May 28, 9:00 A M., A D. 34, then it will end and the new millennial day will begin at 9:00 A M. on May 28th, A D 2084.

I doubt if any man has, in the past, ever spent more time in study, research and devoted more time and energy on this subject than I have. Therefore I have given you my findings on this matter. As to the Gentile time element and how it will end, here is the scripture: "And I saw another mighty angel come down from heaven, clothed with a cloud: and a rainbow was upon his head, and his face was as it were the sun, and his feet as pillars of fire. And he had in his hand a little book open: and he set his right foot upon the sea, and his left foot on the earth. And cried with a loud voice, as when a lion roareth: and when he had cried, seven thunders uttered their voices. And when the seven thunders

OUTER SPACE PEOPLE AND INNER EARTH PEOPLE

had uttered their voices, I was about to write: and I heard a voice from heaven saying unto me, Seal up those things which the seven thunders uttered, and write them not. And the angel which I saw stand upon the earth lifted up his hand to heaven. And sware by him that liveth for ever and ever, who created heaven, and the things that therein are, and the earth, and the things that therein are, and the sea, and the things which are therein, that there should be time no longer. (Rev. 10:1-6.)

At the present rate of speed of the planets in their orbits, it would take 25,800 years to end time and return to eternity, but when a satellite of Yahveh (or man-made) circles the earth seven times in the fraction of a second, the vacuum which it creates in the sky will draw all the water up from the earth. The earth will again become upright at the poles. The mountains will be leveled down, the valleys will be exalted, by the conclusion of the seven peals of thunder. The energy of the sun will increase seven fold (Isa. 26:80), and the light and energy of the moon will become equal to that of the present sun, and time (Gentile times) will end. The Divine time table of Yahveh and the true sacred calendar will be put into effect and will be perfect.

"But in the days of the voice of the seventh angel, when he shall begin to sound, the mystery of Yahveh should be finished, as he hath declared to his servants the prophets. And the voice which I heard from heaven spake unto me again, and said, Go and take the little book which is open in the hand of the angel which standeth upon the sea and upon the earth. And I went unto the angel, and said unto him, Give me the little book. And he said unto me, Take it and eat it up; and it shall make thy belly bitter, but it shall be in they mouth sweet as honey. And I took the little book out of the angel's hand, and ate it up; and it was in my mouth sweet as honey and as soon as I had eaten it my belly was bitter. And he said unto me, Thou must prophesy again before many peoples, and nations, and tongues, and kings." (Rev. 10:7-11.)

You have now heard this prophecy. It has been concealed unto this day. Now it is revealed. The voice of the Seventh Angel (VOTSA) has spoken. So mote it be.

ADVERTISEMENT

Angels Of The Lord

MORE PAGES! LARGE FORMAT! BONUS DVD! ADDED INFORMATION FROM THE PEN OF WILLIAM ORIBELLO!

LEARN THE METHODS NECESSARY TO CALL UPON YOUR GUARDIAN ANGEL FOR GUIDANCE AND PROTECTION

> *PSALMS 90:11-13 DICTATES:* "The Lord hath given his Angels charge over thee, to keep thee in all thy ways."

NOW FOR THE FIRST TIME YOU CAN LEARN ALL THERE IS TO KNOW ABOUT GOD'S SPECIAL MESSENGERS AND COMMAND THEM TO DO YOUR BIDDING

ADD THIS POWERFUL AMULET TO YOUR ORDER

Join Spiritist William Alexander Oribello, Plus Tim Beckley, Rev. Frank Stranges, Arthur Crockett and Sean Casteel As They Reveal The Truth About The Angelic Kingdom. Learn:

♦ Why Angels Were Created.
♦ How Smart Angels Can Be.
♦ The Role Of The Angel Of Death (NOT Evil).
♦ What Their Purpose In The Lord's Scheme Of Things Really Is.
♦ The Actual Language Of The Angels And How To Speak It.
♦ How You Can Call Upon Them Directly For Guidance And Protection In Order To Make Your Own Life More Blissful.
♦ How It is Possible To Keep The Devil At Arm's Distance.
♦ How Angels Are Ranked.
♦ How To Get Them To Utilize Their Fiery Swords.
♦ Learn The Differentiation Between The Various Angels And Their Individual Functions There Are: Archangels. Seraphim. Cherubian. The Thrones. The Dominations, The Virtues. And The Powers.
♦ What Unspoken Blessings You Can Expect To Receive.
♦ Get Them To Fight Your Battles And Bring About Victory In Your Life.
♦ How Angels Are Ranked.
♦ How To Use Them As Your Personal Messenger To Turn In Your Favor The Thoughts And Minds Of Others.
♦ The "Ruling Class" Of The Archangels.
♦ Getting The Attention Of Master Teacher Angels.
♦ The Days And Hours Angels Are Closest To You.
♦ Angels Of The Spirit World.

Order Now: enables you to "call out" to your Guardian Angel in ordinary as well as times of great need. Here is everything you are required to know to bring about a stronger than ever bond with your angel guides and have them answer your cry for help and assistance in matters big and small. Send **$22.00 + $5.00 S/H** now and receive a BONUS DVD with more valuable information.

Timothy Beckley · Box 753 · New Brunswick, NJ 08903

ARCH ANGEL MEDALLION FOR YOUR GUIDANCE, PROTECTION AND PERSONAL GAIN

Love! Finances! Dependence! Reliance!—$38.00

This powerful Arch Angel Amulet, consists of a wide circle exterior, with an Arch Angel spell engraved along the outer edge in a magical script reading "Before me, Behind me, to my right and to my left, I am surrounded by protection." It comes with a small sheet explaining the names of four major Arch Angels as well as the wording with which it is inscribed. Though it does not come with a chain, this amulet is approximately 1 3/8" in diameter and made of the finest lead-free pewter. Design may vary from that in ad.

SAVE WITH THIS SPECIAL OFFER Angel Of The Lord Expanded Edition and your own Arch Angel Amulet for just **$55.00 + $5.00 S/H**

ADVERTISEMENT

NEWLY EXPANDED, LARGE FORMAT EDITION WILLIAM ALEXANDER ORIBELLO'S
CANDLE BURNING MAGIC WITH THE PSALMS
THE SCRIPTURES TEACH US THAT... "IT IS FAR BETTER TO LIGHT A CANDLE THAN TO CURSE THE DARKNESS."

IF YOU ARE LOOKING FOR SPIRITUAL GUIDANCE IN YOUR LIFE THIS MAY BE THE MOST IMPORTANT BOOK YOU WILL EVER OWN!

All you need to fulfill your inner most desires, dreams and wishes is a match, ordinary candles, oils and the ability to recite a specific Psalm from Scripture. Candle Burning Magic with The Psalms is the only book to combine both of these important elements.

In an easy to read style, William Oribello – one of the most dynamic spiritists of the past century — unlocks for the serious learner the secret code encrypted in the Psalms which will bring about positive results in the area of personal spiritual growth, as well as with everyday matters. Here are Psalms you can read aloud or to yourself along with the specific colored candles you need to burn.

OVER 150 PROVEN RITUALS USING GOD'S INSPIRED WORDS
OVERCOME DEPRESSION · EXPERIENCE GREAT JOY · OVERCOME ATTACKERS AND ROBBERS · BE PROTECTED FROM SUFFERING · KEEP BAD LUCK AWAY · RECEIVE INSTRUCTIONS IN DREAMS · RECEIVE GREAT STRENGTH · REGAIN PEACE WITH A PERSON YOU HAVE HAD A FALLING OUT WITH · RECEIVE DIVINE GRACE, LOVE AND MERCY · HELP IN COURT CASES · OBTAIN GREAT FINANCIAL REWARDS · HAVE A STRONG WILL · ATTRACT LOVE AND FRIENDSHIP · BANISH MARRIAGE PROBLEMS · · BRING ABOUT GOOD FORTUNE · DRAW PROSPERITY AND MONEY INTO YOUR LIFE

☐ Order the new large format, 200 page, edition of
CANDLE BURNING MAGIC WITH THE PSALMS for just $20.00 + $5.00 S/H

WANT TO LEARN MORE? FOR THE SERIOUS STUDENT ONLY!
NOW HEAR FOR THE FIRST TIME REV. ORIBELLO DELIVER A DRAMATIC LECTURE/SERMON ON THE MAGIC OF THE INNER LIGHT

☐ This special **MAGIC OF INNER LIGHT** package includes (1) Rare **Audio CD-MAGIC OF THE INNER LIGHT**, available no where else, on which Rev Oribello delivers a firey sermon/lecture. Two personal monographs available here only. (2) **COSMIC MYSTERIES UNVEILED** which provides a concise means of getting on "The Path," utilizing a simplified system of inner development, mental imagery and symbolic illustrations.

And ☐ **PERSONALITY UNMASKED**, revealing how you can find out what other people are really like. This entire *"For Serious Students Only"* package is just $29.95 + $5.00 S/H

( ) **SPECIAL COMBO** - All items this page - Candle Psalms Book, and Inner Light package — just $45.00 + $5.00 S/H

Timothy Beckley · Box 753 · New Brunswick, NJ 08903

ADVERTISEMENT

NEWLY OFFERED: THE SECRET HISTORY OF EXTRATERRESTRIALS EXPLORES THE INFLUENCE AND ROLE OF ETS IN THE MILITARY, GOVERNMENT, TECHNOLOGY, HISTORY, AND THE COMING NEW AGE.

Includes the Iraqi Stargate, the Hybrid Project of alien interbreeding. Surveys contact with ETs, abductions, alien technology and exopolitics, genetic tampering by ETs, and the history behind the Nazis and UFO and their link to underground bases in the Antarctica. This book sketches out a breathtaking vision of the planetary revolution just around the corner. — 328 pages. 8 color pages.
Order Secret History Of ETs by Ken Kasten,
$18.95 + $5.00 S/H

Timothy Beckley · Box 753 · New Brunswick, NJ 08903

WHO WAS THE "MYSTERIOUS ALIEN" WITH AMAZING POWERS?

FIND OUT THE SECRETS OF THE "STRANGER AT THE PENTAGON"

**70 MINUTE DVD
And Rare Report:
MY FRIEND BEYOND EARTH**

The late Dr. Frank E. Stranges says Val Thor was a guest of the U.S. military for several years.

Left to right: Jill, Donn & Valiant Thor. All three were reportedly from Venus. Photographed in 1959 at Highbridge, New Jersey.

**LEARN: WHY HE HAD NO FINGERPRINTS
THE REASON HE CAME TO EARTH
WHY HE COULD NOT BE HARMED
WHAT HIS RELIGIOUS BELIEFS WERE
WHERE HE IS TODAY**

For your copy of STRANGER AT THE PENTAGON THE VIDEO VERSION, send $17.50 + $5.00 S/H and we will include a bonus of the very rare booklet *My Friend Beyond Earth.*

Timothy Green Beckley · Box 753
New Brunswick, New Jersey 08903

PSYCHIC GEM FROM SPACE

Researchers claim Moldavite opens Interdimensional Doorways

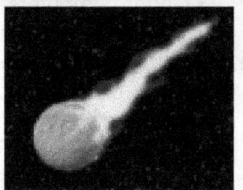

The rare stone Moldavite can only be found along the remote Moldau River in Czechoslovakia. Scientists have determined that it fell to Earth 15 million years ago.

The stone is believed to give its wearer enhanced "powers of perception" bordering on the supernatural. It vibrates 80 times faster than quartz and enables the participant to tie a direct line into the higher dimensional communique systems.

It is also a way of immediately clearning and aligning the entire chakara system and, according to the level of awareness reached, it will make the connection to the so-called 8th chakra or "telepathic receiver band."

❑ **MOLDIVATE GEMSTONE KIT** - Includes a small pendant and a copy of the 178 page *MOLDAVITE STARBORN STONE* by Robert Simmons as well as the remarkable *"Divine Fire"* audio CD narrated by Brad Steiger. — $42.00 + $5.00 S/H
❑ **LARGER STONE AND KIT** — $62.00 + $5.00 S/H

Timothy Beckley · Box 753
New Brunswick, NJ 08903

Credit Card Hotline:
732-602-3407.
PayPal orders may be addressed to
MRUFO8@hotmail.com

ADVERTISEMENT

AVAILABLE AGAIN IN THREE POPULAR SIZES!
Nikola Tesla's "Miracle" PURPLE ENERGY PLATES

The Plates Function As Transceivers, Creating A Field Of Energy Around Themselves That Will Penetrate Any Material Substance. This Energy Is Very Beneficial To All Life...Plant, Animal Or Human!

In the 1940s, electrical engineer Ralph Bergstresser met the wizard Nikola Tesla in an effort to explore the energetic options to help end WWII. Bergstresser was impressed with the knowledge and deep humanitarian ideals of Tesla. Tesla gave Ralph inspiration regarding his knowledge and access of "free energy" when he offered a curious clue. "If you want to understand the secrets of nature look to vibration and frequency."

Tesla died shortly after the meeting but Bergstresser spent the next 20 years breaking through the veil of matter to access Tesla's ideas. In 1965 he introduced the Tesla Purple Energy Plates to the world. He chose an inexpensive medium that, when altered, would act as a transceiver to draw in and radiate Universal Life Force or "Free Energy."

The Tesla Purple Energy Plates are a beautiful violet color and are a window into the 4th and 5th dimensional fields. They radiate their energy for a distance of 10 to 18 inches.

Experimentation has shown there are many uses for the plates. Here are only a few of them:

- Place a small size plate into a pocket or purse for more energy. Actual physical contact is not required.
- Place a large plate in refrigerator (center shelf is best). Food, except meat and fish, will stay fresh longer.
- Place a plate beneath a sick houseplant, or water sick plants with water that has been place on a plate overnight.
- Place a small plate in dog or cat bed, or under food dish.
- To energize crystals, place on a Purple Plate for 12 hours.
- Use a plate on injured area of any living thing.
- Under computers to block harmful radiation.

IMPORTANT NOTICE: The FDA and AMA prohibit making claims related to the mental or physical illness of individuals using unapproved methods of treatment. Purported "benefits" have been reported by private users employing no medical training. Users of Tesla Purple Plates should, under no circumstances, terminate any professional care they may be currently undergoing.

- Travelers can carry a small plate to energize their drinking water and eliminate illness or upset stomach.
- Small plates placed on forehead to alleviate headache, on joints to alleviate gout and arthritis, on stomach to stop nausea.
- Place on forehead to help remember dreams and promote deeper meditation.

ORDER YOUR PLATES TODAY IN ANY ONE OF THREE SIZES

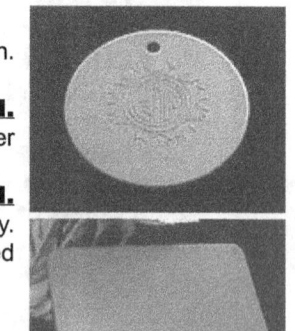

❑ **PURPLE DISC—1½ INCHES IN DIAMETER**—Attach to pet collar or under water dish. Create a necklace for yourself or put one in each shoe. Carry in purse, wallet or pocket.
—**$17.00 OR 3 FOR $40.00 + $5.00 S/H.**

❑ **SMALL PLATE—4½ INCHES X 2¾ INCHES**—Best for using on a painful area. Put under glass or bottled water, or under your sheet, on pillow, or in your favorite chair
—**$25.00 OR 3 FOR $68.00 + $5.00 S/H.**

❑ **LARGE PLATE—12" X 12"** (approx)—Because of its size, this plate carries more energy. Excellent for refrigerator shelf. Under a bag of groceries. Under a gallon of water to drink or to feed plants. Multiple uses—**$75.00 OR 3 FOR $200.00 + $8.00 S/H.**

NOTE: Each plate comes with report on how best to utilize the awesome power of the plates.

WANT TO LEARN MORE ABOUT TESLA?
❑ **THE LOST JOURNALS OF NIKOLA TESLA—Time Travel, Alternative Energy, And The Secret Of NAZI Flying Saucers.** New edition. 4 chapters added. Author Tim Swartz investigates the stolen files of Tesla, removed ny the FBI following Tesla's death. —**$24.00 + $5.00 S/H**

❑ **THE SECRETS OF NIKOLA TESLA DVD COMBO**—Two full length features on one DVD tells the complete story! Here is the truth personified about an amazing man that big business tried to silence.—**$18.00 + $5.00 S/H**

Timothy Beckley • Box 753 • New Brunswick, NJ 08903

Credit card payment through PayPal • All cards accepted • No registration email: MRUFO8@hotmail.com and we send PayPal invoice. Fastest method, safe, secure, easy • USA bank checks, Int'l or postal money orders or Western Union

ADVERTISEMENT

OVER 900 PAGES OF SUPPRESSED BIBLICAL HISTORY FROM THE ORIGINS OF HUMANKIND TO THE LAST JUDGEMENT!

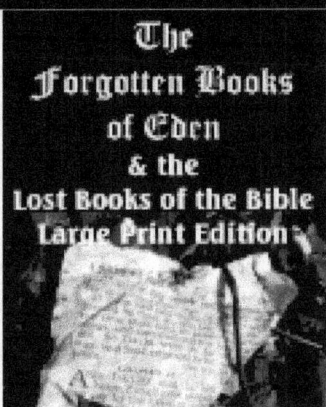

THE FORGOTTEN BOOKS OF EDEN
THE LOST BOOKS OF THE BIBLE—Large Print Edition
Suppressed By The Church ... But Now Fully Revealed
The Uncensored Truth About The Origins of Humankind And The Ageless Conflict Between Good And Evil

Here is the story of Adam and Eve which is the most ancient in the world; a story that has survived because it embodies the fight between man and the Devil. Adapted from the work of unknown Egyptians parts of this version are found in the Talmud, the Koran, and elsewhere, showing the vital role it played in the original literature of human wisdom. This adaptation has been passed down and was first written in Arabic and then translated into Ethiopic. It is a detailed history of Adam and Eve and their descendents found nowhere else and how the "Family Tree" ties all of the Old Testament together.

This large print edition also includes 26 Apocryphal books from the first 400 years of Christianity that were not included in the Testaments. The question remains: Why were these divinely inspired works kept out of the Bible by the church? You will find the answers within these pages.

We have combined **THE LOST BOOKS OF THE BIBLE** with another forbidden work known as **THE FORGOTTEN BOOKS OF EDEN** which includes the true story of Adam and Eve's conflict with Satan, as well as the Psalms of Solomon, the Testaments of the Twelve Patriarchs and the Secrets of Eden.

Order your copy of **FORGOTTEN BOOKS OF EDEN/LOST BOOKS OF THE BIBLE** now for just **$39.95 + $5.00 S/H.**

THE FORBIDDEN BOOKS OF THE NEW TESTAMENT

THE MATERIAL IN THE FORBIDDEN BOOKS OF THE NEW TESTAMENT HAS BEEN TRANSLATED FROM ITS ORIGINAL TONGUES BY THE WORLD'S GREATEST SCHOLARS, THE TASK TAKING WELL OVER 100 YEARS

There have been many facts about the life and times of Jesus which have not been included in the New Testament. The documents contained in this large size—8.5x11—450 page edition, were written soon after Christ's crucifixion during the early spread of Christianity, but before the church was able to censor some of the documents for a variety of reasons. Now after over 1500 years of suppression, the shroud of secrecy has been lifted and sincere students of the Bible will be able to read these original chapters and verses, and decide for themselves their authority.

The Birth of Christ — The Early Life of Mary — The Birth of John—The Virgin Birth — The Baptism of Jesus in the Jordan— Christ Praying In The Garden—Peter Cutting Off the Ear of Mulches—The Kiss of Judas — Christ on the Cross—The Resurrection of our Lord — Jesus Ascending to Heaven—The Red Sea Swallowing Up the Army of Pharaoh—Christ's Descent Into Hell — The Last Judgment.

450+ pages 8.5x11 Format Large print Edition — $39.95 + $5.00 S/H
978-1-60611-028-7 · 1-60611-027-6

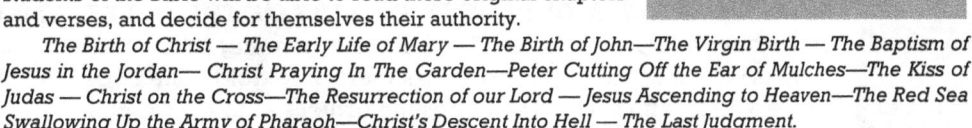

Timothy Beckley · Box 753 · New Brunswick, NJ 0890
Credit Card Customers Call 732 602-3407
PayPal MRUFO8@hotmail.com
Please refer to the order form inside the back cover of this isue for detailed ordering and shipping information. NJ residents add sales tax.

TWO HUGE BOOKS. BUY THEM AS A SET FOR $62.00 + $8.00 S/H OR PURCHASE THEM INDIVIDUALLY

ADVERTISEMENT

A FILM BY TIMOTHY GREEN BECKLEY
SECRETS OF THE VATICAN

THE VATICAN has been shrouded in mystery and intrigue for centuries. Except for the highest Cardinals and Bishops, the public and even members of the priesthood are not privy to the inner workings of the church. It is rumored that there are, in secret archives, centuries-old artifacts that, if revealed, could embarrass the standard-bearers of the faith.

SEARCHING for the truth has always been Conspiracy Journal's main goal. With this in mind, we recently "invaded" the walls of the Vatican with our hidden cameras on a fact-finding mission. On our return, we followed up our investigation by interviewing such astute researchers as Jordan Maxwell, Brad Steiger and Patricia Ress. The result is an astounding professionally produced video which is available for immediate shipment.

FILMED WITHIN THE WALLS OF THE HOLY CITY WITH SECRET CAMERAS

SOME OF THE EXCITING CONTENTS INCLUDE:

· Does the Vatican conceal knowledge that the crucifixion was a fraud? · Is there a secret cabal of Satanists within the Vatican to further the evil conspiracy of the New World Order? · Learn about strange events today! · Can exorcism be a futile effort that often results in the death of the possessed? · What secrets is the Vatican keeping about the perilous future of our world? · Is the Vatican link to the Hubble Telescope evidence that they are aware of a world-destroying comet headed our way?

EXAMINE with these researchers the reports of Vatican conspiracies, anti-semitism, the sinking of the Titantic, the assassination of Lincoln, the true author of Mein Kampf, Satanic Rituals, Celibacy and Madness, Demon Possession, Mystery Cults of Babylon and MORE!

SECRETS OF THE VATICAN—$20.00 + $5.00 S/H

WANT TO LEARN MORE?—THE SECRETS OF THE POPES—This illustrated book by Arthur Crockett includes: St. Malachi's stunning prophecies about the Last Pope · The Pope who tried to turn worthless metal into gold · The Pope who claimed he had a conversation with Jesus · The Pope who professed to read minds · The Pope who forsaw the end of the world · And the startling story of "Pope Joan", who is believed to have been a woman!

ORDER "SECRETS OF THE POPES" FOR JUST $17.50 + $5.00 S/H

SUPER SPECIAL OFFER! SECRETS OF THE VATICAN DVD WITH 2 AUDIO CDS AND THE BOOK, SECRETS OF THE POPES FOR ONLY $32.00 + $5.00 S/H

Payment via PayPal (easiest way) Order by email to MRUFO8@hotmail.com. We will send a PayPal invoice. Or send USA bank check, International or Postal Money Order or Western Union. NO CASH!

ORDER FROM:
Timothy Beckley · Box 753
New Brunswick, NJ 08903

ADVERTISEMENT

CIA AND NAZI COLLABORATION EXPOSED! GERMAN SCIENTISTS UTILIZE TESLA TECHNOLOGY TO CONSTRUCT FLYING SAUCERS

Soon after cessation of hostilities closed World War II, hundreds of former Nazi and SS members were secretly smugged into America to work on military and space programs. They were employed by nearly every one of the military-industrial complex companies, developing bombs, missiles, rockets, aircraft and advanced ground vehicles.

Many former Nazis went to work for the CIA, and, indeed, actually formed the foundation of that agency because they kept accurate records of their enemies (Russia), and the CIA purchased this knowledge and contact information from them.

Both the U.S. and USSR made adequate use of Tesla technologies to create weapons and communications devices previously undreamed of, including — if the records are true — aerial disc platforms, or "Flying Saucers." Intelligence records show that German scientists had built and test-flown several different types of flying discs. The complete plans for one type were captured at the BMW auto factory in Prague at the close of the war.

FIRE FROM THE SKY exposes how it all happened and the consequences with which we all must live today. It also explains the circumstances under which UFO researchers and the public have been manipulated into certain belief patterns, including aspects of the abduction phenomenon which utilizes a high degree of mind control.

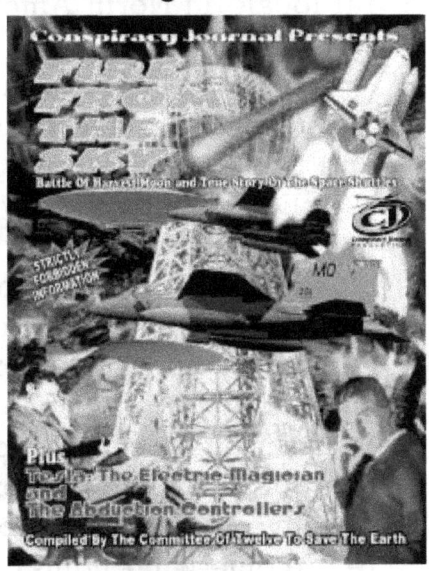

OUR SPECIAL PRICE:
$25.00 + $5.00 S/H

EXCLUSIVE BOOK & AUDIO CD SET

( ) WANT TO KNOW MORE?? EVIL AGENDA OF THE SECRET GOVERNMENT — EXPOSING PROJECT PAPER CLIP AND THE UNDERGROUND UFO BASES OF HITLER'S ELITE.
Tim Swartz reveals how the Controllers have imitated REAL alien abductions and are breeding a Hybrid Zombie Race.
Add $15.00 to your order!

PARTIAL LIST OF CONTENTS: In The Begining; USS Thresher and the U-2; Total Russian Defense; Project Paperclip; Operation Sunrise; Project Overcast; German Scientists and Aliens; NICAP; Then Came 1947; Antarctica; Admiral Byrd and Operation Highjump; Hitler Escaped!; Polar Defenses; UFOs: Nazi or Alien?; Russian Space Program; Scalar Weapons Activated; Rudolph Hess and Secret Space Base; Werner Heisenberg; Who Created The Atomic Bomb?; German Submarines in the South Atlantic; German Flying Saucers; Falklands Islands War; The Kennedy/Nazi Connection; Cover and Concealment; Nikola Tesla: The Forgotten Genius; Nikola Tesla— The Greatest Hacker Of All Time & MORE!

Timothy Beckley
Box 753 • New Brunswick, NJ
08903

ADVERTISEMENT

NEW AMAZING BOOK!
VISIT THE MOST MYSTERIOUS PLACE ON EARTH!

Sacred Site? Entrance To The Inner Earth? Doorway To Another Dimension? Hidden UFO Base? Time Warp? "Black Hole?"

MYSTERIES OF MOUNT SHASTA
Home Of The Ancient Gods And Underground Dwellers!
ADVENTURE IN WONDER AND TERROR

Come along with paranormal journalist Tim Beckley as he explores what has a reputation for being the most Supernatural locale in North America, if not the world.

You can visit Mt Shasta, climb high up if you are able to take the thin atmosphere and don't mind carrying well needed supplies. What you may find could be nothing unusual (believers say a hypnotic cloak clouds the minds of "non deserving" souls.) Or you could come away with an entirely new attitude on life, just like author Dana Howard who stated, "Mount Shasta is one of several conditioning stations for visitors from outer space." Those who live near the base of the mountain report blue-white lights glowing through the tall pines, and huge mother ships have been seen hovering over its highest peak, flashing in and out of this dimensional reality.

· Here are stories of Lemurians and survivors of other "lost civilizations" who roam the woods freely and occasionally wander into n town to trade gold for supplies.

· Little men who seldom come out except at night to collect edibles and then return to their cavern homes.

· Native Americans residing in the backwoods say they have not only heard the screams of Bigfoot, but have seen these hairy creatures closeup!

· The location of the capitol of the subterranean world known as Telos, occupied by the Ascended Masters of Wisdom. This city is connected to the Hollow Earth through a worldwide network of secret tunnels.

· Accounts of miraculous healings, including those whose eye sight have been regenerated after being struck by mysterious blue beams of light coming from inside the mountain.

The number of unexplained events associated with Mt Shasta are now literally in the hundreds. This large size book of nearly 200, 8x11 pages, makes for exciting reading as well as information you won't find being printed even in the nearby daily and weekly newspapers. Order **MYSTERIES OF MT SHASTA** for just **$29.95 + $5.00 S/H** and join us on an exciting journey into the nether world.

**Mount Shasta Book
Just $29.95 + $5.00 S/H**

Global Communications
Box 753 · New Brunswick, NJ 08903

GEORGE HUNT WILLIAMSON came to realize that in America if you try to buck the status quo or change the system you can easily be slandered and identified as a dangerous dissident whether it be a communist, a fascist, or a neo Nazi. Many of the UFO contactees of the early days of the UFO/New Age movement were thusly labeled.

Williamson – aka Brother Philip – was at the forefront of those the government was keeping an eagle eye on for fear the Russians might be using him as a highly sophisticated mind managed and manipulated "Mind Soldier." *TRAVELING THE PATH BACK TO THE ROAD IN THE SKY* includes the entire text of Williamson's most accredited work linking ancient civilizations with the remote beginnings of humanity and visitations from outer space.

In addition, a vast update on Williamson's conflicted personality and his FBI papers has been added to this volume, as well as a fascinating commentary by Brad Steiger, who was to meet with Williamson to receive some important information when *"Brother Philip passed away unexpectedly."* —

J. EDGAR HOOVER'S G-MEN IDENTIFIED GEORGE HUNT WILLIAMSON AS A COMMUNIST OR AT PARAMOUNT A "MIND CONTROLLED SOLDIER" OF THE SOVIET UNION. . . OTHER UFO CONTACTS FROM THE EARLY UFO ERA WERE THUSLY LABELED!

Timothy Beckley · Box 753 · New Brunswick, NJ 08903 · PayPal: MRUFO8@hotmail.com

OVER 90 TITLES AVAILABLE ON KINDLE. KINDLE BOOKS CAN BE DOWNLOADED FROM ANY PC.

TIME TRAVEL

It has been the dream of philosophers and scientist alike. The fantasies of every small boy and the musings of writers and poets throughout the ages; to be able to shed the shackles of seconds, minutes and hours, to go beyond the confines of today and the shadows of yesterday.

Time travel...the very words seem to conjure up the infinite possibilities of the past and future revealed.

Whether by mechanical means like the controversial Montuk Project, or by using the untapped powers of the human mind, time travel is a reality that offers mankind the potential of freedom from the limitations of our universe.

Timothy Beckley
P. O. Box 753
New Brunswick, NJ 08903

TIME SLIPS - REAL TIME MACHINES - AND HOW-TO EXPERIMENTS TO GO FORWARDS OR BACKWARDS THROUGH TIME AND SPACE. OR JUST ENJOY THINKING OF ALL THE POSSIBILITIES. . . 4 BOOKS FOR YOUR AMAZEMENT NOW AVAILABLE

OVER 90 TITLES AVAILABLE ON KINDLE. KINDLE BOOKS CAN BE DOWNLOADED FROM ANY PC.

THE ULTRA-TERRESTRIAL INVASION OF EARTH HAS BEGUN!

BONUS: AUDIO CD

The Ultra-Terrestrials Are Here And They Are Walking Among Us!

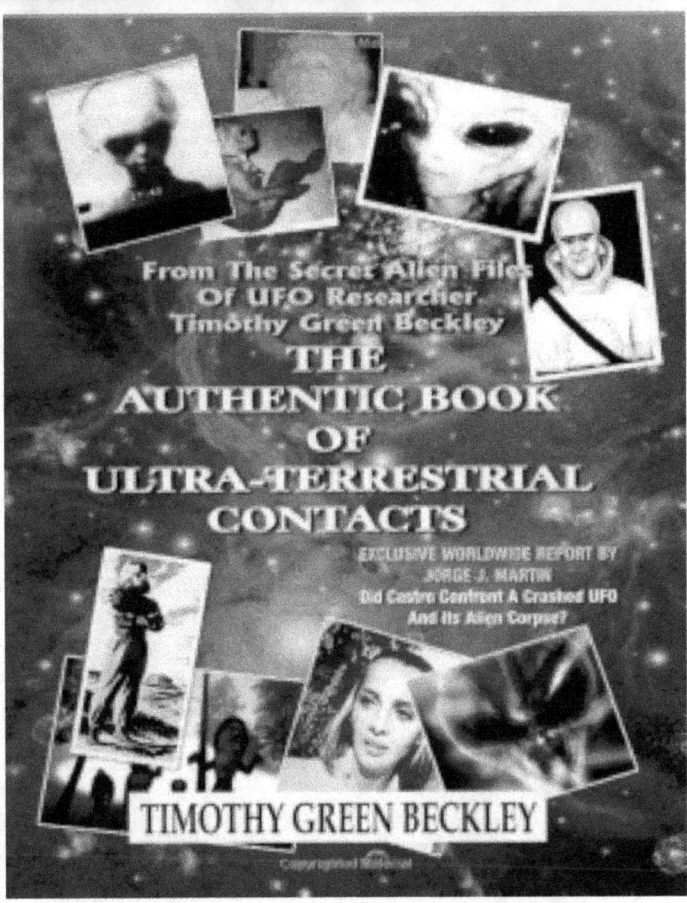

Throughout history we have been surrounded by invisible beings who can upon occasion materialize and take up a variety of shapes and facades – even resembling humans so that they can walk on the surface undetected. Some of these beings may come in peace... while others are here for their own nefarious purposes, perhaps going so far as to control our minds, possess our body and do bloodcurdling experiments upon us. In 1966, a Gallipulis, Ohio, nurse saw a dome shaped UFO land in a remote field. She was compelled to walk toward the craft. Several seconds passed before a number of beings emerged from the UFO and walked up to the woman, who found herself unable to move. The woman said the aliens looked exactly like earthlings and spoke to her for several minutes in perfect English. Eventually, the ship departed and the woman wandered off in a daze. Months later, while walking along the street, she saw these same two men. She ran into the local sheriff's office in an attempt to drag him out to see the "space people" for himself. He refused. Since then she has been constantly ridiculed by her neighbors.

YES! They can pass for humans, but they are NOT and their true forms may be too horrific to comprehend.

PLUS! This volume contains dozens of strange cases taken from the files of "Mr UFO" over decades. Recently, Beckley – who is a frequent guest on Coast to Coast AM and the ParaCast.Com—appeared on William Shatner's Weird or What? TV show where he revealed the true origins of a strange little creature that had been captured in an animal trap in Mexico and mistaken for an "alien baby," which it definitely is NOT! Amazingly, Tim Beckley reveals how to contact the peaceful Guardians, and set up a telepathic bond with the Watchers.

FREE CD NARRATED BY BRAD STEIGER

As a BONUS anyone ordering this book will receive at no additional cost a 60 minute audio CD which discuses the various forms of alien contact and how to acquire the most positive benefits from a UFO sighting or close encounter.

( ) ORDER – THE BOOK OF AUTHENTIC ULTRA-TERRESTRIAL CONTACTS, $20.00 + $5.00 S/H

Also Recommended:
( ) **Round Trip To Hell In A Flying Saucer** - $22
( ) **Evil Empire Of The Ets** — $20
( ) **Trilogy of the Unknown** — $20
All Items This Ad Just — $72.00 + $8.00 S/H

Make All Payments To:
TIMOTHY G. BECKLEY · BOX 753
NEW BRUNSWICK, NJ 08903
PayPal: MRUFO8@hotmail.com

THE LAST BOOKS of Tuella
With Material From The Ashtar Command:
Master Symbol of the Solar Cross & A New Book of Revelations

HERE ARE THE SECRET MASTER KEYS TO THE GREAT AWAKENING... FOR THE FIRST TIME THE SPIRITUAL HIERARCHY EXPOSES THE UNIVERSAL LAWS OF .. LIFE – MAGNETIC RESONANCE – ACTION AND REACTION – LIGHT — VIBRATION – MIND – HARMONY – DIMENSIONS – LOVE – POLARITY – ATTRACTION – MANIFESTATION

Following the death of the well respected channel Tuella – primary representative for the Ashtar Command on Earth – her important last manuscript, *THE MASTER SYMBOL OF THE SOLAR CROSS* became impossible to obtain. This work contains the key symbols that offer us the basic laws governing every phase of our awareness as a complete unit of being. Here are the Universal Laws that can make us co-creative spirits of God. Here is the Great Awakening that will enable us to evolve toward a consciousness of the basic oneness of all life. This is the Great Lesson of absolute necessity of our living in accordance with the Laws of Creation. OVER 300 LARGE SIZE PAGES, THIS WORK COMES WITH AN ACTUAL CHANNELING SESSION – CONVERTED TO AUDIO CD – as given by the space entity known as Monka, as well as the only recorded lecture give by Tuella known to exist. *MASTER SYMBOL OF THE SOLAR CROSS* was $50.00 – now just $29.95

Also Newly Revised: A NEW BOOK OF REVELATIONS —
A HARVESTING OF SOULS AT EARTH'S FINAL MOMENT: A GRAND DECEPTION FOR THE "LAST DAYS"

You are about the participate in the most fabulous transformation of humankind ever experienced. Here are shocking revelations from the highest spiritual powers in the universe that will balance your chakras and tune-up your soul. These are the final messages and warnings from the Ashtar Command, the Space Brotherhood, and the Masters of Universal Wisdom. This work corrects many of the misconceptions and inaccurate translations made of the Old and New Testaments and lays the foundation for *"A New Book of Revelations"* as transcribed to Tuella, the official representative for outer space and inner consciousness. Now is the time to get ready for the *GREAT CHANGES* to happen in our lifetime!
Order *A NEW BOOK OF REVELATIONS* for just $20.00

Both Titles $44.00 + $5.00 S/H

**SUPER SPECIAL
ALL ITEMS THIS PAGE
JUST $99.00 + $8.00 S/H**

Two Books Above And These Four Books

OTHER ASHTAR COMMAND BOOKS AVAILABLE
☐ PROJECT WORLD EVACUATION - $20.00
☐ ASHTAR REVEALING HIS SECRET IDENTITY - $20.00
☐ ON EARTH ASSIGNMENT - $20.00
☐ THE SPACE PEOPLE SPEAK - $14.00

Timothy Beckley, Box 753, New Brunswick, NJ 08903
24/7 credit card answering machine: 732 602-3407   - PayPal Orders MrUFO8@hotmail.com

www.ingramcontent.com/pod-product-compliance
Lightning Source LLC
Chambersburg PA
CBHW080242170426
43192CB00014BA/2528